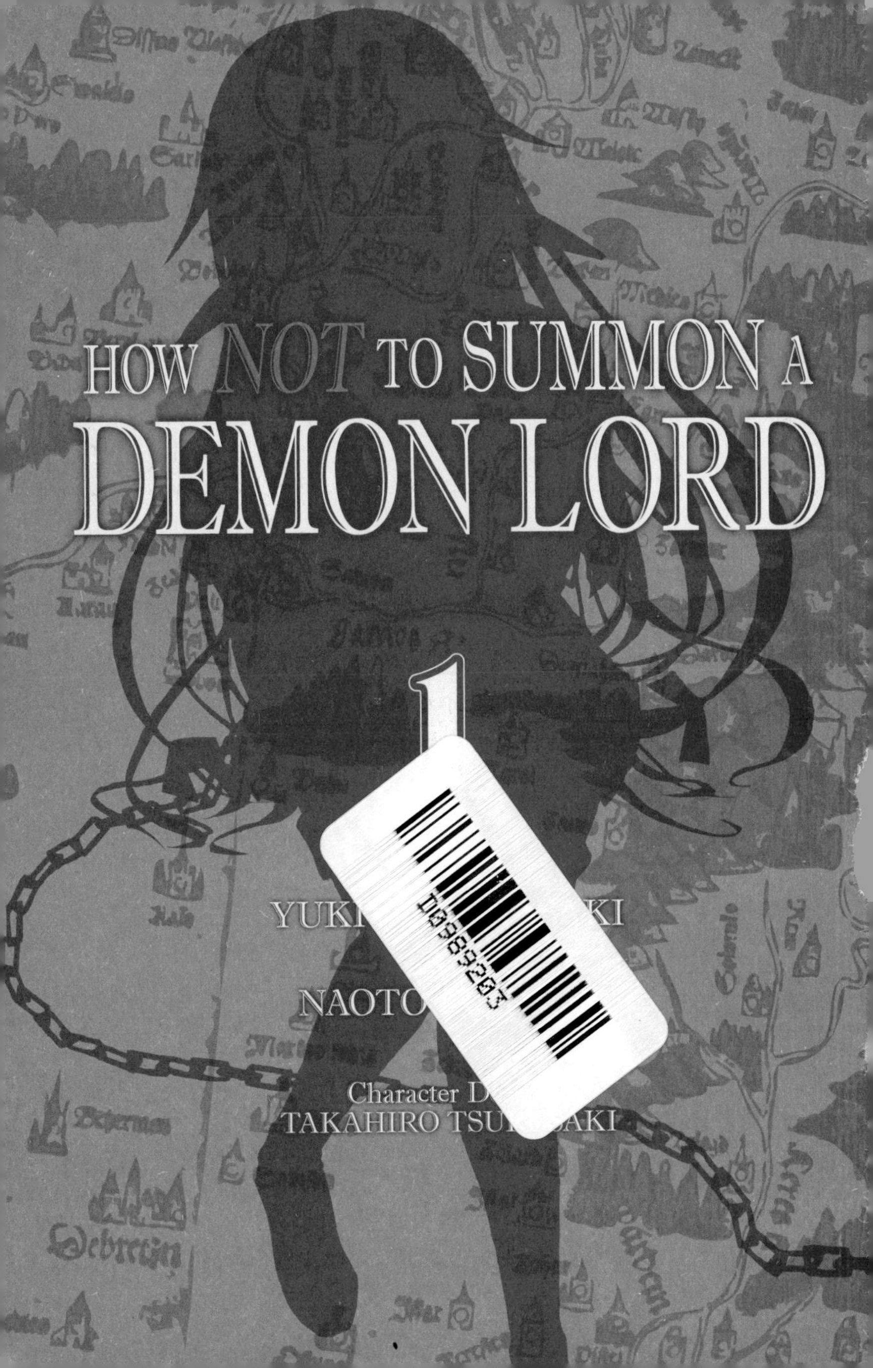
HOW NOT TO SUMMON A
DEMON LORD
1
YUKI KI
NAOTO
Character D
TAKAHIRO TSU SAKI

HOW NOT TO SUMMON A DEMON LORD

1

CONTENTS

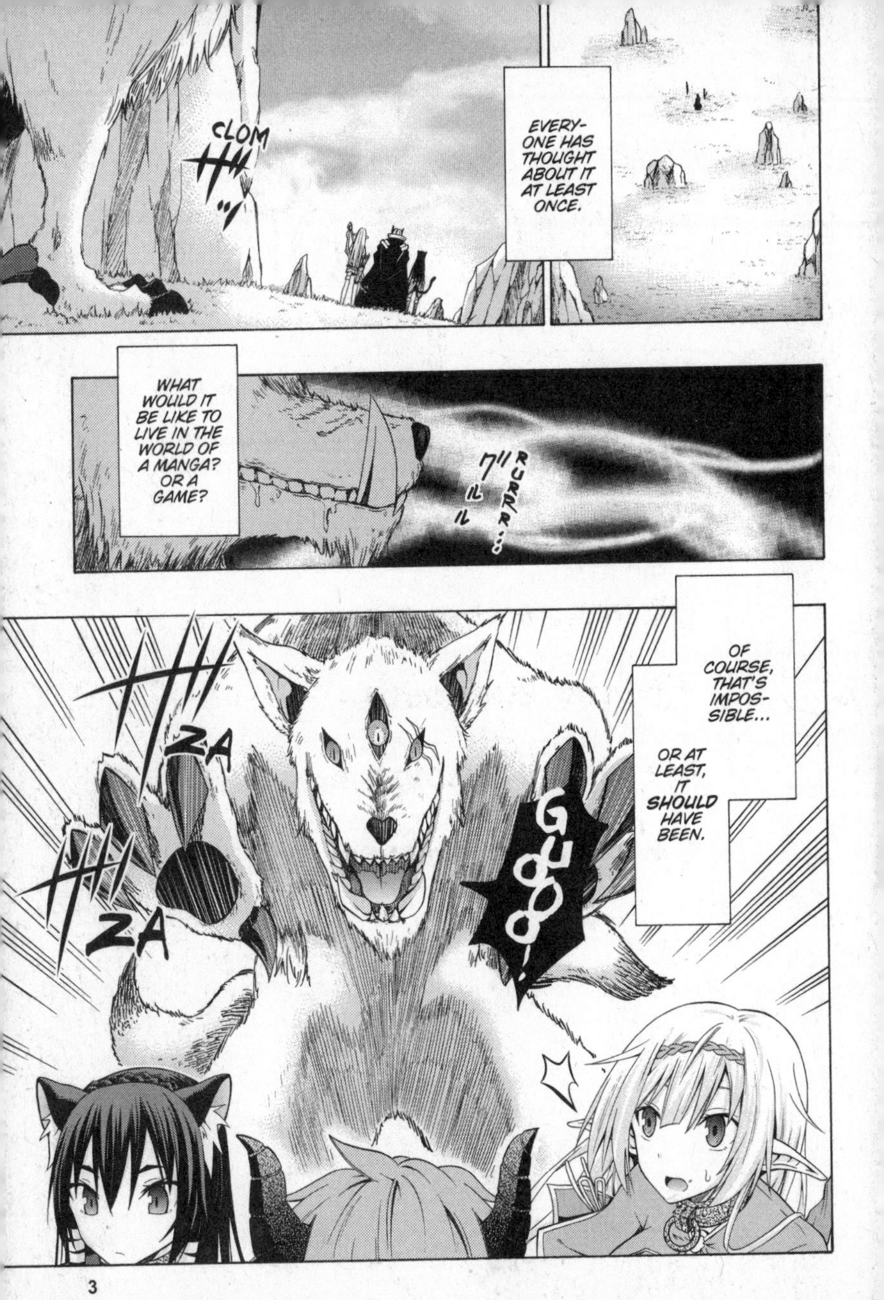
EVERY-ONE HAS THOUGHT ABOUT IT AT LEAST ONCE.
CLOM
WHAT WOULD IT BE LIKE TO LIVE IN THE WORLD OF A MANGA? OR A GAME?
RURRR...
グルル
OF COURSE, THAT'S IMPOSSIBLE...
OR AT LEAST, IT SHOULD HAVE BEEN.
GUOOO!
ZA
ZA

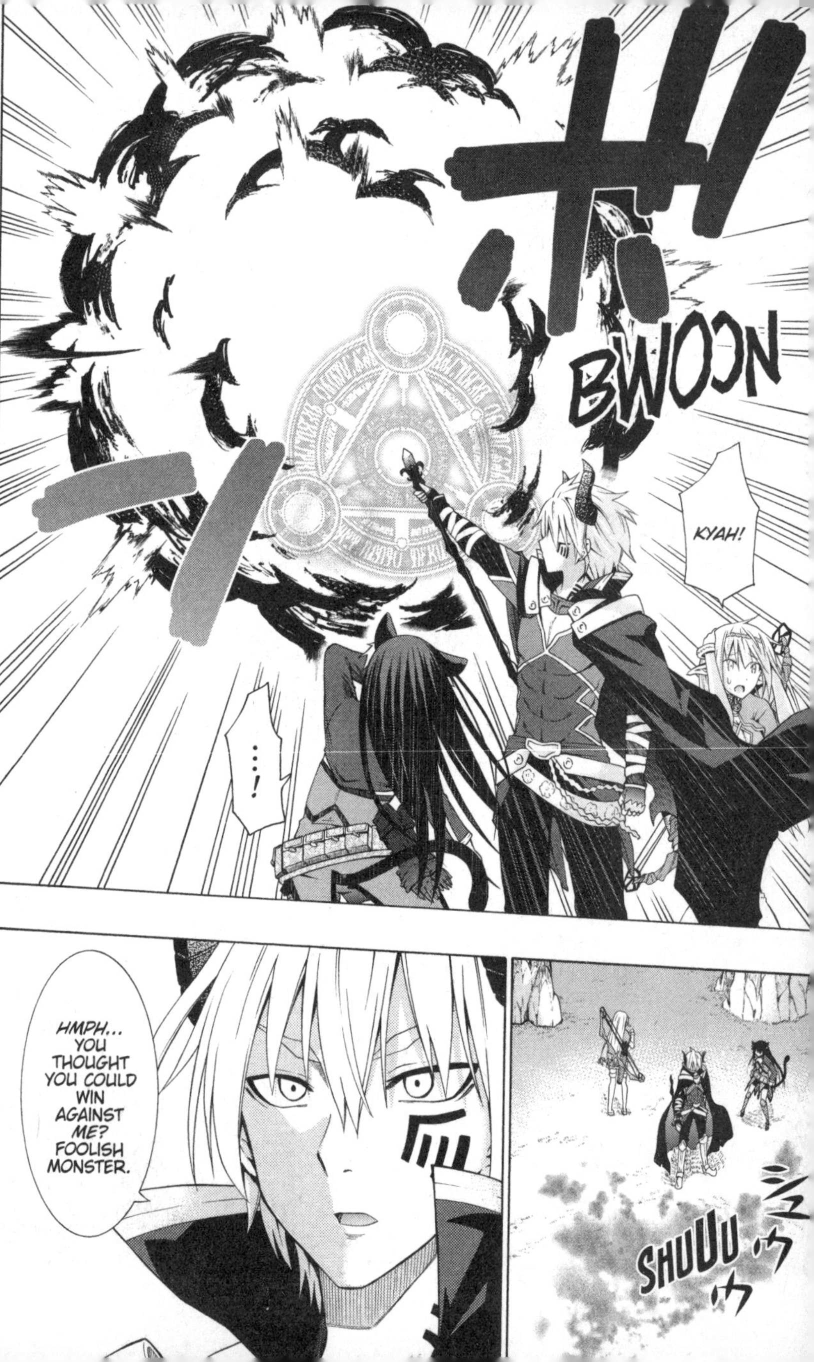
BWOON
KYAH!
...!
SHUUU
HMPH... YOU THOUGHT YOU COULD WIN AGAINST ME? FOOLISH MONSTER.

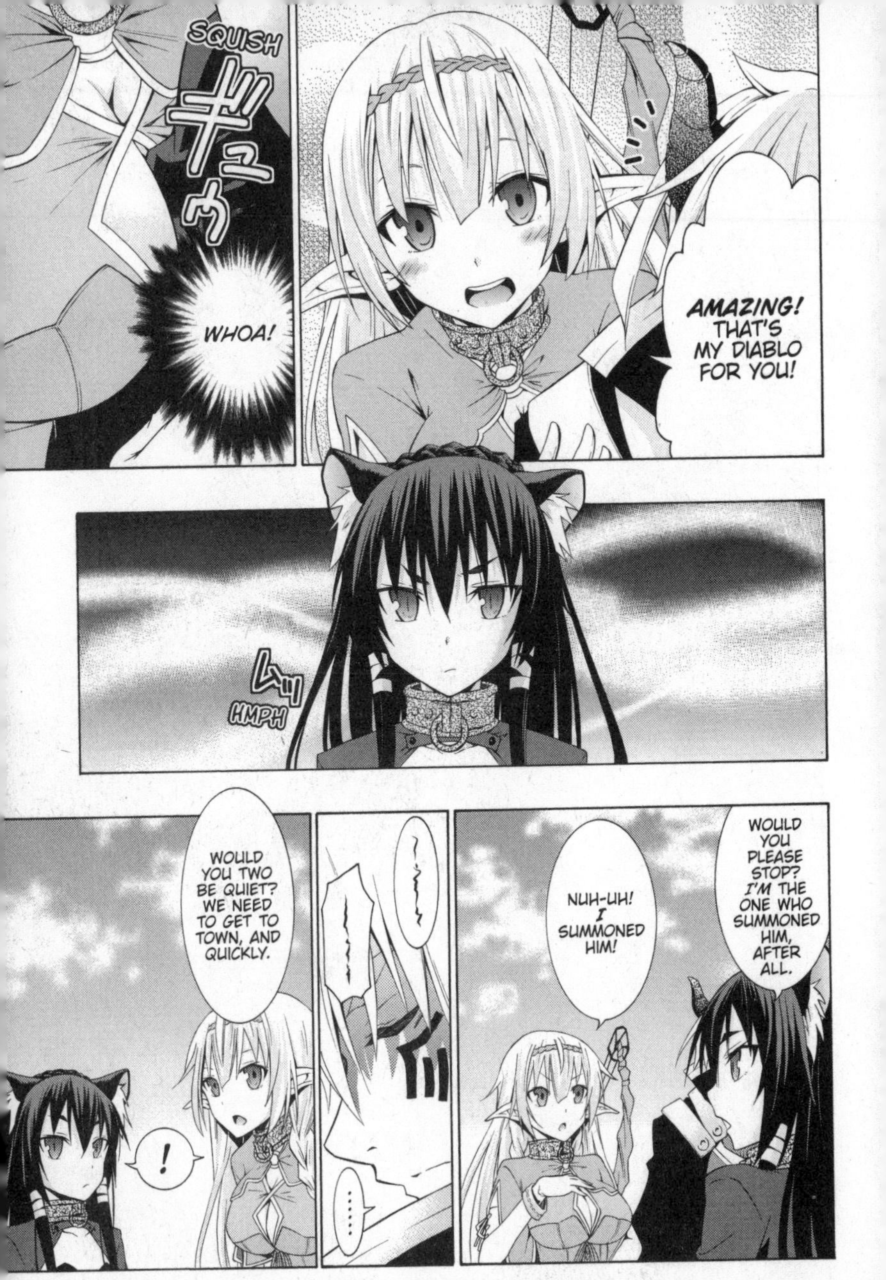
AMAZING! THAT'S MY DIABLO FOR YOU!
SQUISH
WHOA!
HMPH
WOULD YOU PLEASE STOP? I'M THE ONE WHO SUMMONED HIM, AFTER ALL.
NUH-UH! I SUMMONED HIM!
WOULD YOU TWO BE QUIET? WE NEED TO GET TO TOWN, AND QUICKLY.
!

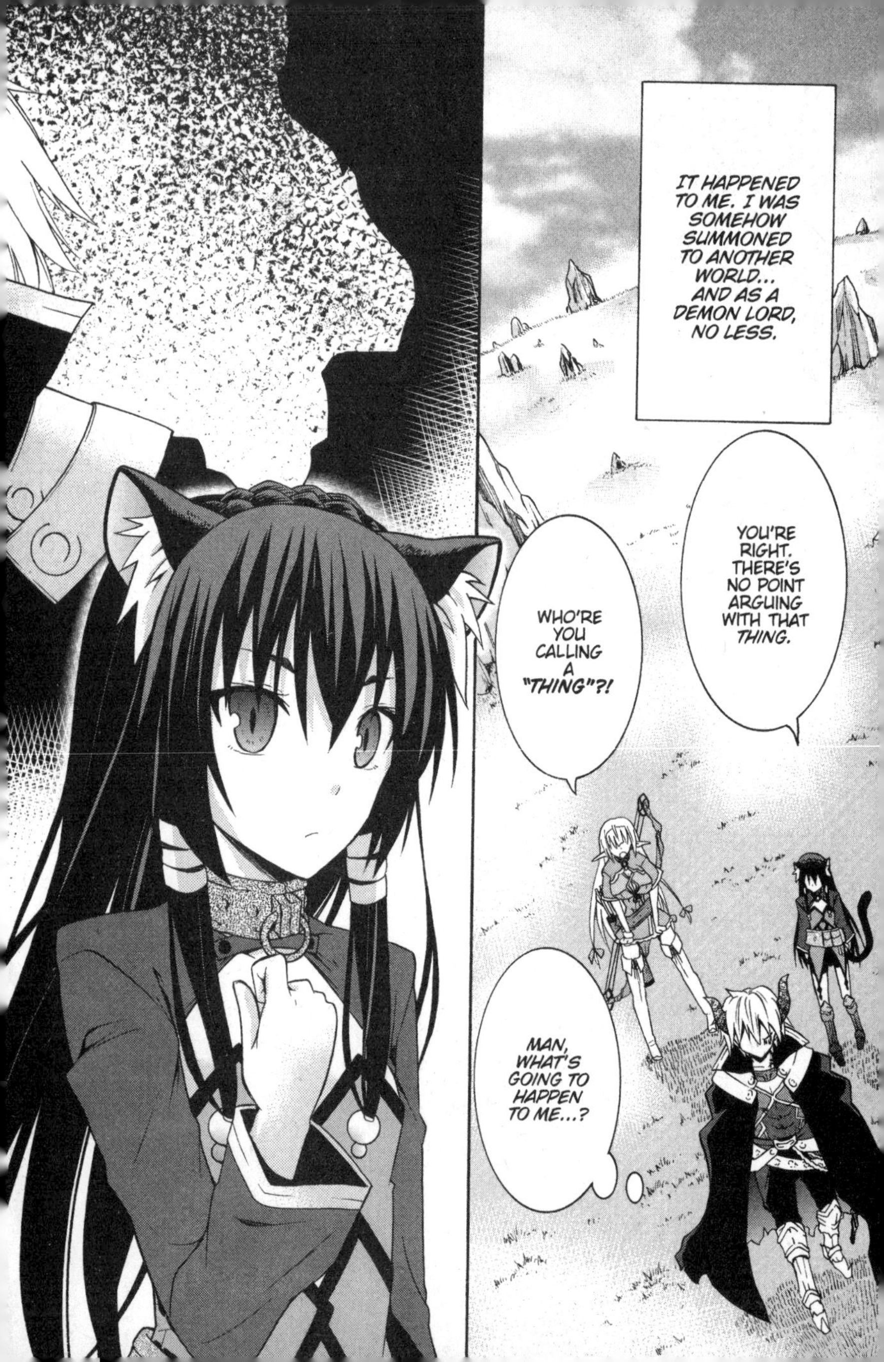
IT HAPPENED TO ME. I WAS SOMEHOW SUMMONED TO ANOTHER WORLD... AND AS A DEMON LORD, NO LESS.
YOU'RE RIGHT. THERE'S NO POINT ARGUING WITH THAT *THING.*
WHO'RE YOU CALLING A *"THING"*?!
MAN, WHAT'S GOING TO HAPPEN TO ME...?

1 BEING SUMMONED I

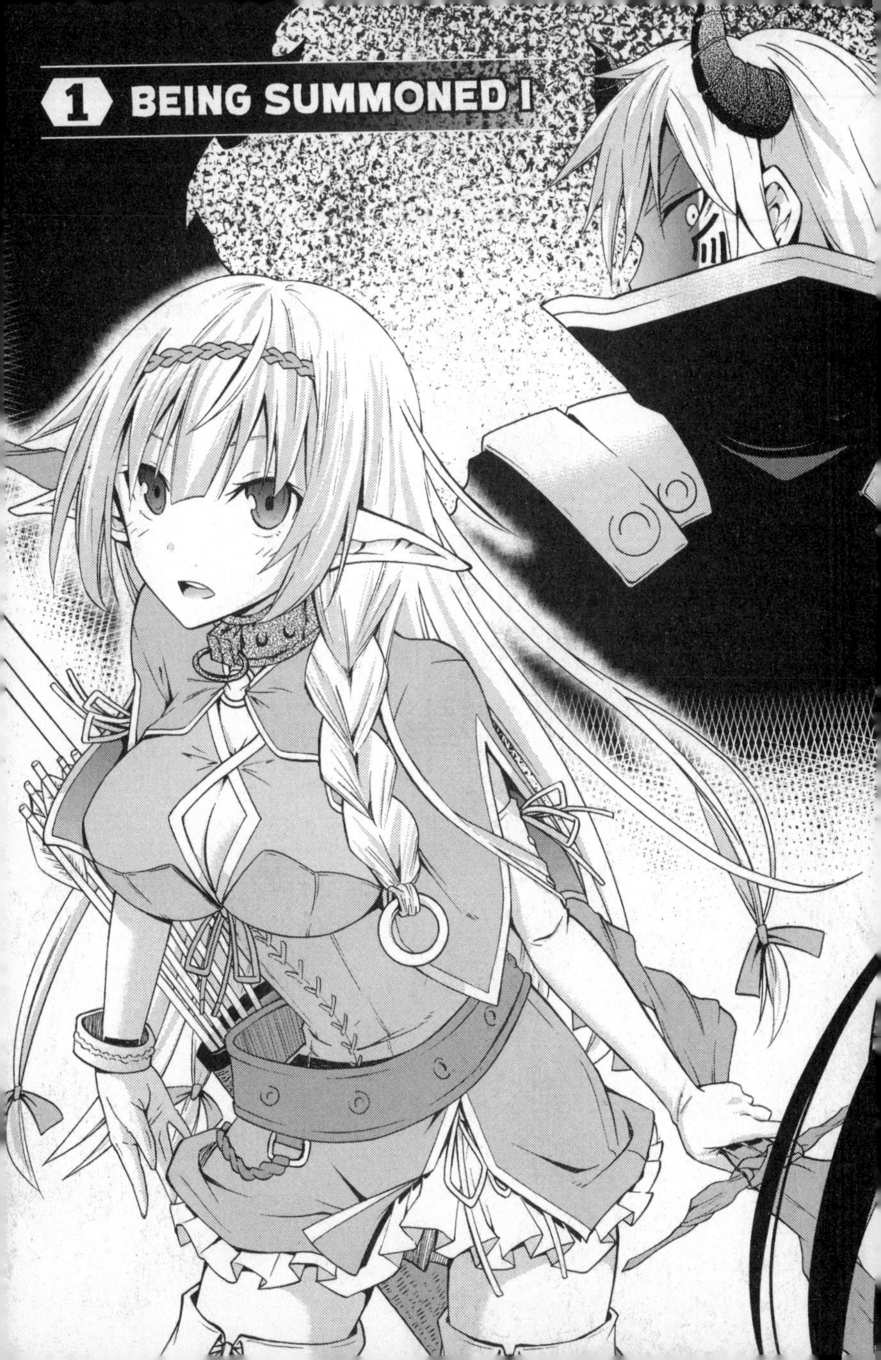

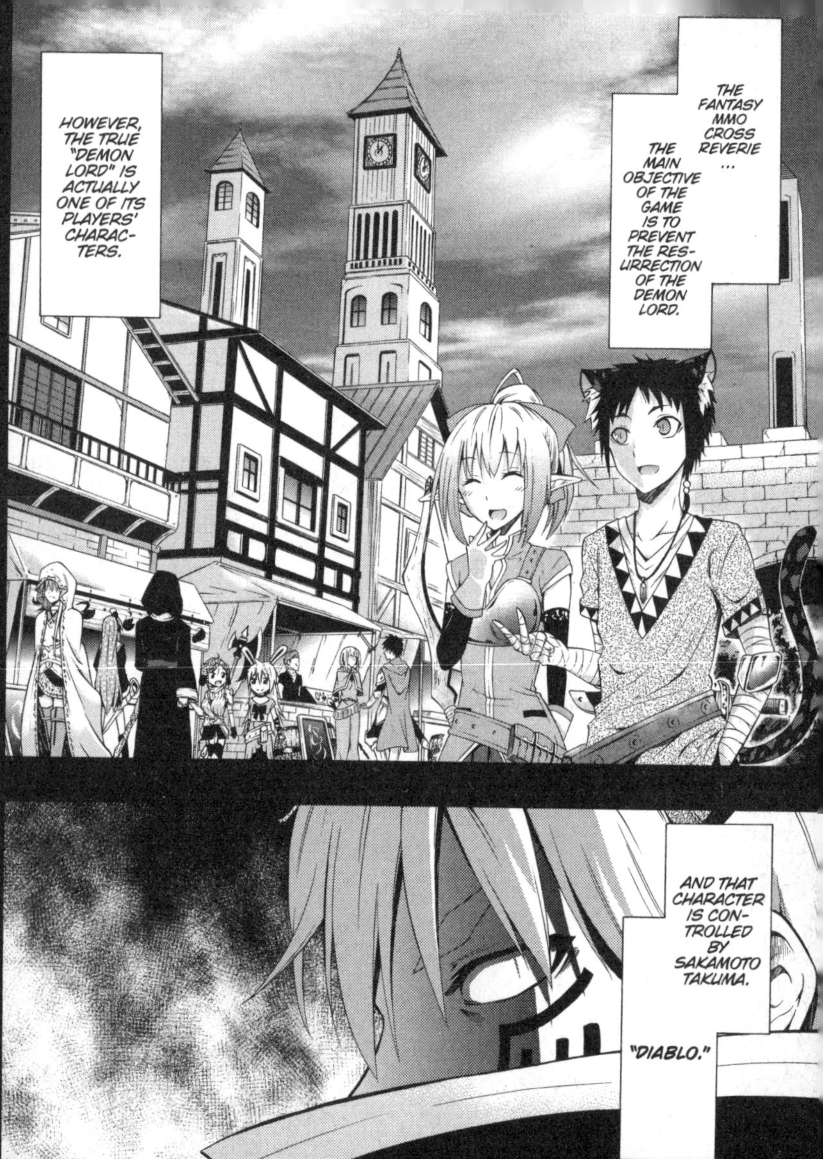
THE FANTASY MMO CROSS REVERIE ...
THE MAIN OBJECTIVE OF THE GAME IS TO PREVENT THE RESURRECTION OF THE DEMON LORD.
HOWEVER, THE TRUE "DEMON LORD" IS ACTUALLY ONE OF ITS PLAYERS' CHARACTERS.
AND THAT CHARACTER IS CONTROLLED BY SAKAMOTO TAKUMA.
"DIABLO."

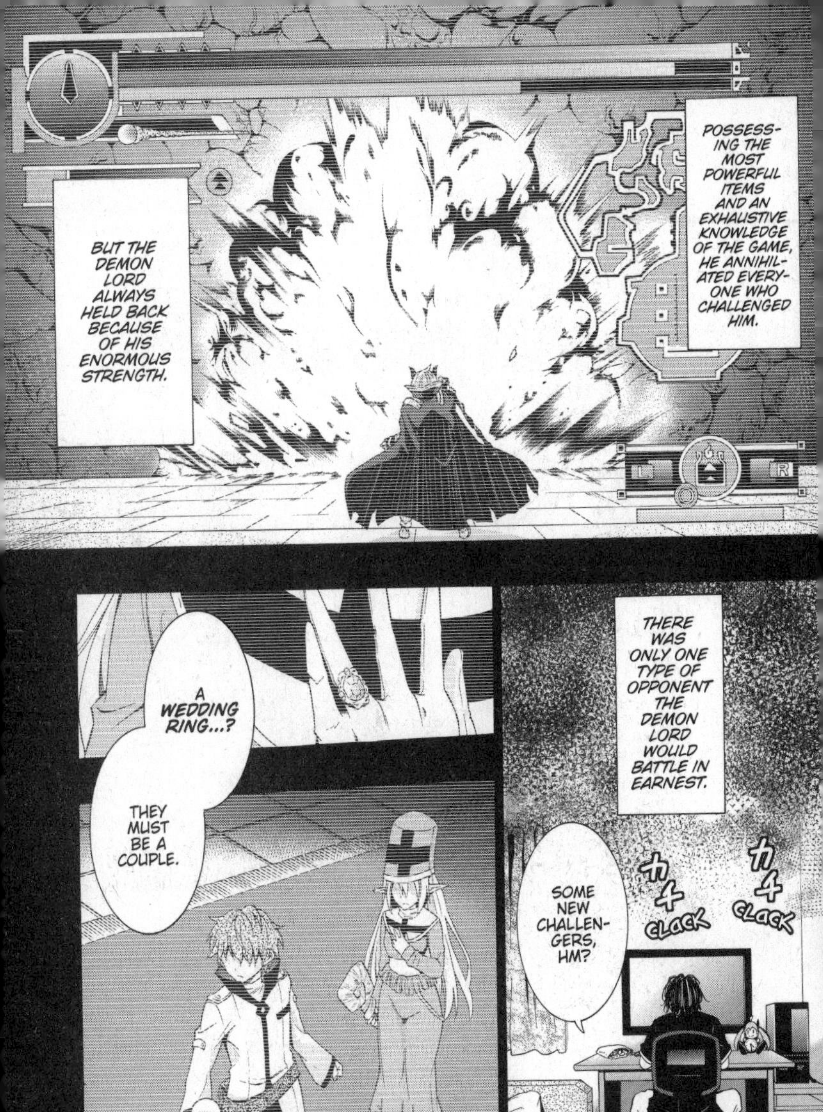

POSSESSING THE MOST POWERFUL ITEMS AND AN EXHAUSTIVE KNOWLEDGE OF THE GAME, HE ANNIHILATED EVERYONE WHO CHALLENGED HIM.
BUT THE DEMON LORD ALWAYS HELD BACK BECAUSE OF HIS ENORMOUS STRENGTH.
THERE WAS ONLY ONE TYPE OF OPPONENT THE DEMON LORD WOULD BATTLE IN EARNEST.
カタ CLACK
カタ CLACK
SOME NEW CHALLENGERS, HM?
A WEDDING RING...?
THEY MUST BE A COUPLE.

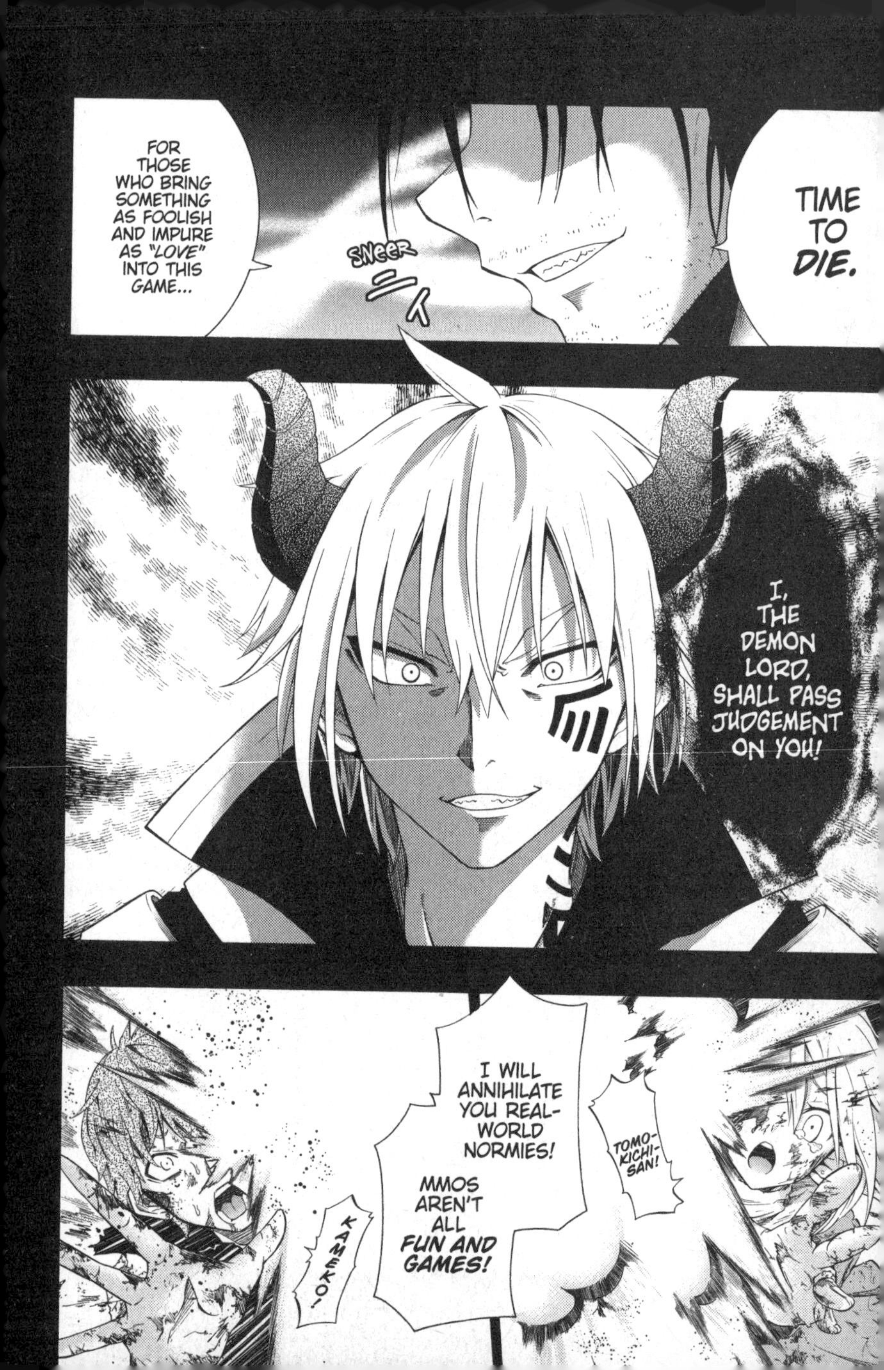
FOR THOSE WHO BRING SOMETHING AS FOOLISH AND IMPURE AS "LOVE" INTO THIS GAME...
SNEER
ニイ
TIME TO DIE.
I, THE DEMON LORD, SHALL PASS JUDGEMENT ON YOU!
TOMO-KICHI-SAN!
I WILL ANNIHILATE YOU REAL-WORLD NORMIES!
MMOS AREN'T ALL FUN AND GAMES!
KAMEKO!

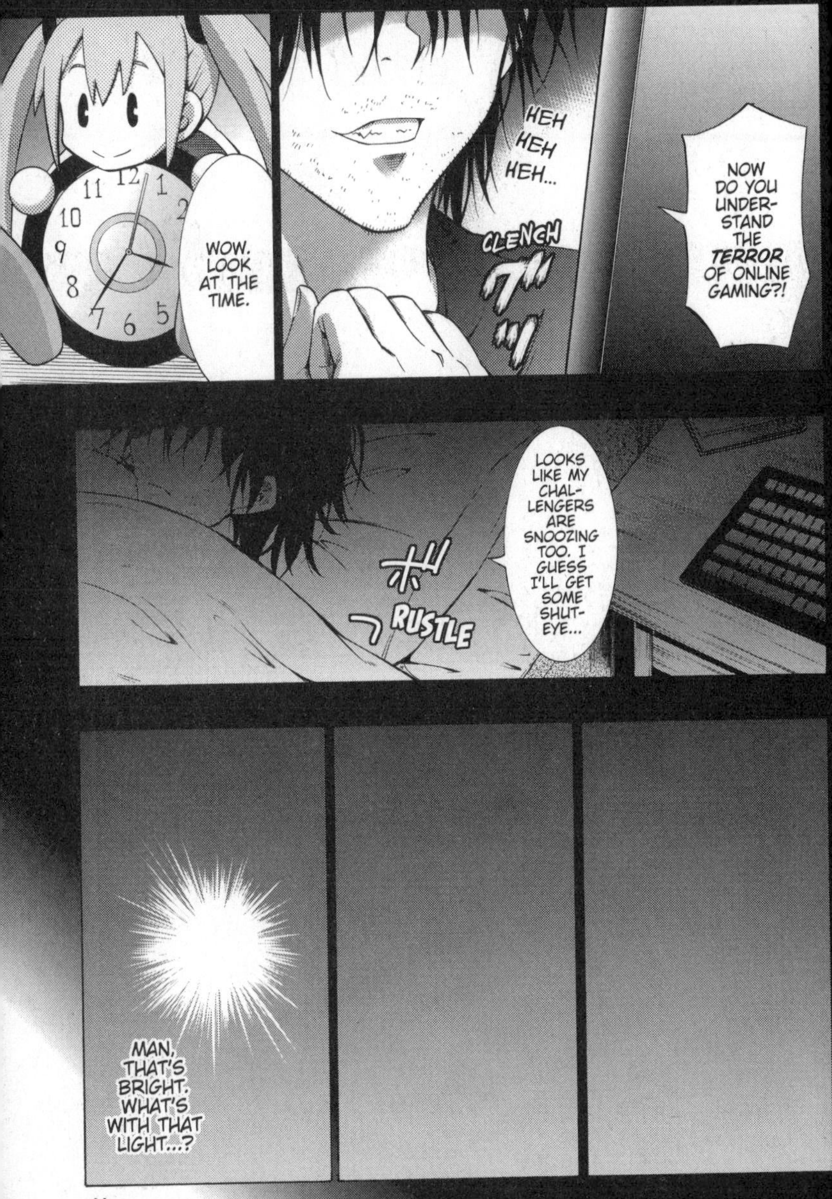
NOW DO YOU UNDERSTAND THE TERROR OF ONLINE GAMING?!
HEH HEH HEH...
CLENCH
WOW. LOOK AT THE TIME.
LOOKS LIKE MY CHALLENGERS ARE SNOOZING TOO. I GUESS I'LL GET SOME SHUT-EYE...
RUSTLE
MAN, THAT'S BRIGHT. WHAT'S WITH THAT LIGHT...?

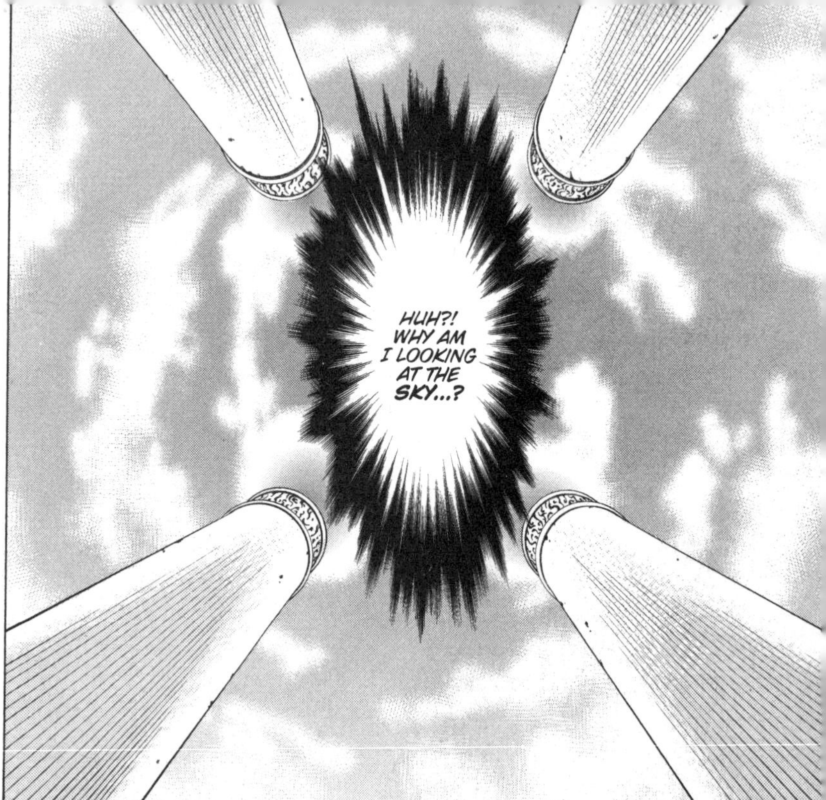
HUH?! WHY AM I LOOKING AT THE SKY...?

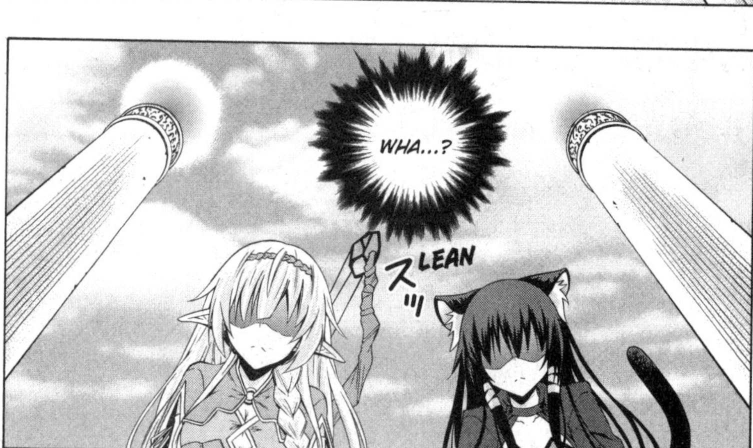
WHA...?
LEAN
スッ

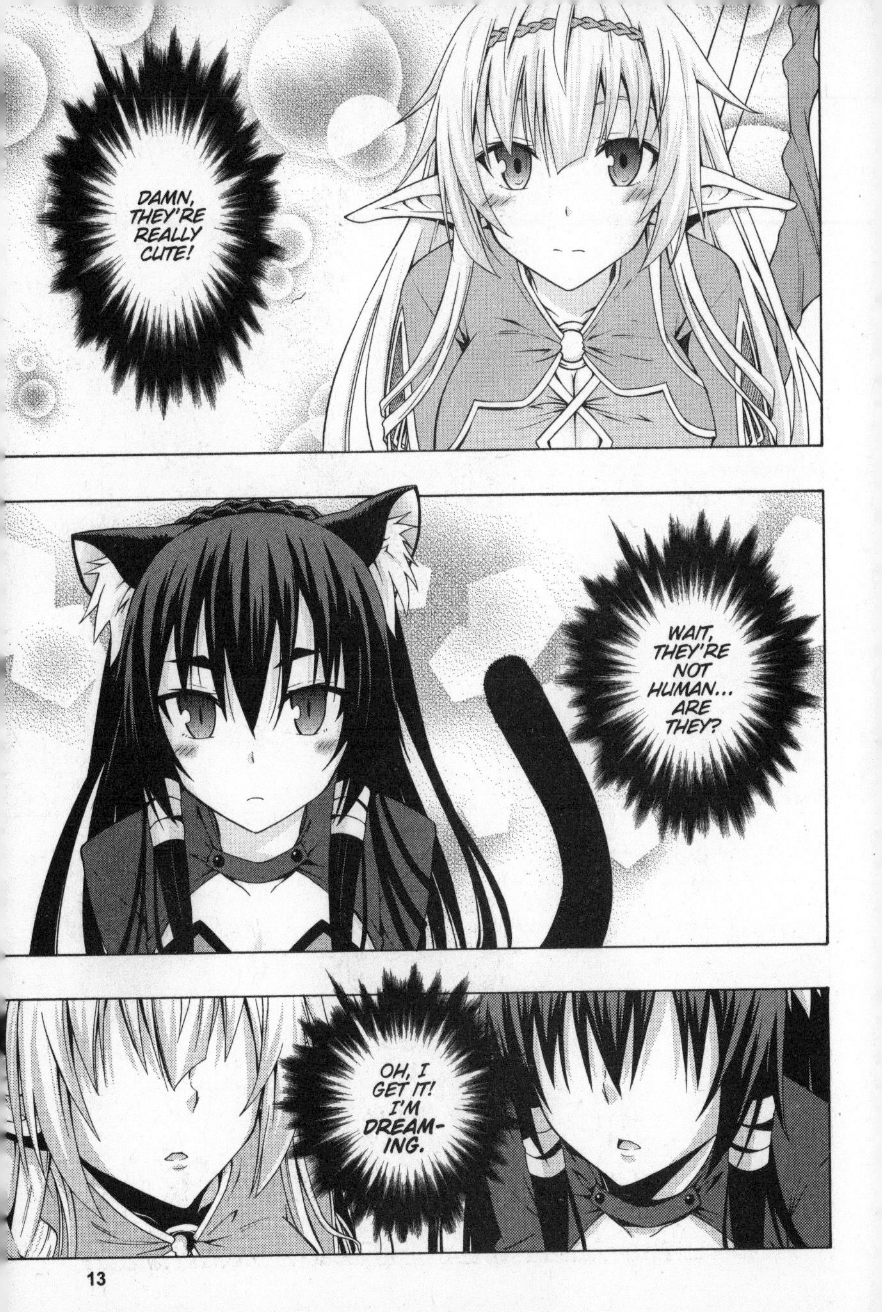
DAMN, THEY'RE REALLY CUTE!
WAIT, THEY'RE NOT HUMAN... ARE THEY?
OH, I GET IT! I'M DREAMING.

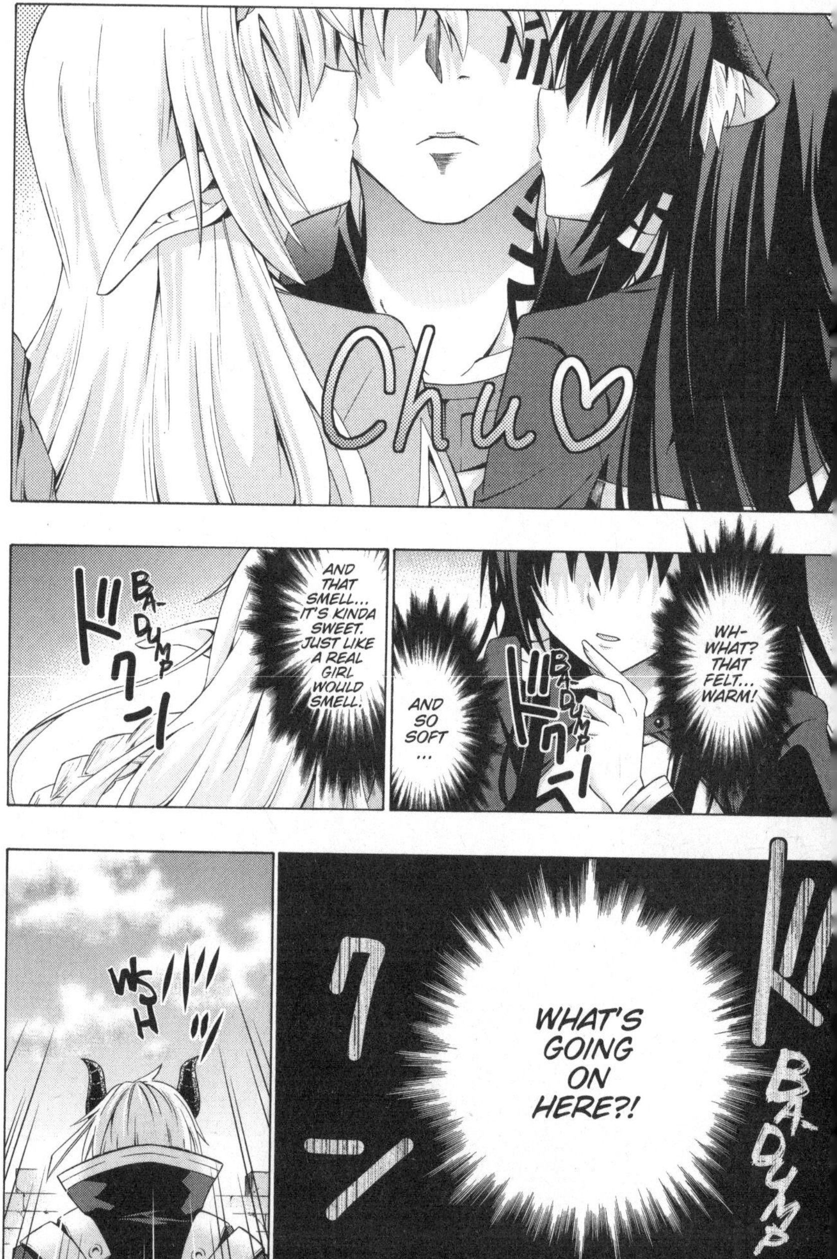
Chu♡
WH-WHAT? THAT FELT... WARM!
AND SO SOFT...
BA-DUMP
AND THAT SMELL... IT'S KINDA SWEET. JUST LIKE A REAL GIRL WOULD SMELL.
BA-DUMP
WHAT'S GOING ON HERE?!
BA-DUMP
WSH

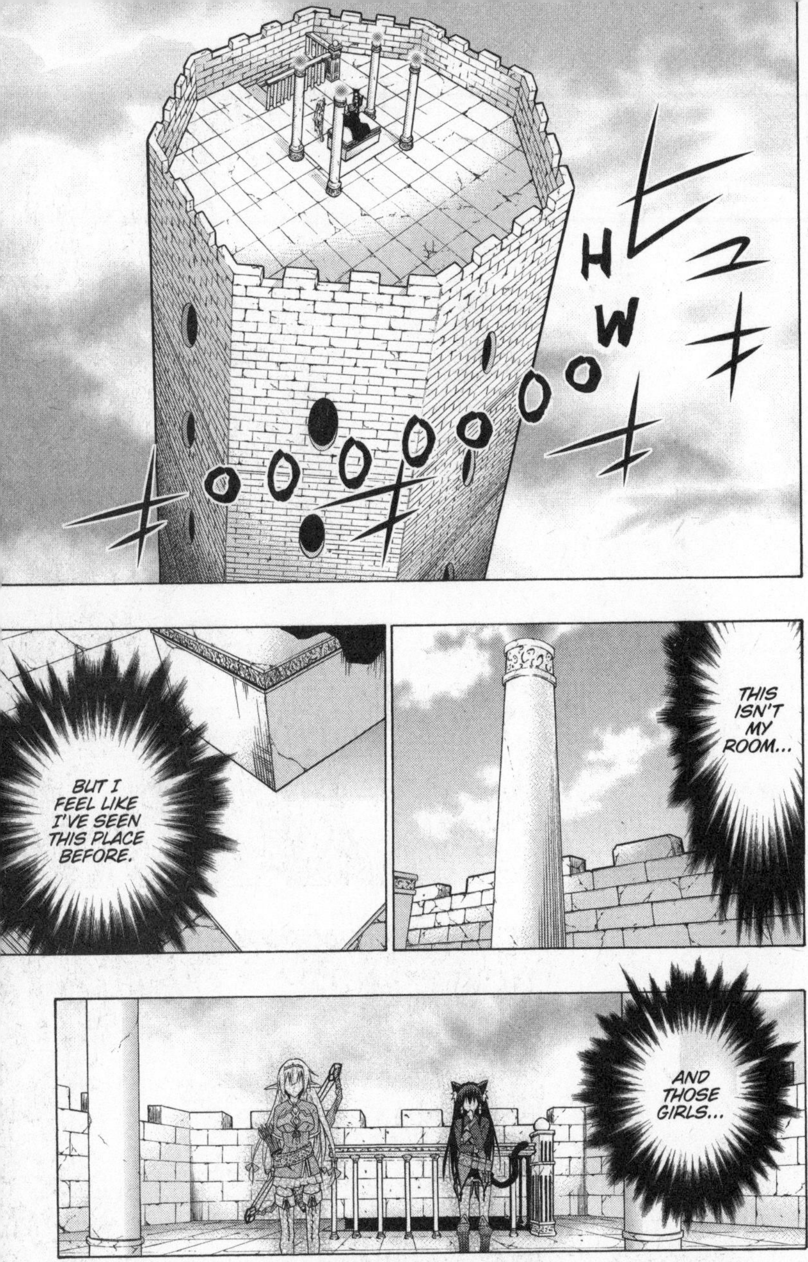
HWOOOOOOO
THIS ISN'T MY ROOM...
BUT I FEEL LIKE I'VE SEEN THIS PLACE BEFORE.
AND THOSE GIRLS...

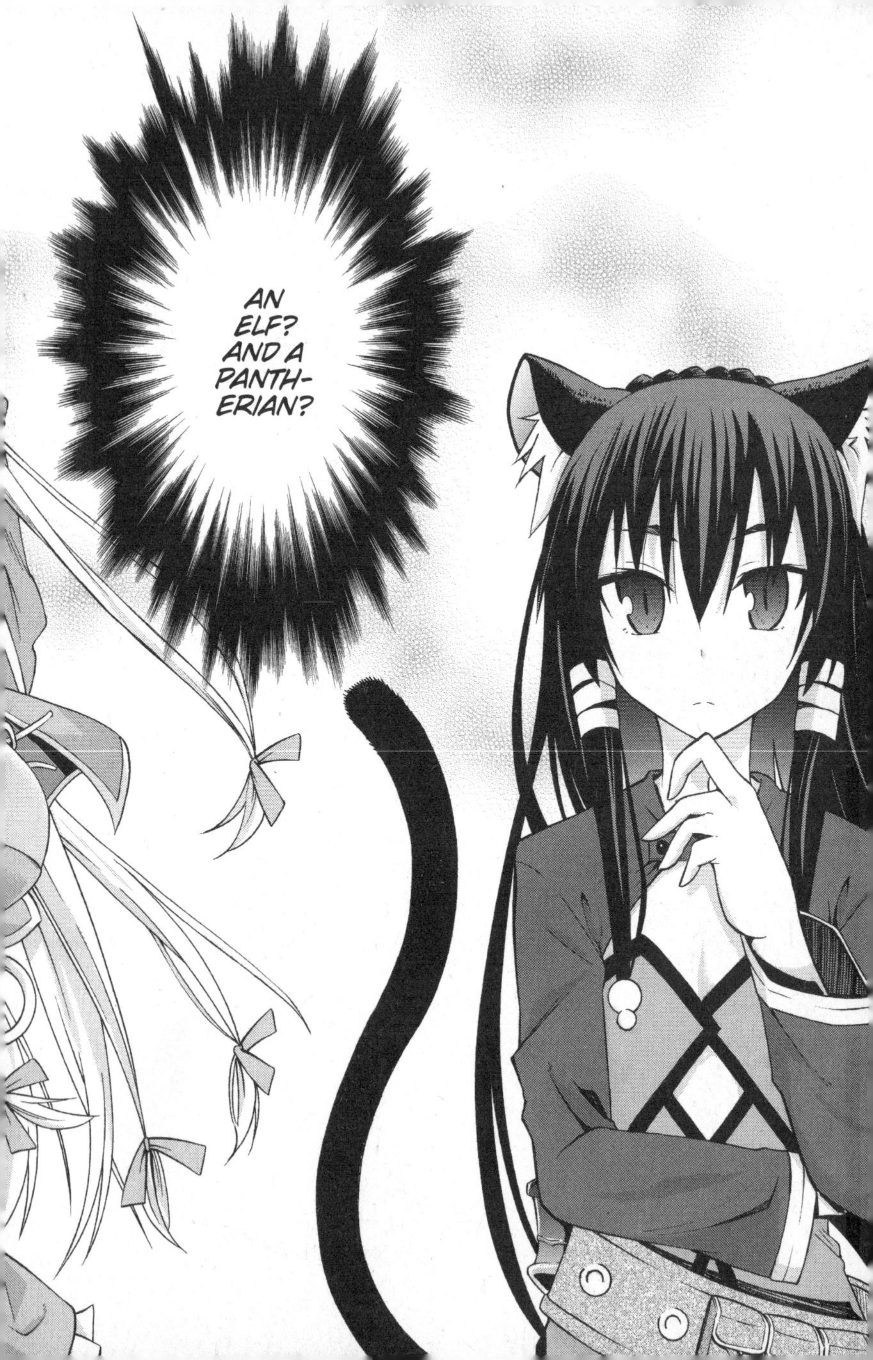
AN ELF? AND A PANTH-ERIAN?

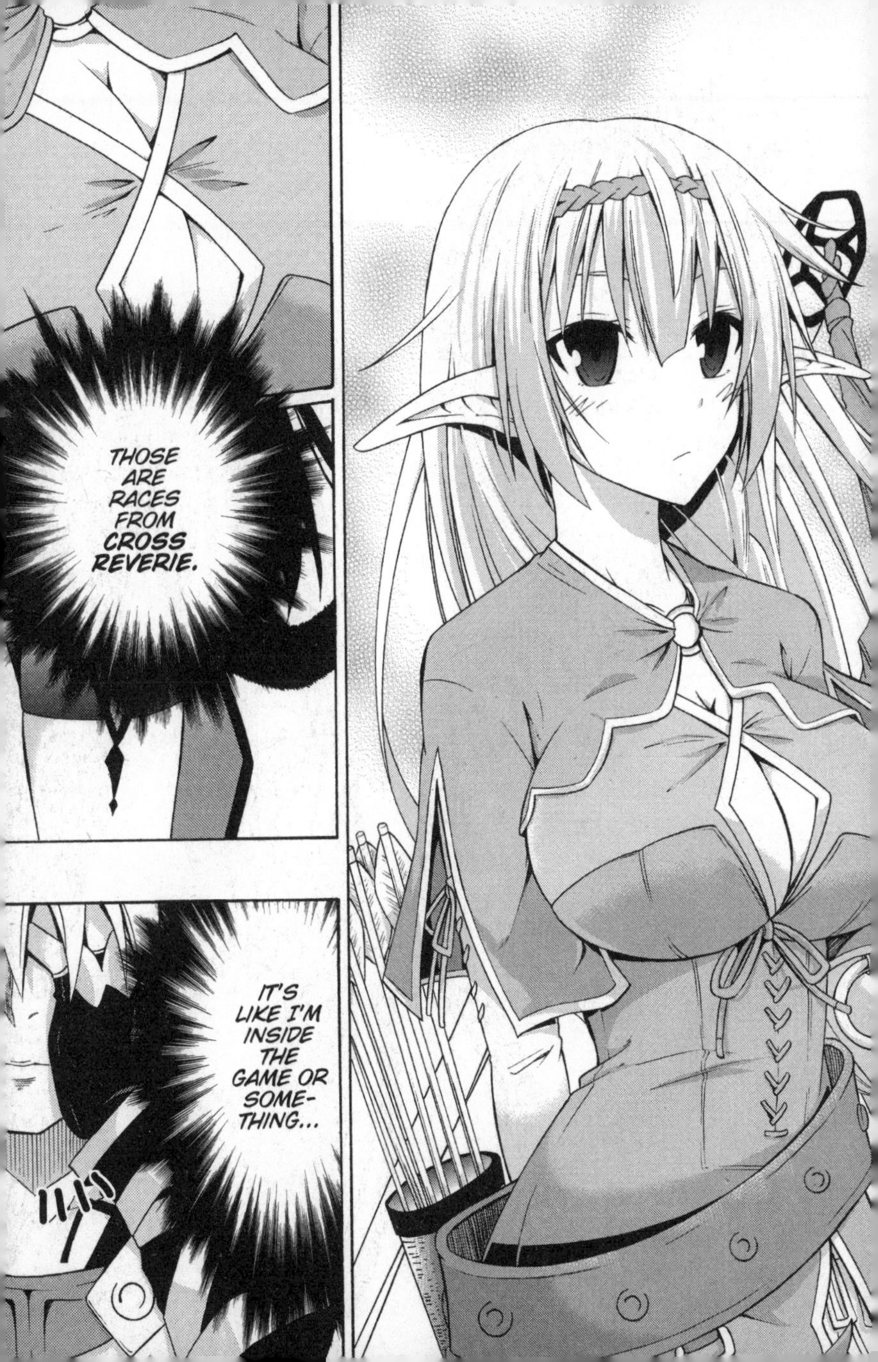
THOSE ARE RACES FROM CROSS REVERIE.
IT'S LIKE I'M INSIDE THE GAME OR SOME-THING...

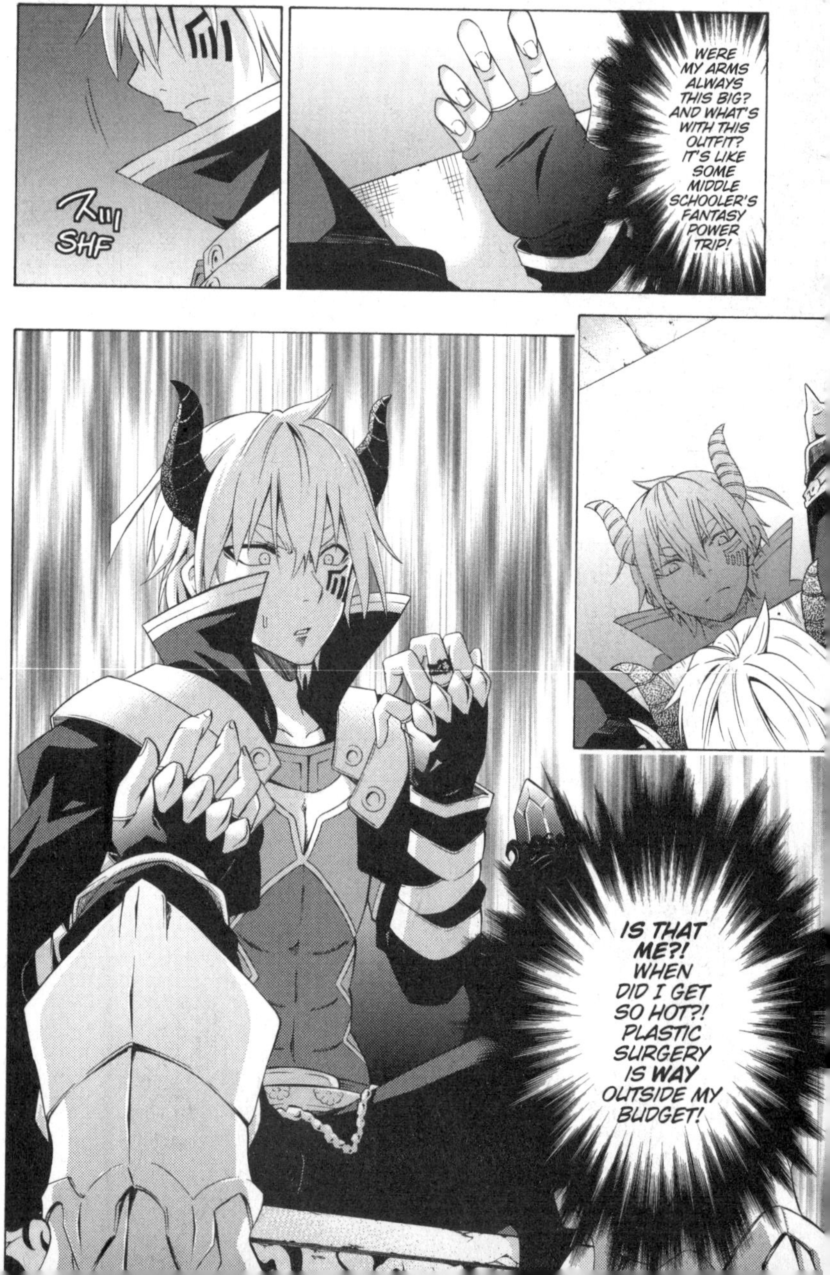
WERE MY ARMS ALWAYS THIS BIG? AND WHAT'S WITH THIS OUTFIT? IT'S LIKE SOME MIDDLE SCHOOLER'S FANTASY POWER TRIP!
スッ
SHF
IS THAT ME?! WHEN DID I GET SO HOT?! PLASTIC SURGERY IS WAY OUTSIDE MY BUDGET!

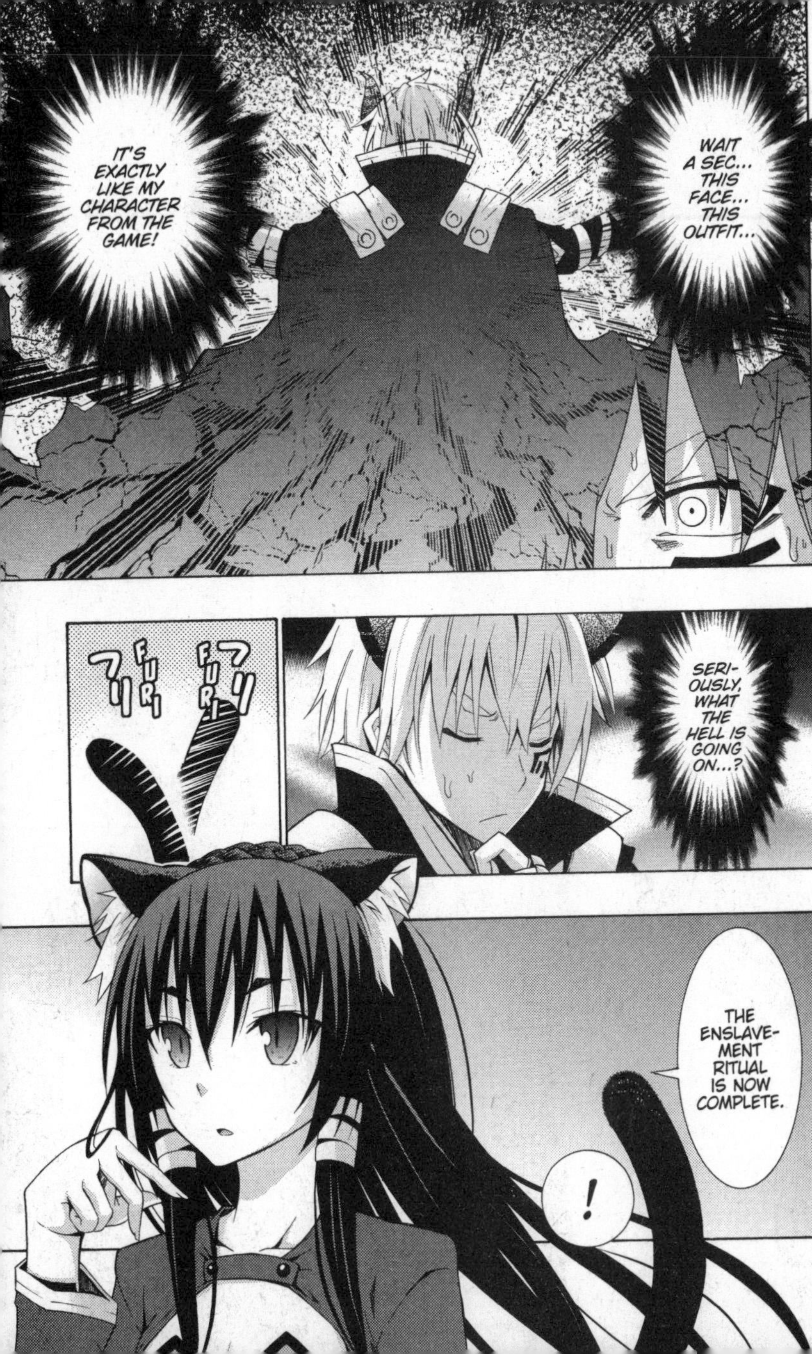
WAIT A SEC... THIS FACE... THIS OUTFIT...
IT'S EXACTLY LIKE MY CHARACTER FROM THE GAME!
SERI-OUSLY, WHAT THE HELL IS GOING ON...?
フリ FURI
フリ FURI
THE ENSLAVE-MENT RITUAL IS NOW COMPLETE.
!

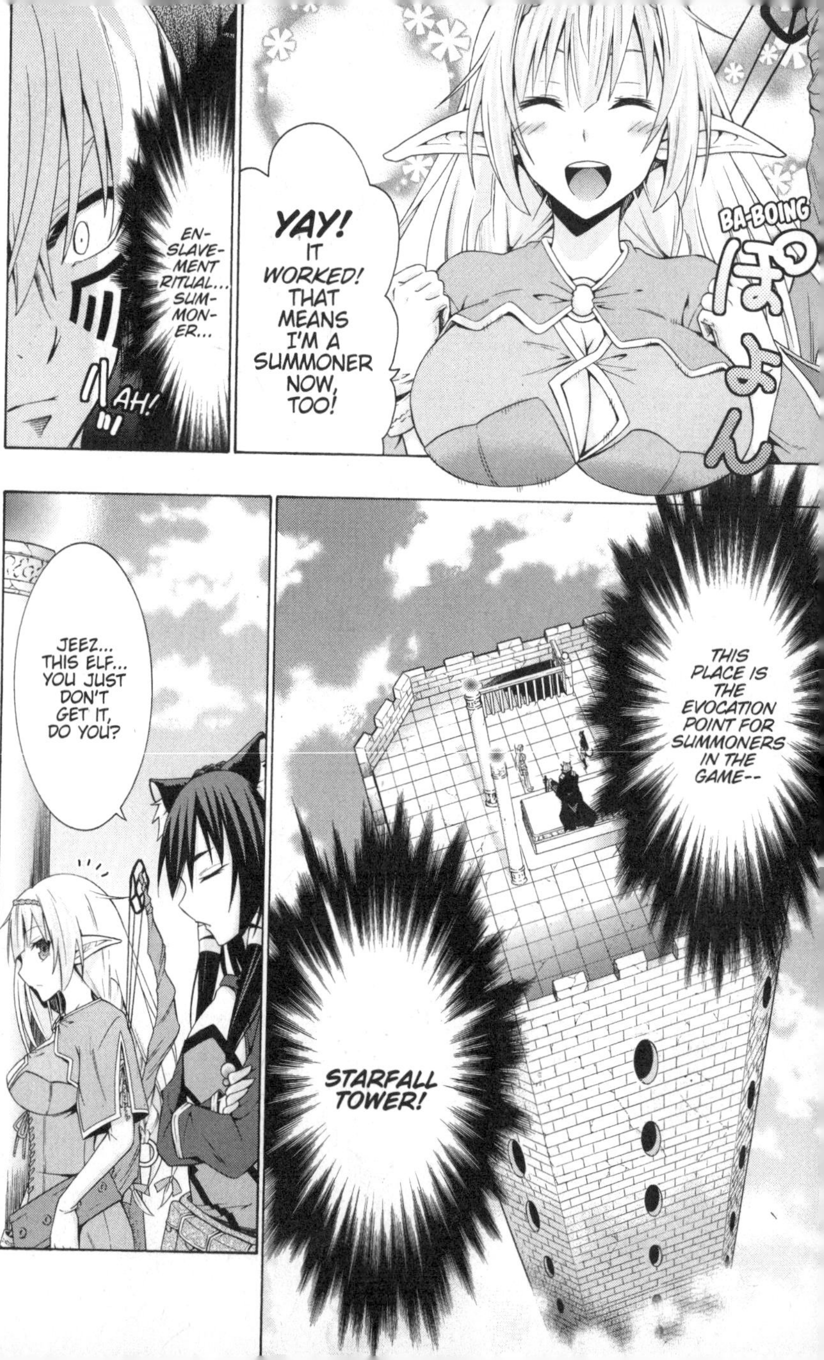
BA-BOING
ぽよん
YAY! IT WORKED! THAT MEANS I'M A SUMMONER NOW, TOO!
EN-SLAVE-MENT RITUAL... SUM-MON-ER...
AH!
THIS PLACE IS THE EVOCATION POINT FOR SUMMONERS IN THE GAME--
STARFALL TOWER!
JEEZ... THIS ELF... YOU JUST DON'T GET IT, DO YOU?

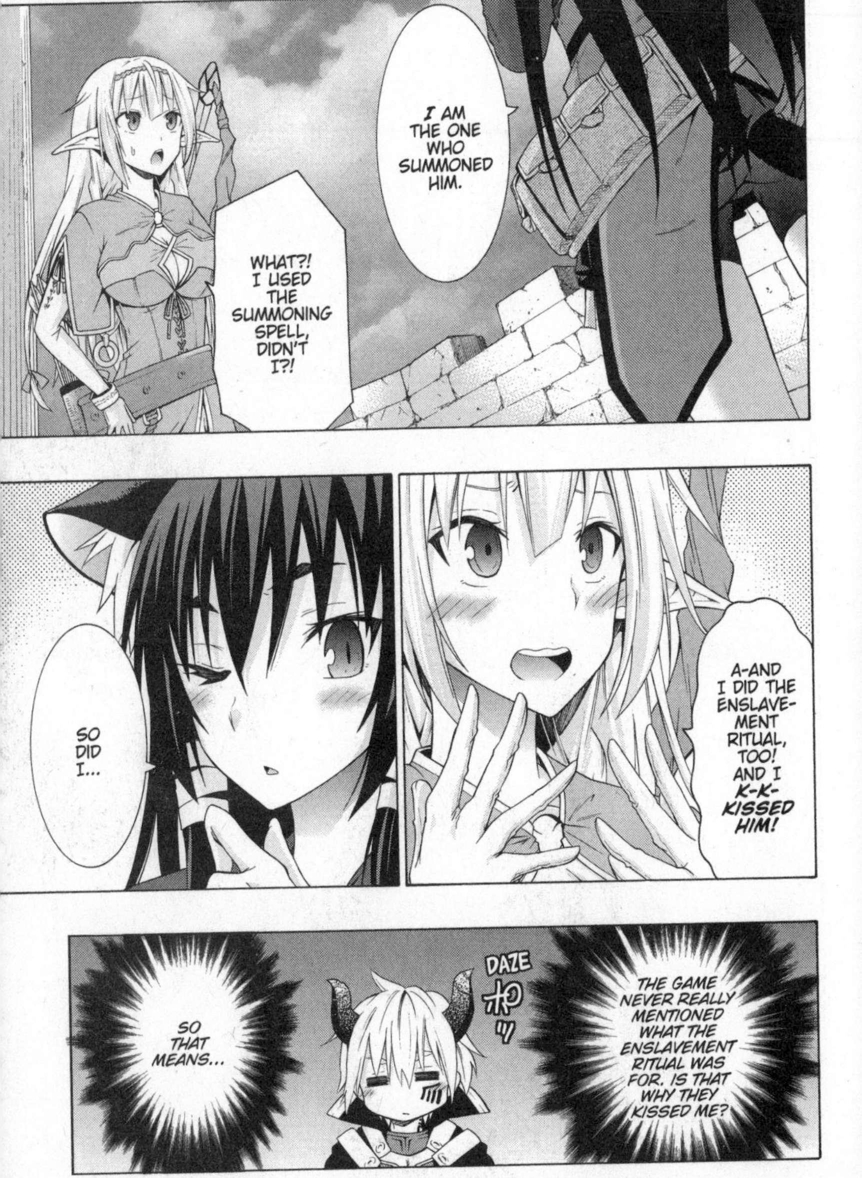
I AM THE ONE WHO SUMMONED HIM.
WHAT?! I USED THE SUMMONING SPELL, DIDN'T I?!
A-AND I DID THE ENSLAVE-MENT RITUAL, TOO! AND I K-K-KISSED HIM!
SO DID I...
THE GAME NEVER REALLY MENTIONED WHAT THE ENSLAVEMENT RITUAL WAS FOR. IS THAT WHY THEY KISSED ME?
DAZE
ホッ
SO THAT MEANS...

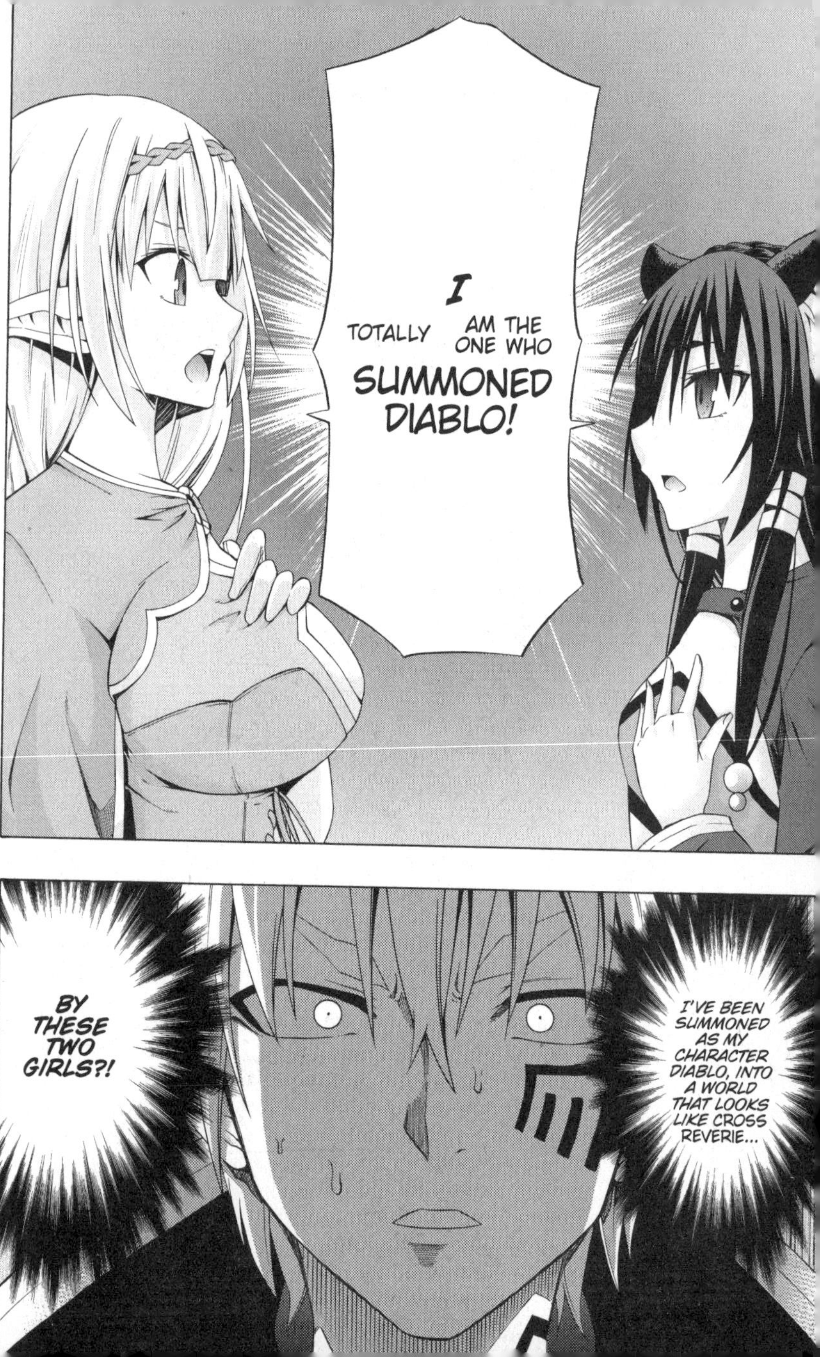
I TOTALLY AM THE ONE WHO SUMMONED DIABLO!
I'VE BEEN SUMMONED AS MY CHARACTER DIABLO, INTO A WORLD THAT LOOKS LIKE CROSS REVERIE...
BY THESE TWO GIRLS?!

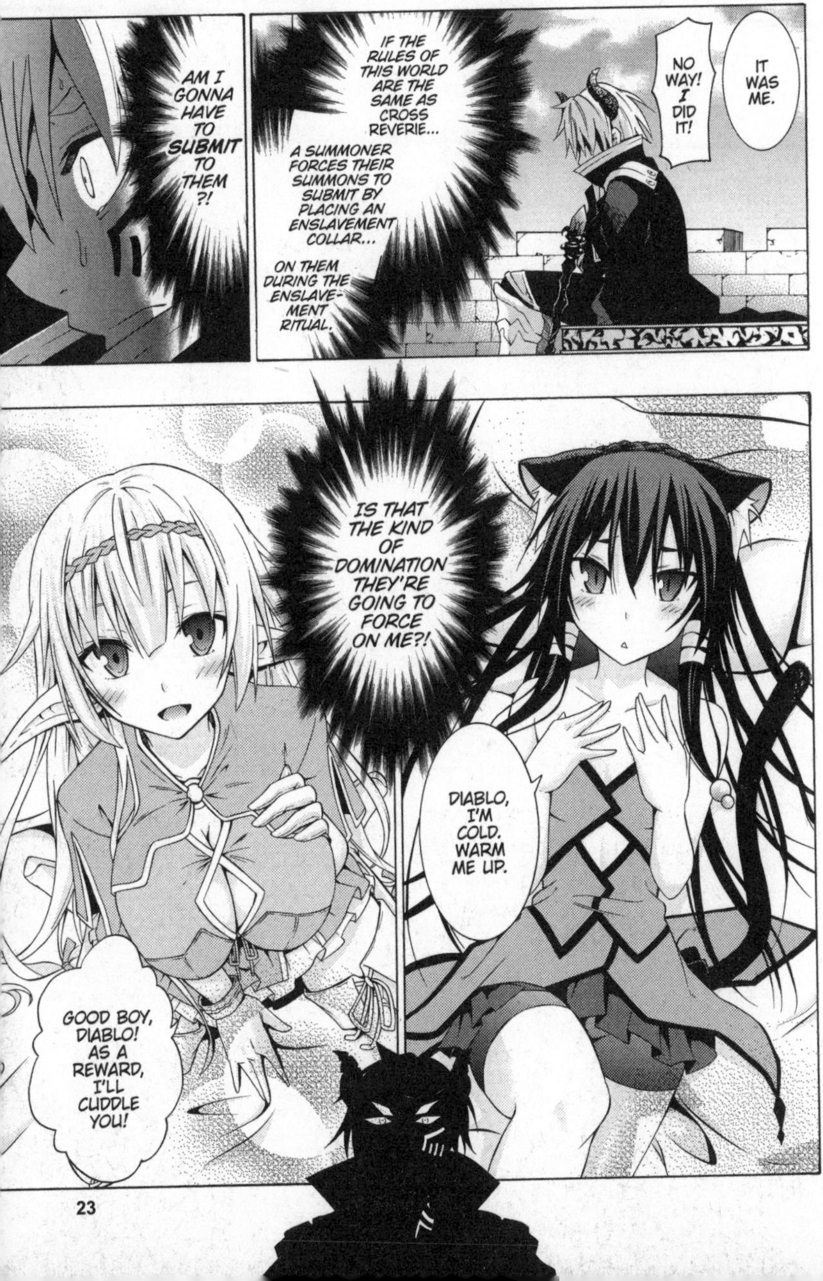
IT WAS ME.
NO WAY! I DID IT!
IF THE RULES OF THIS WORLD ARE THE SAME AS CROSS REVERIE...
A SUMMONER FORCES THEIR SUMMONS TO SUBMIT BY PLACING AN ENSLAVEMENT COLLAR...
ON THEM DURING THE ENSLAVE-MENT RITUAL.
AM I GONNA HAVE TO SUBMIT TO THEM?!
IS THAT THE KIND OF DOMINATION THEY'RE GOING TO FORCE ON ME?!
DIABLO, I'M COLD. WARM ME UP.
GOOD BOY, DIABLO! AS A REWARD, I'LL CUDDLE YOU!

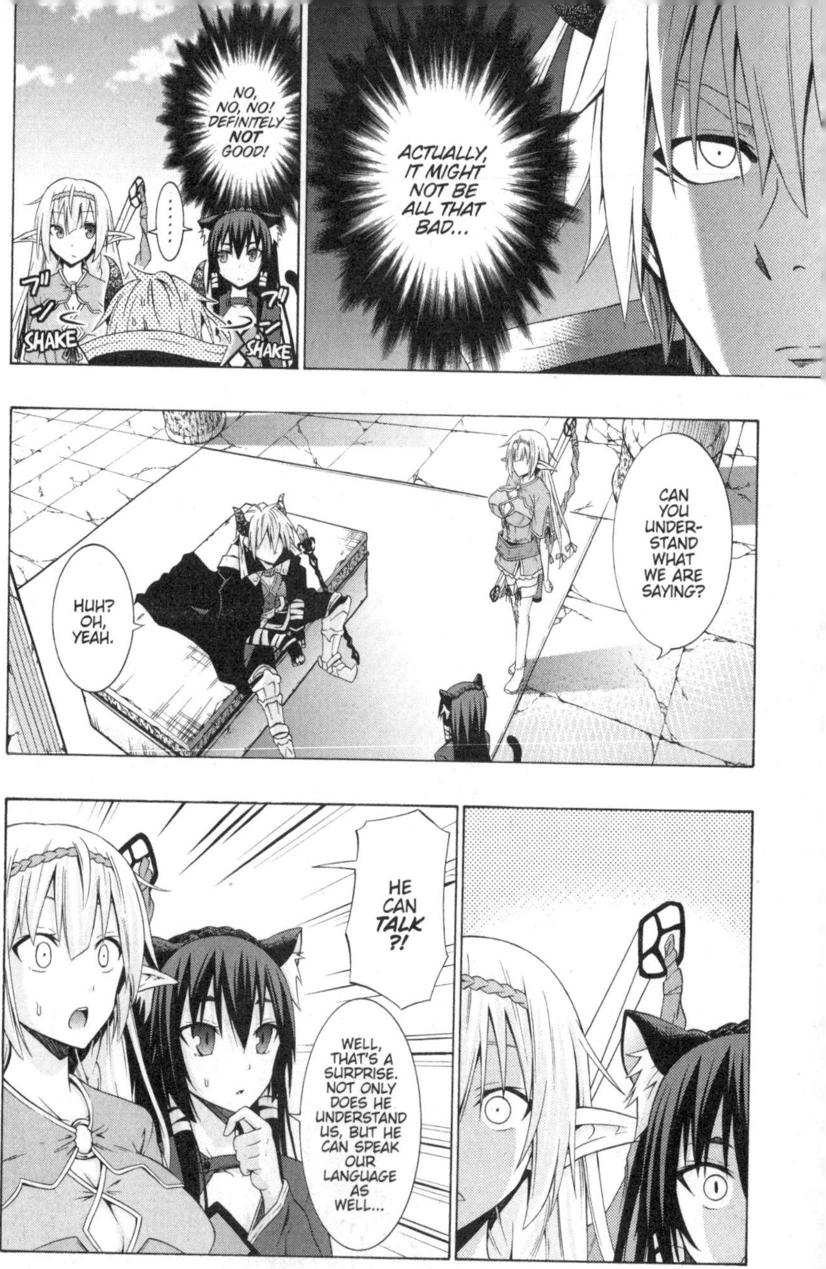
ACTUALLY, IT MIGHT NOT BE ALL THAT BAD...
NO, NO, NO! DEFINITELY NOT GOOD!
......
SHAKE
SHAKE
CAN YOU UNDER-STAND WHAT WE ARE SAYING?
HUH? OH, YEAH.
HE CAN TALK?!
WELL, THAT'S A SURPRISE. NOT ONLY DOES HE UNDERSTAND US, BUT HE CAN SPEAK OUR LANGUAGE AS WELL...

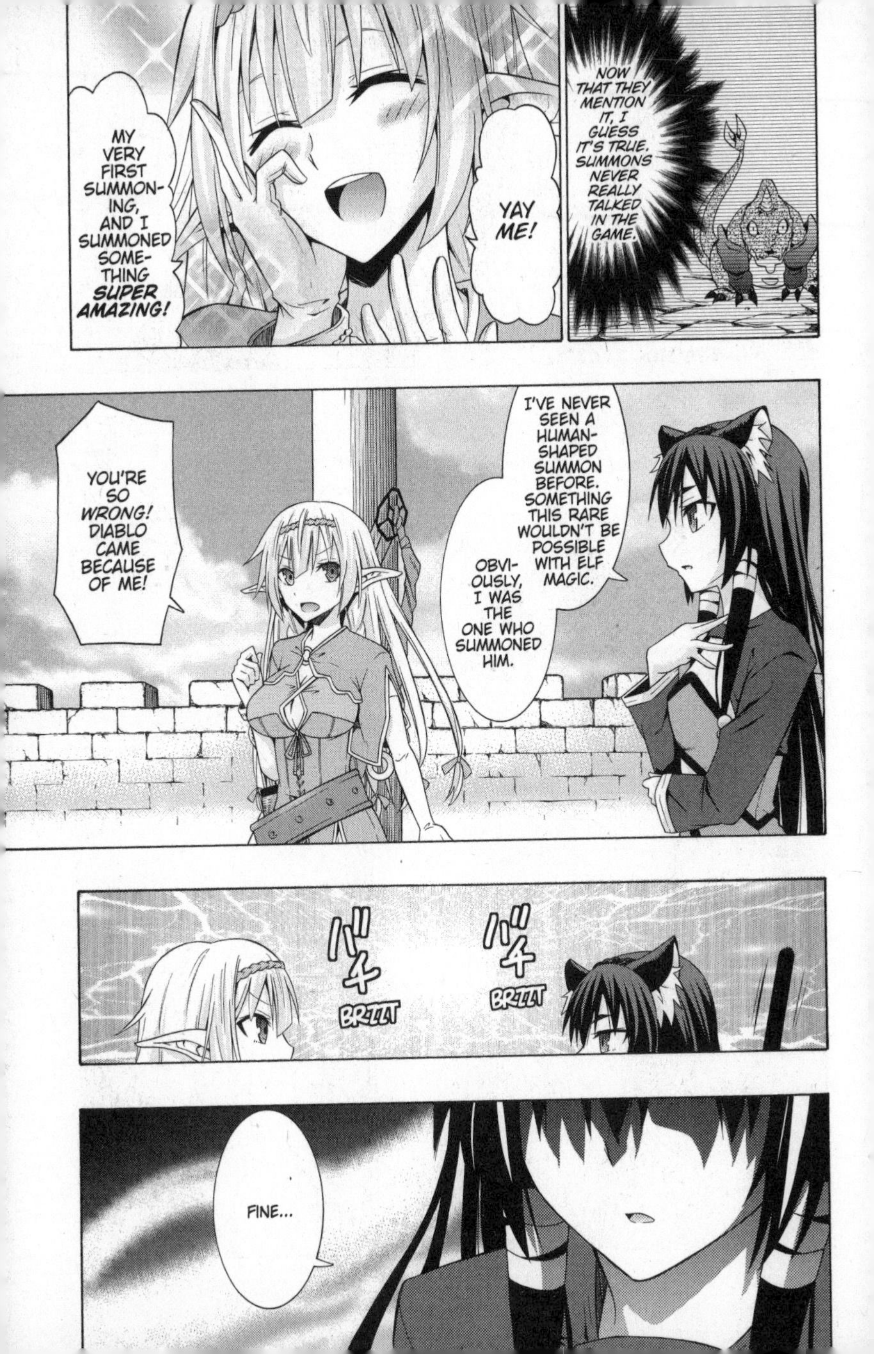
NOW THAT THEY MENTION IT, I GUESS IT'S TRUE. SUMMONS NEVER REALLY TALKED IN THE GAME.
MY VERY FIRST SUMMONING, AND I SUMMONED SOMETHING SUPER AMAZING!
YAY ME!
I'VE NEVER SEEN A HUMAN-SHAPED SUMMON BEFORE. SOMETHING THIS RARE WOULDN'T BE POSSIBLE WITH ELF MAGIC.
OBVIOUSLY, I WAS THE ONE WHO SUMMONED HIM.
YOU'RE SO WRONG! DIABLO CAME BECAUSE OF ME!
バチ
BRZZZT
バチ
BRZZZT
FINE...

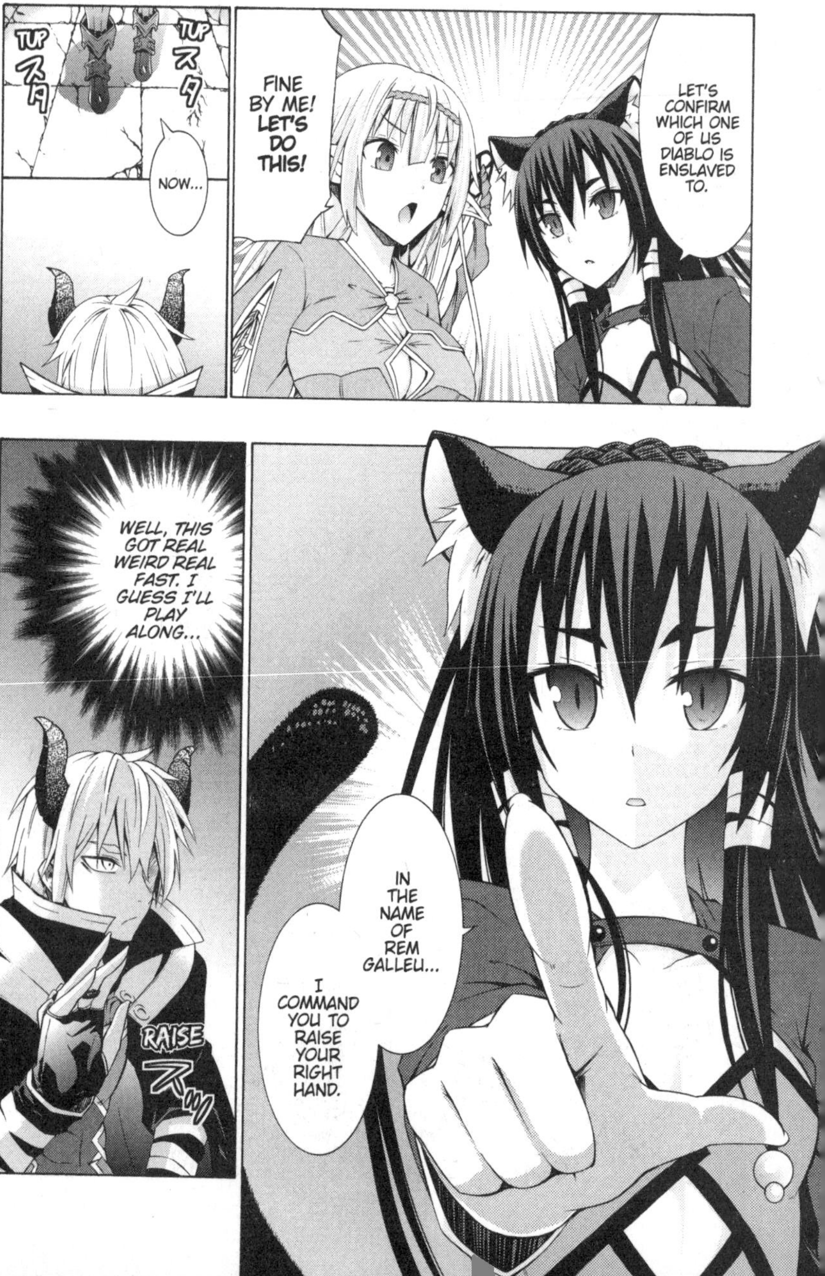
LET'S CONFIRM WHICH ONE OF US DIABLO IS ENSLAVED TO.
FINE BY ME! LET'S DO THIS!
TUP スタ
TUP スタ
NOW...
IN THE NAME OF REM GALLEU...
I COMMAND YOU TO RAISE YOUR RIGHT HAND.
WELL, THIS GOT REAL WEIRD REAL FAST. I GUESS I'LL PLAY ALONG...
RAISE スッ

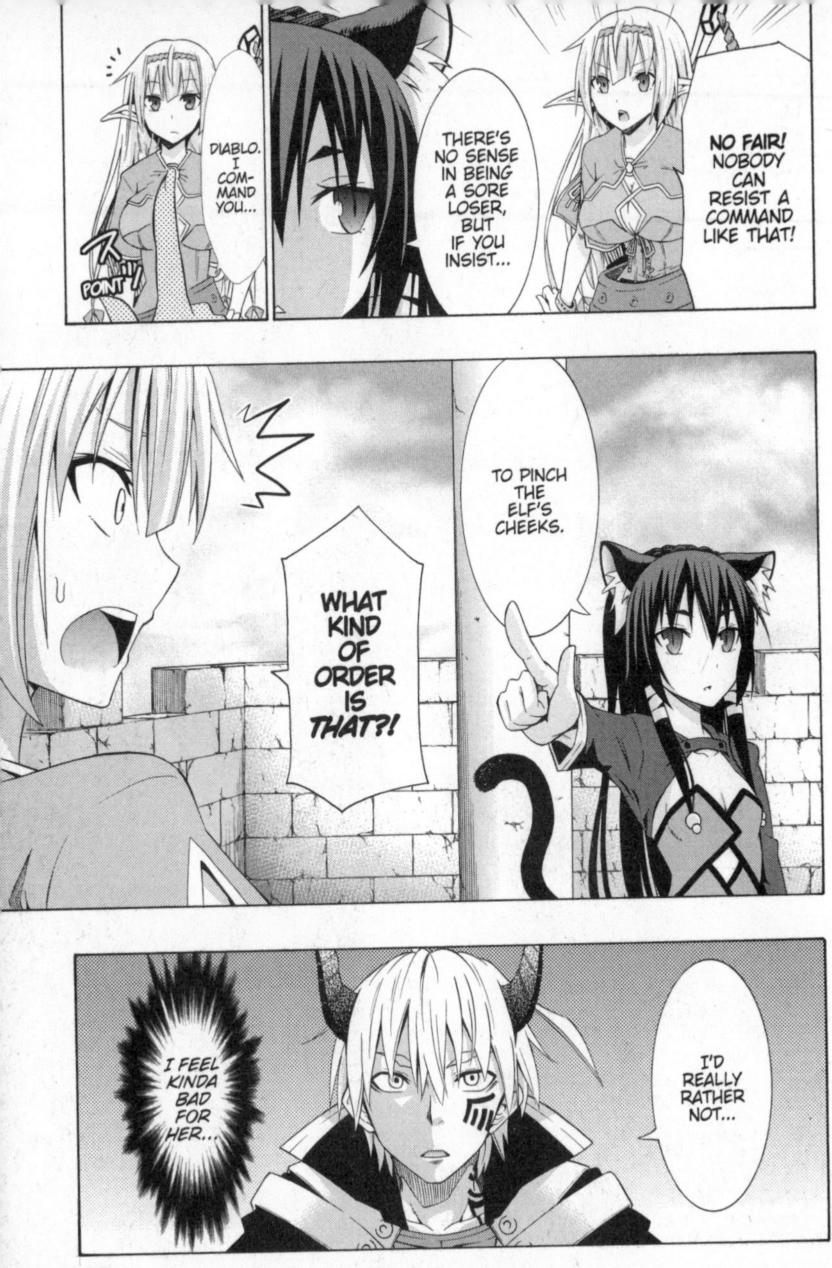
NO FAIR! NOBODY CAN RESIST A COMMAND LIKE THAT!
THERE'S NO SENSE IN BEING A SORE LOSER, BUT IF YOU INSIST...
DIABLO. I COM-MAND YOU...
POINT
TO PINCH THE ELF'S CHEEKS.
WHAT KIND OF ORDER IS *THAT?!*
I'D REALLY RATHER NOT...
I FEEL KINDA BAD FOR HER...

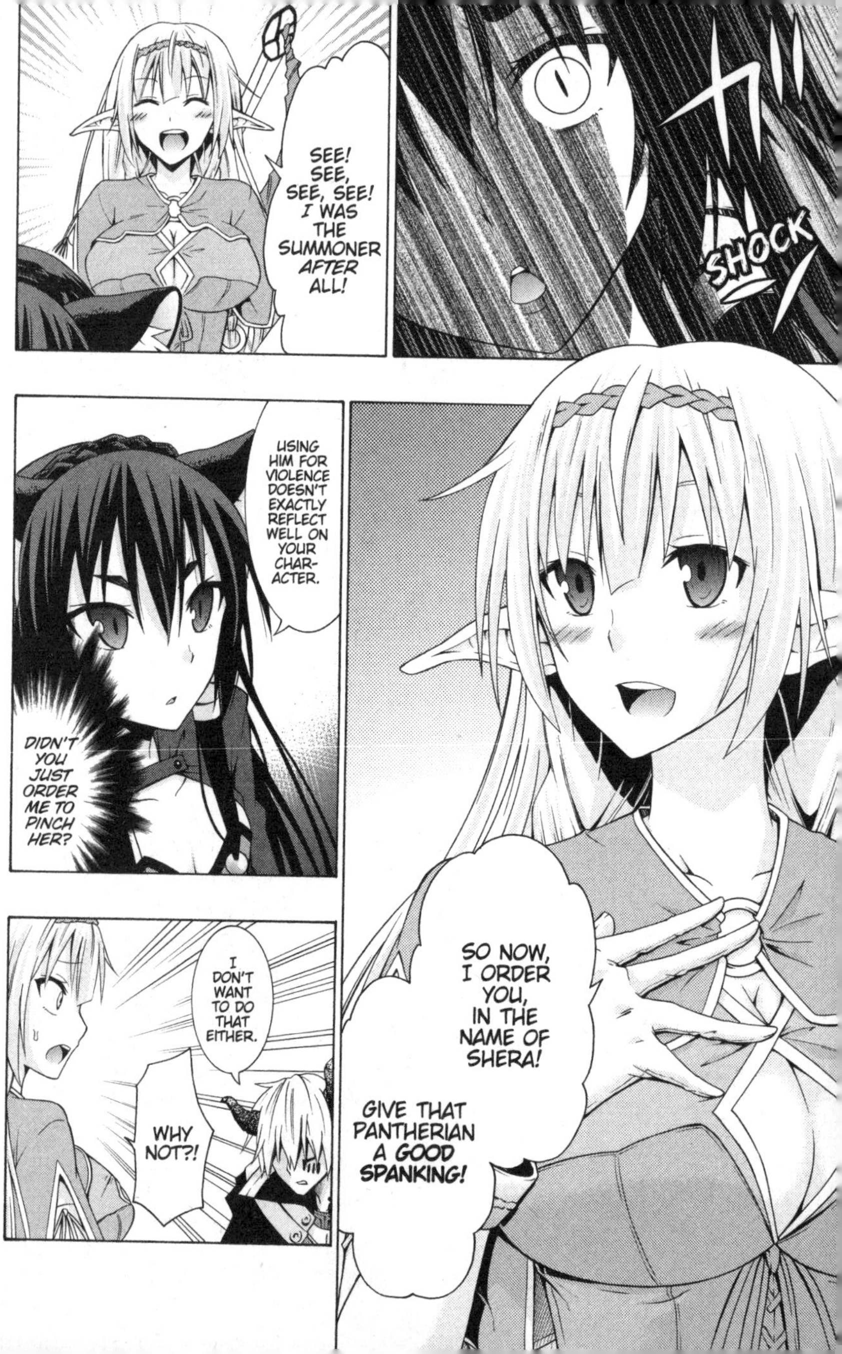
SHOCK
SEE! SEE, SEE, SEE! I WAS THE SUMMONER AFTER ALL!
SO NOW, I ORDER YOU, IN THE NAME OF SHERA!
GIVE THAT PANTHERIAN A GOOD SPANKING!
USING HIM FOR VIOLENCE DOESN'T EXACTLY REFLECT WELL ON YOUR CHAR-ACTER.
DIDN'T YOU JUST ORDER ME TO PINCH HER?
I DON'T WANT TO DO THAT EITHER.
WHY NOT?!

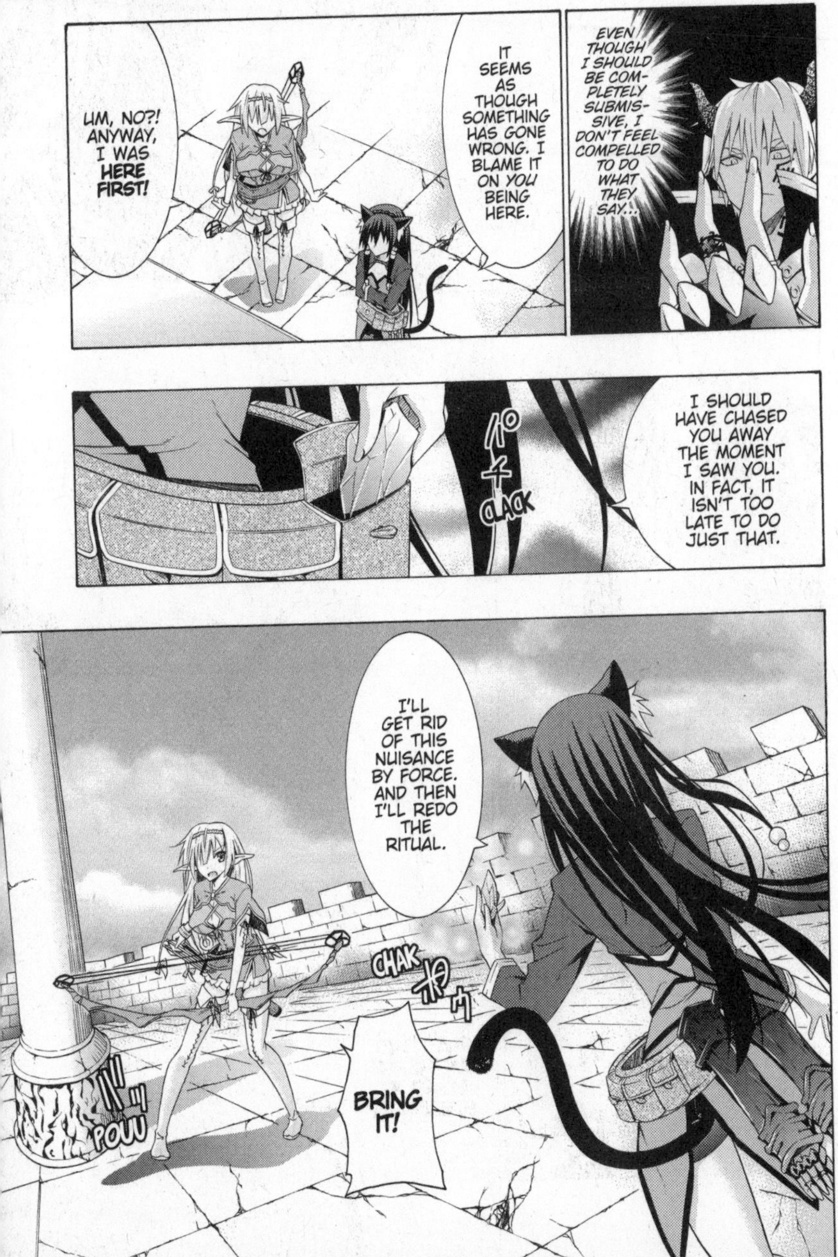
EVEN THOUGH I SHOULD BE COMPLETELY SUBMISSIVE, I DON'T FEEL COMPELLED TO DO WHAT THEY SAY...
IT SEEMS AS THOUGH SOMETHING HAS GONE WRONG. I BLAME IT ON *YOU* BEING HERE.
UM, NO?! ANYWAY, I WAS **HERE FIRST!**
I SHOULD HAVE CHASED YOU AWAY THE MOMENT I SAW YOU. IN FACT, IT ISN'T TOO LATE TO DO JUST THAT.
パチ
CLACK
I'LL GET RID OF THIS NUISANCE BY FORCE. AND THEN I'LL REDO THE RITUAL.
CHAK
BRING IT!
POUU

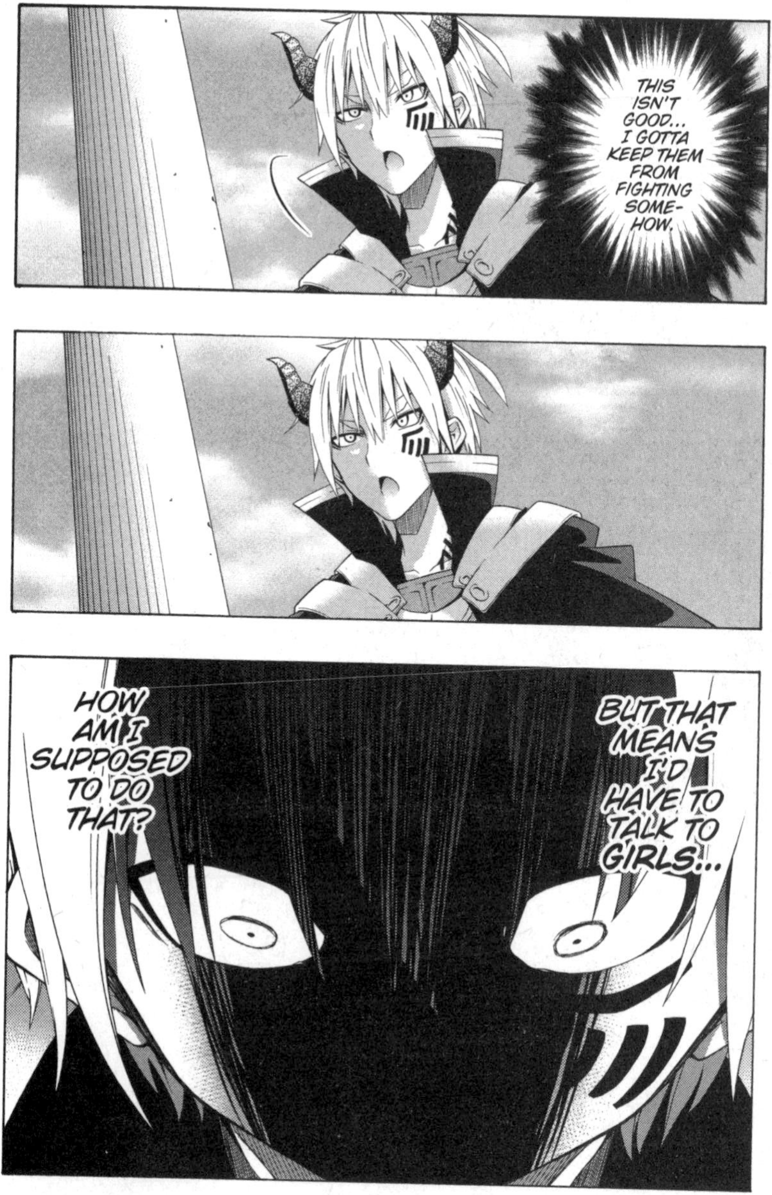
THIS ISN'T GOOD... I GOTTA KEEP THEM FROM FIGHTING SOME-HOW.
BUT THAT MEANS I'D HAVE TO TALK TO GIRLS...
HOW AM I SUPPOSED TO DO THAT?

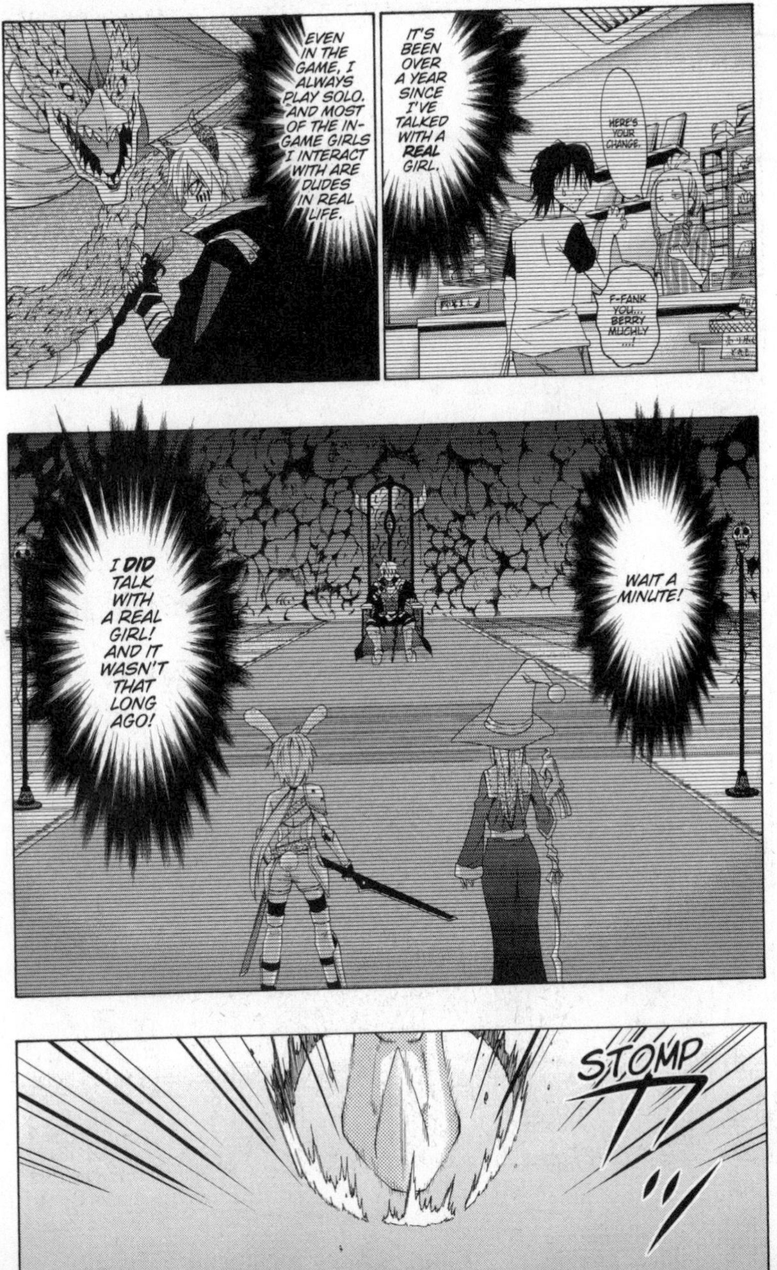
IT'S BEEN OVER A YEAR SINCE I'VE TALKED WITH A REAL GIRL.
HERE'S YOUR CHANGE.
F-FANK YOU... BERRY MUCHLY ...!
EVEN IN THE GAME, I ALWAYS PLAY SOLO. AND MOST OF THE IN-GAME GIRLS I INTERACT WITH ARE DUDES IN REAL LIFE.
WAIT A MINUTE!
I DID TALK WITH A REAL GIRL! AND IT WASN'T THAT LONG AGO!
STOMP

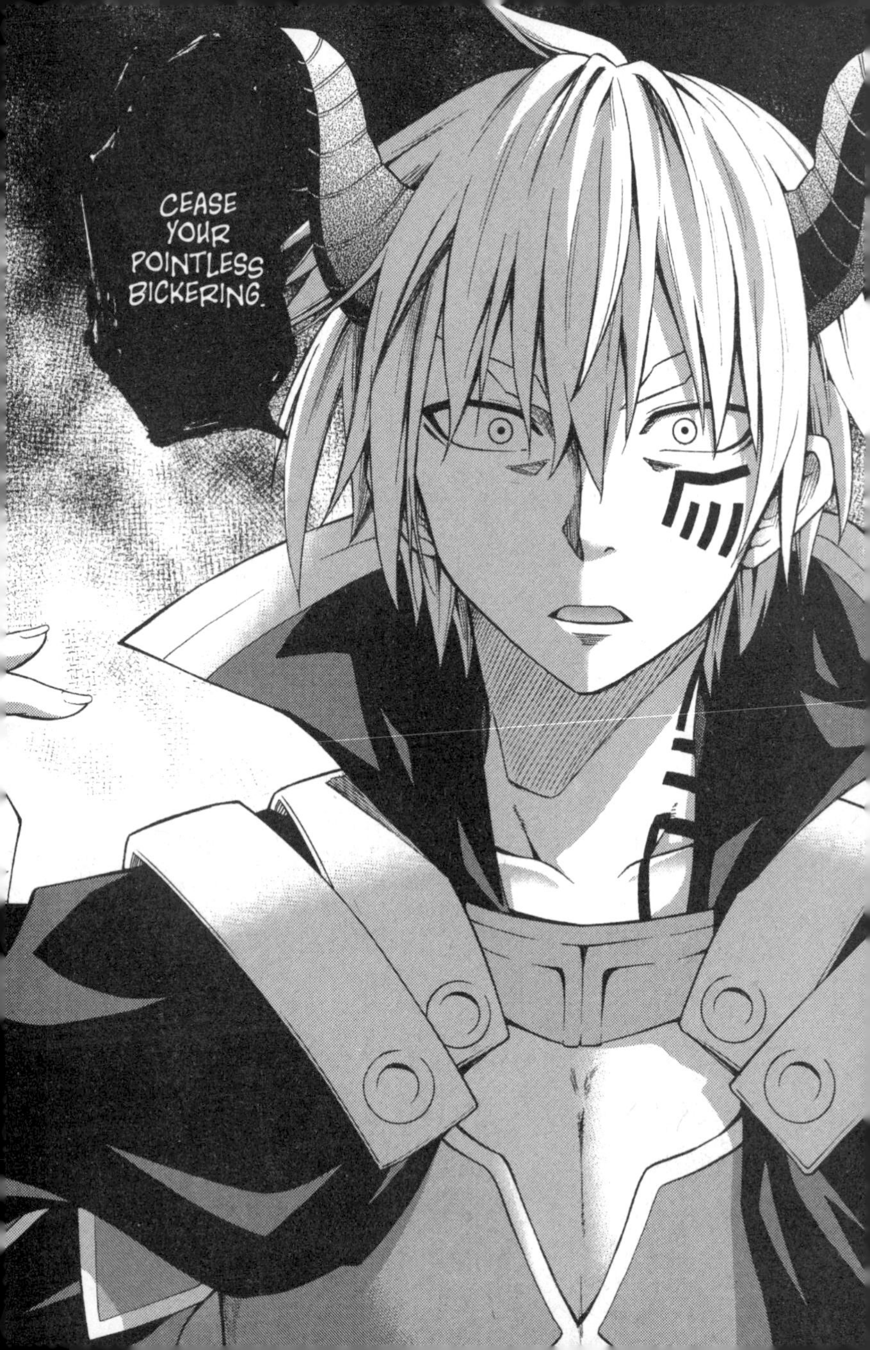
CEASE YOUR POINTLESS BICKERING.

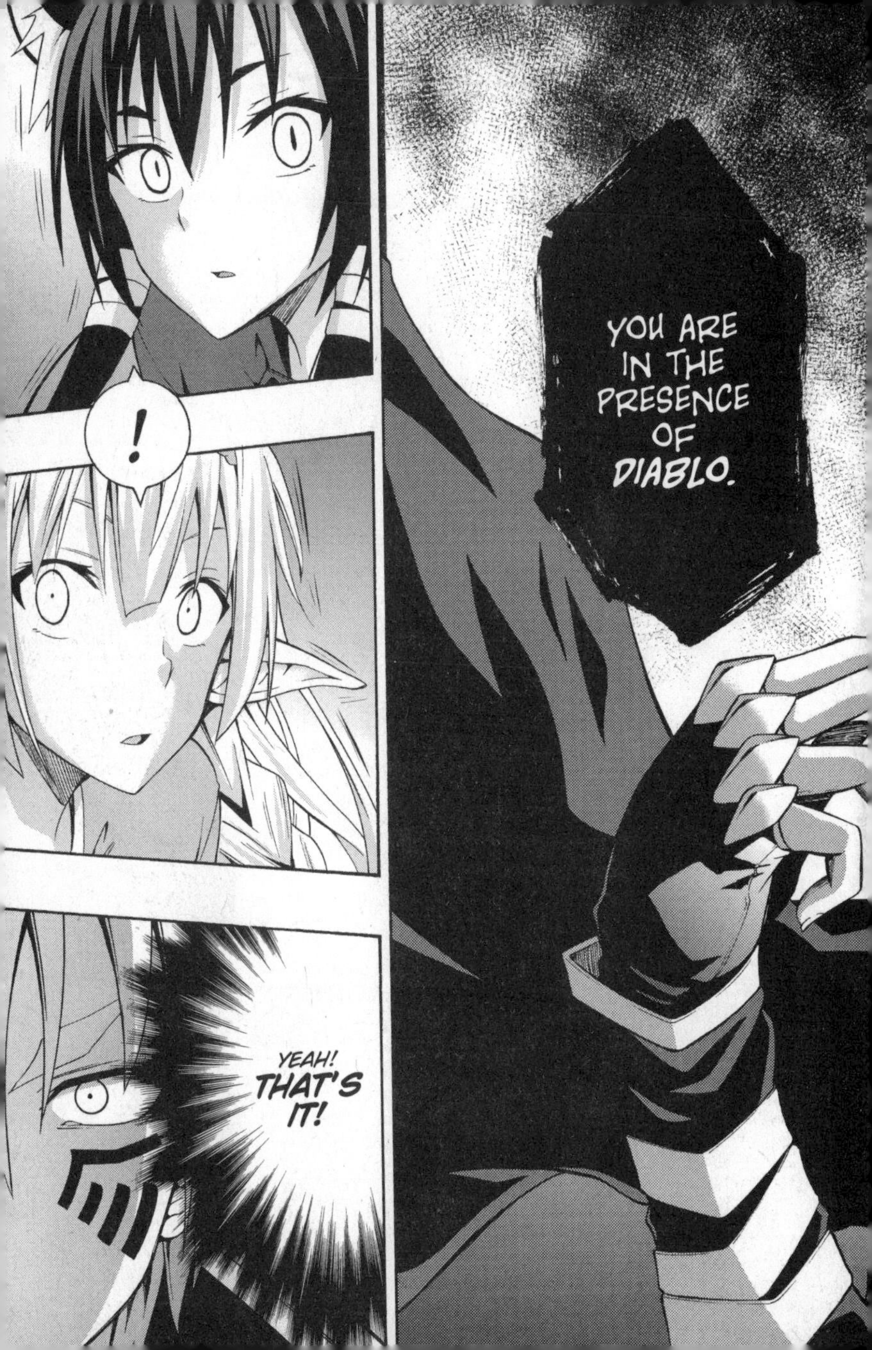
YOU ARE IN THE PRESENCE OF DIABLO.
!
YEAH! THAT'S IT!

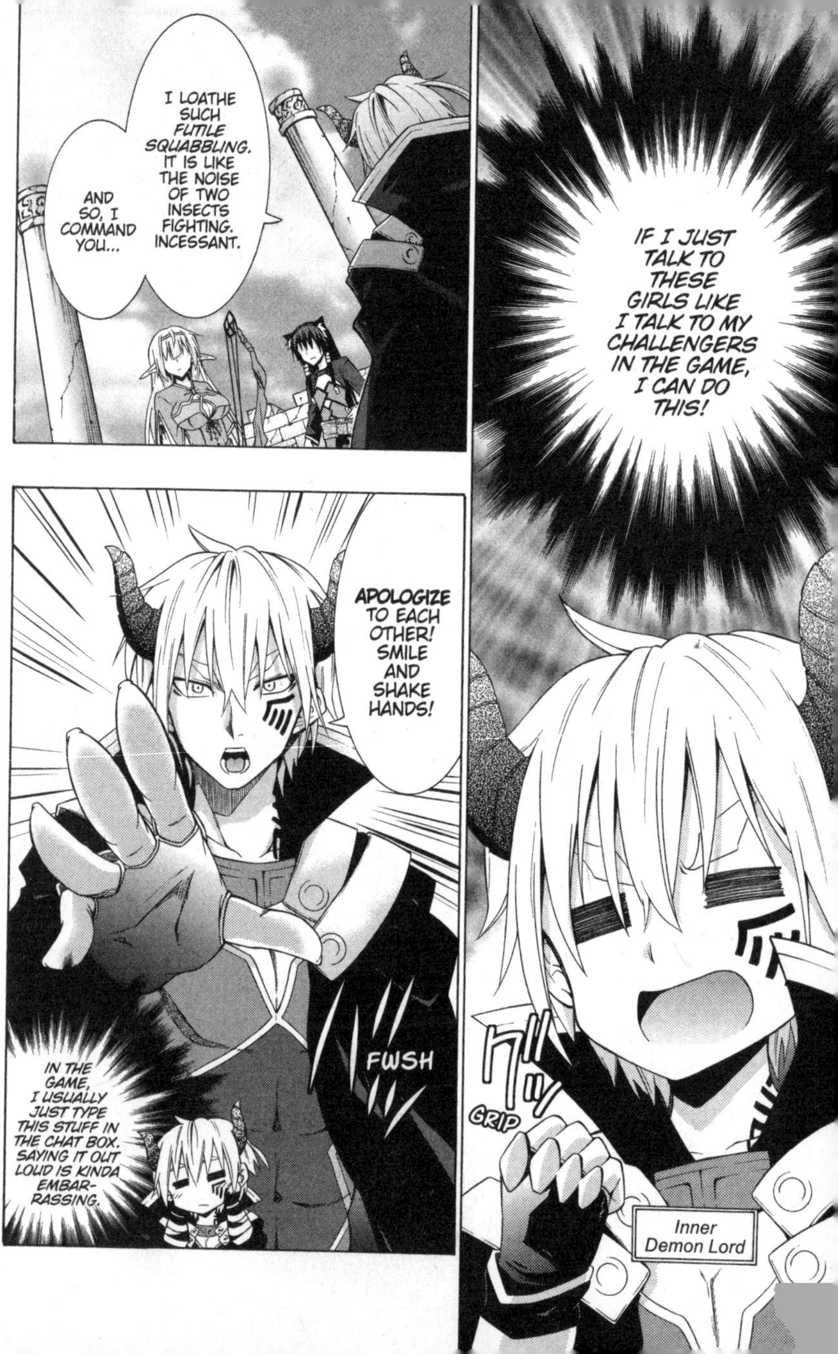
IF I JUST TALK TO THESE GIRLS LIKE I TALK TO MY CHALLENGERS IN THE GAME, I CAN DO THIS!
GRIP
Inner Demon Lord
I LOATHE SUCH FUTILE SQUABBLING. IT IS LIKE THE NOISE OF TWO INSECTS FIGHTING. INCESSANT.
AND SO, I COMMAND YOU...
APOLOGIZE TO EACH OTHER! SMILE AND SHAKE HANDS!
FWSH
IN THE GAME, I USUALLY JUST TYPE THIS STUFF IN THE CHAT BOX. SAYING IT OUT LOUD IS KINDA EMBARRASSING.

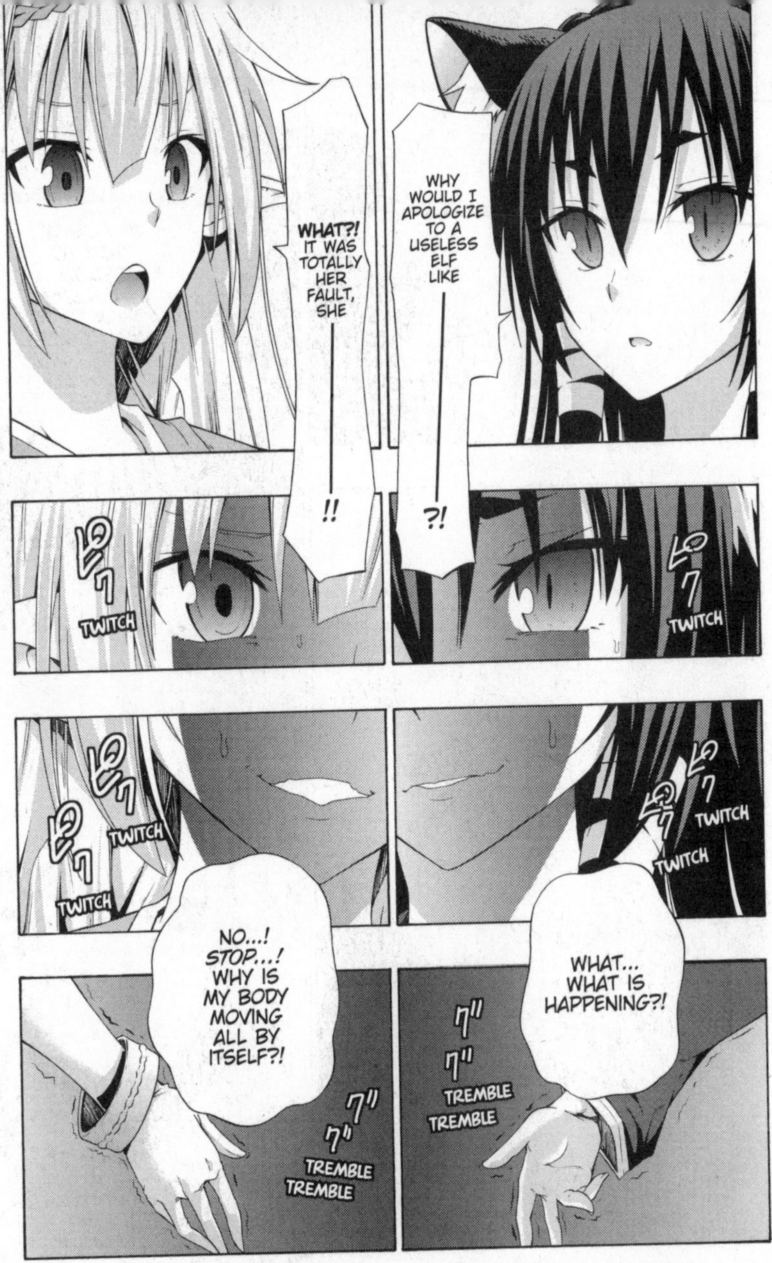
WHY WOULD I APOLOGIZE TO A USELESS ELF LIKE
WHAT?! IT WAS TOTALLY HER FAULT, SHE
?!
ピク
TWITCH
!!
ピク
TWITCH
ピク ピク
TWITCH TWITCH
ピク ピク
TWITCH TWITCH
WHAT... WHAT IS HAPPENING?!
グ グ
TREMBLE TREMBLE
NO...! STOP...! WHY IS MY BODY MOVING ALL BY ITSELF?!
グ グ
TREMBLE TREMBLE

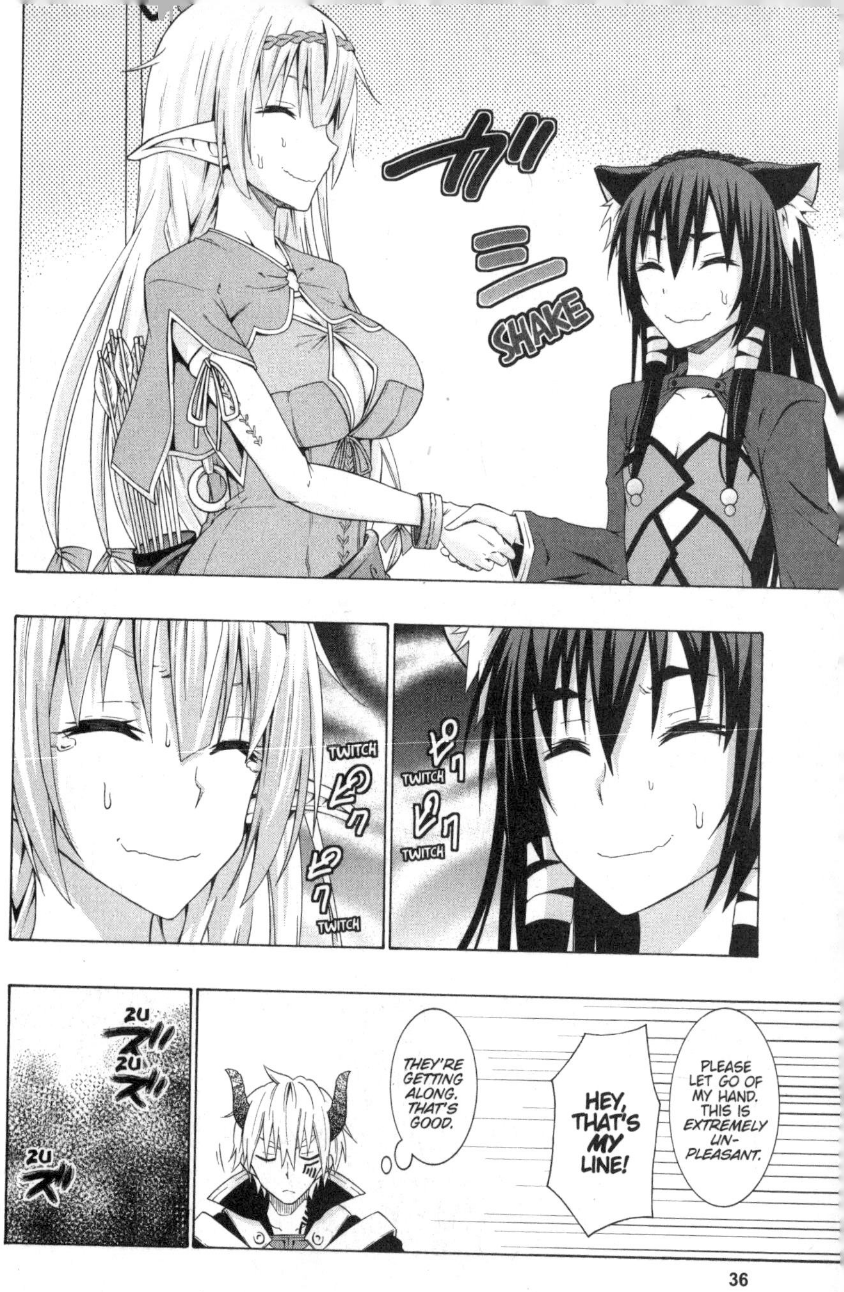
SHAKE
TWITCH
TWITCH
TWITCH
TWITCH
PLEASE LET GO OF MY HAND. THIS IS EXTREMELY UN-PLEASANT.
HEY, THAT'S MY LINE!
THEY'RE GETTING ALONG. THAT'S GOOD.
ZU
ZU
ZU

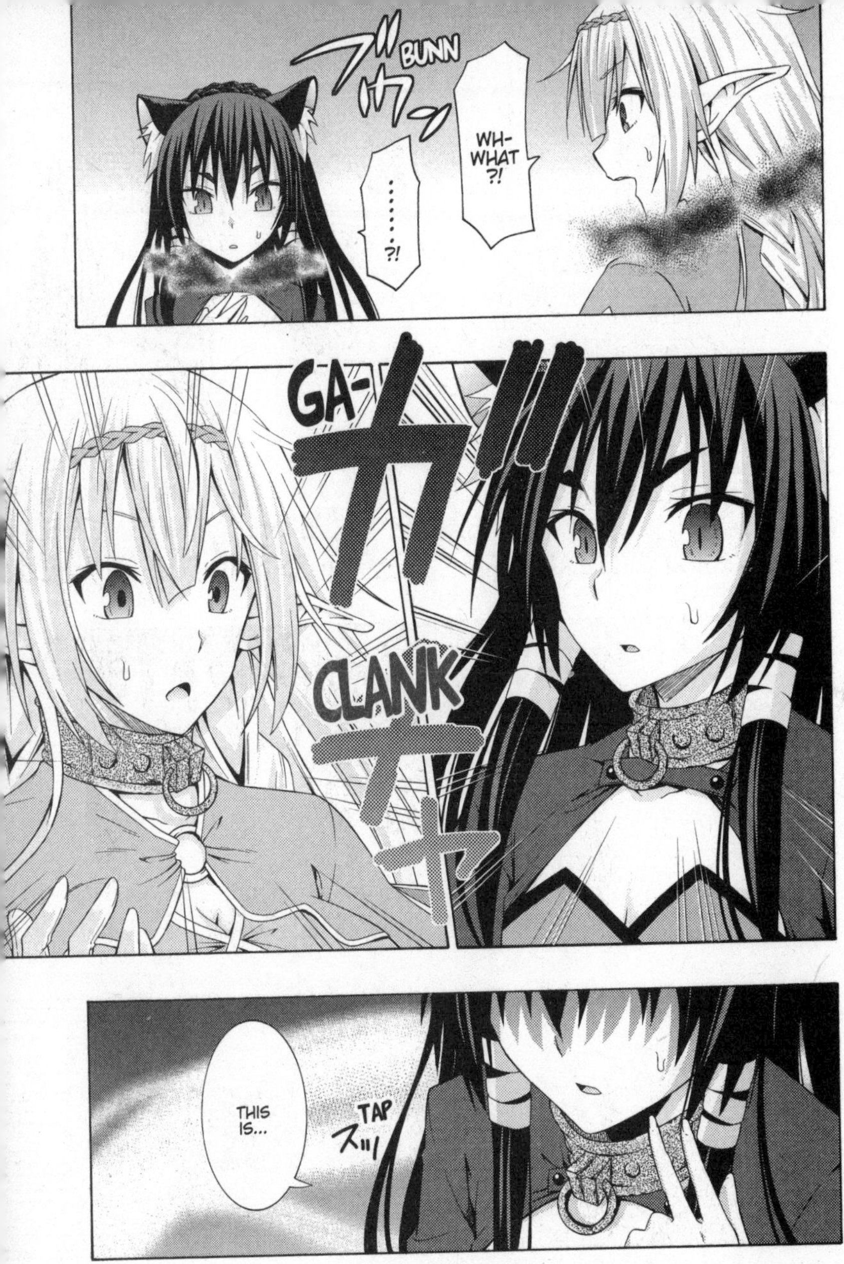

WH-WHAT?!
BUNN
......?!
GA-
CLANK
TAP
THIS IS...

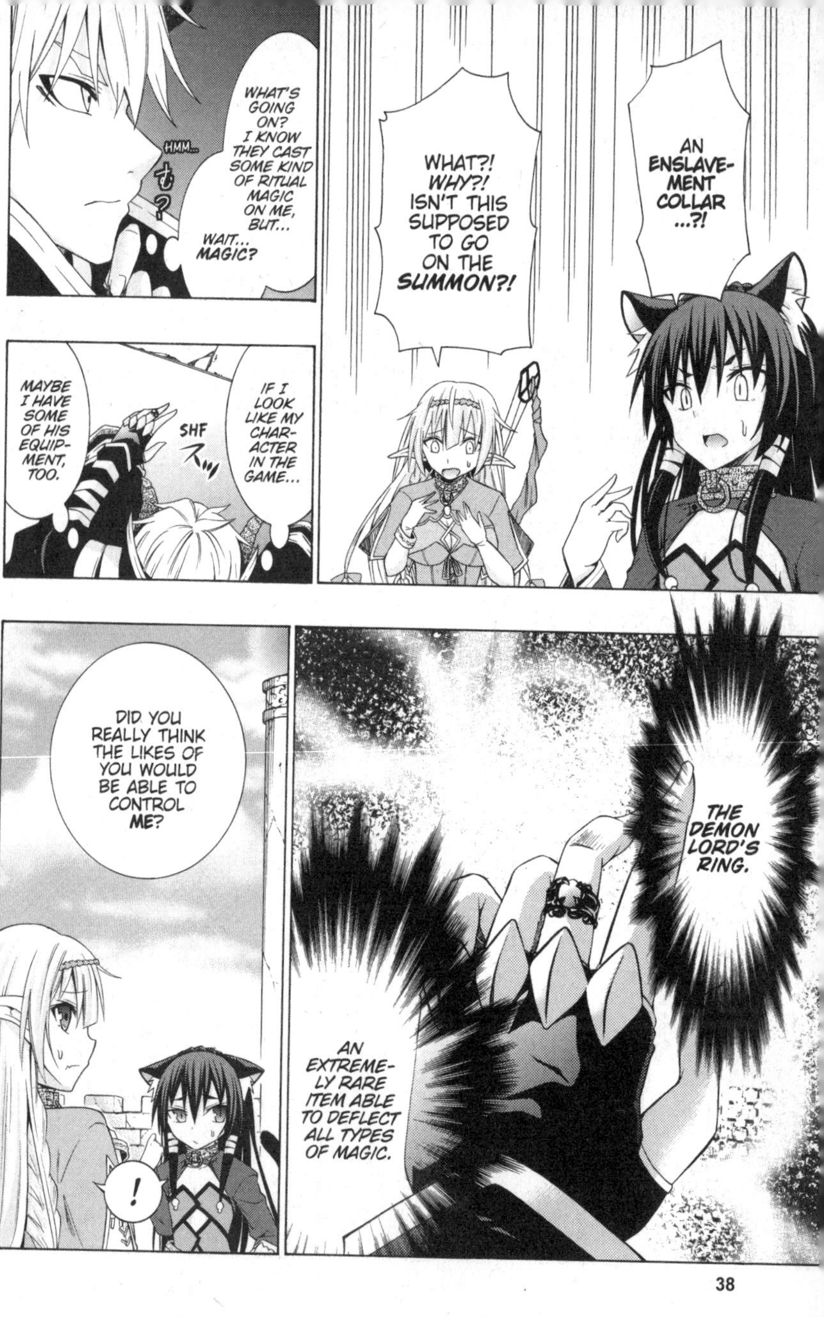
AN ENSLAVE-MENT COLLAR ...?!
WHAT?! WHY?! ISN'T THIS SUPPOSED TO GO ON THE SUMMON?!
WHAT'S GOING ON? I KNOW THEY CAST SOME KIND OF RITUAL MAGIC ON ME, BUT...
HMM... む?
WAIT... MAGIC?
IF I LOOK LIKE MY CHAR-ACTER IN THE GAME...
SHF スッ
MAYBE I HAVE SOME OF HIS EQUIP-MENT, TOO.
THE DEMON LORD'S RING.
AN EXTREME-LY RARE ITEM ABLE TO DEFLECT ALL TYPES OF MAGIC.
DID YOU REALLY THINK THE LIKES OF YOU WOULD BE ABLE TO CONTROL ME?
!

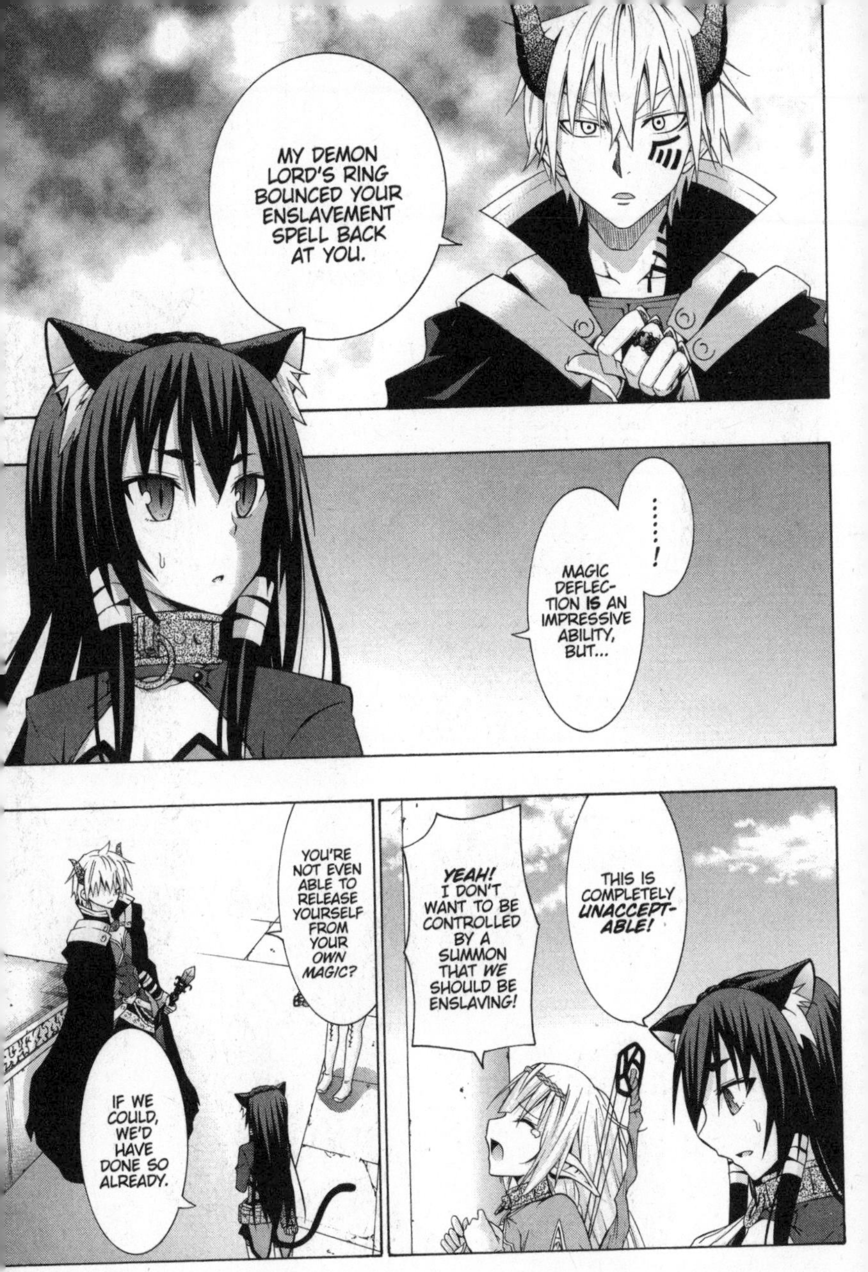
MY DEMON LORD'S RING BOUNCED YOUR ENSLAVEMENT SPELL BACK AT YOU.
......!
MAGIC DEFLECTION **IS** AN IMPRESSIVE ABILITY, BUT...
THIS IS COMPLETELY ***UNACCEPTABLE!***
YEAH! I DON'T WANT TO BE CONTROLLED BY A SUMMON THAT *WE* SHOULD BE ENSLAVING!
YOU'RE NOT EVEN ABLE TO RELEASE YOURSELF FROM YOUR *OWN MAGIC?*
IF WE COULD, WE'D HAVE DONE SO ALREADY.

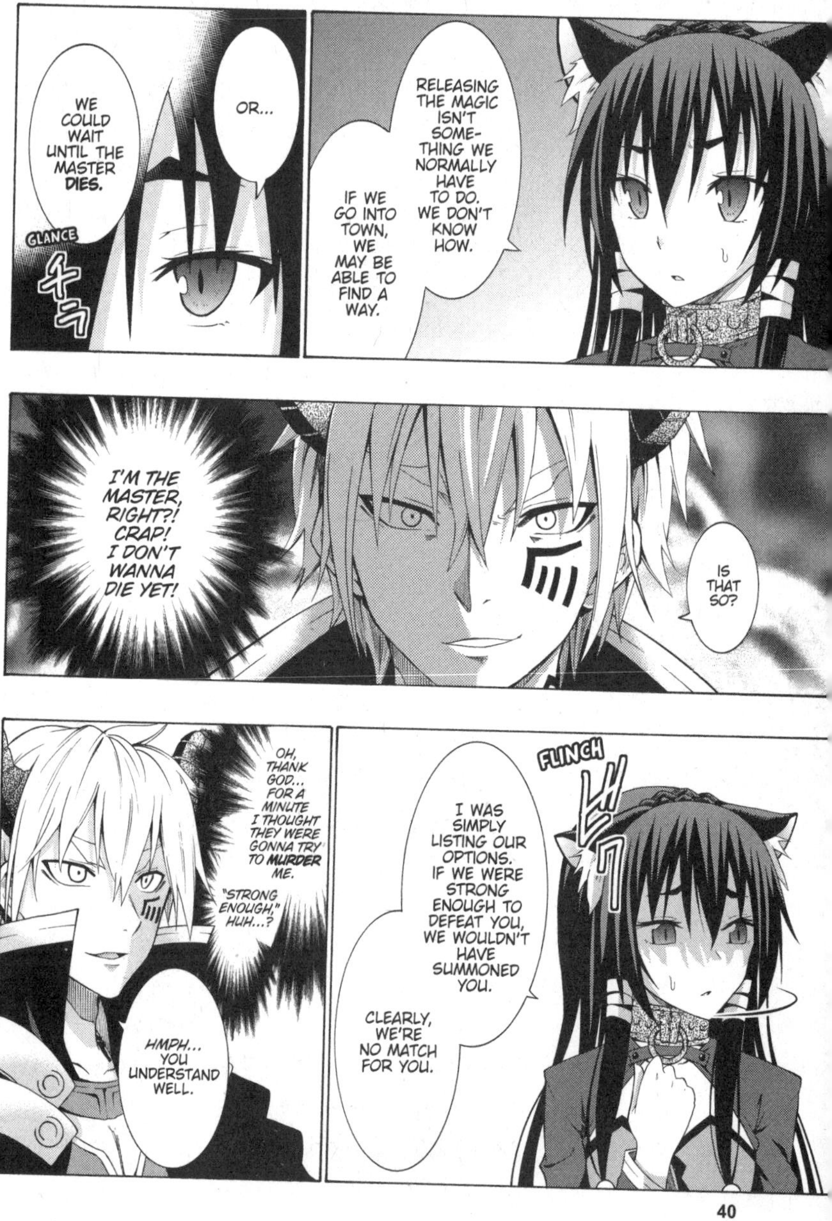
RELEASING THE MAGIC ISN'T SOMETHING WE NORMALLY HAVE TO DO. WE DON'T KNOW HOW.
IF WE GO INTO TOWN, WE MAY BE ABLE TO FIND A WAY.
OR...
WE COULD WAIT UNTIL THE MASTER **DIES.**
GLANCE
IS THAT SO?
I'M THE MASTER, RIGHT?! CRAP! I DON'T WANNA DIE YET!
FLINCH
I WAS SIMPLY LISTING OUR OPTIONS. IF WE WERE STRONG ENOUGH TO DEFEAT YOU, WE WOULDN'T HAVE SUMMONED YOU.
CLEARLY, WE'RE NO MATCH FOR YOU.
OH, THANK GOD... FOR A MINUTE I THOUGHT THEY WERE GONNA TRY TO ***MURDER*** *ME.*
"STRONG ENOUGH," HUH...?
HMPH... YOU UNDERSTAND WELL.

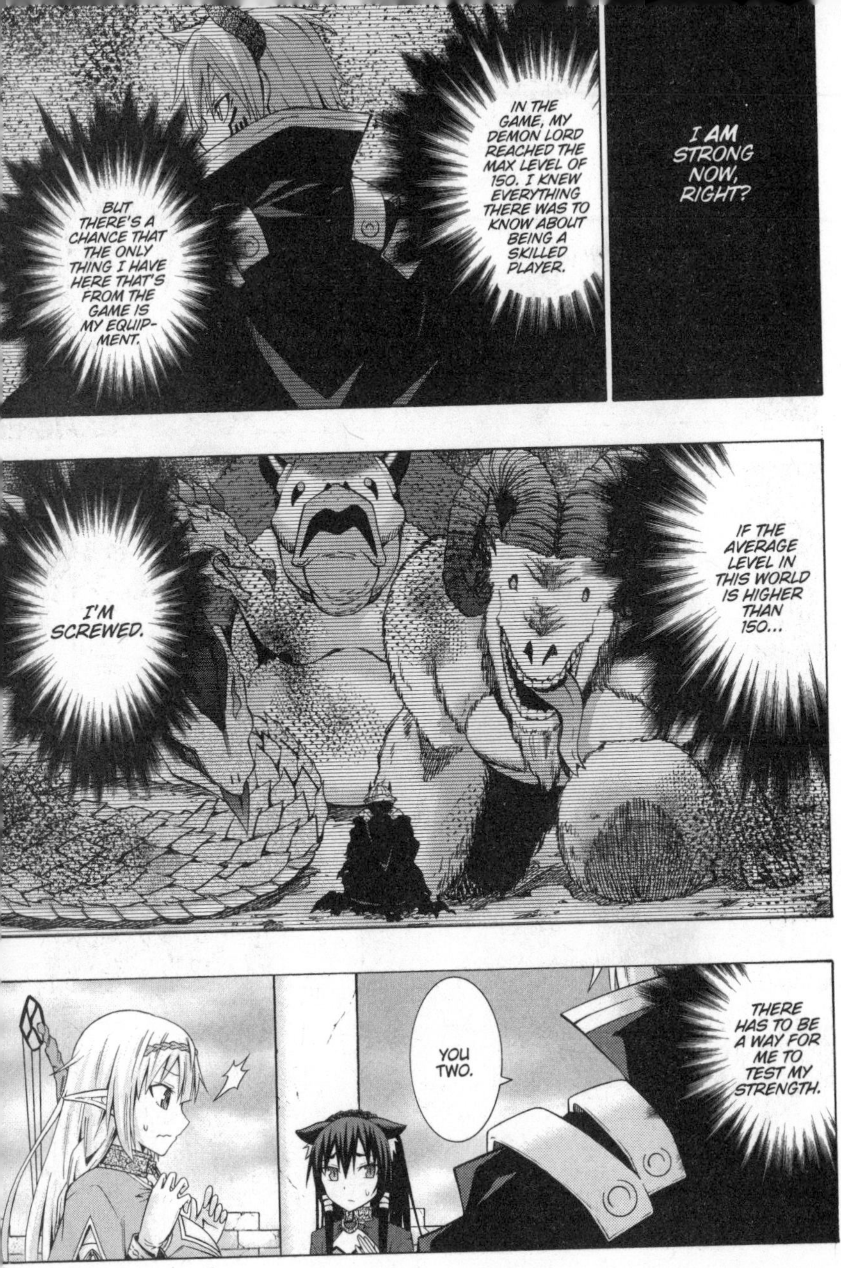
I AM STRONG NOW, RIGHT?
IN THE GAME, MY DEMON LORD REACHED THE MAX LEVEL OF 150. I KNEW EVERYTHING THERE WAS TO KNOW ABOUT BEING A SKILLED PLAYER.
BUT THERE'S A CHANCE THAT THE ONLY THING I HAVE HERE THAT'S FROM THE GAME IS MY EQUIPMENT.
IF THE AVERAGE LEVEL IN THIS WORLD IS HIGHER THAN 150...
I'M SCREWED.
THERE HAS TO BE A WAY FOR ME TO TEST MY STRENGTH.
YOU TWO.

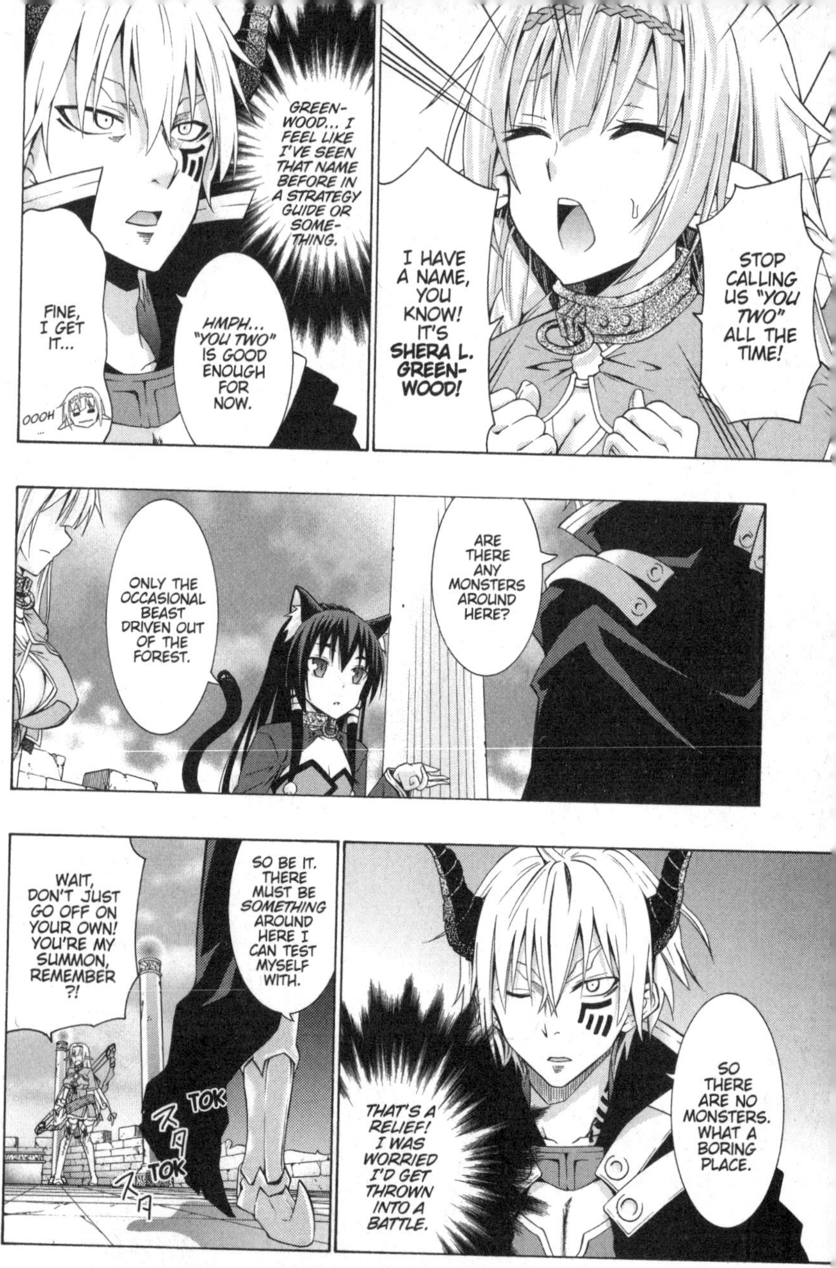
STOP CALLING US "YOU TWO" ALL THE TIME!
I HAVE A NAME, YOU KNOW! IT'S **SHERA L. GREENWOOD!**
GREENWOOD... I FEEL LIKE I'VE SEEN THAT NAME BEFORE IN A STRATEGY GUIDE OR SOMETHING.
HMPH... "YOU TWO" IS GOOD ENOUGH FOR NOW.
FINE, I GET IT...
OOOH...
ARE THERE ANY MONSTERS AROUND HERE?
ONLY THE OCCASIONAL BEAST DRIVEN OUT OF THE FOREST.
SO THERE ARE NO MONSTERS. WHAT A BORING PLACE.
THAT'S A RELIEF! I WAS WORRIED I'D GET THROWN INTO A BATTLE.
SO BE IT. THERE MUST BE SOMETHING AROUND HERE I CAN TEST MYSELF WITH.
WAIT, DON'T JUST GO OFF ON YOUR OWN! YOU'RE MY SUMMON, REMEMBER?!
TOK
TOK

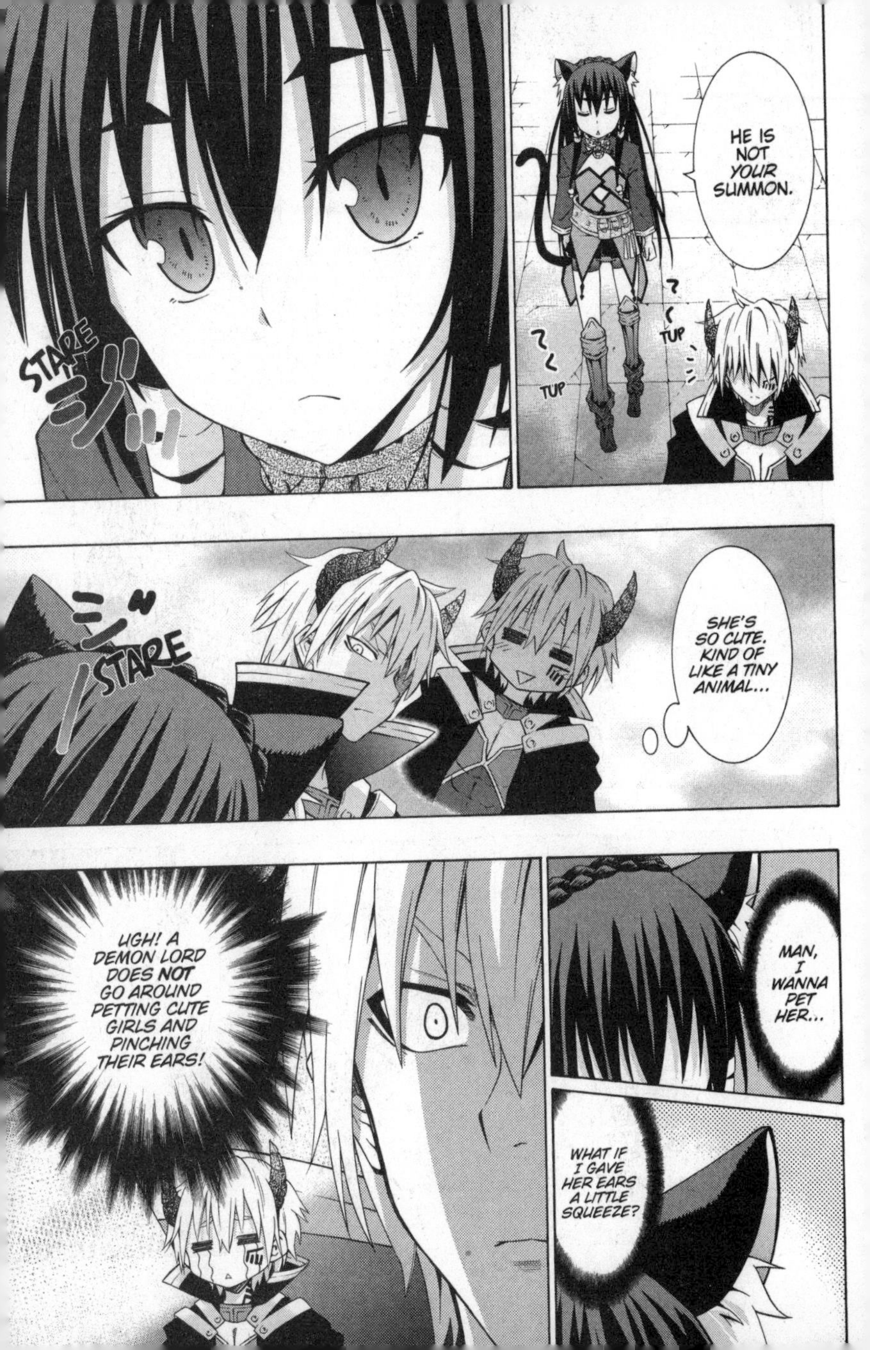
HE IS NOT YOUR SUMMON.
TUP
TUP
STARE
SHE'S SO CUTE. KIND OF LIKE A TINY ANIMAL...
STARE
MAN, I WANNA PET HER...
WHAT IF I GAVE HER EARS A LITTLE SQUEEZE?
UGH! A DEMON LORD DOES NOT GO AROUND PETTING CUTE GIRLS AND PINCHING THEIR EARS!

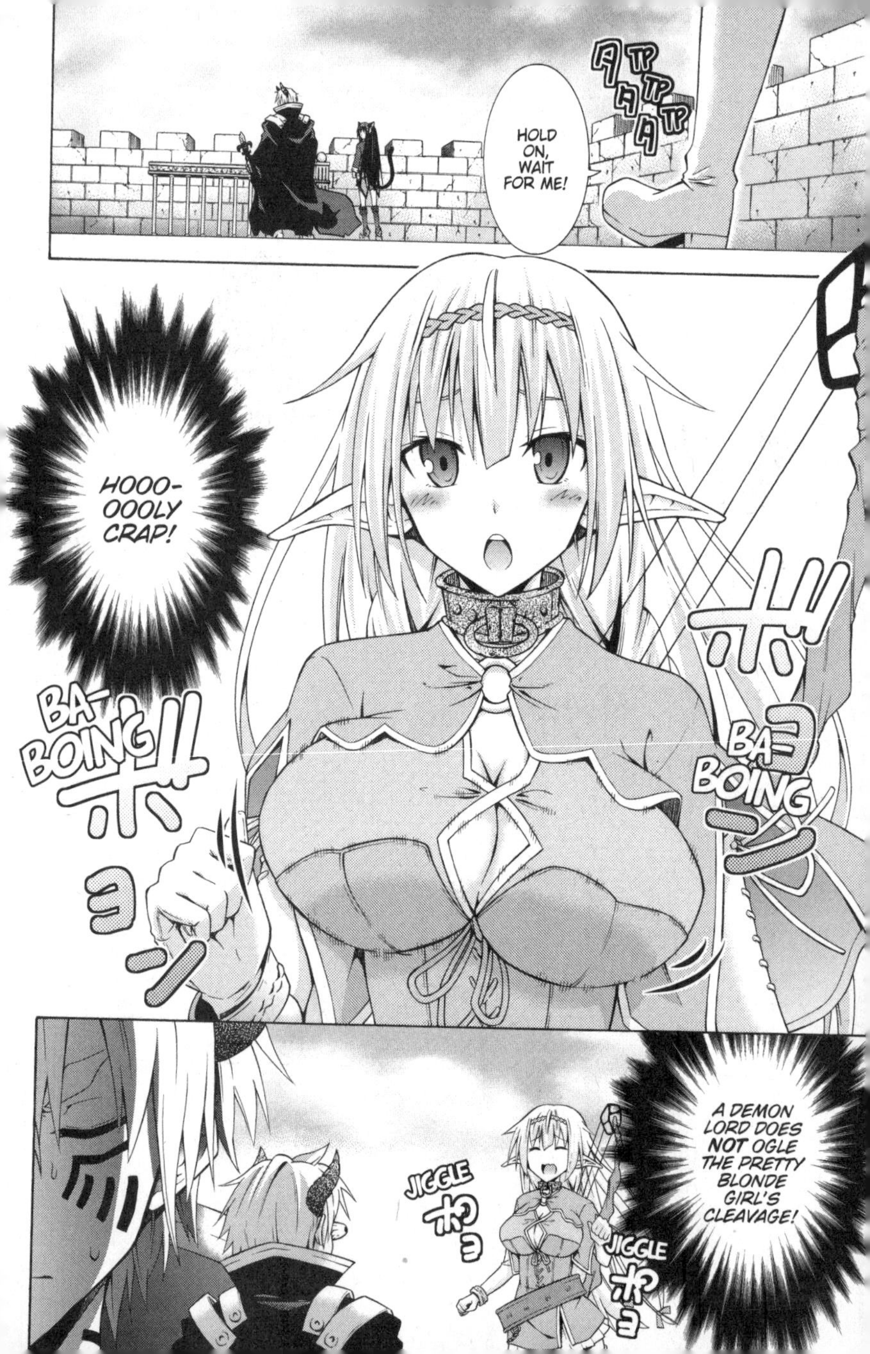
TP TP TP
HOLD ON, WAIT FOR ME!
HOOOO-OOOLY CRAP!
BA-BOING
BA-BOING
A DEMON LORD DOES NOT OGLE THE PRETTY BLONDE GIRL'S CLEAVAGE!
JIGGLE
JIGGLE

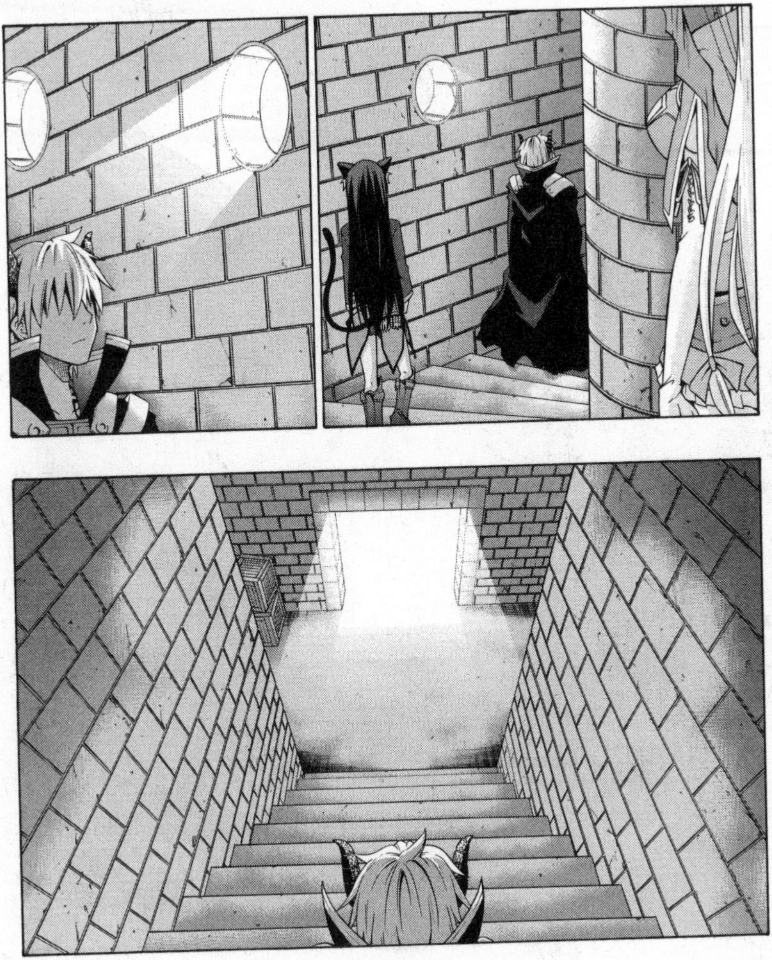

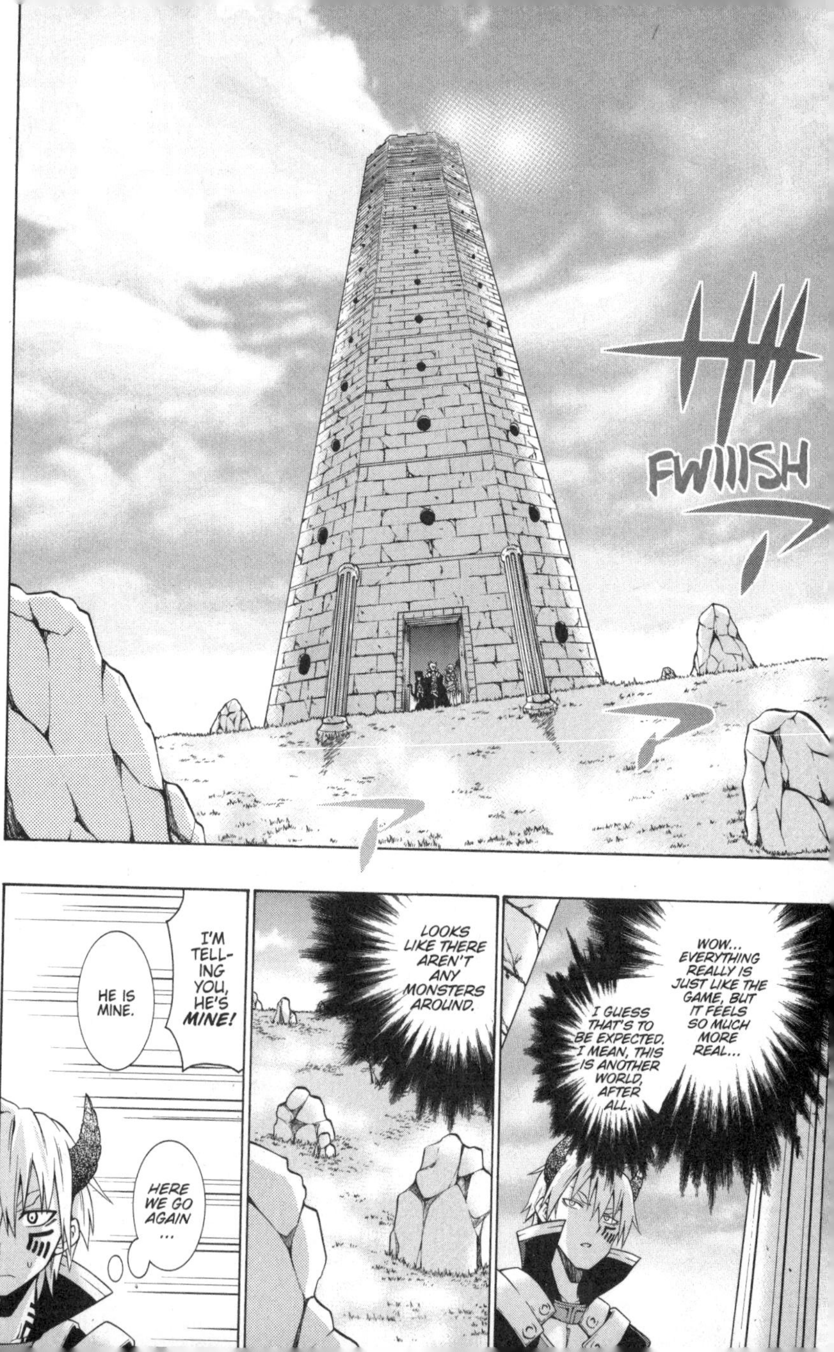
FWIIISH
WOW... EVERYTHING REALLY IS JUST LIKE THE GAME, BUT IT FEELS SO MUCH MORE REAL...
I GUESS THAT'S TO BE EXPECTED. I MEAN, THIS IS ANOTHER WORLD, AFTER ALL.
LOOKS LIKE THERE AREN'T ANY MONSTERS AROUND.
I'M TELLING YOU, HE'S MINE!
HE IS MINE.
HERE WE GO AGAIN ...

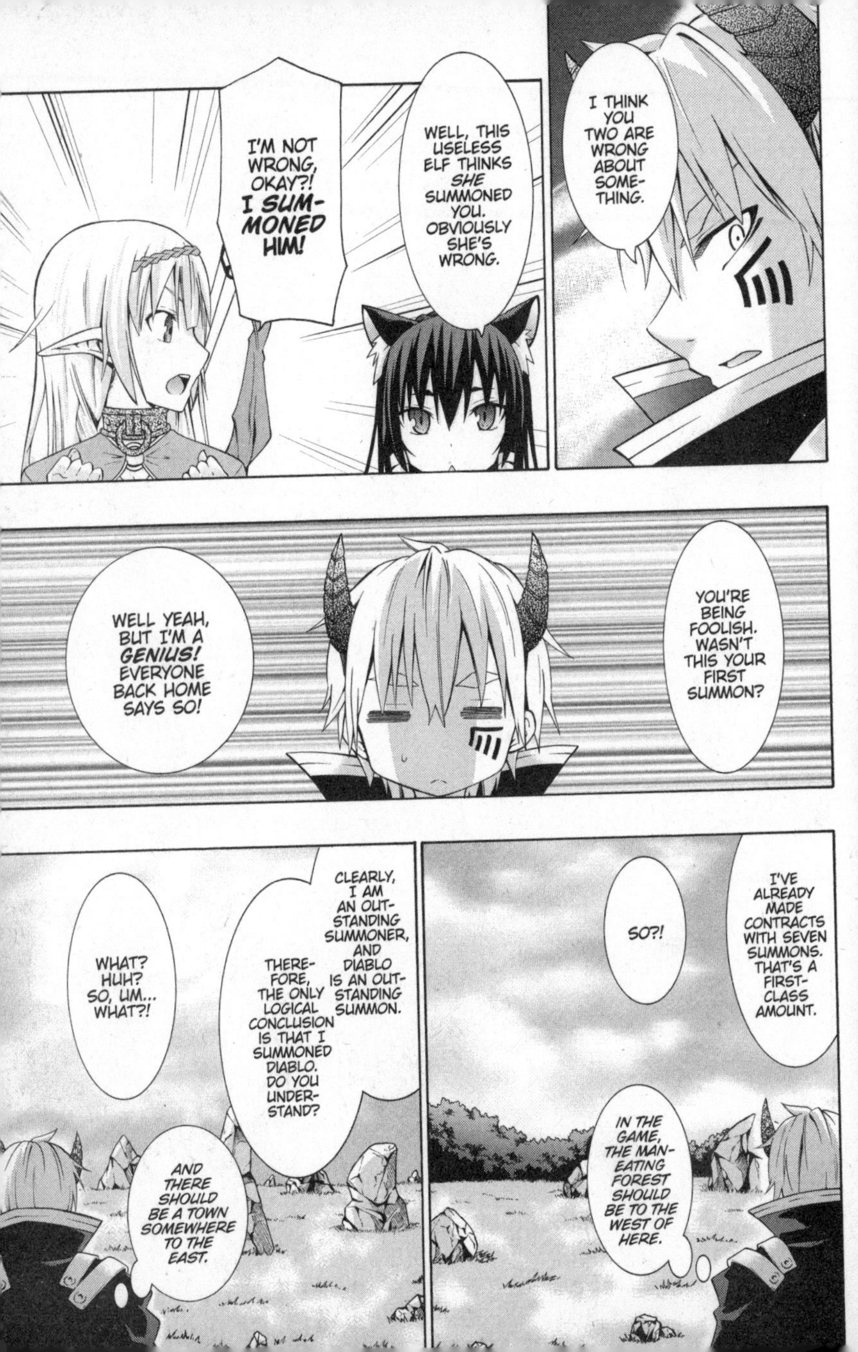
I THINK YOU TWO ARE WRONG ABOUT SOMETHING.
WELL, THIS USELESS ELF THINKS *SHE* SUMMONED YOU. OBVIOUSLY SHE'S WRONG.
I'M NOT WRONG, OKAY?! **I SUMMONED HIM!**
YOU'RE BEING FOOLISH. WASN'T THIS YOUR FIRST SUMMON?
WELL YEAH, BUT I'M A ***GENIUS!*** EVERYONE BACK HOME SAYS SO!
I'VE ALREADY MADE CONTRACTS WITH SEVEN SUMMONS. THAT'S A FIRST-CLASS AMOUNT.
SO?!
IN THE GAME, THE MAN-EATING FOREST SHOULD BE TO THE WEST OF HERE.
CLEARLY, I AM AN OUTSTANDING SUMMONER, AND DIABLO IS AN OUTSTANDING SUMMON. THEREFORE, THE ONLY LOGICAL CONCLUSION IS THAT I SUMMONED DIABLO. DO YOU UNDERSTAND?
WHAT? HUH? SO, UM... WHAT?!
AND THERE SHOULD BE A TOWN SOMEWHERE TO THE EAST.

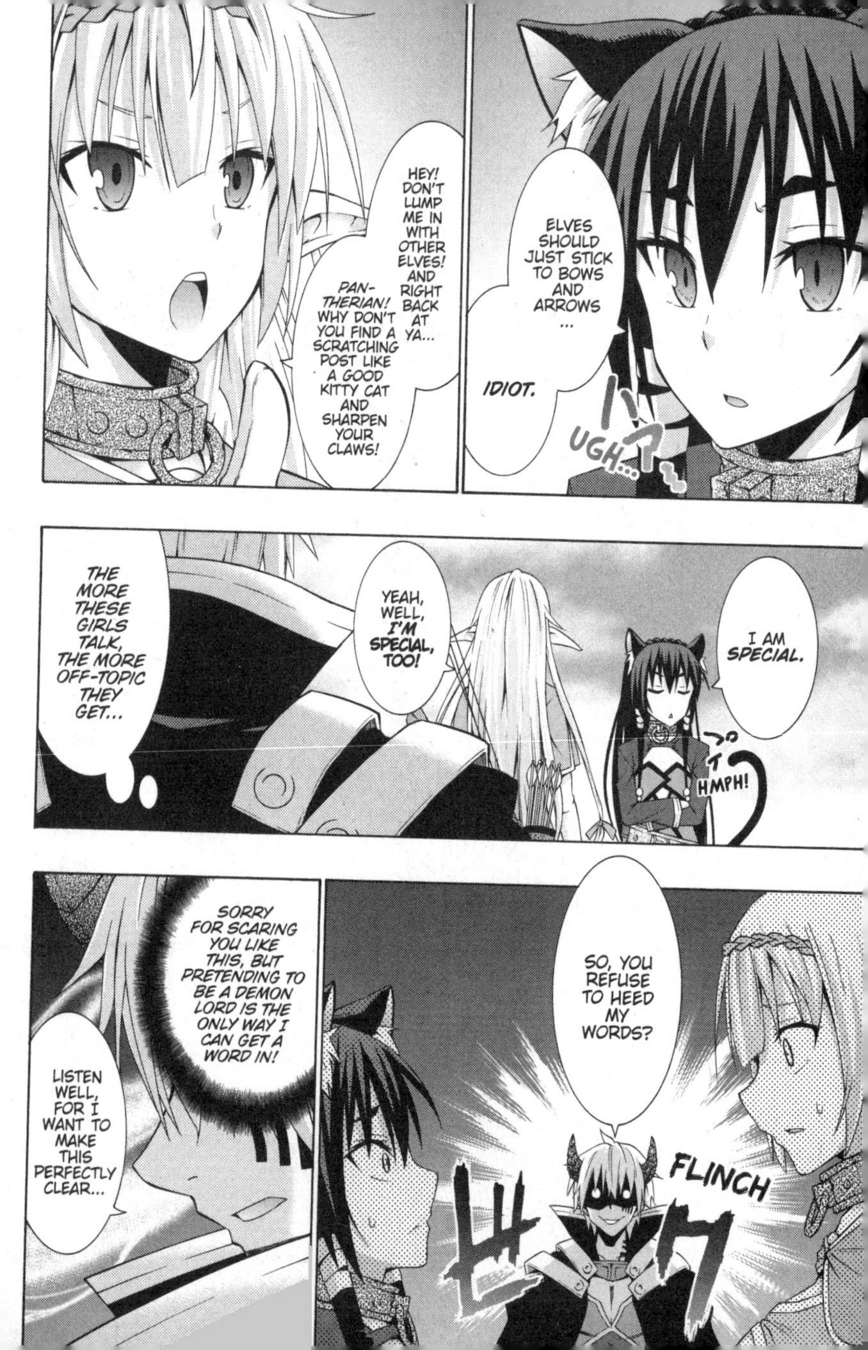
ELVES SHOULD JUST STICK TO BOWS AND ARROWS...
IDIOT.
UGH...
HEY! DON'T LUMP ME IN WITH OTHER ELVES! AND RIGHT BACK AT YA...
PAN-THERIAN! WHY DON'T YOU FIND A SCRATCHING POST LIKE A GOOD KITTY CAT AND SHARPEN YOUR CLAWS!
I AM SPECIAL.
HMPH!
YEAH, WELL, I'M SPECIAL, TOO!
THE MORE THESE GIRLS TALK, THE MORE OFF-TOPIC THEY GET...
SO, YOU REFUSE TO HEED MY WORDS?
FLINCH
SORRY FOR SCARING YOU LIKE THIS, BUT PRETENDING TO BE A DEMON LORD IS THE ONLY WAY I CAN GET A WORD IN!
LISTEN WELL, FOR I WANT TO MAKE THIS PERFECTLY CLEAR...

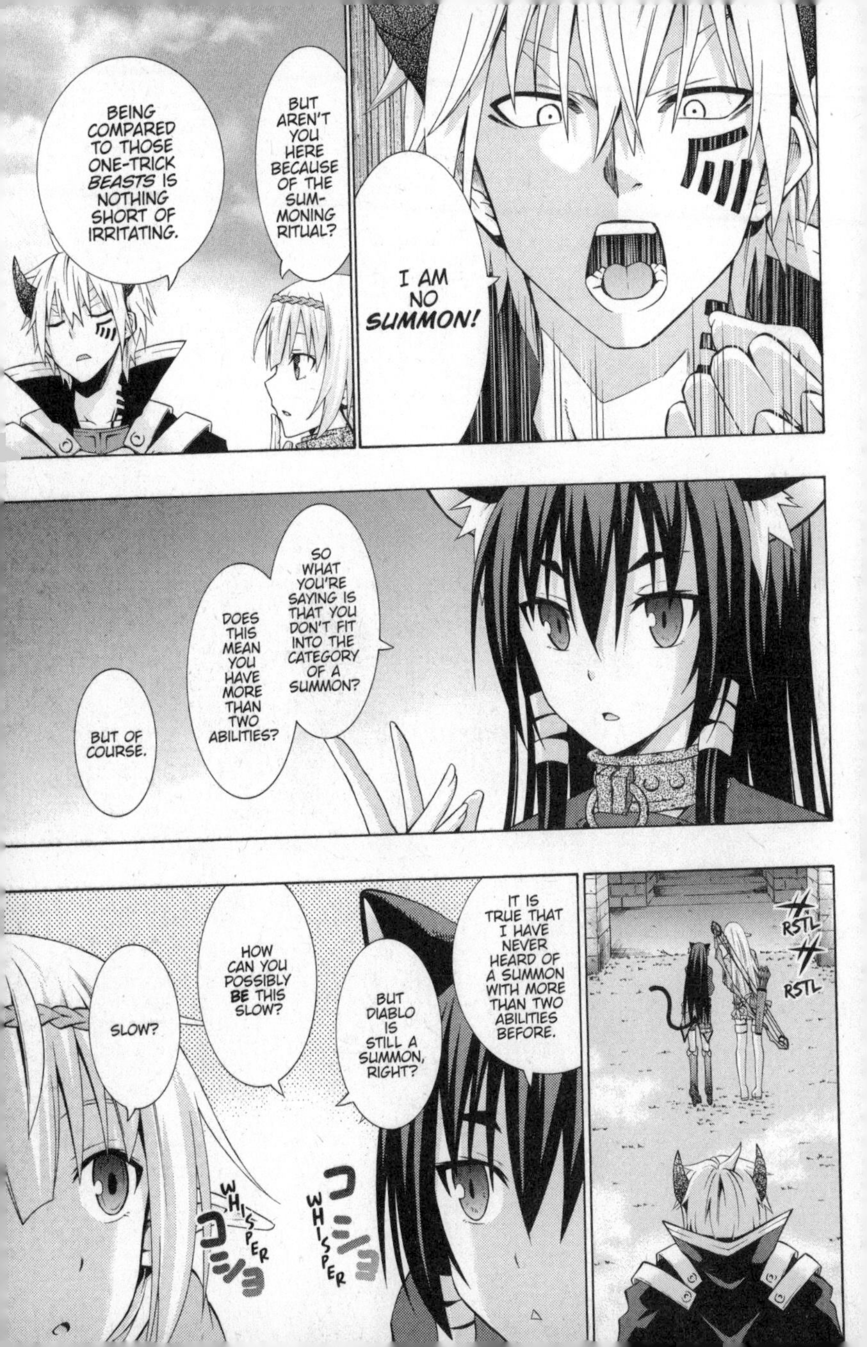
I AM NO SUMMON!
BUT AREN'T YOU HERE BECAUSE OF THE SUMMONING RITUAL?
BEING COMPARED TO THOSE ONE-TRICK BEASTS IS NOTHING SHORT OF IRRITATING.
SO WHAT YOU'RE SAYING IS THAT YOU DON'T FIT INTO THE CATEGORY OF A SUMMON?
DOES THIS MEAN YOU HAVE MORE THAN TWO ABILITIES?
BUT OF COURSE.
IT IS TRUE THAT I HAVE NEVER HEARD OF A SUMMON WITH MORE THAN TWO ABILITIES BEFORE.
RSTL
RSTL
BUT DIABLO IS STILL A SUMMON, RIGHT?
HOW CAN YOU POSSIBLY BE THIS SLOW?
SLOW?
WHISPER
WHISPER

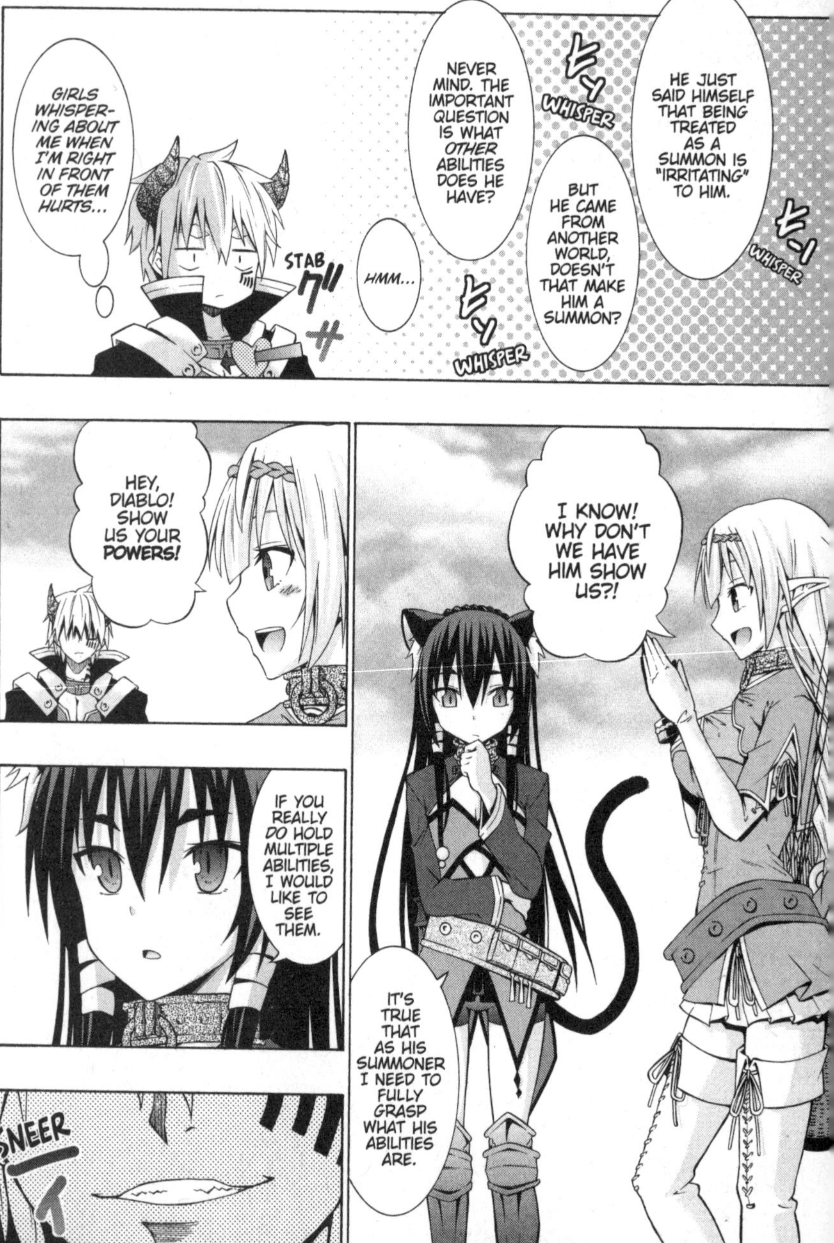
HE JUST SAID HIMSELF THAT BEING TREATED AS A SUMMON IS "IRRITATING" TO HIM.
WHISPER
BUT HE CAME FROM ANOTHER WORLD, DOESN'T THAT MAKE HIM A SUMMON?
WHISPER
NEVER MIND. THE IMPORTANT QUESTION IS WHAT *OTHER* ABILITIES DOES HE HAVE?
HMM...
WHISPER
STAB
GIRLS WHISPERING ABOUT ME WHEN I'M RIGHT IN FRONT OF THEM HURTS...
I KNOW! WHY DON'T WE HAVE HIM SHOW US?!
IT'S TRUE THAT AS HIS SUMMONER I NEED TO FULLY GRASP WHAT HIS ABILITIES ARE.
HEY, DIABLO! SHOW US YOUR **POWERS!**
IF YOU REALLY *DO* HOLD MULTIPLE ABILITIES, I WOULD LIKE TO SEE THEM.
SNEER

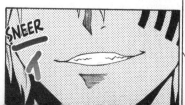

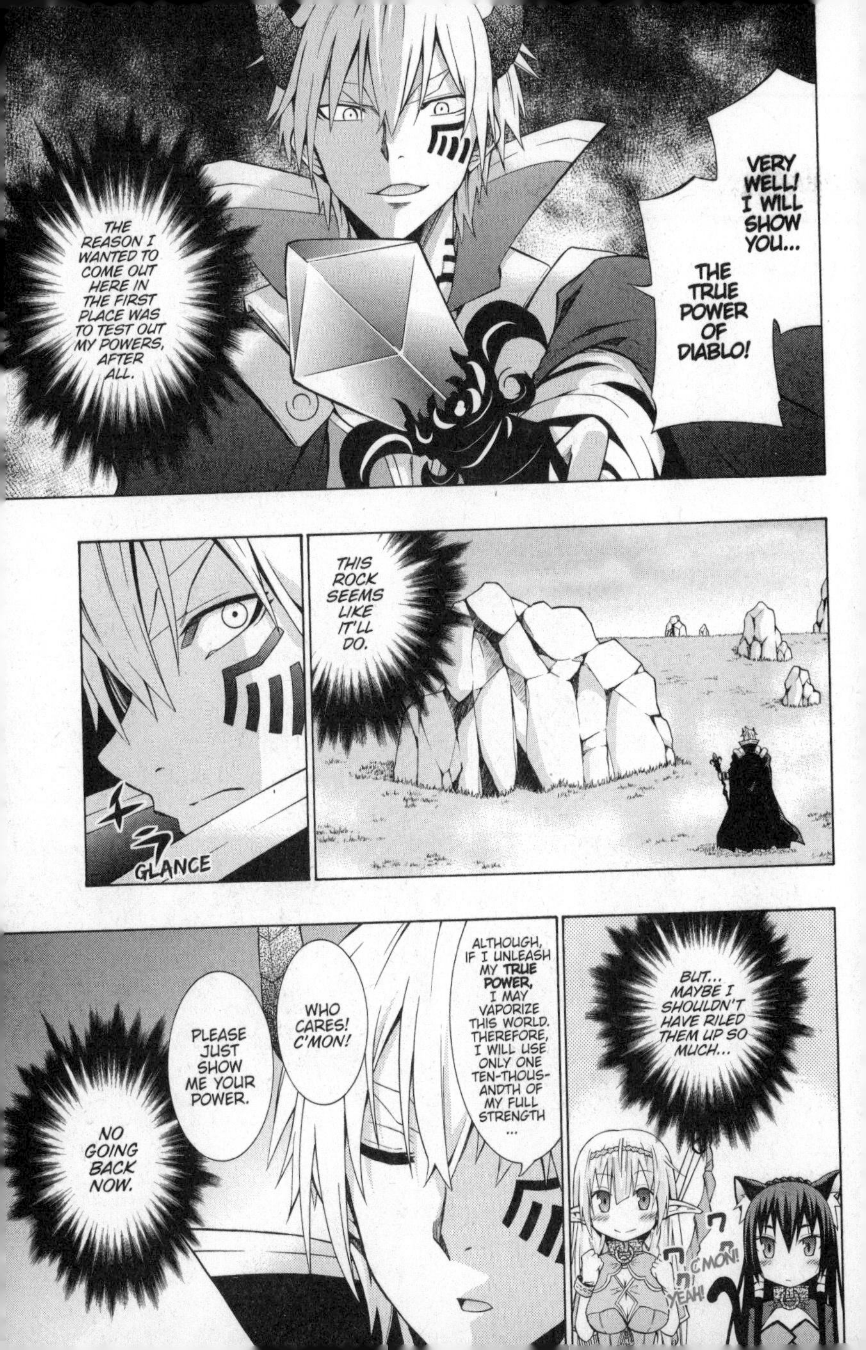
VERY WELL! I WILL SHOW YOU...
THE TRUE POWER OF DIABLO!
THE REASON I WANTED TO COME OUT HERE IN THE FIRST PLACE WAS TO TEST OUT MY POWERS, AFTER ALL.
THIS ROCK SEEMS LIKE IT'LL DO.
GLANCE
BUT... MAYBE I SHOULDN'T HAVE RILED THEM UP SO MUCH...
C'MON!
YEAH!
ALTHOUGH, IF I UNLEASH MY TRUE POWER, I MAY VAPORIZE THIS WORLD. THEREFORE, I WILL USE ONLY ONE TEN-THOUS-ANDTH OF MY FULL STRENGTH...
WHO CARES! C'MON!
PLEASE JUST SHOW ME YOUR POWER.
NO GOING BACK NOW.

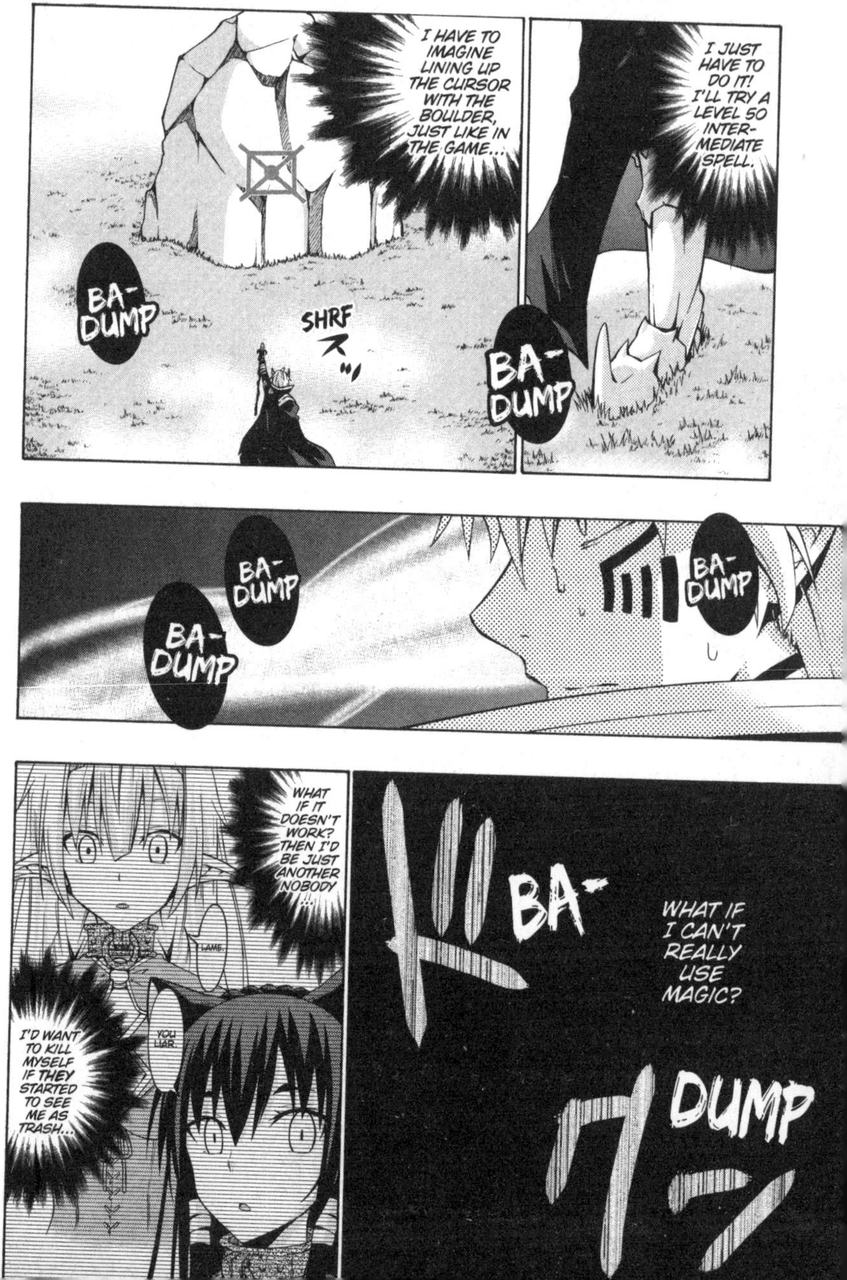
I JUST HAVE TO DO IT! I'LL TRY A LEVEL 50 INTERMEDIATE SPELL.
BA-DUMP
I HAVE TO IMAGINE LINING UP THE CURSOR WITH THE BOULDER, JUST LIKE IN THE GAME...
SHRF
BA-DUMP
BA-DUMP
BA-DUMP
BA-DUMP
WHAT IF I CAN'T REALLY USE MAGIC?
BA-
DUMP
WHAT IF IT DOESN'T WORK? THEN I'D BE JUST ANOTHER NOBODY...!
LAME.
YOU LIAR.
I'D WANT TO KILL MYSELF IF THEY STARTED TO SEE ME AS TRASH...

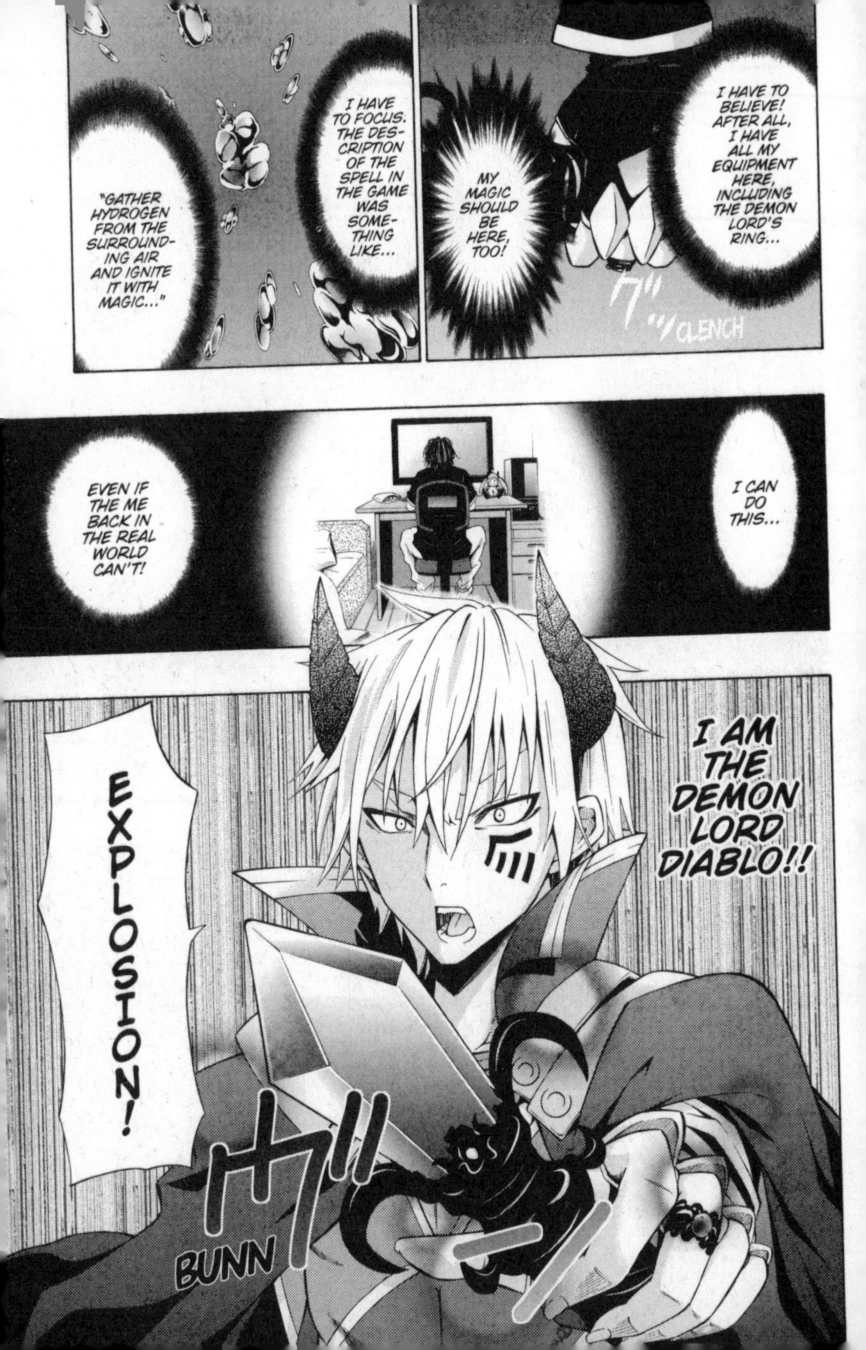
I HAVE TO BELIEVE! AFTER ALL, I HAVE ALL MY EQUIPMENT HERE, INCLUDING THE DEMON LORD'S RING...
MY MAGIC SHOULD BE HERE, TOO!
CLENCH
I HAVE TO FOCUS. THE DESCRIPTION OF THE SPELL IN THE GAME WAS SOMETHING LIKE...
"GATHER HYDROGEN FROM THE SURROUNDING AIR AND IGNITE IT WITH MAGIC..."
I CAN DO THIS...
EVEN IF THE ME BACK IN THE REAL WORLD CAN'T!
I AM THE DEMON LORD DIABLO!!
EXPLOSION!
BUNN

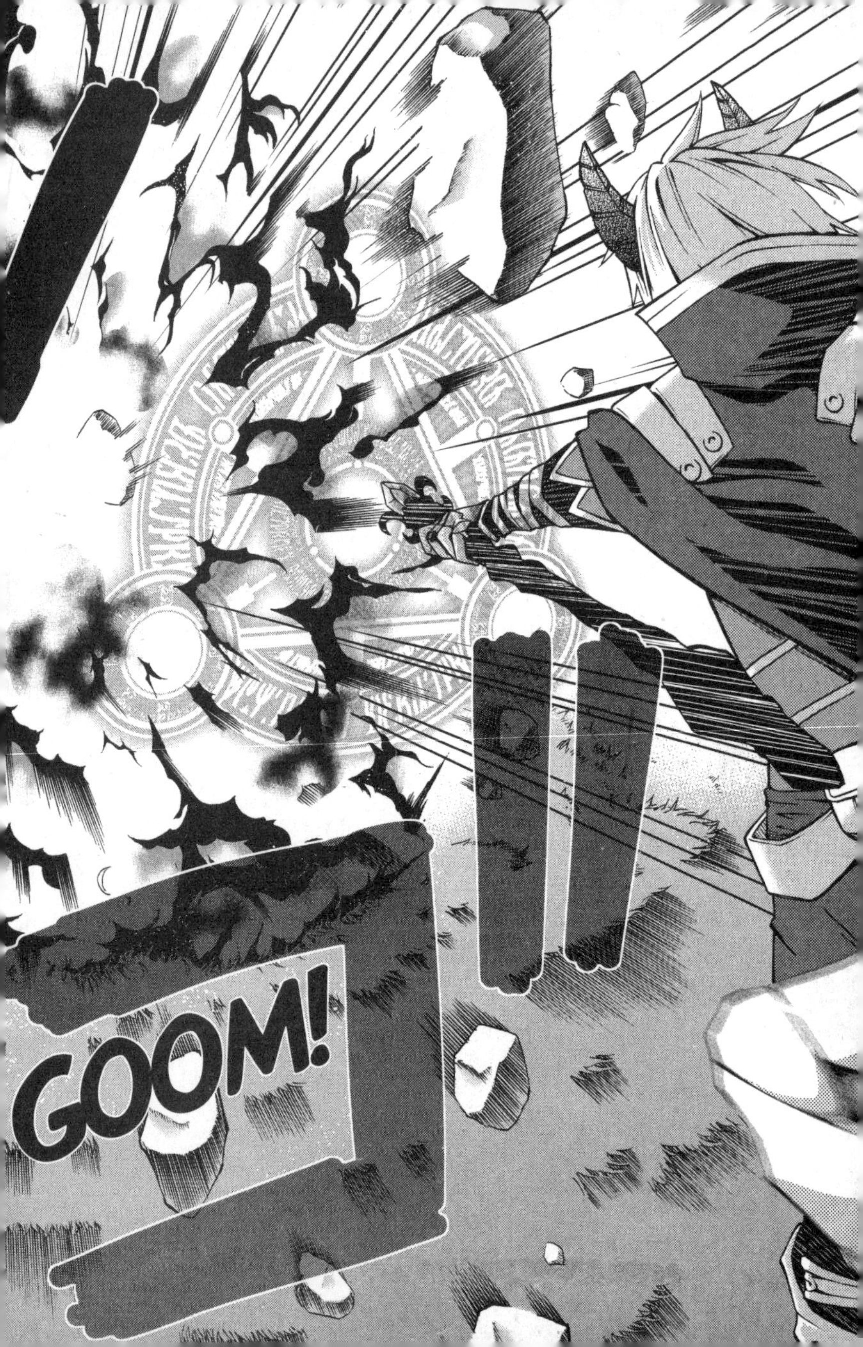
GOOM!

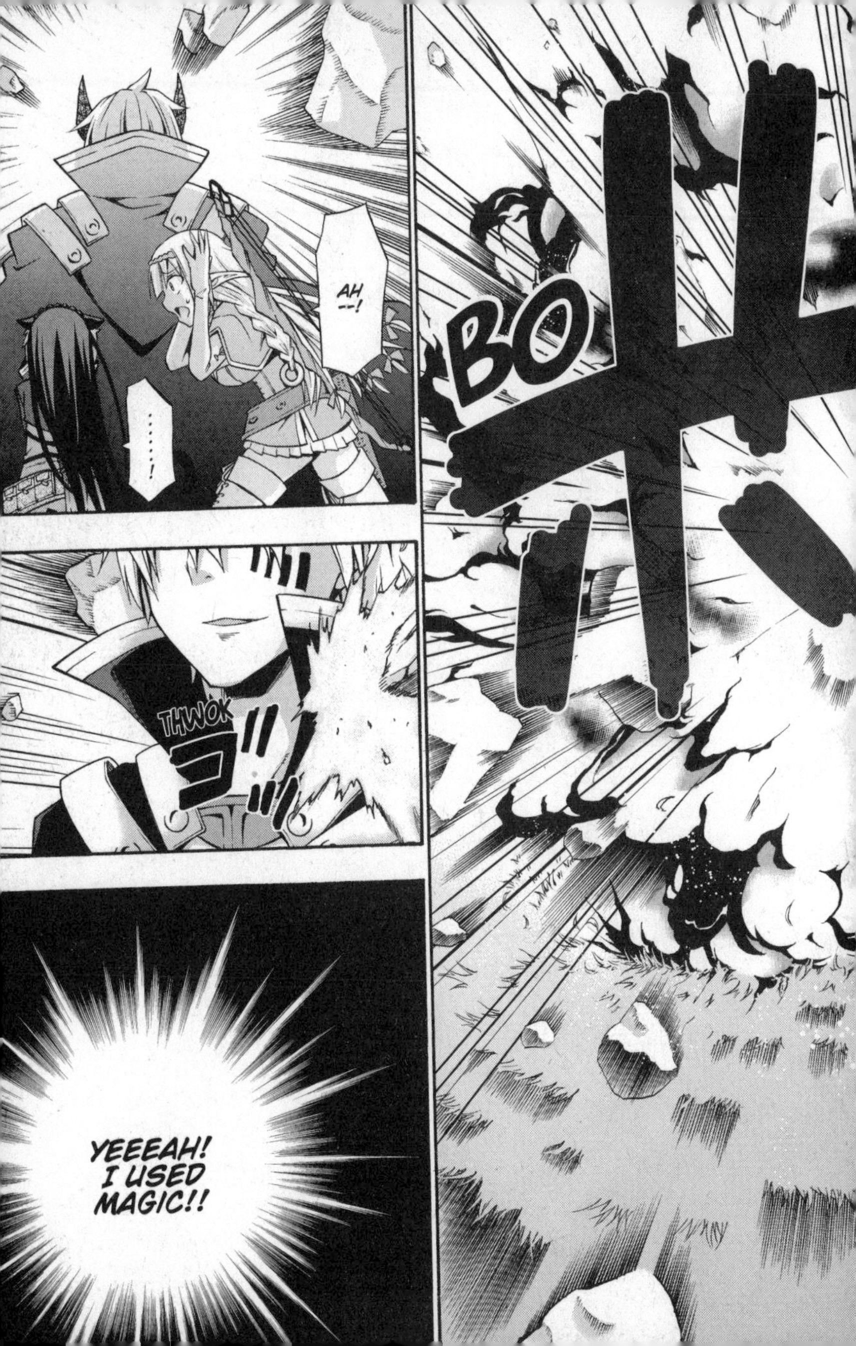
BO
AH --!
......!
THWOK
YEEEAH! I USED MAGIC!!

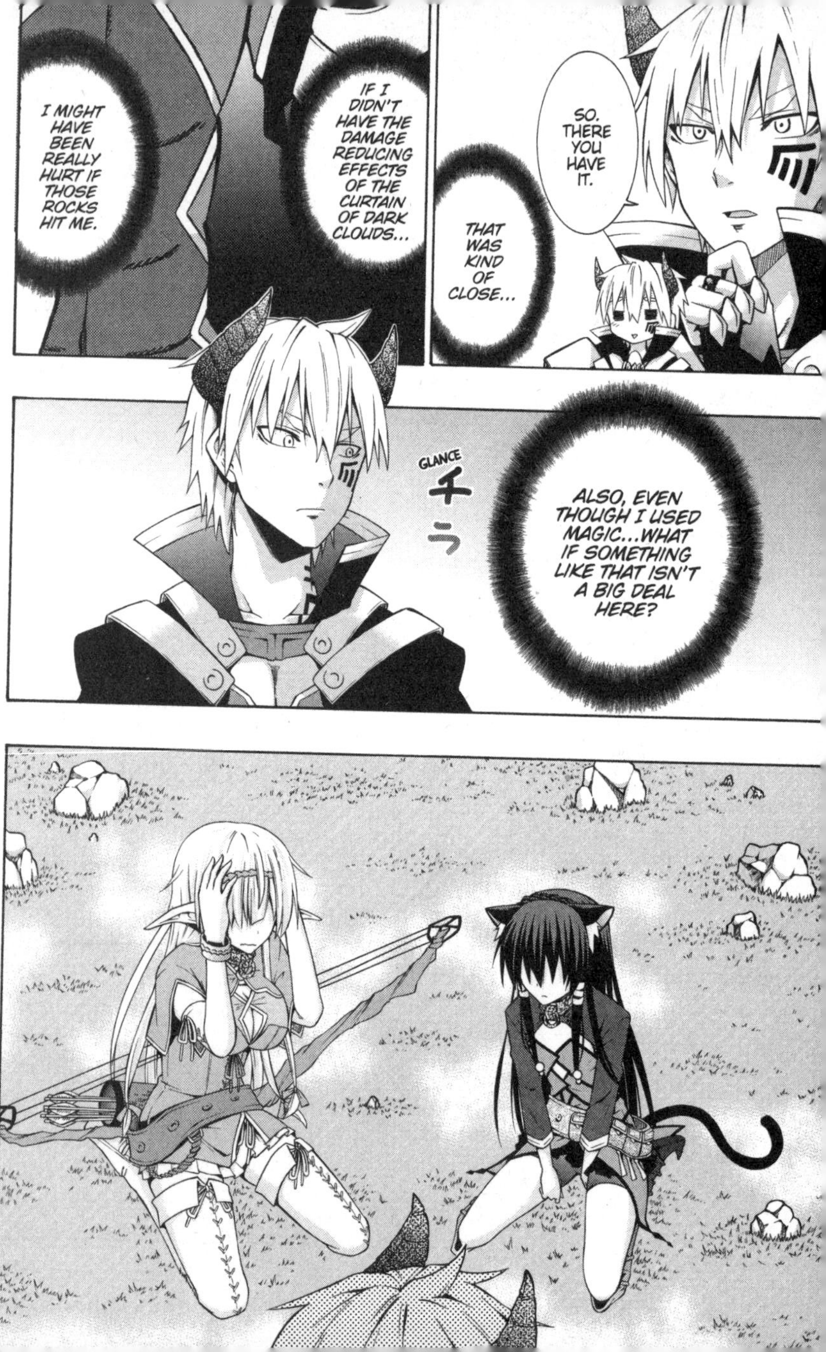
SO. THERE YOU HAVE IT.
THAT WAS KIND OF CLOSE...
IF I DIDN'T HAVE THE DAMAGE REDUCING EFFECTS OF THE CURTAIN OF DARK CLOUDS...
I MIGHT HAVE BEEN REALLY HURT IF THOSE ROCKS HIT ME.
ALSO, EVEN THOUGH I USED MAGIC...WHAT IF SOMETHING LIKE THAT ISN'T A BIG DEAL HERE?
GLANCE
チラ

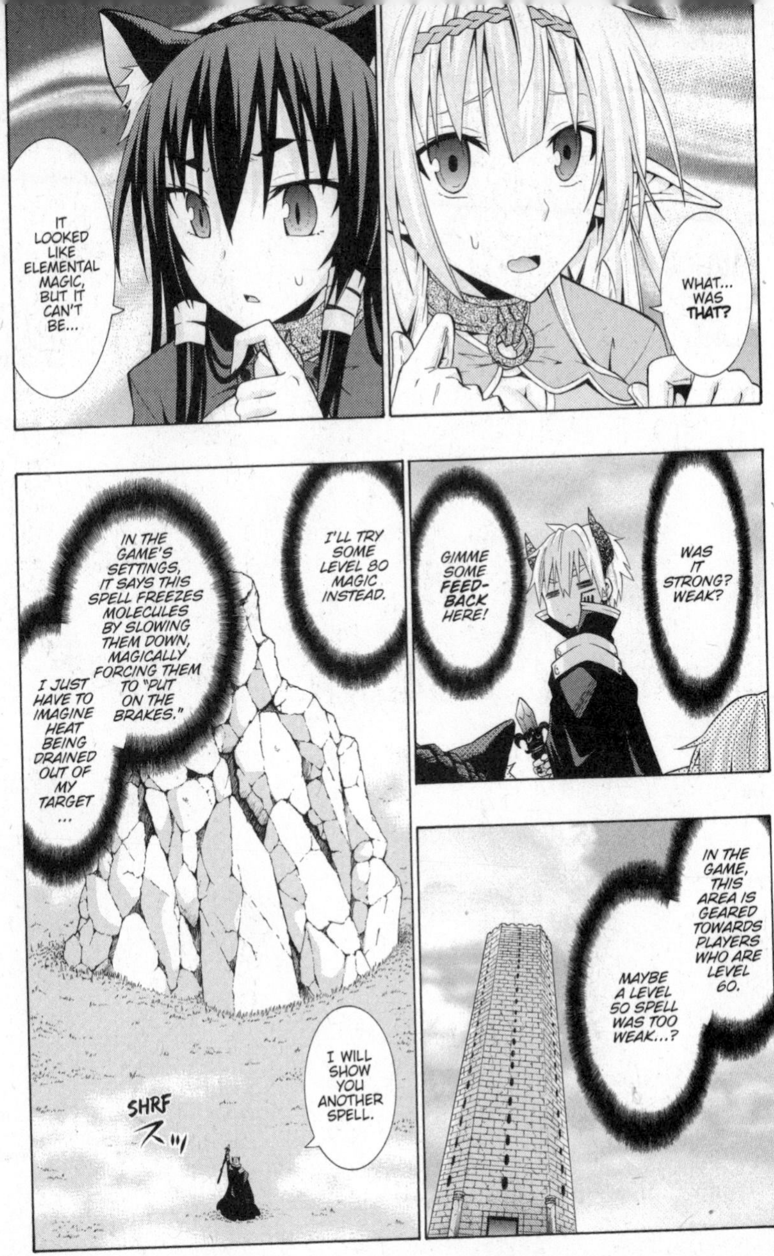
WHAT... WAS THAT?
IT LOOKED LIKE ELEMENTAL MAGIC, BUT IT CAN'T BE...
WAS IT STRONG? WEAK?
GIMME SOME FEED-BACK HERE!
IN THE GAME, THIS AREA IS GEARED TOWARDS PLAYERS WHO ARE LEVEL 60.
MAYBE A LEVEL 50 SPELL WAS TOO WEAK...?
I'LL TRY SOME LEVEL 80 MAGIC INSTEAD.
IN THE GAME'S SETTINGS, IT SAYS THIS SPELL FREEZES MOLECULES BY SLOWING THEM DOWN, MAGICALLY FORCING THEM TO "PUT ON THE BRAKES."
I JUST HAVE TO IMAGINE HEAT BEING DRAINED OUT OF MY TARGET ...
I WILL SHOW YOU ANOTHER SPELL.
SHRF
スッ

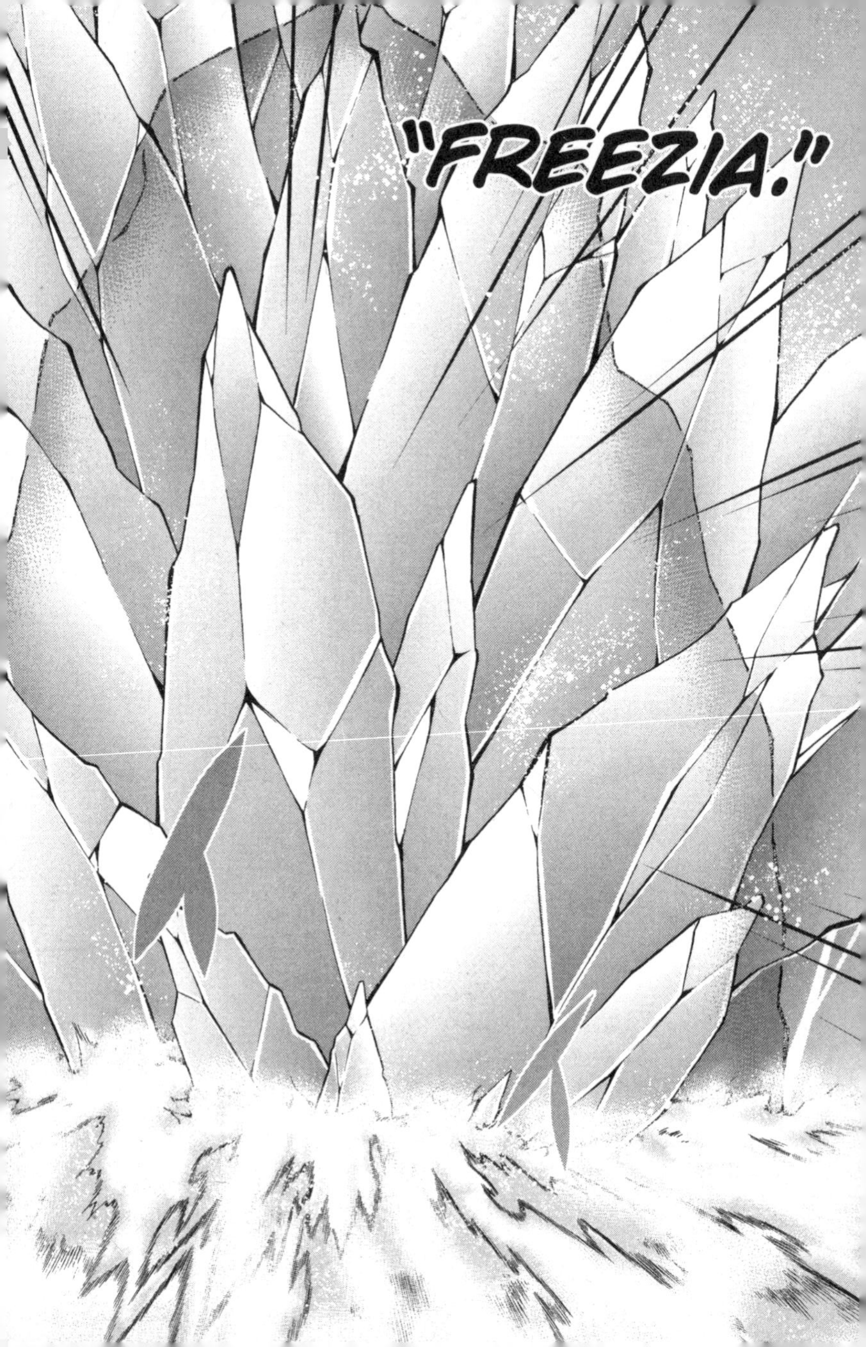
"FREEZIA."

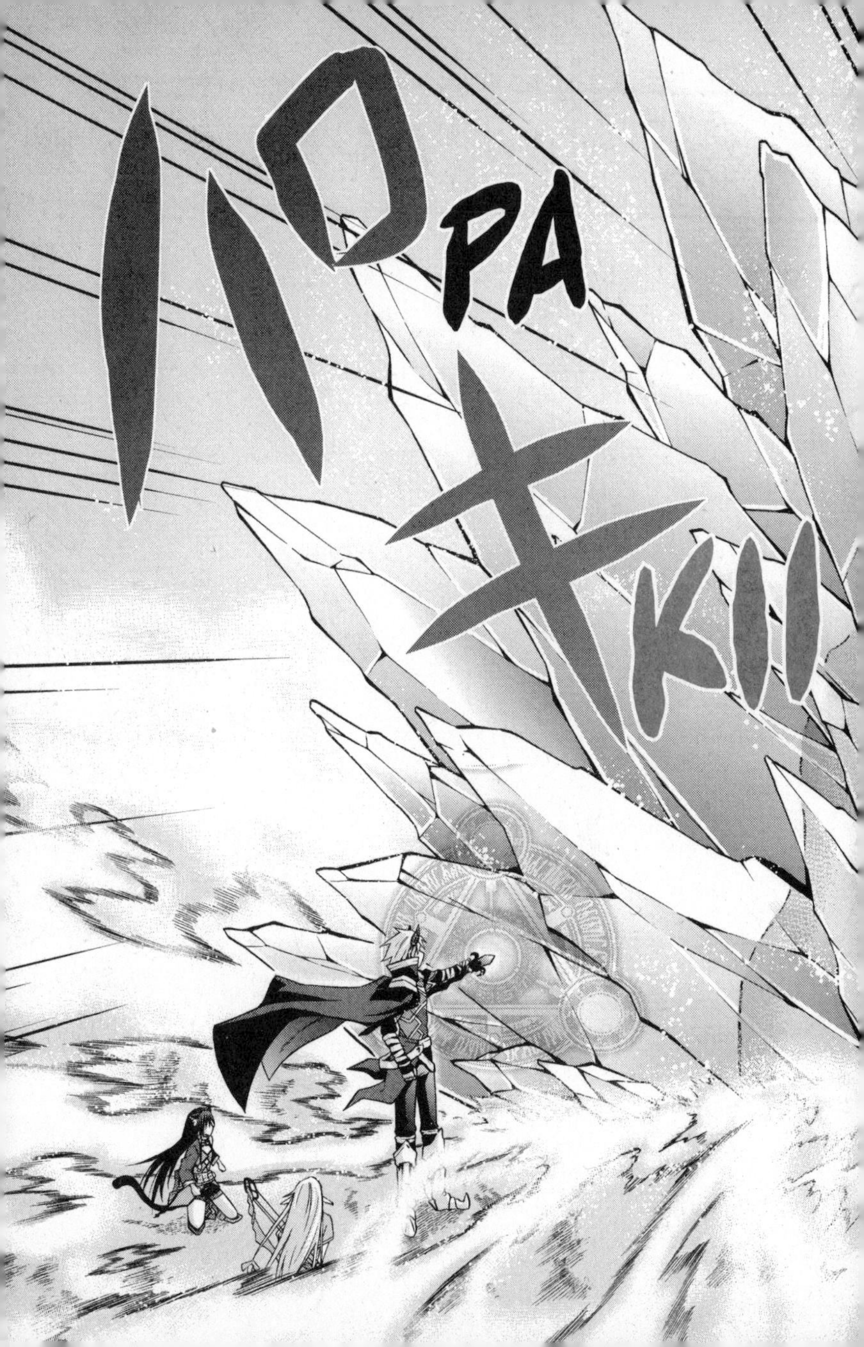
PA
KII

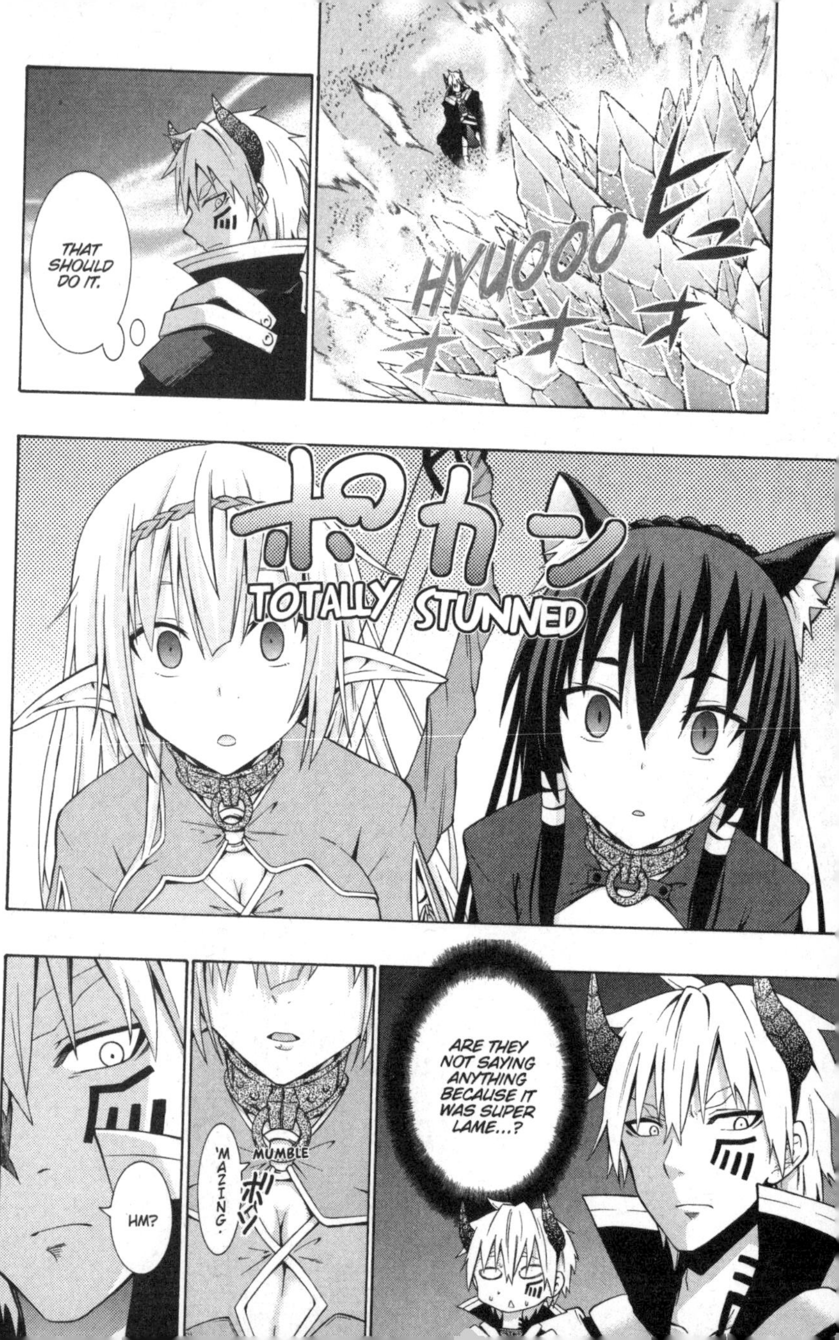
HYUOOO
ヒュオオオ
THAT SHOULD DO IT.
ポカーン
TOTALLY STUNNED
ARE THEY NOT SAYING ANYTHING BECAUSE IT WAS SUPER LAME...?
MUMBLE
'MAZING.
HM?

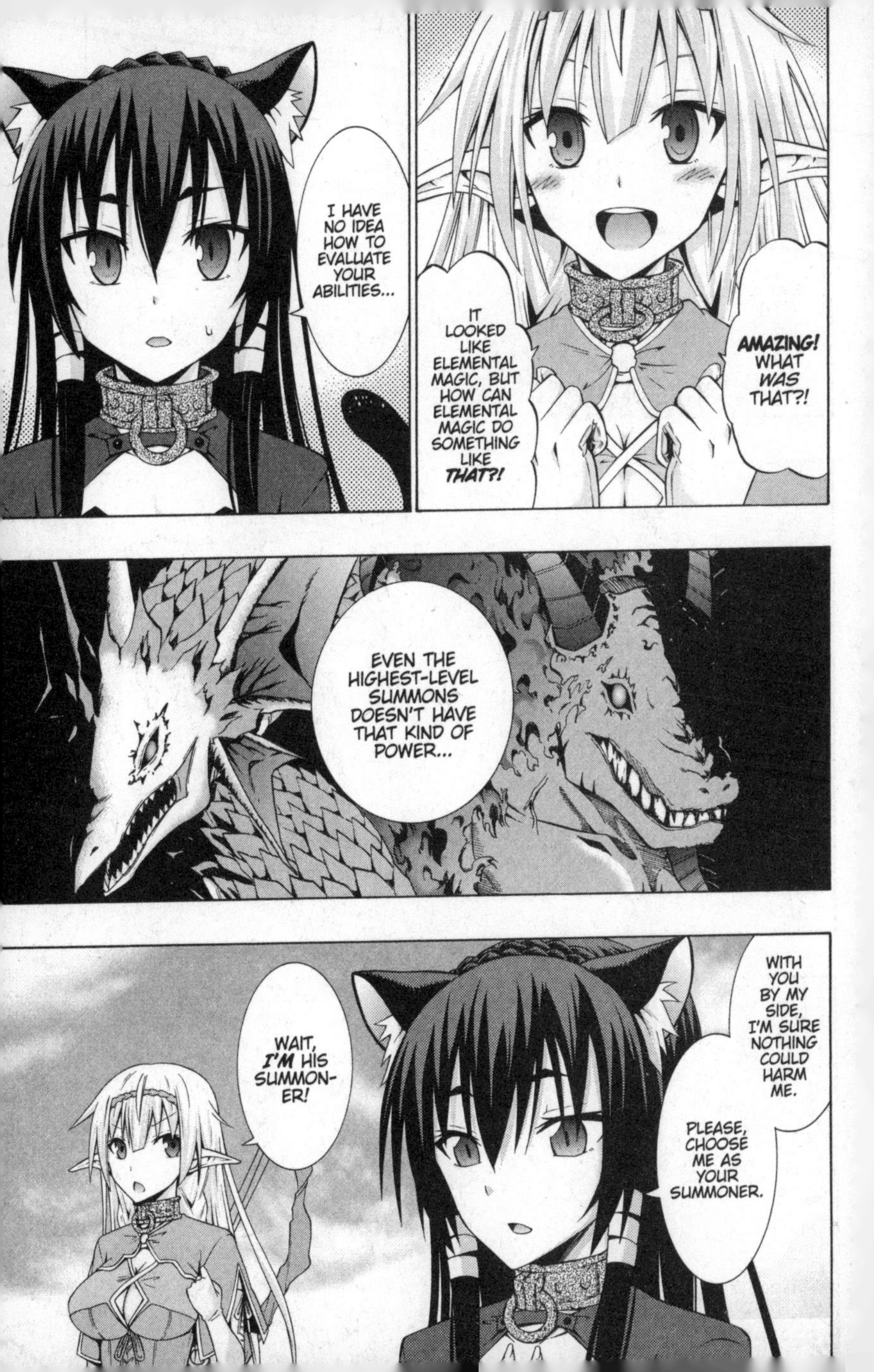
AMAZING! WHAT WAS THAT?!
IT LOOKED LIKE ELEMENTAL MAGIC, BUT HOW CAN ELEMENTAL MAGIC DO SOMETHING LIKE THAT?!
I HAVE NO IDEA HOW TO EVALUATE YOUR ABILITIES...
EVEN THE HIGHEST-LEVEL SUMMONS DOESN'T HAVE THAT KIND OF POWER...
WITH YOU BY MY SIDE, I'M SURE NOTHING COULD HARM ME.
PLEASE, CHOOSE ME AS YOUR SUMMONER.
WAIT, I'M HIS SUMMON-ER!

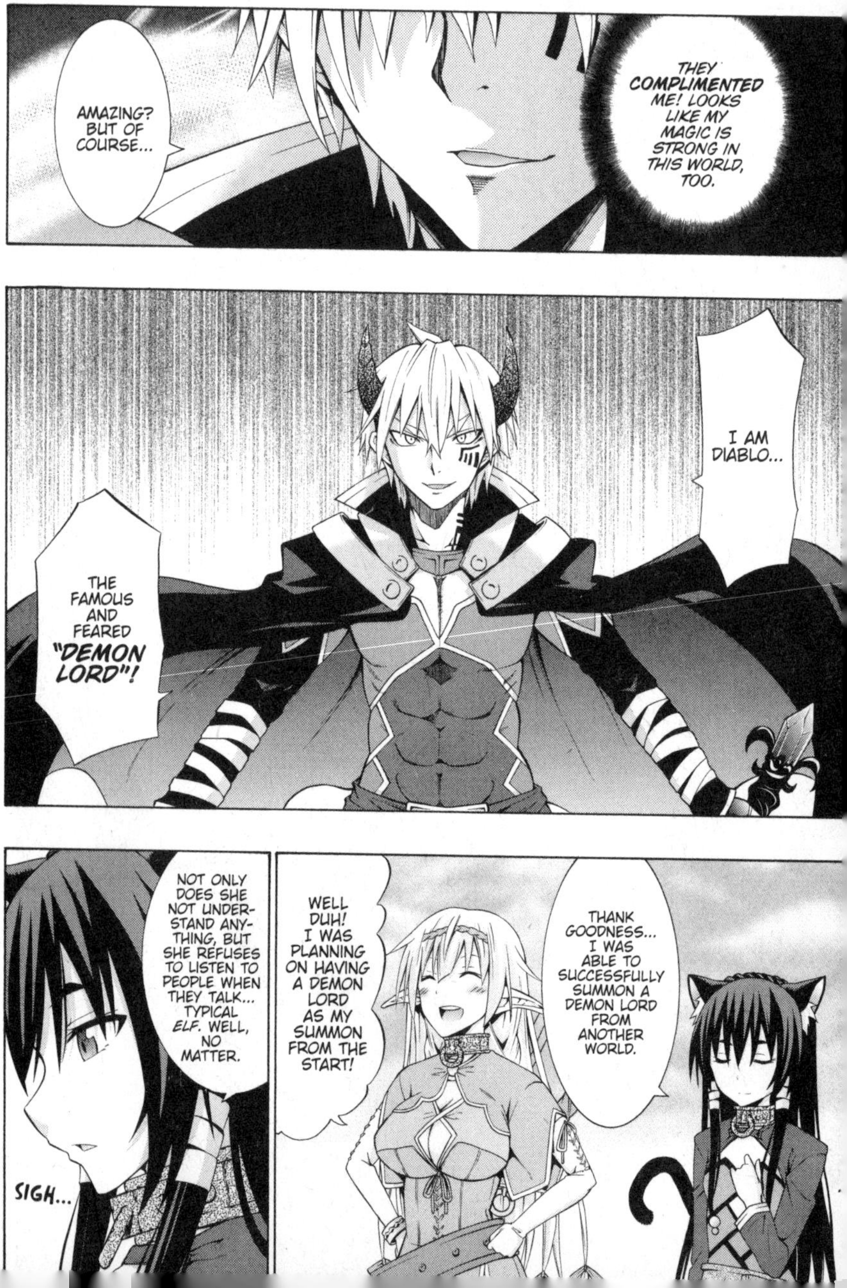
THEY COMPLIMENTED ME! LOOKS LIKE MY MAGIC IS STRONG IN THIS WORLD, TOO.
AMAZING? BUT OF COURSE...
I AM DIABLO...
THE FAMOUS AND FEARED "DEMON LORD"!
THANK GOODNESS... I WAS ABLE TO SUCCESSFULLY SUMMON A DEMON LORD FROM ANOTHER WORLD.
WELL DUH! I WAS PLANNING ON HAVING A DEMON LORD AS MY SUMMON FROM THE START!
NOT ONLY DOES SHE NOT UNDERSTAND ANYTHING, BUT SHE REFUSES TO LISTEN TO PEOPLE WHEN THEY TALK... TYPICAL ELF. WELL, NO MATTER.
SIGH...

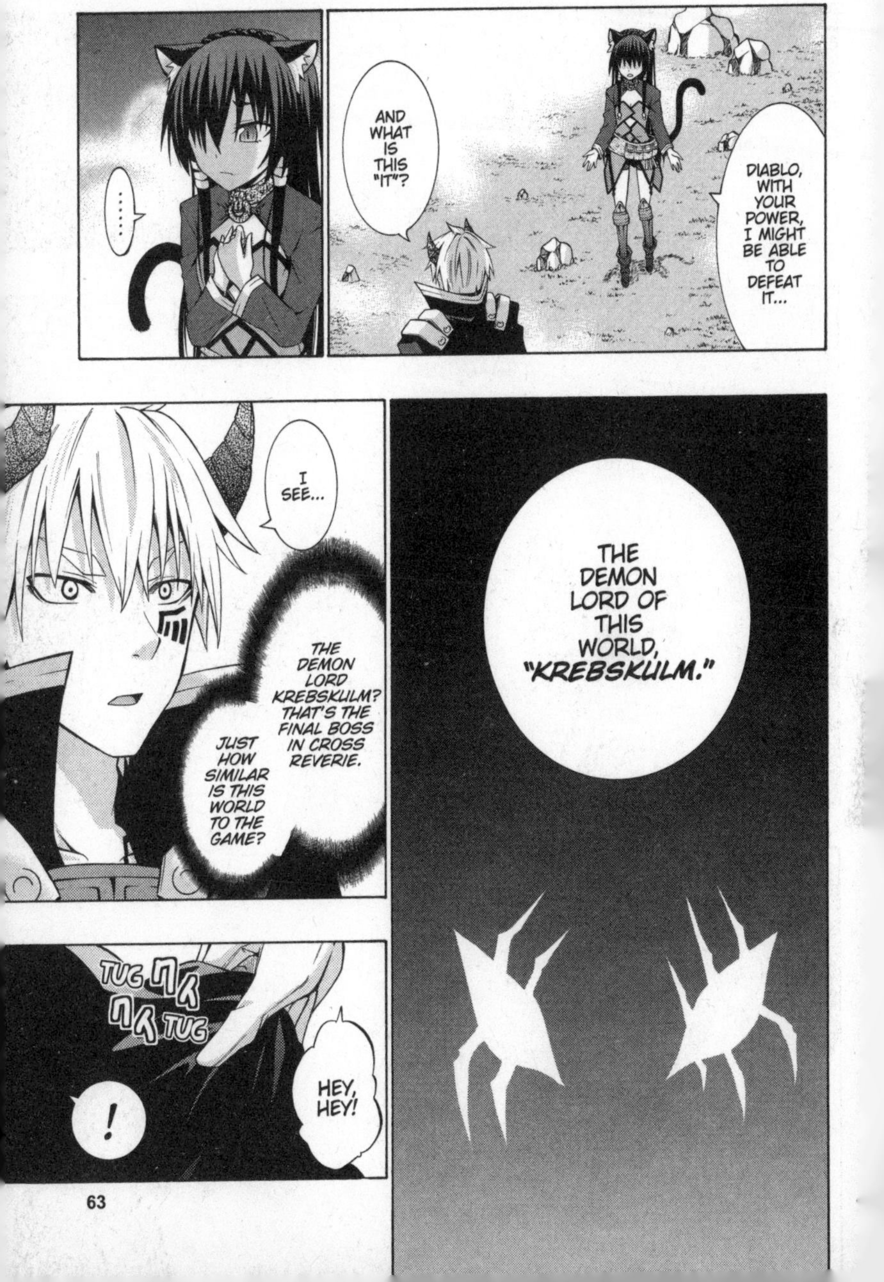
DIABLO, WITH YOUR POWER, I MIGHT BE ABLE TO DEFEAT IT...
AND WHAT IS THIS "IT"?
......
THE DEMON LORD OF THIS WORLD, "KREBSKULM."
I SEE...
THE DEMON LORD KREBSKULM? THAT'S THE FINAL BOSS IN CROSS REVERIE.
JUST HOW SIMILAR IS THIS WORLD TO THE GAME?
TUG
TUG
HEY, HEY!
!

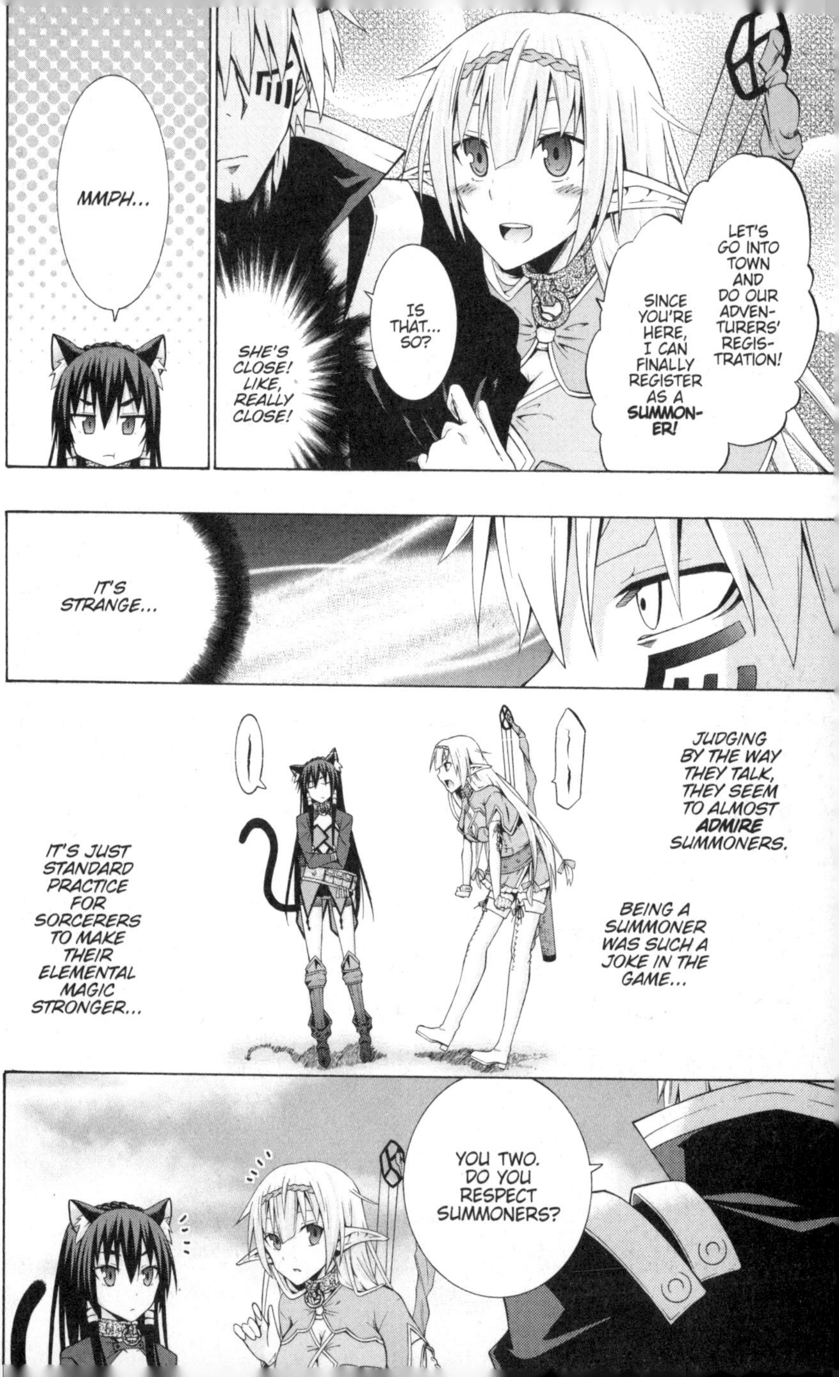
LET'S GO INTO TOWN AND DO OUR ADVENTURERS' REGISTRATION!
SINCE YOU'RE HERE, I CAN FINALLY REGISTER AS A **SUMMONER!**
IS THAT... SO?
SHE'S CLOSE! LIKE, REALLY CLOSE!
MMPH...
IT'S JUST STRANGE...
JUDGING BY THE WAY THEY TALK, THEY SEEM TO ALMOST **ADMIRE** SUMMONERS.
BEING A SUMMONER WAS SUCH A JOKE IN THE GAME...
!
!
IT'S JUST STANDARD PRACTICE FOR SORCERERS TO MAKE THEIR ELEMENTAL MAGIC STRONGER...
YOU TWO. DO YOU RESPECT SUMMONERS?

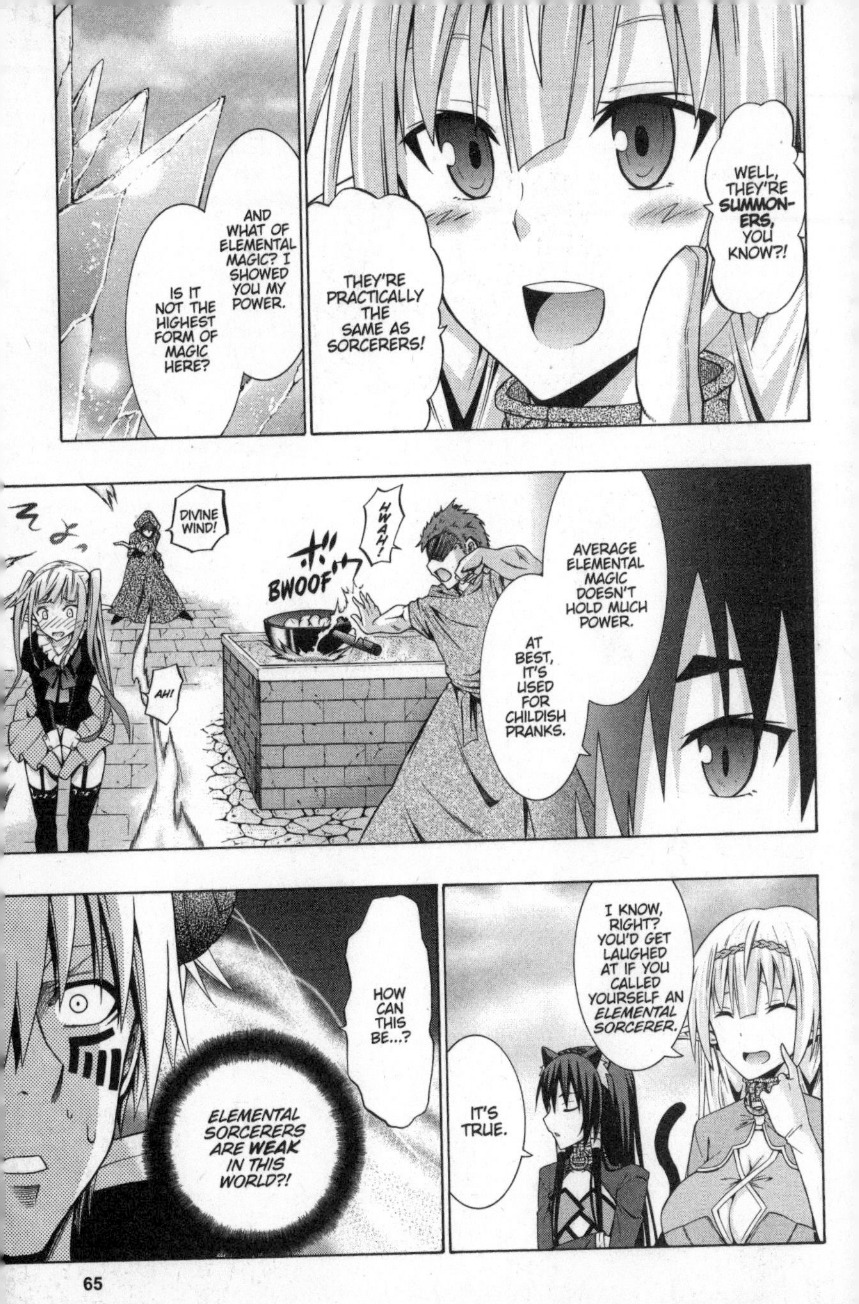
WELL, THEY'RE SUMMONERS, YOU KNOW?!
THEY'RE PRACTICALLY THE SAME AS SORCERERS!
AND WHAT OF ELEMENTAL MAGIC? I SHOWED YOU MY POWER.
IS IT NOT THE HIGHEST FORM OF MAGIC HERE?
AVERAGE ELEMENTAL MAGIC DOESN'T HOLD MUCH POWER.
AT BEST, IT'S USED FOR CHILDISH PRANKS.
HWAH!
BWOOF
DIVINE WIND!
AH!
I KNOW, RIGHT? YOU'D GET LAUGHED AT IF YOU CALLED YOURSELF AN ELEMENTAL SORCERER.
IT'S TRUE.
HOW CAN THIS BE...?
ELEMENTAL SORCERERS ARE WEAK IN THIS WORLD?!

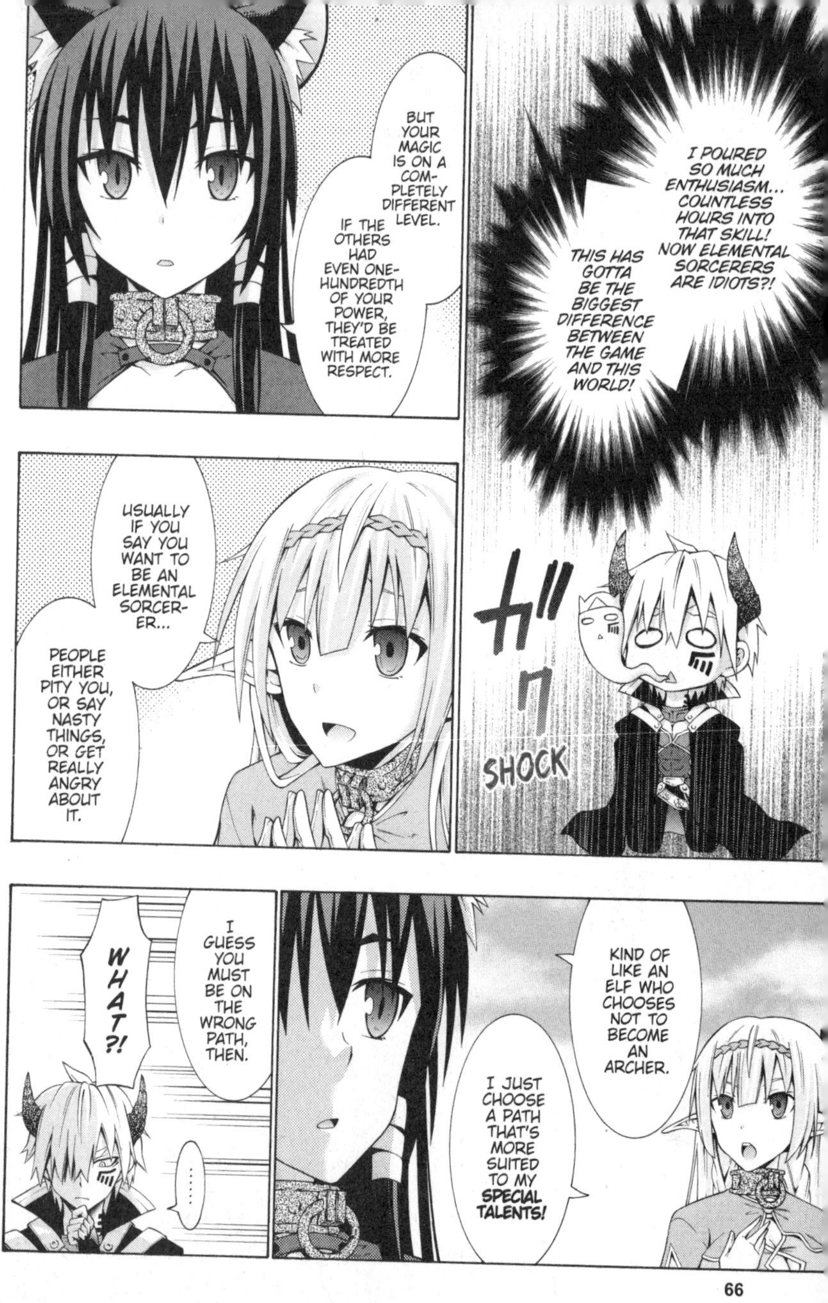

I POURED SO MUCH ENTHUSIASM... COUNTLESS HOURS INTO THAT SKILL! NOW ELEMENTAL SORCERERS ARE IDIOTS?!
THIS HAS GOTTA BE THE BIGGEST DIFFERENCE BETWEEN THE GAME AND THIS WORLD!
ガク
SHOCK
BUT YOUR MAGIC IS ON A COM-PLETELY DIFFERENT LEVEL.
IF THE OTHERS HAD EVEN ONE-HUNDREDTH OF YOUR POWER, THEY'D BE TREATED WITH MORE RESPECT.
USUALLY IF YOU SAY YOU WANT TO BE AN ELEMENTAL SORCER-ER...
PEOPLE EITHER PITY YOU, OR SAY NASTY THINGS, OR GET REALLY ANGRY ABOUT IT.
KIND OF LIKE AN ELF WHO CHOOSES NOT TO BECOME AN ARCHER.
I JUST CHOOSE A PATH THAT'S MORE SUITED TO MY **SPECIAL TALENTS!**
I GUESS YOU MUST BE ON THE WRONG PATH, THEN.
WHAT?!
......

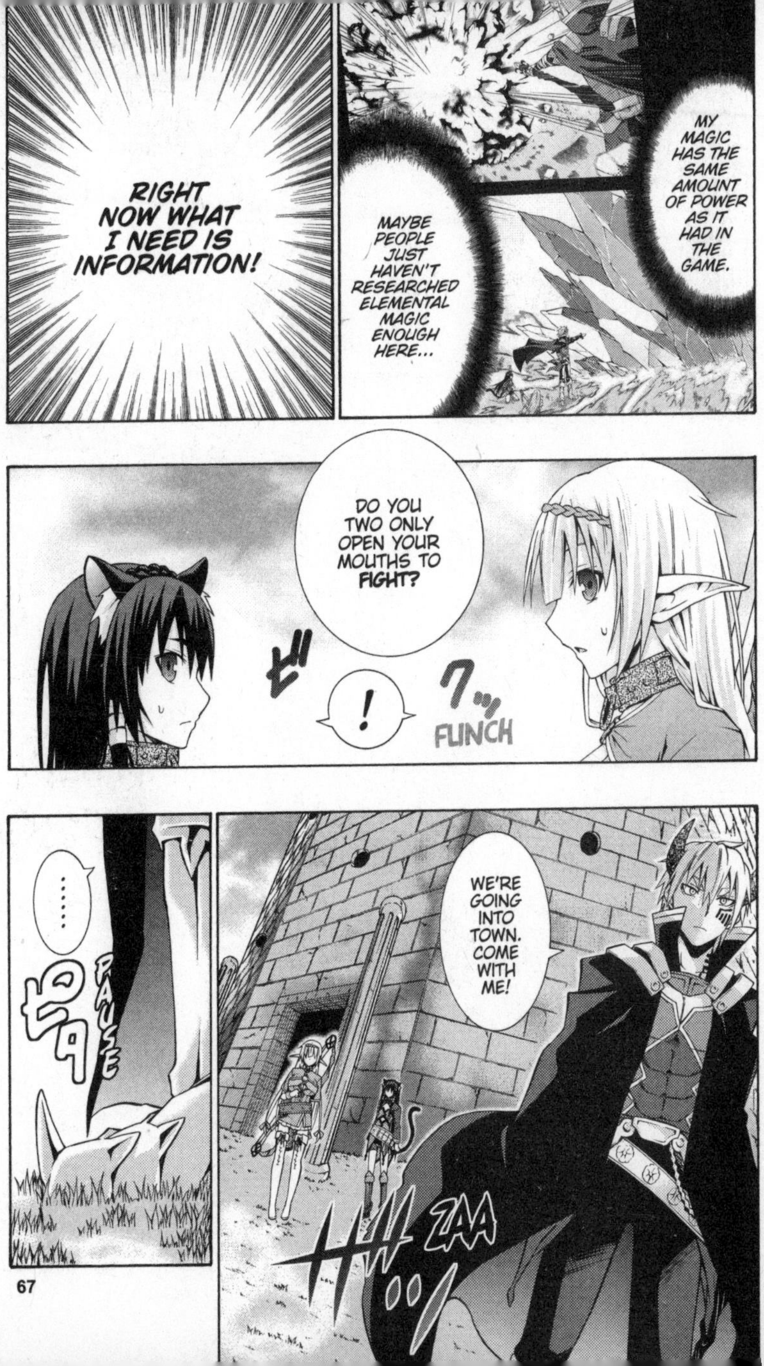
MY MAGIC HAS THE SAME AMOUNT OF POWER AS IT HAD IN THE GAME.
MAYBE PEOPLE JUST HAVEN'T RESEARCHED ELEMENTAL MAGIC ENOUGH HERE...
RIGHT NOW WHAT I NEED IS INFORMATION!
DO YOU TWO ONLY OPEN YOUR MOUTHS TO FIGHT?
FLINCH
!
WE'RE GOING INTO TOWN. COME WITH ME!
ZAA
......
PAUSE

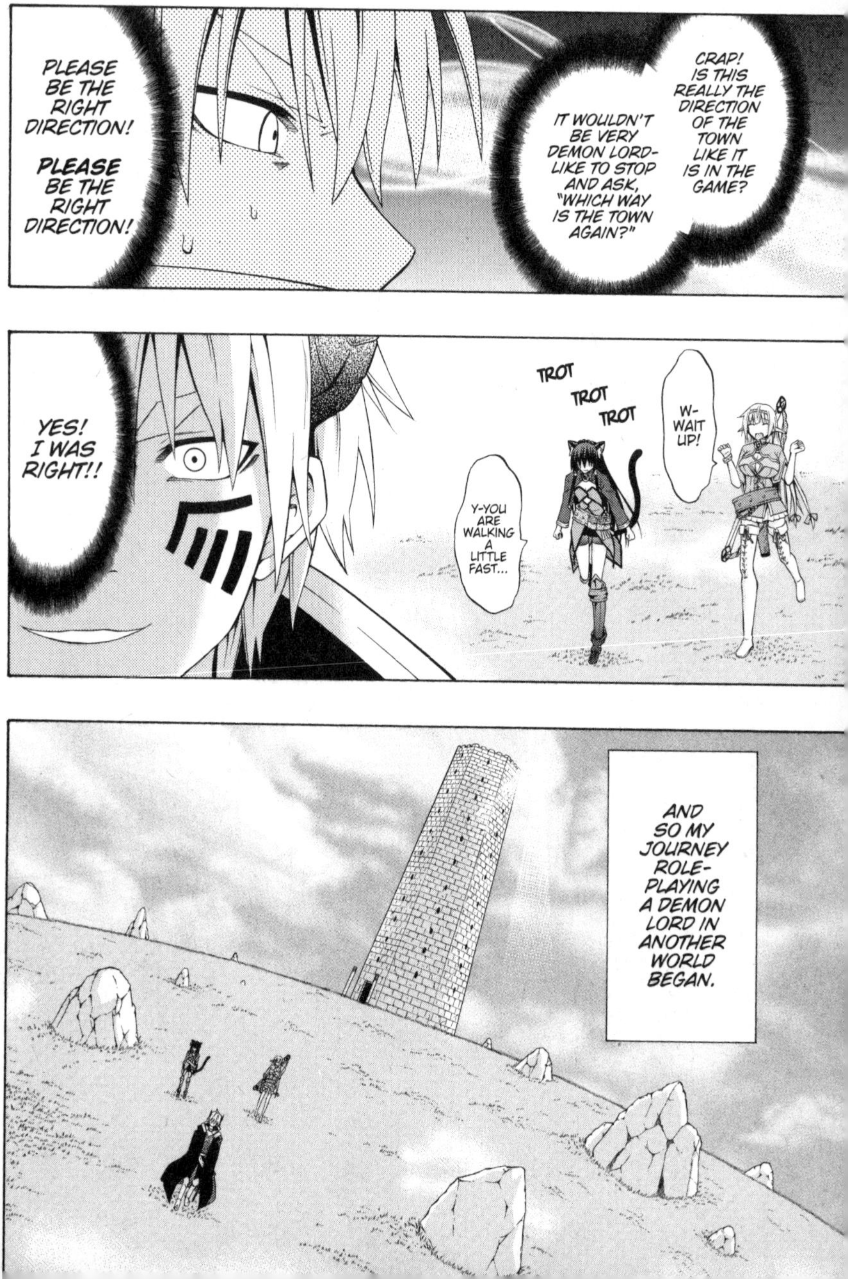
CRAP! IS THIS REALLY THE DIRECTION OF THE TOWN LIKE IT IS IN THE GAME?
IT WOULDN'T BE VERY DEMON LORD-LIKE TO STOP AND ASK, "WHICH WAY IS THE TOWN AGAIN?"
PLEASE BE THE RIGHT DIRECTION!
PLEASE BE THE RIGHT DIRECTION!
W-WAIT UP!
TROT
TROT
TROT
Y-YOU ARE WALKING A LITTLE FAST...
YES! I WAS RIGHT!!
AND SO MY JOURNEY ROLE-PLAYING A DEMON LORD IN ANOTHER WORLD BEGAN.

HOW NOT TO SUMMON A DEMON LORD

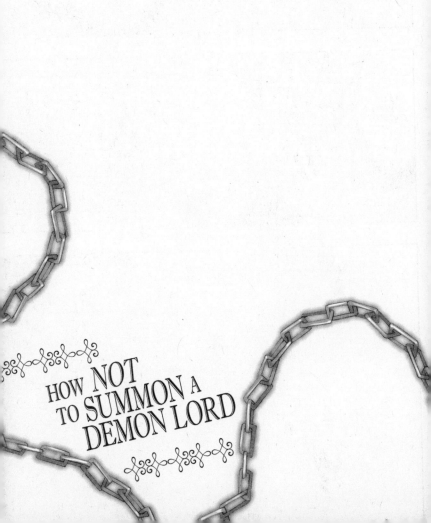

2 BEING SUMMONED II

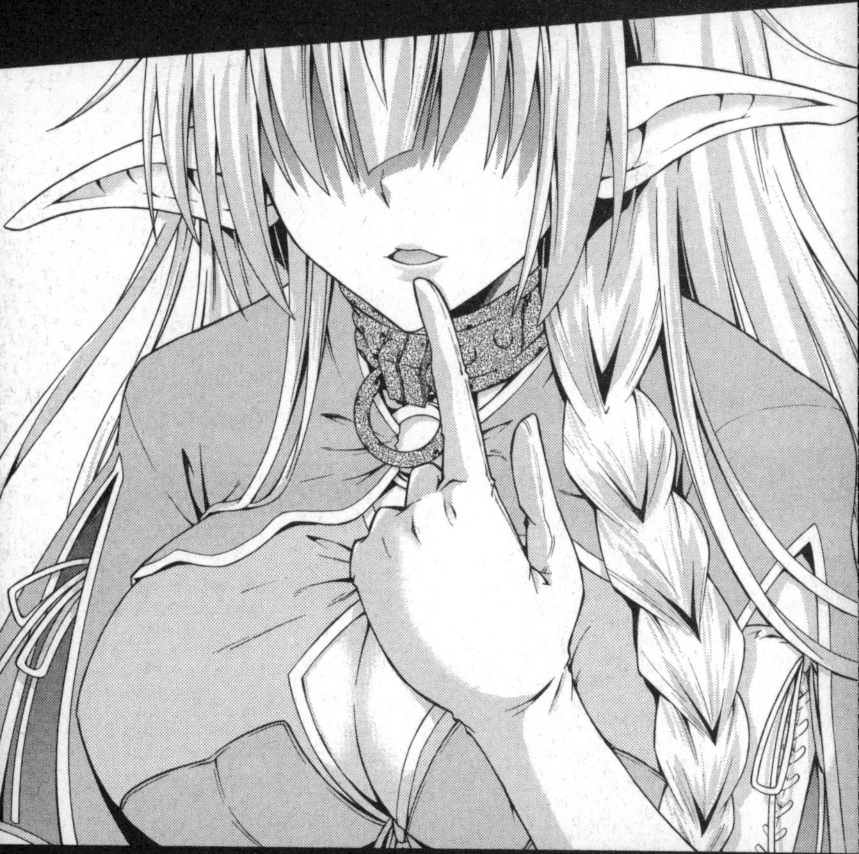

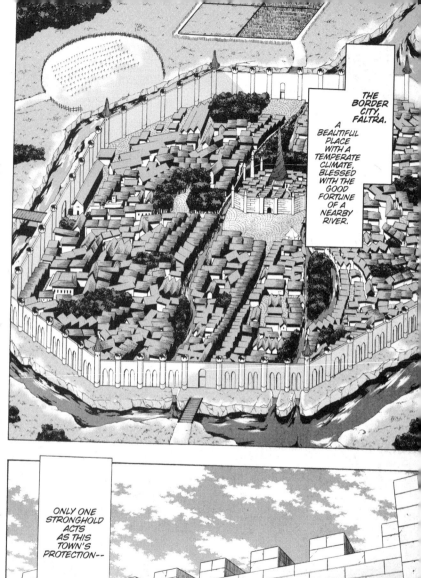

THE BORDER CITY, FALTRA.

A BEAUTIFUL PLACE WITH A TEMPERATE CLIMATE, BLESSED WITH THE GOOD FORTUNE OF A NEARBY RIVER.

ONLY ONE STRONGHOLD ACTS AS THIS TOWN'S PROTECTION--

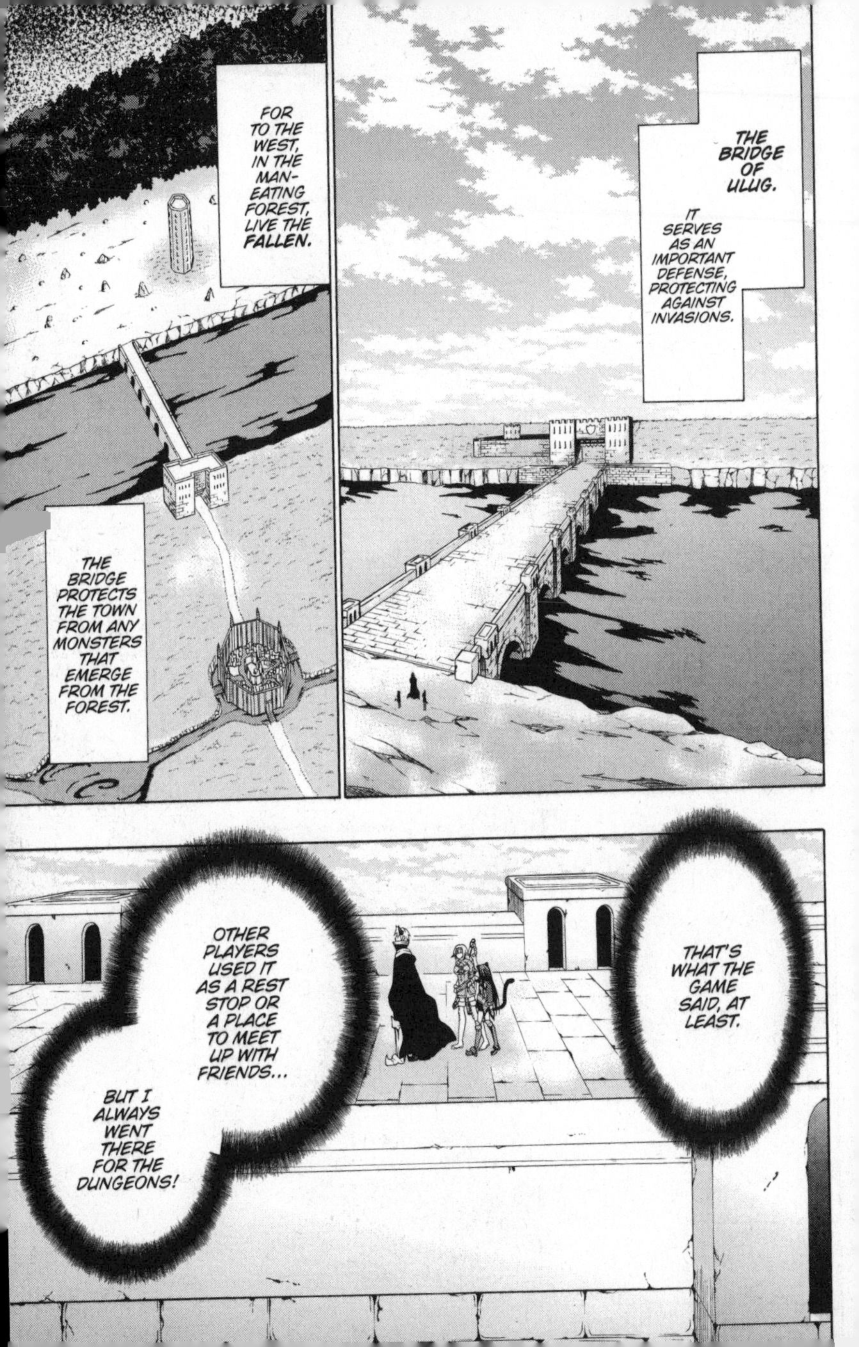
THE BRIDGE OF ULUG.
IT SERVES AS AN IMPORTANT DEFENSE, PROTECTING AGAINST INVASIONS.
FOR TO THE WEST, IN THE MAN-EATING FOREST, LIVE THE FALLEN.
THE BRIDGE PROTECTS THE TOWN FROM ANY MONSTERS THAT EMERGE FROM THE FOREST.
THAT'S WHAT THE GAME SAID, AT LEAST.
OTHER PLAYERS USED IT AS A REST STOP OR A PLACE TO MEET UP WITH FRIENDS...
BUT I ALWAYS WENT THERE FOR THE DUNGEONS!

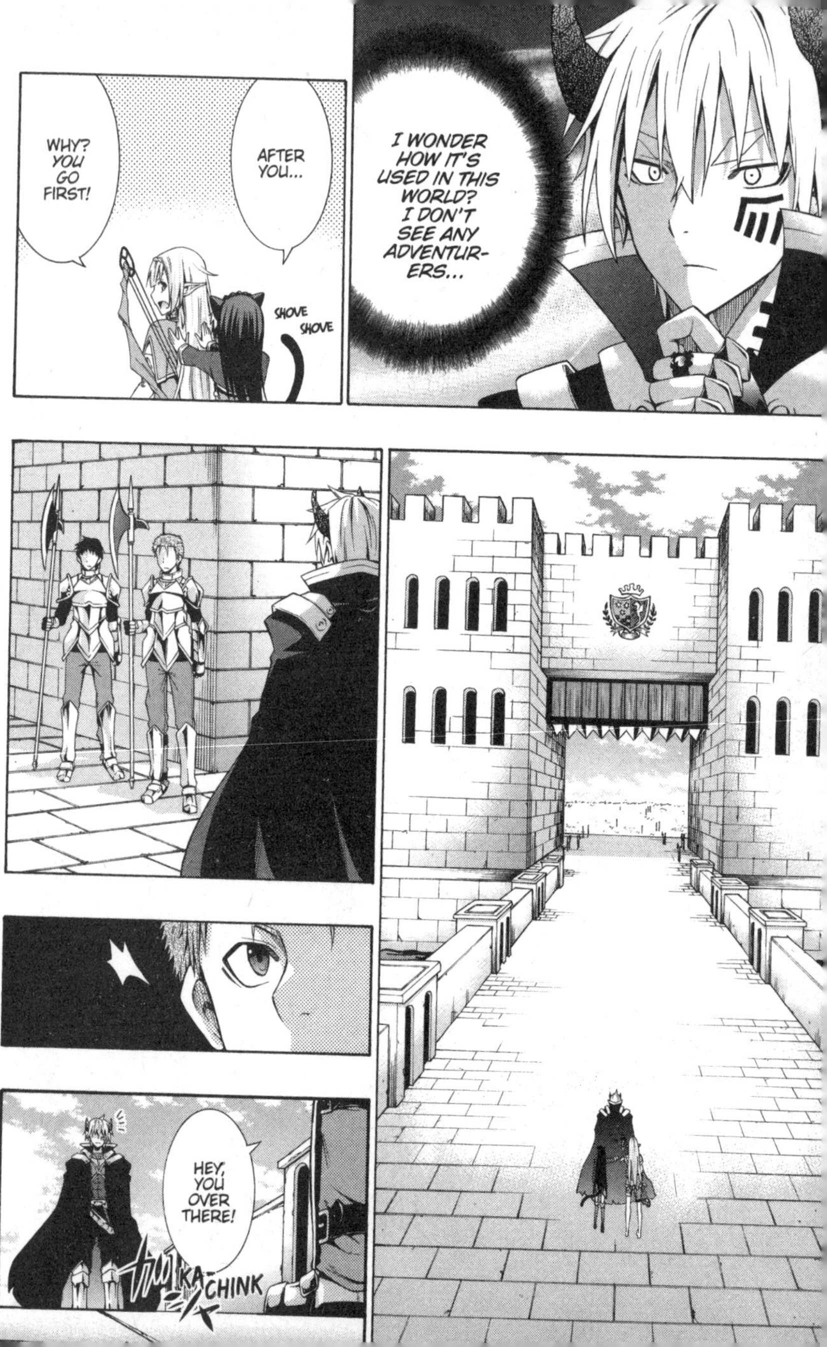
I WONDER HOW IT'S USED IN THIS WORLD? I DON'T SEE ANY ADVENTURERS...
AFTER YOU...
WHY? YOU GO FIRST!
SHOVE SHOVE
HEY, YOU OVER THERE!
KA-CHINK

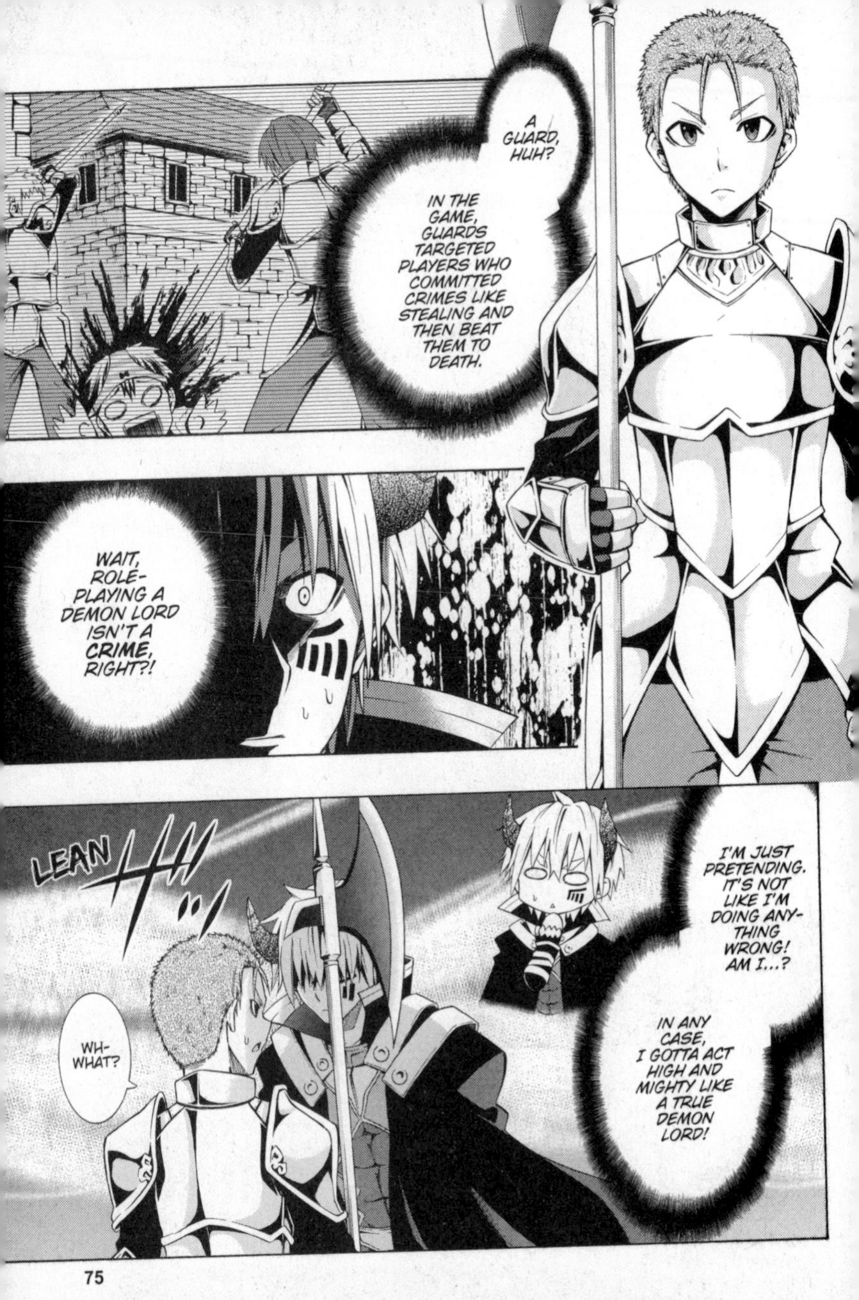
A GUARD, HUH?
IN THE GAME, GUARDS TARGETED PLAYERS WHO COMMITTED CRIMES LIKE STEALING AND THEN BEAT THEM TO DEATH.
WAIT, ROLE-PLAYING A DEMON LORD ISN'T A CRIME, RIGHT?!
I'M JUST PRETENDING. IT'S NOT LIKE I'M DOING ANY-THING WRONG! AM I...?
IN ANY CASE, I GOTTA ACT HIGH AND MIGHTY LIKE A TRUE DEMON LORD!
LEAN
WH-WHAT?

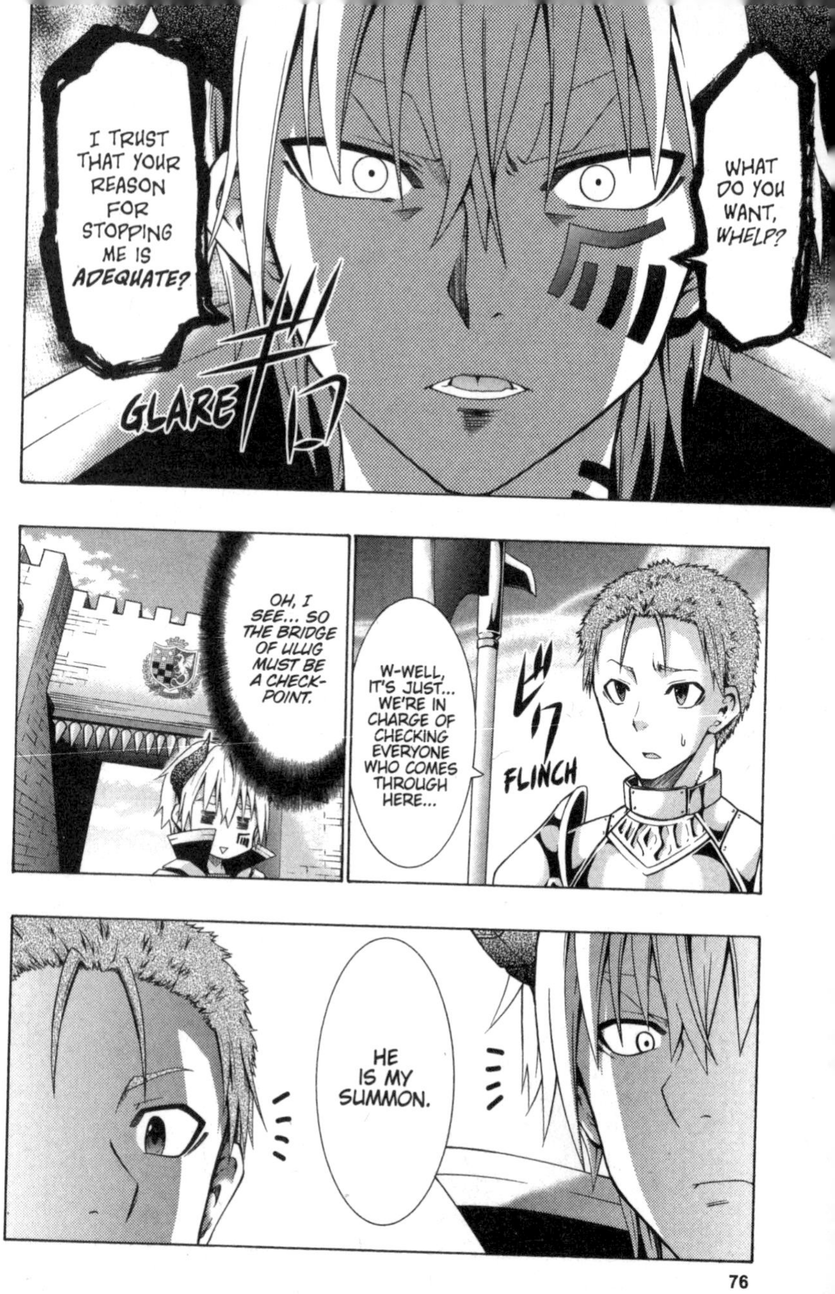
WHAT DO YOU WANT, WHELP?
I TRUST THAT YOUR REASON FOR STOPPING ME IS ADEQUATE?
GLARE
W-WELL, IT'S JUST... WE'RE IN CHARGE OF CHECKING EVERYONE WHO COMES THROUGH HERE...
FLINCH
OH, I SEE... SO THE BRIDGE OF ULUG MUST BE A CHECK-POINT.
HE IS MY SUMMON.

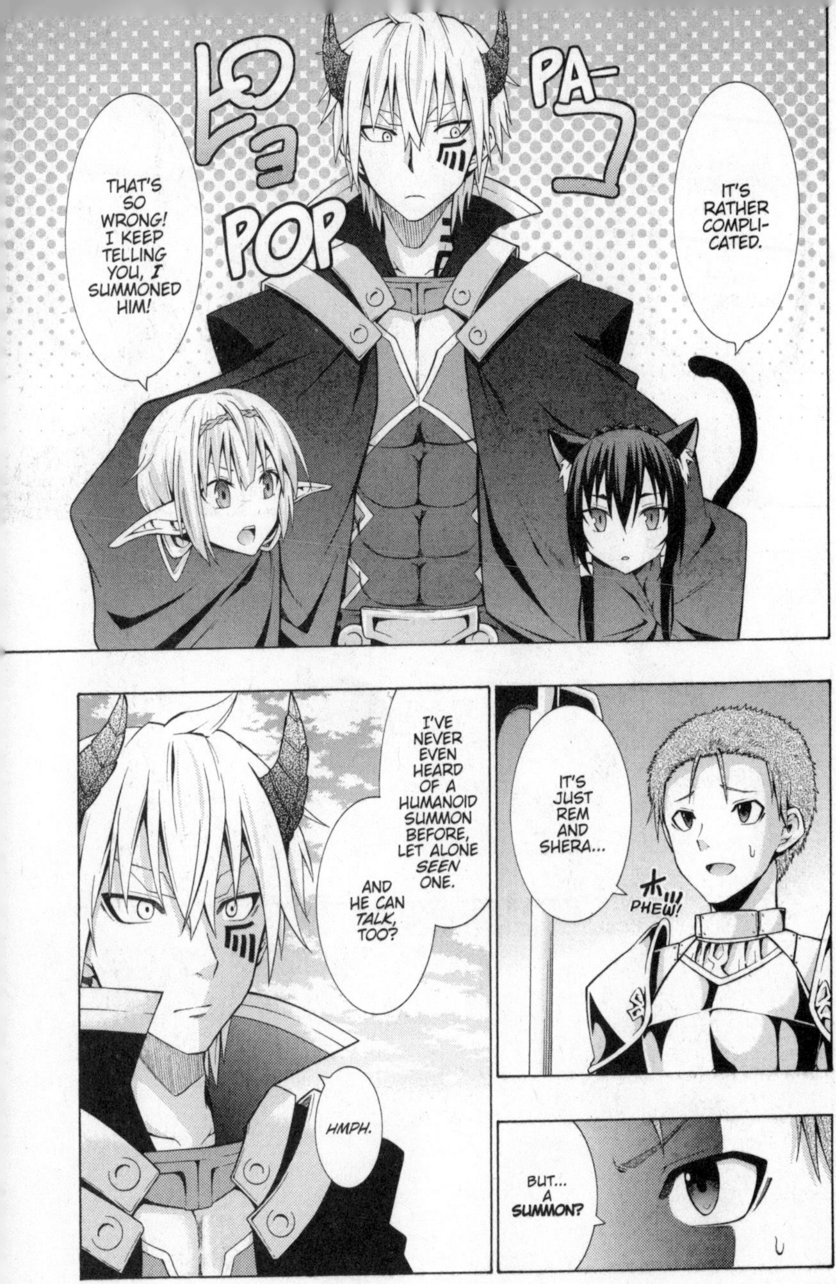
PA-
IT'S RATHER COMPLICATED.
THAT'S SO WRONG! I KEEP TELLING YOU, *I* SUMMONED HIM!
POP
IT'S JUST REM AND SHERA...
PHEW!
BUT... A SUMMON?
I'VE NEVER EVEN HEARD OF A HUMANOID SUMMON BEFORE, LET ALONE *SEEN* ONE.
AND HE CAN *TALK*, TOO?
HMPH.

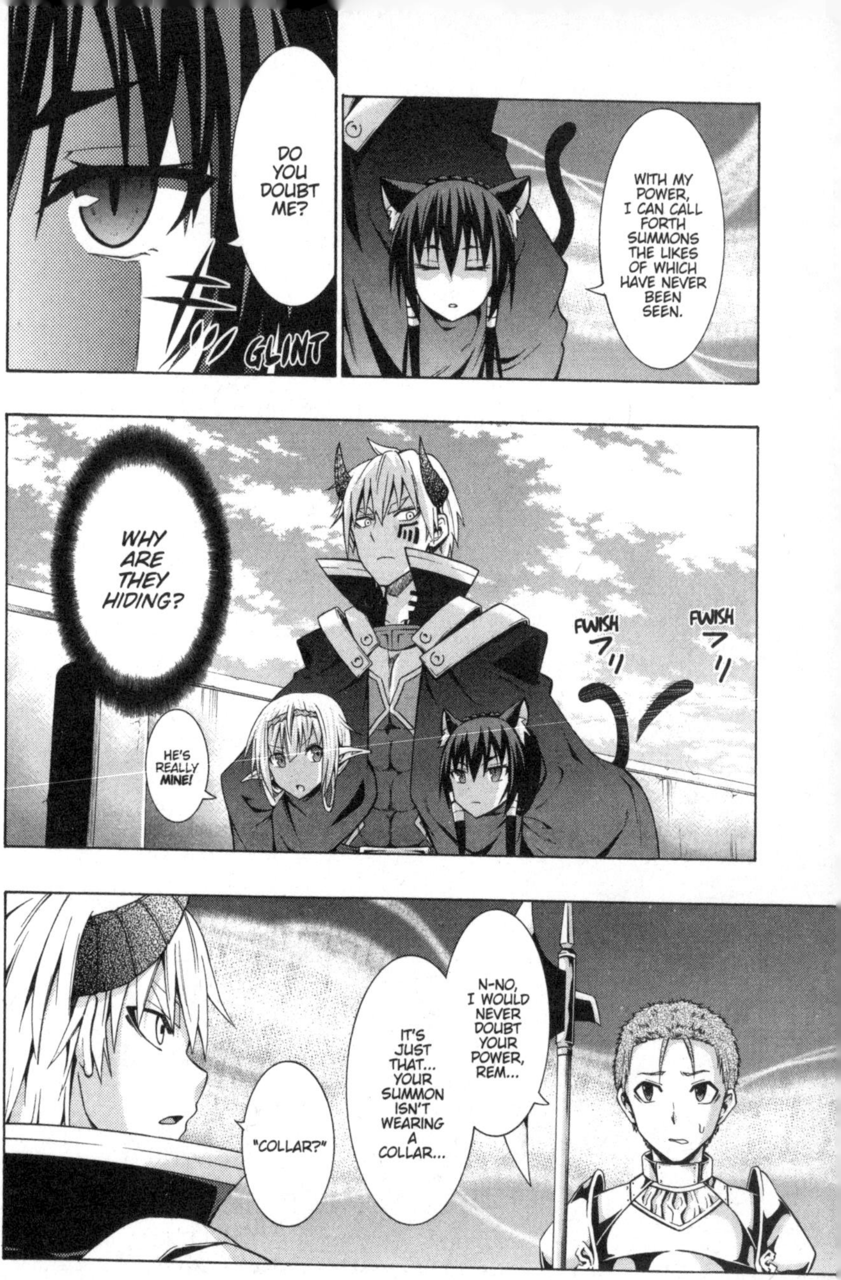
WITH MY POWER, I CAN CALL FORTH SUMMONS THE LIKES OF WHICH HAVE NEVER BEEN SEEN.
DO YOU DOUBT ME?
GLINT
FWISH
FWISH
WHY ARE THEY HIDING?
HE'S REALLY MINE!
N-NO, I WOULD NEVER DOUBT YOUR POWER, REM...
IT'S JUST THAT... YOUR SUMMON ISN'T WEARING A COLLAR...
"COLLAR?"

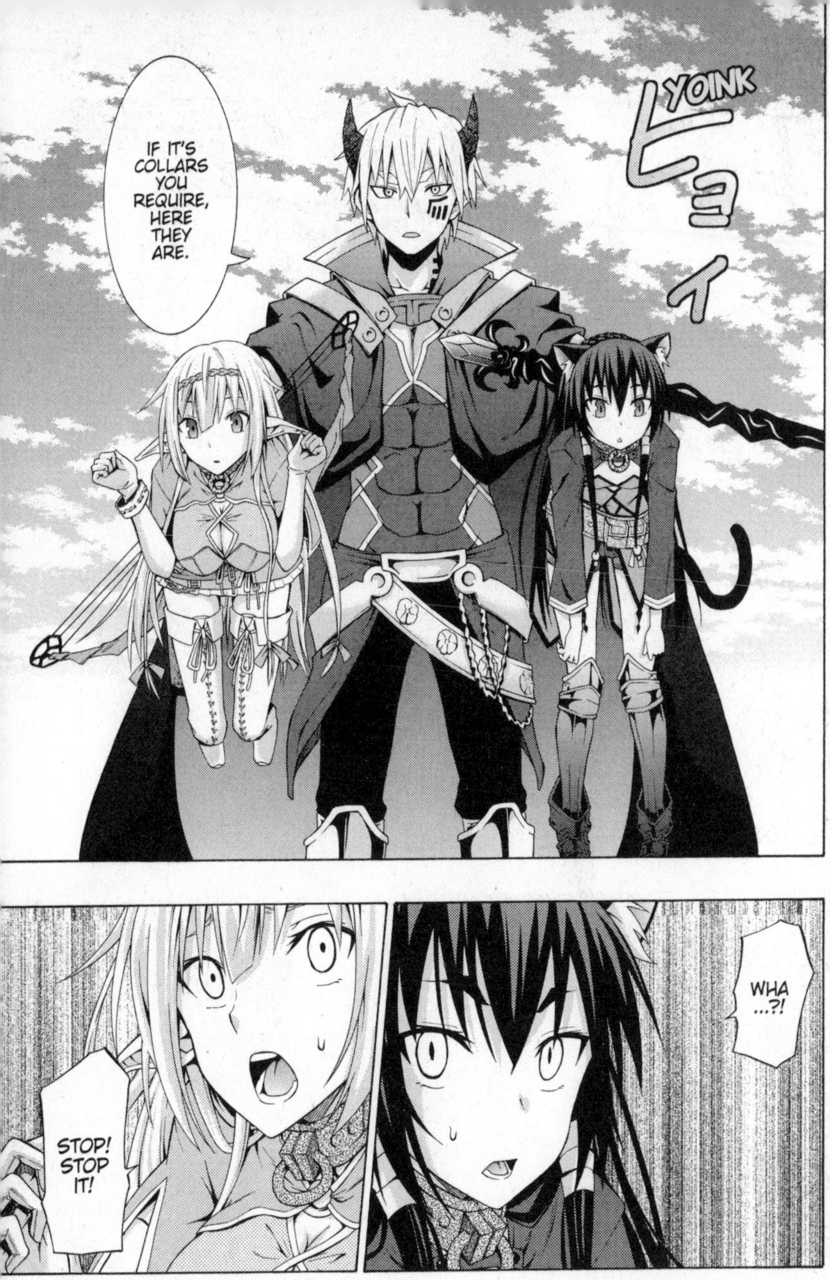
YOINK
ヒョイ
IF IT'S COLLARS YOU REQUIRE, HERE THEY ARE.
WHA ...?!
STOP! STOP IT!

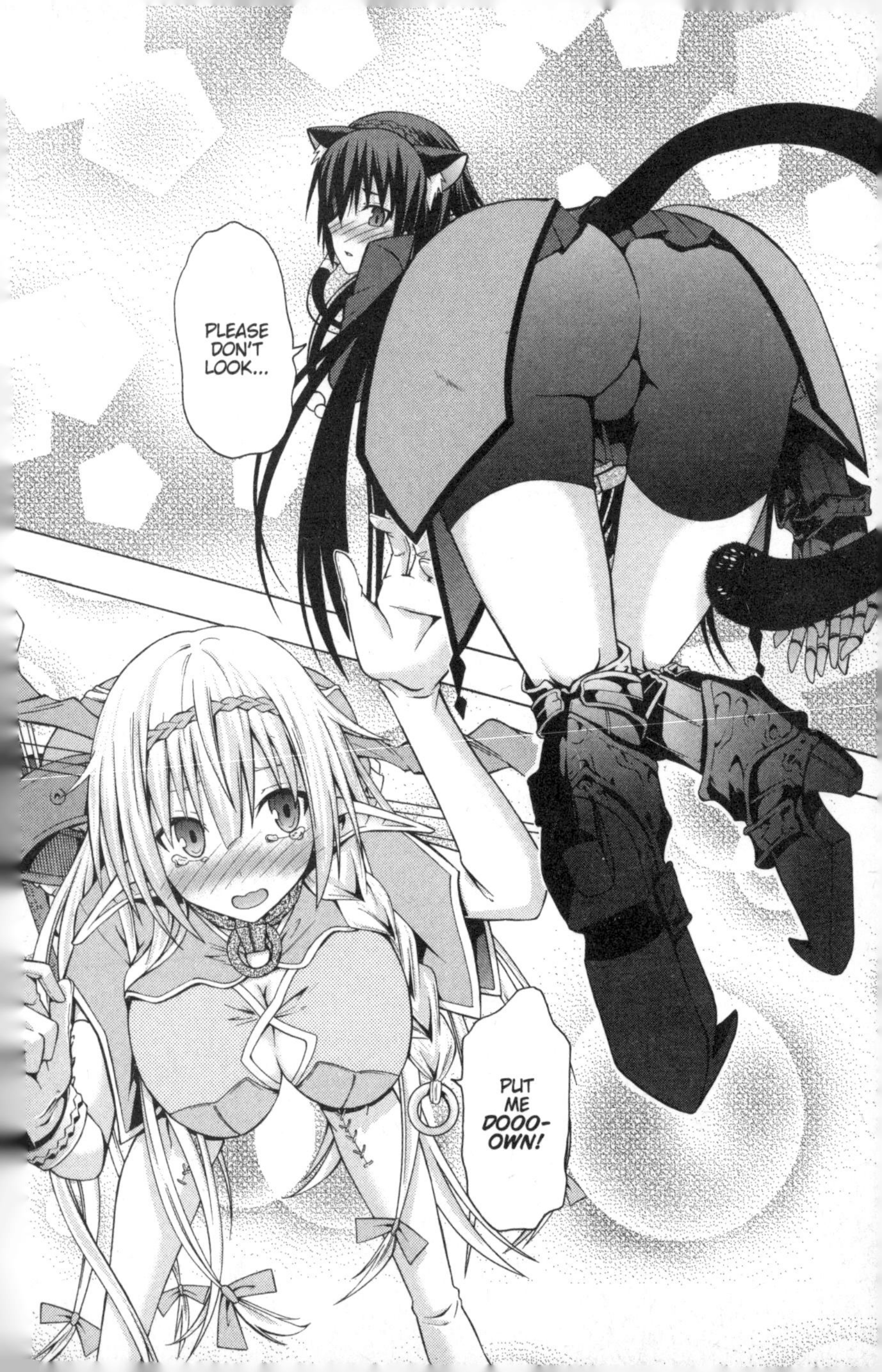
PLEASE DON'T LOOK...
PUT ME DOOOO-OWN!

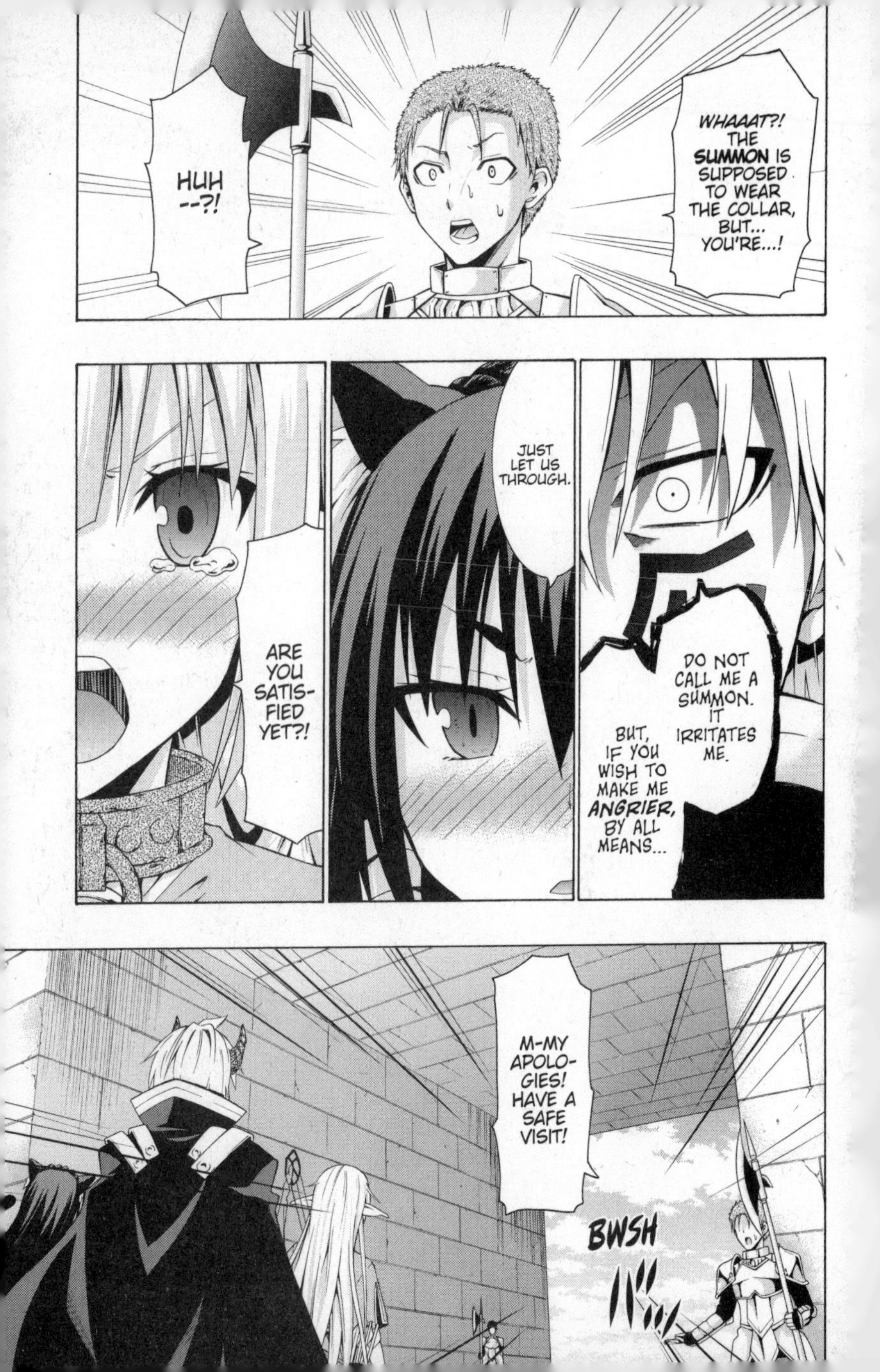
WHAAAT?! THE SUMMON IS SUPPOSED TO WEAR THE COLLAR, BUT... YOU'RE...!
HUH--?!
DO NOT CALL ME A SUMMON. IT IRRITATES ME.
BUT, IF YOU WISH TO MAKE ME ANGRIER, BY ALL MEANS...
JUST LET US THROUGH.
ARE YOU SATIS-FIED YET?!
M-MY APOLO-GIES! HAVE A SAFE VISIT!
BWSH

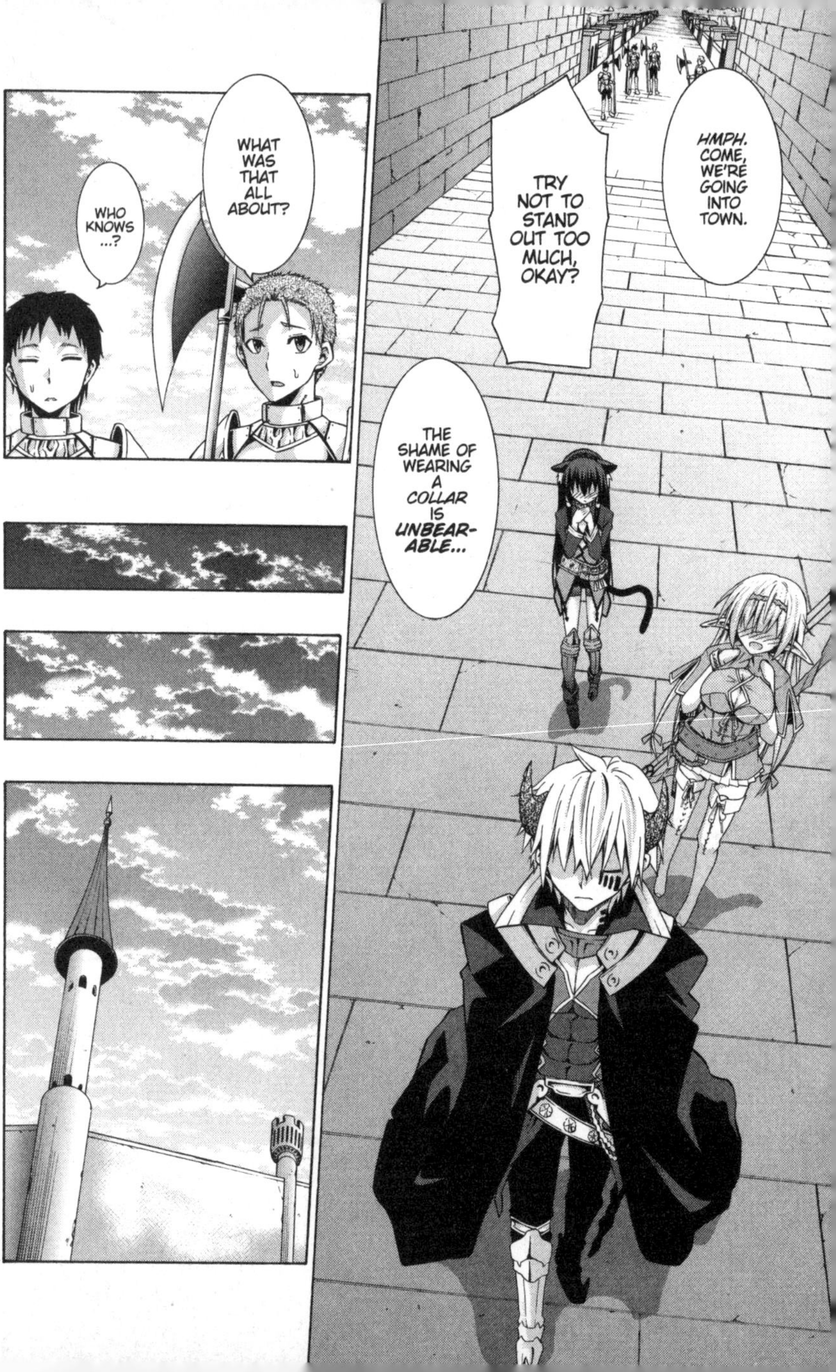
HMPH. COME, WE'RE GOING INTO TOWN.
TRY NOT TO STAND OUT TOO MUCH, OKAY?
THE SHAME OF WEARING A COLLAR IS *UNBEARABLE...*
WHAT WAS THAT ALL ABOUT?
WHO KNOWS ...?

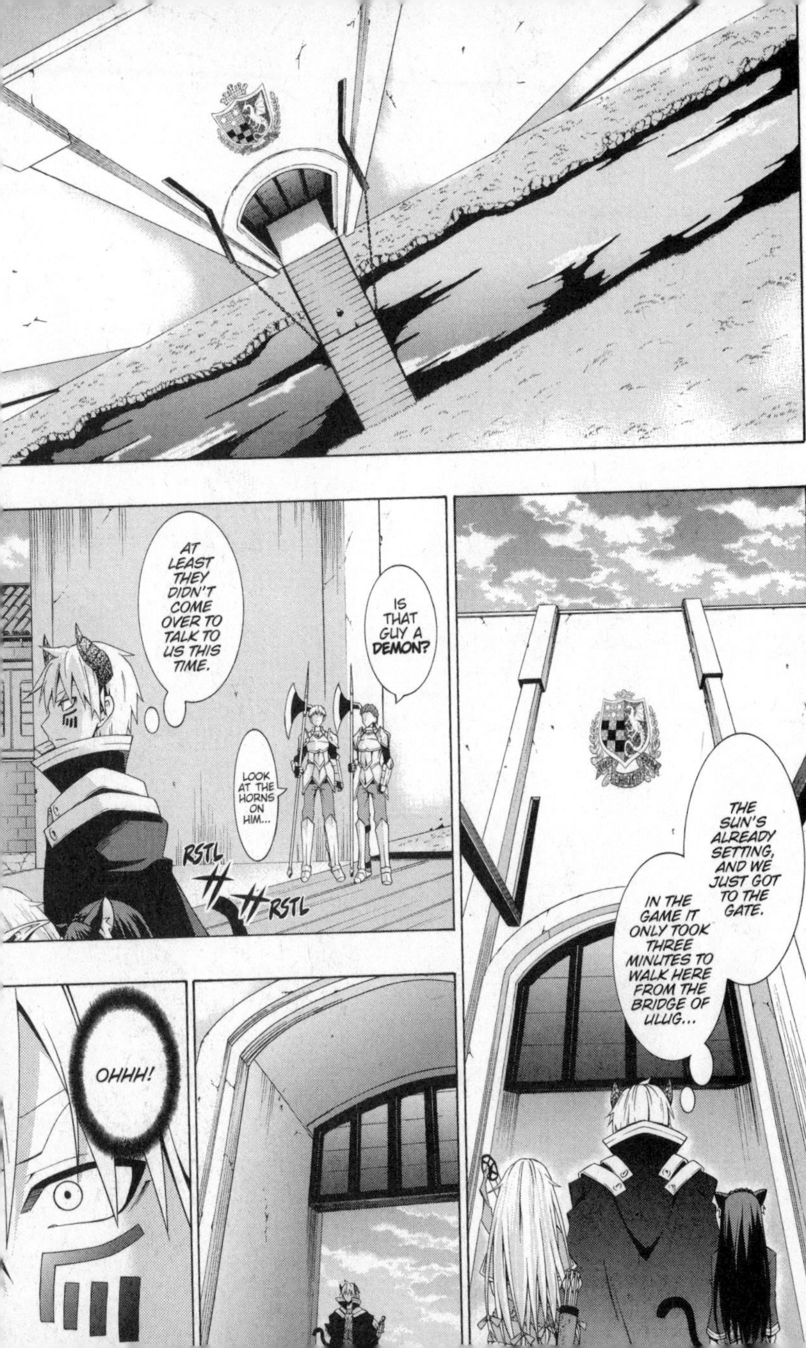
THE SUN'S ALREADY SETTING, AND WE JUST GOT TO THE GATE.
IN THE GAME IT ONLY TOOK THREE MINUTES TO WALK HERE FROM THE BRIDGE OF ULUG...
IS THAT GUY A DEMON?
AT LEAST THEY DIDN'T COME OVER TO TALK TO US THIS TIME.
LOOK AT THE HORNS ON HIM...
RSTL
RSTL
OHHH!

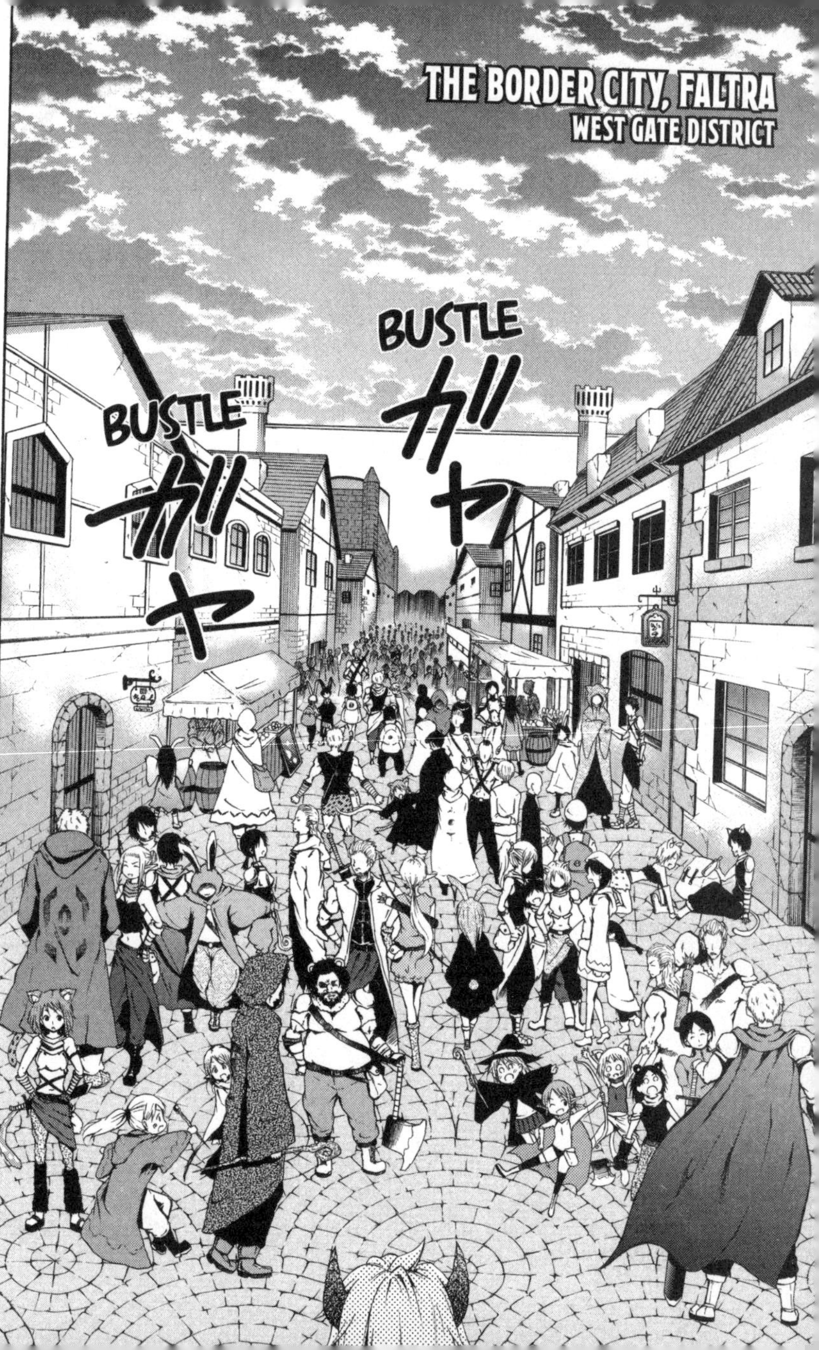
THE BORDER CITY, FALTRA
WEST GATE DISTRICT
BUSTLE
ガヤ
BUSTLE
ガヤ

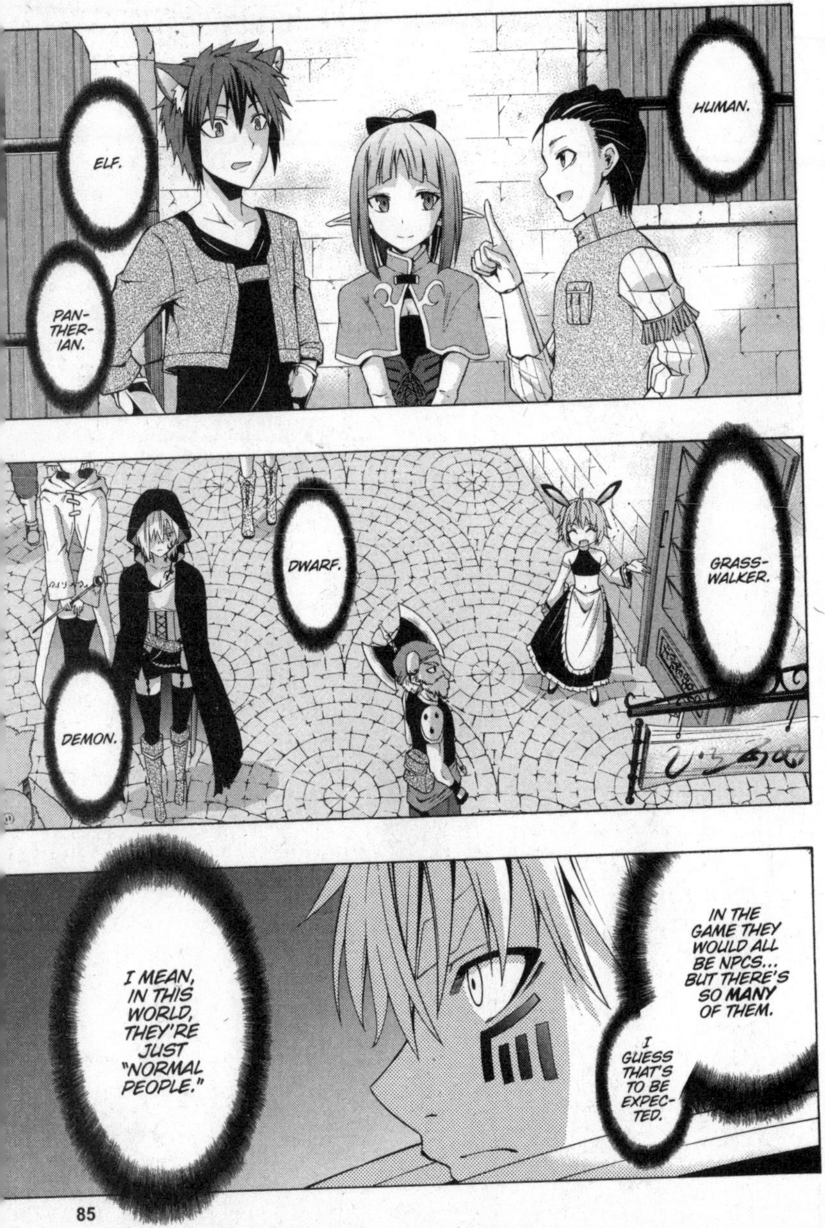
HUMAN.
ELF.
PANTHERIAN.
GRASSWALKER.
DWARF.
DEMON.
IN THE GAME THEY WOULD ALL BE NPCS... BUT THERE'S SO MANY OF THEM.
I GUESS THAT'S TO BE EXPECTED.
I MEAN, IN THIS WORLD, THEY'RE JUST "NORMAL PEOPLE."

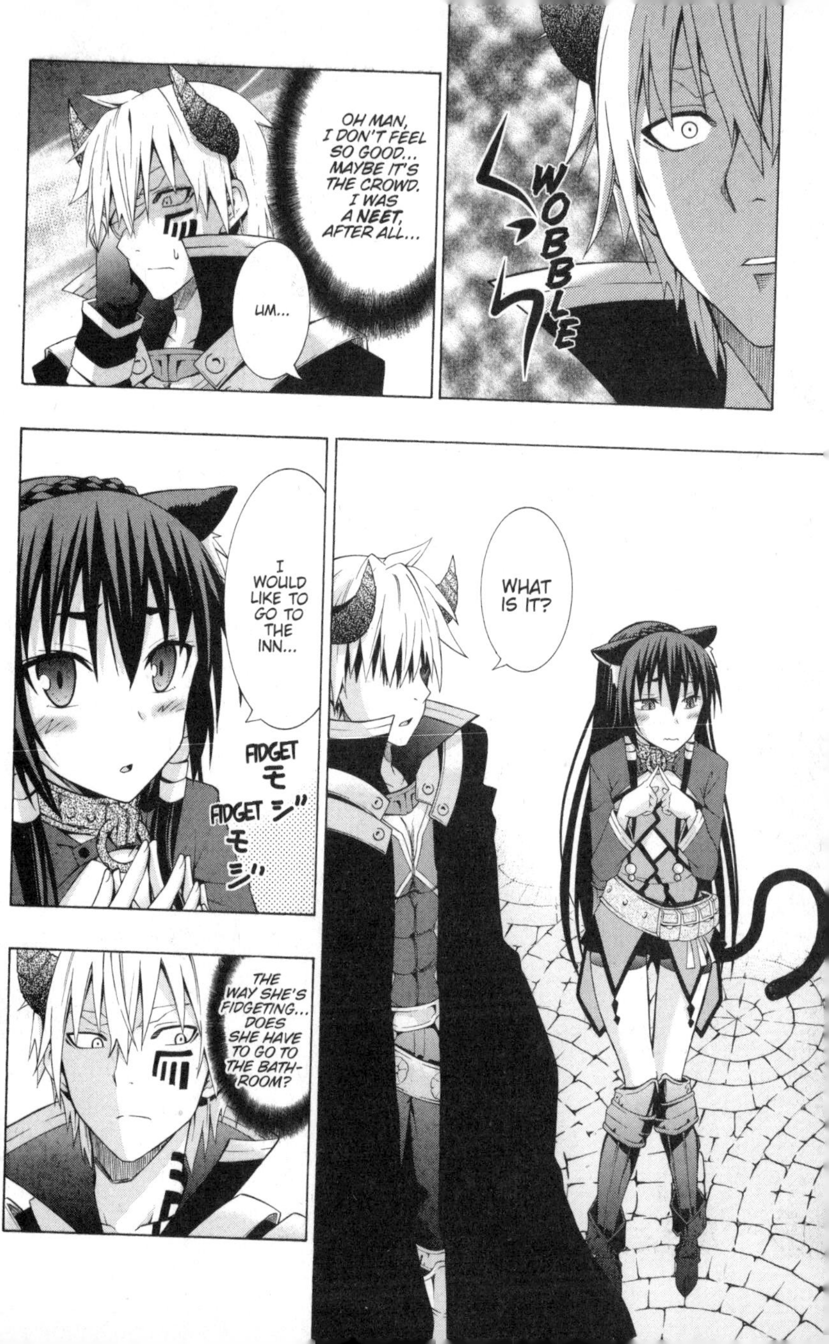
WOBBLE
OH MAN, I DON'T FEEL SO GOOD... MAYBE IT'S THE CROWD. I WAS A NEET, AFTER ALL...
UM...
WHAT IS IT?
I WOULD LIKE TO GO TO THE INN...
FIDGET モジ
FIDGET モジ
THE WAY SHE'S FIDGETING... DOES SHE HAVE TO GO TO THE BATH-ROOM?

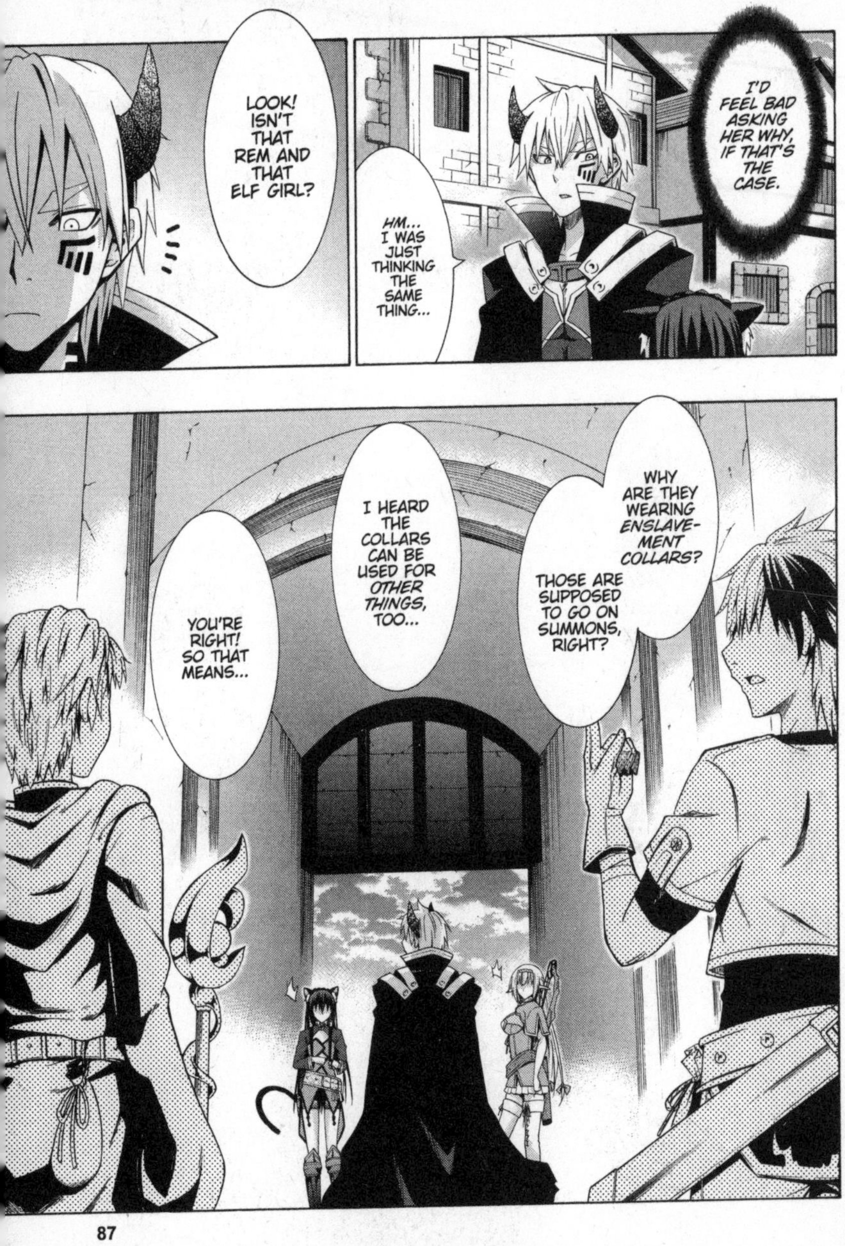
I'D FEEL BAD ASKING HER WHY, IF THAT'S THE CASE.
HM... I WAS JUST THINKING THE SAME THING...
LOOK! ISN'T THAT REM AND THAT ELF GIRL?
WHY ARE THEY WEARING ENSLAVEMENT COLLARS?
THOSE ARE SUPPOSED TO GO ON SUMMONS, RIGHT?
I HEARD THE COLLARS CAN BE USED FOR OTHER THINGS, TOO...
YOU'RE RIGHT! SO THAT MEANS...

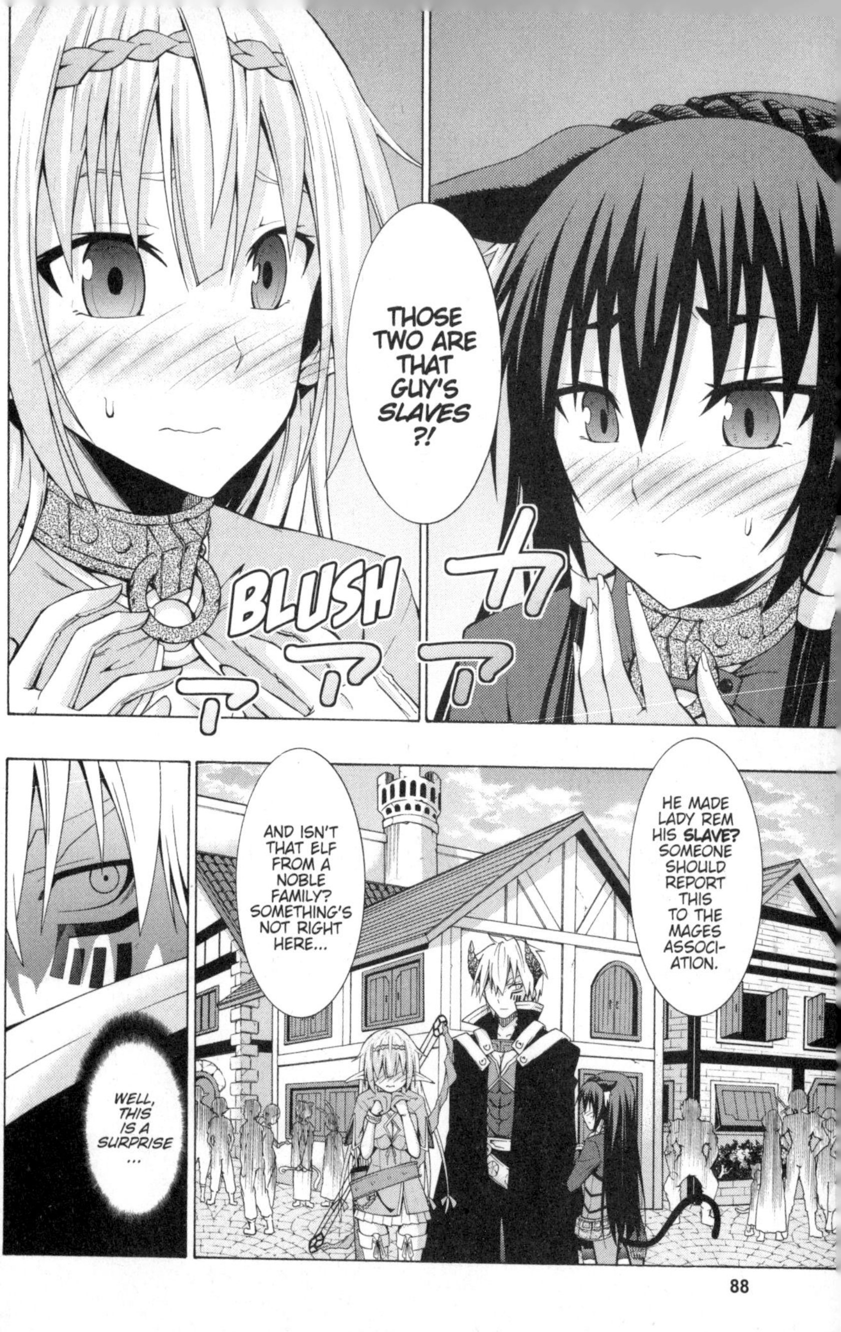
THOSE TWO ARE THAT GUY'S SLAVES?!
BLUSH
HE MADE LADY REM HIS SLAVE? SOMEONE SHOULD REPORT THIS TO THE MAGES ASSOCIATION.
AND ISN'T THAT ELF FROM A NOBLE FAMILY? SOMETHING'S NOT RIGHT HERE...
WELL, THIS IS A SURPRISE...

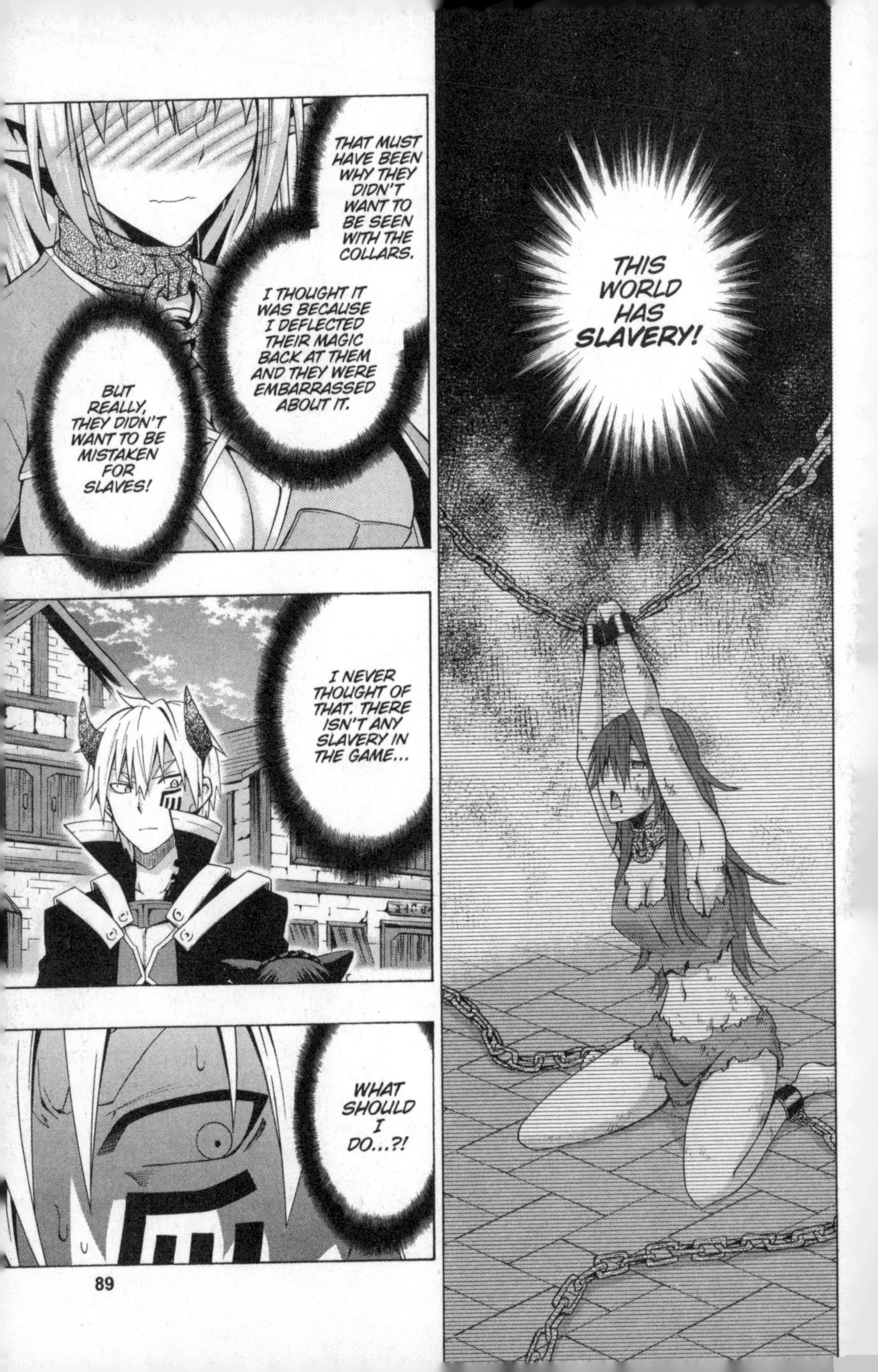
THIS WORLD HAS SLAVERY!
THAT MUST HAVE BEEN WHY THEY DIDN'T WANT TO BE SEEN WITH THE COLLARS.
I THOUGHT IT WAS BECAUSE I DEFLECTED THEIR MAGIC BACK AT THEM AND THEY WERE EMBARRASSED ABOUT IT.
BUT REALLY, THEY DIDN'T WANT TO BE MISTAKEN FOR SLAVES!
I NEVER THOUGHT OF THAT. THERE ISN'T ANY SLAVERY IN THE GAME...
WHAT SHOULD I DO...?!

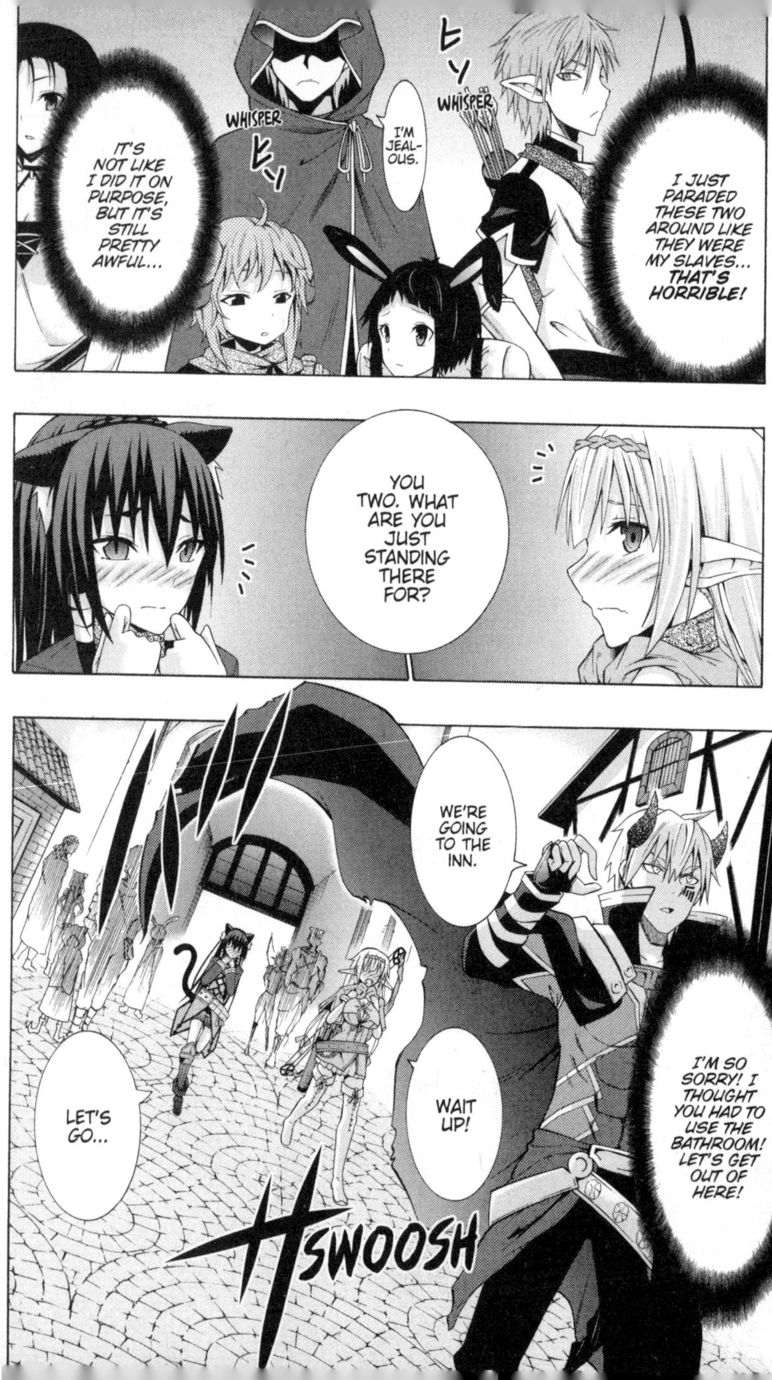
I JUST PARADED THESE TWO AROUND LIKE THEY WERE MY SLAVES... **THAT'S HORRIBLE!**
WHISPER
ヒソ
I'M JEAL-OUS.
WHISPER
ヒソ
IT'S NOT LIKE I DID IT ON PURPOSE, BUT IT'S STILL PRETTY AWFUL...
YOU TWO. WHAT ARE YOU JUST STANDING THERE FOR?
WE'RE GOING TO THE INN.
I'M SO SORRY! I THOUGHT YOU HAD TO USE THE BATHROOM! LET'S GET OUT OF HERE!
WAIT UP!
LET'S GO...
SWOOSH

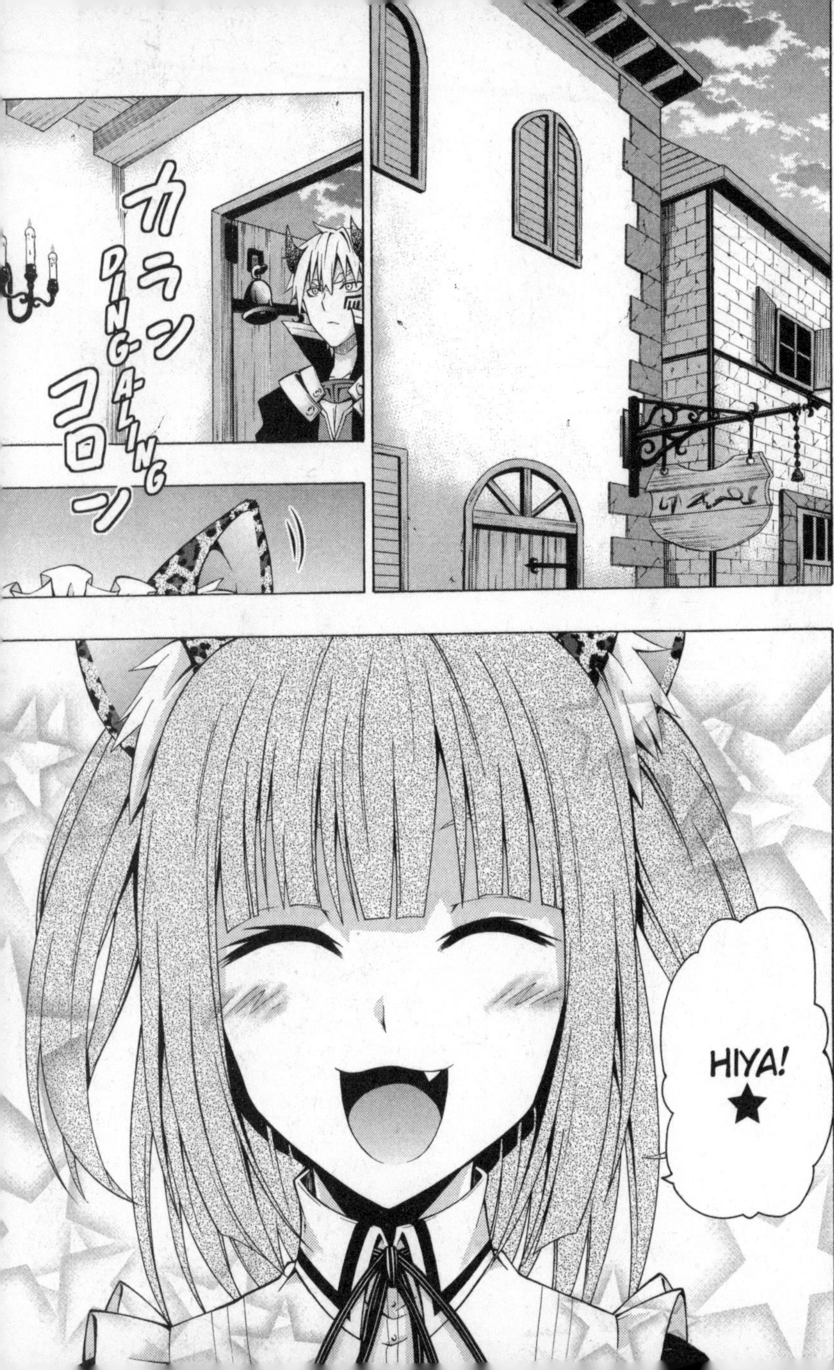
カランコローン
DING-A-LING
HIYA! ★

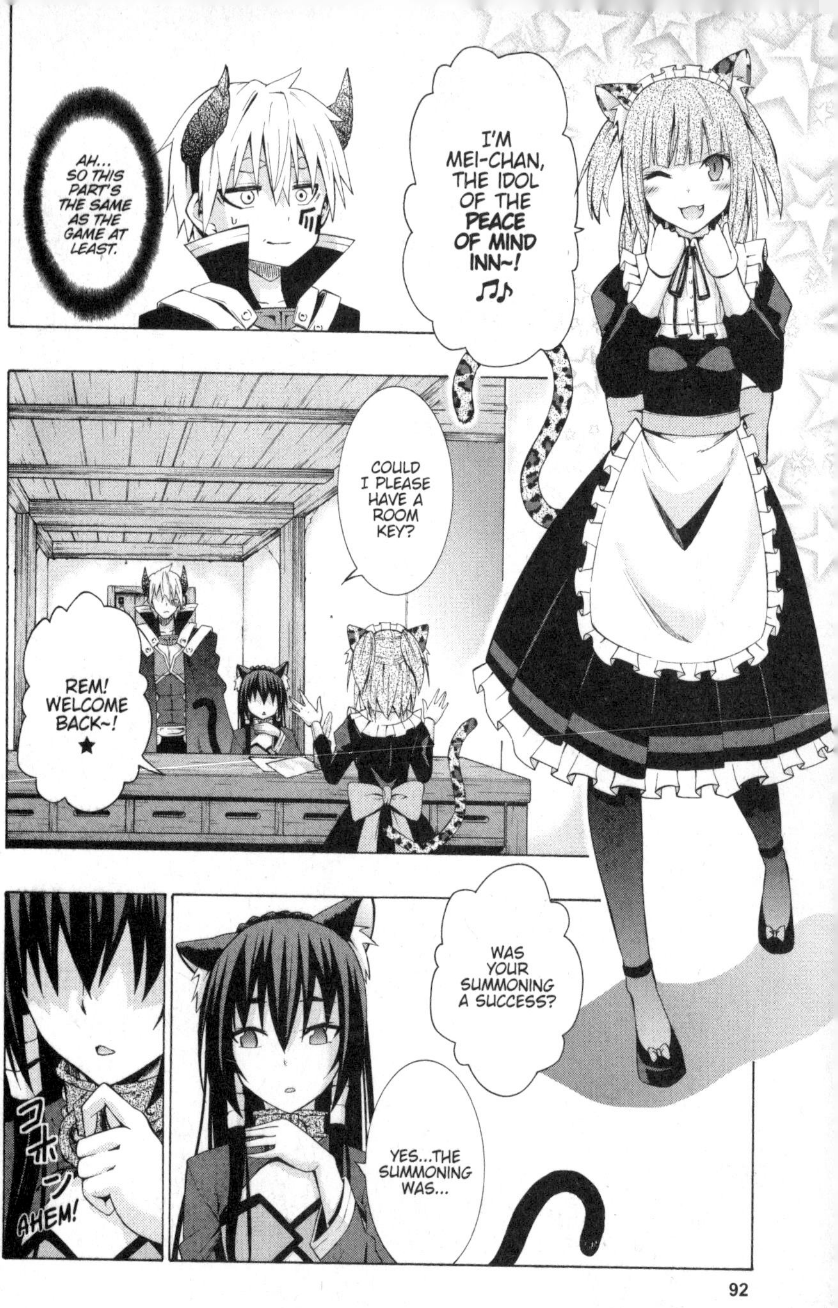
I'M MEI-CHAN, THE IDOL OF THE PEACE OF MIND INN~! ♫♪
AH... SO THIS PART'S THE SAME AS THE GAME AT LEAST.
COULD I PLEASE HAVE A ROOM KEY?
REM! WELCOME BACK~! ★
WAS YOUR SUMMONING A SUCCESS?
YES...THE SUMMONING WAS...
コホン
AHEM!

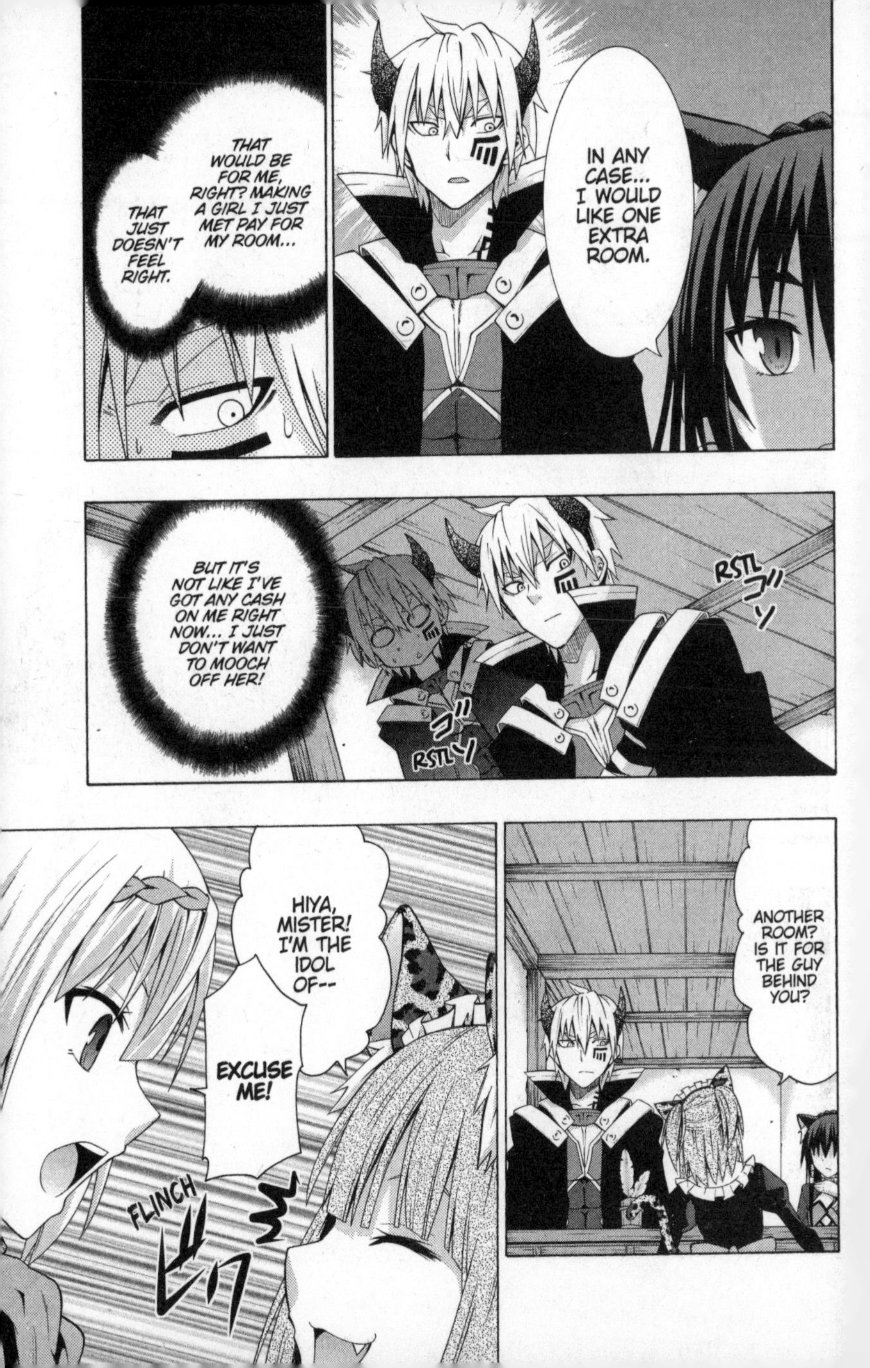
IN ANY CASE... I WOULD LIKE ONE EXTRA ROOM.
THAT WOULD BE FOR ME, RIGHT? MAKING A GIRL I JUST MET PAY FOR MY ROOM...
THAT JUST DOESN'T FEEL RIGHT.
RSTL ゴソ
BUT IT'S NOT LIKE I'VE GOT ANY CASH ON ME RIGHT NOW... I JUST DON'T WANT TO MOOCH OFF HER!
RSTL ゴソ
ANOTHER ROOM? IS IT FOR THE GUY BEHIND YOU?
HIYA, MISTER! I'M THE IDOL OF--
EXCUSE ME!
FLINCH ビクッ

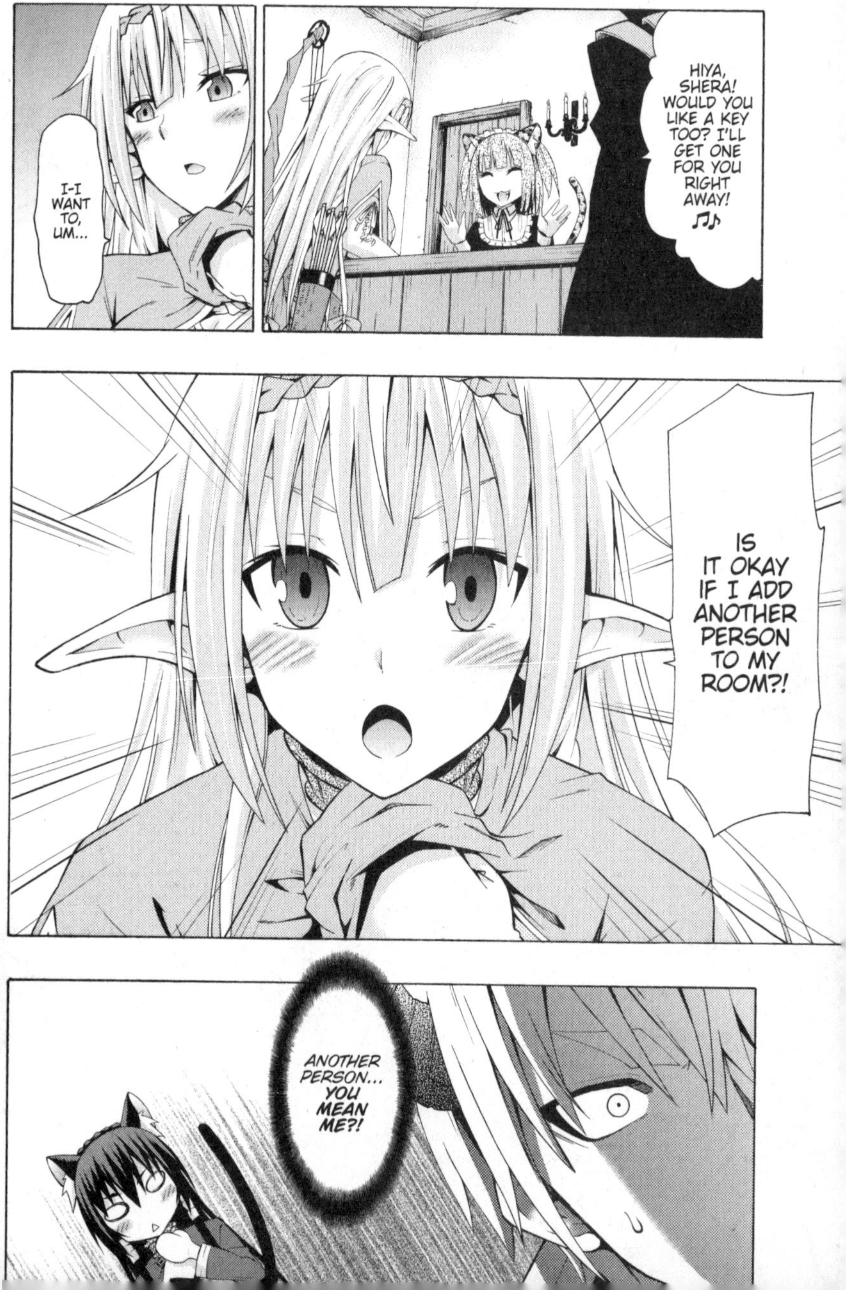
HIYA, SHERA! WOULD YOU LIKE A KEY TOO? I'LL GET ONE FOR YOU RIGHT AWAY! ♫♪
I-I WANT TO, UM...
IS IT OKAY IF I ADD ANOTHER PERSON TO MY ROOM?!
ANOTHER PERSON... YOU MEAN ME?!

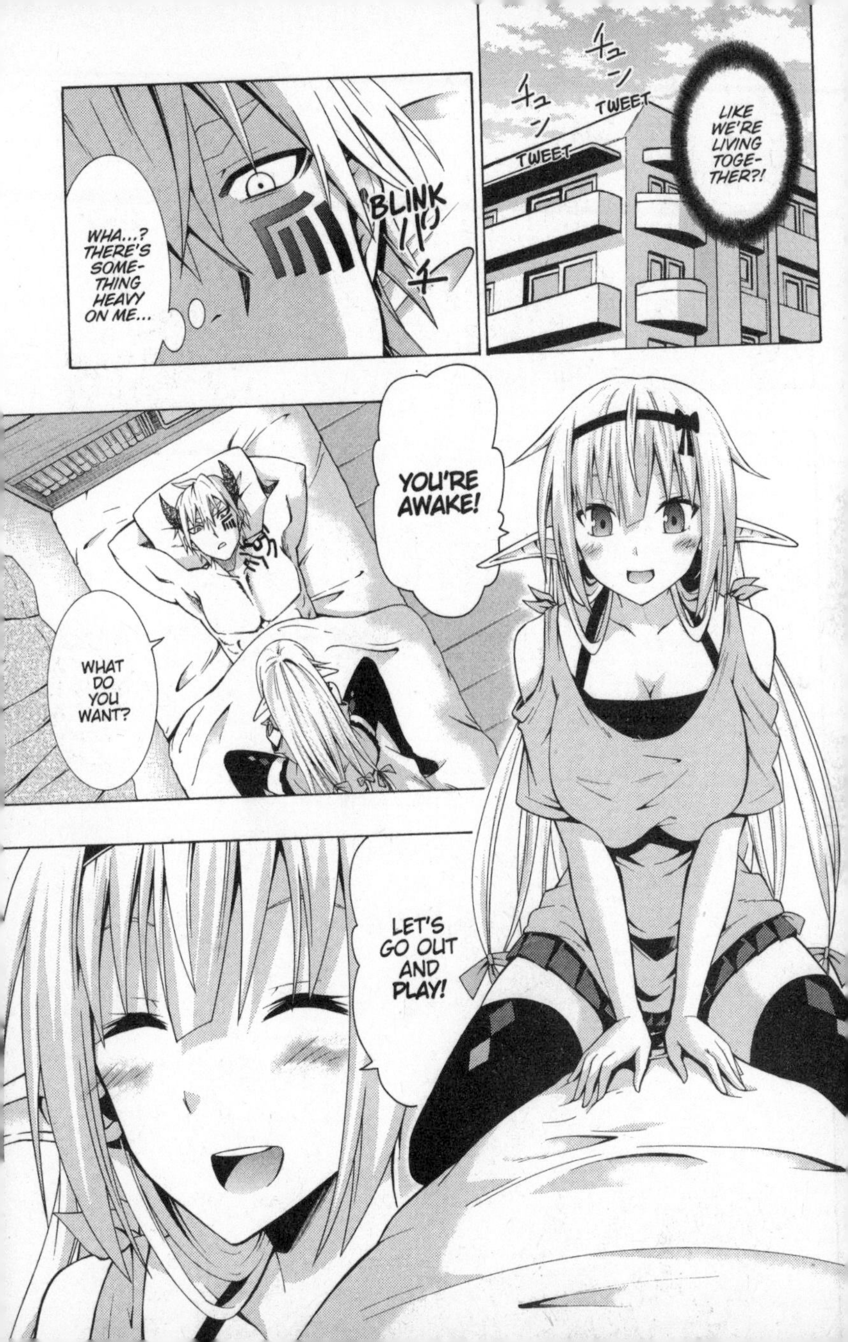チュン
TWEET
チュン
TWEET
LIKE WE'RE LIVING TOGE-THER?!
BLINK
パチ
WHA...? THERE'S SOME-THING HEAVY ON ME...
YOU'RE AWAKE!
WHAT DO YOU WANT?
LET'S GO OUT AND PLAY!

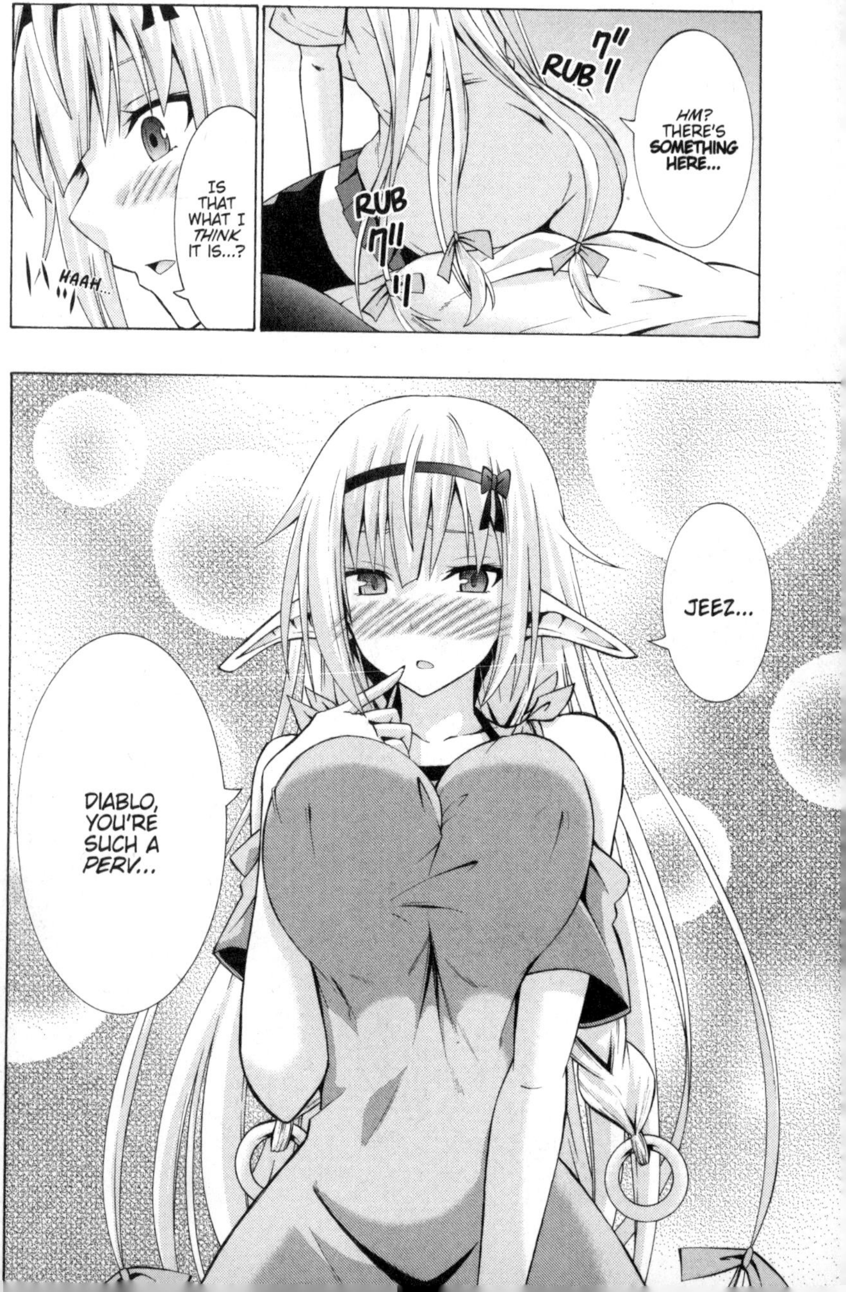
RUB
HM? THERE'S SOMETHING HERE...
RUB
IS THAT WHAT I THINK IT IS...?
HAAH...
JEEZ...
DIABLO, YOU'RE SUCH A PERV...

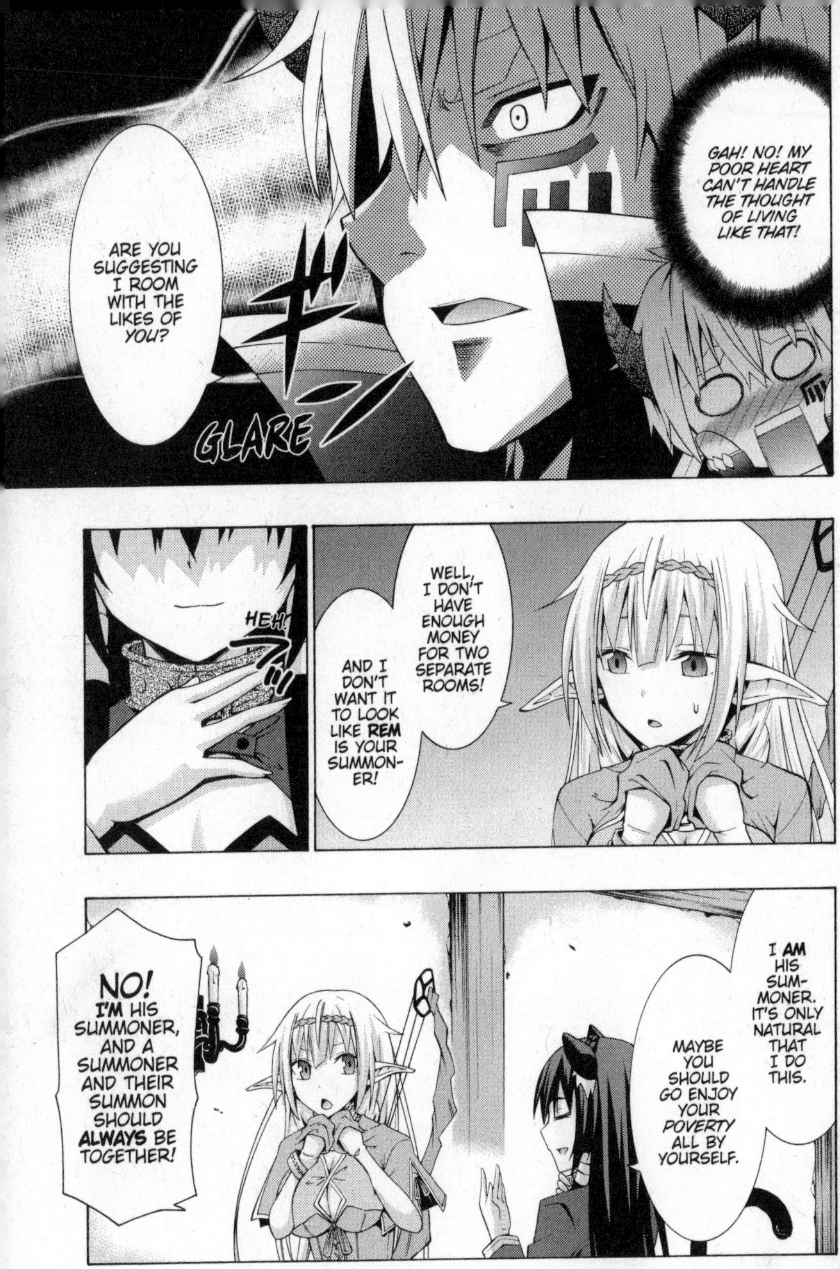
GAH! NO! MY POOR HEART CAN'T HANDLE THE THOUGHT OF LIVING LIKE THAT!
ARE YOU SUGGESTING I ROOM WITH THE LIKES OF YOU?
GLARE
WELL, I DON'T HAVE ENOUGH MONEY FOR TWO SEPARATE ROOMS!
AND I DON'T WANT IT TO LOOK LIKE REM IS YOUR SUMMONER!
HEH!
I AM HIS SUMMONER. IT'S ONLY NATURAL THAT I DO THIS.
MAYBE YOU SHOULD GO ENJOY YOUR POVERTY ALL BY YOURSELF.
NO! I'M HIS SUMMONER, AND A SUMMONER AND THEIR SUMMON SHOULD ALWAYS BE TOGETHER!

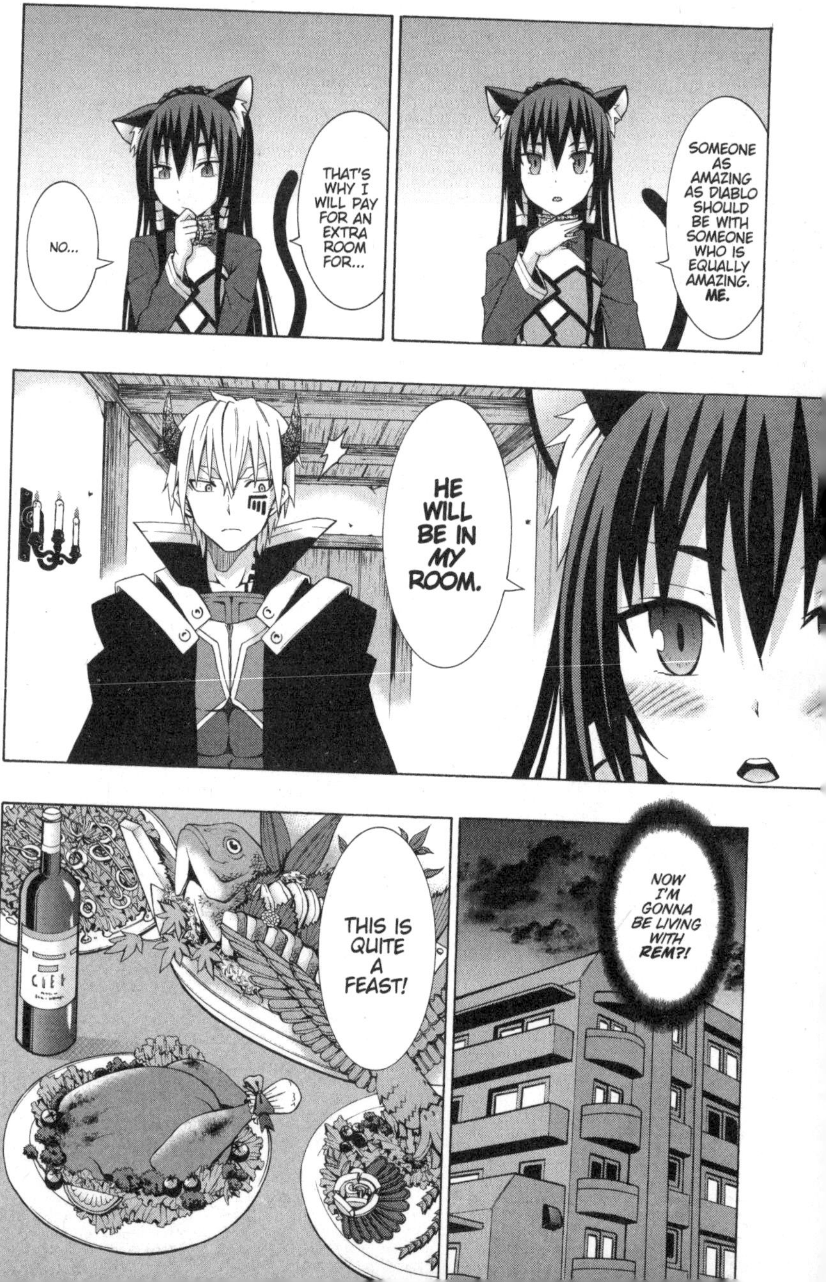
SOMEONE AS AMAZING AS DIABLO SHOULD BE WITH SOMEONE WHO IS EQUALLY AMAZING. ME.
THAT'S WHY I WILL PAY FOR AN EXTRA ROOM FOR...
NO...
HE WILL BE IN MY ROOM.
NOW I'M GONNA BE LIVING WITH REM?!
THIS IS QUITE A FEAST!

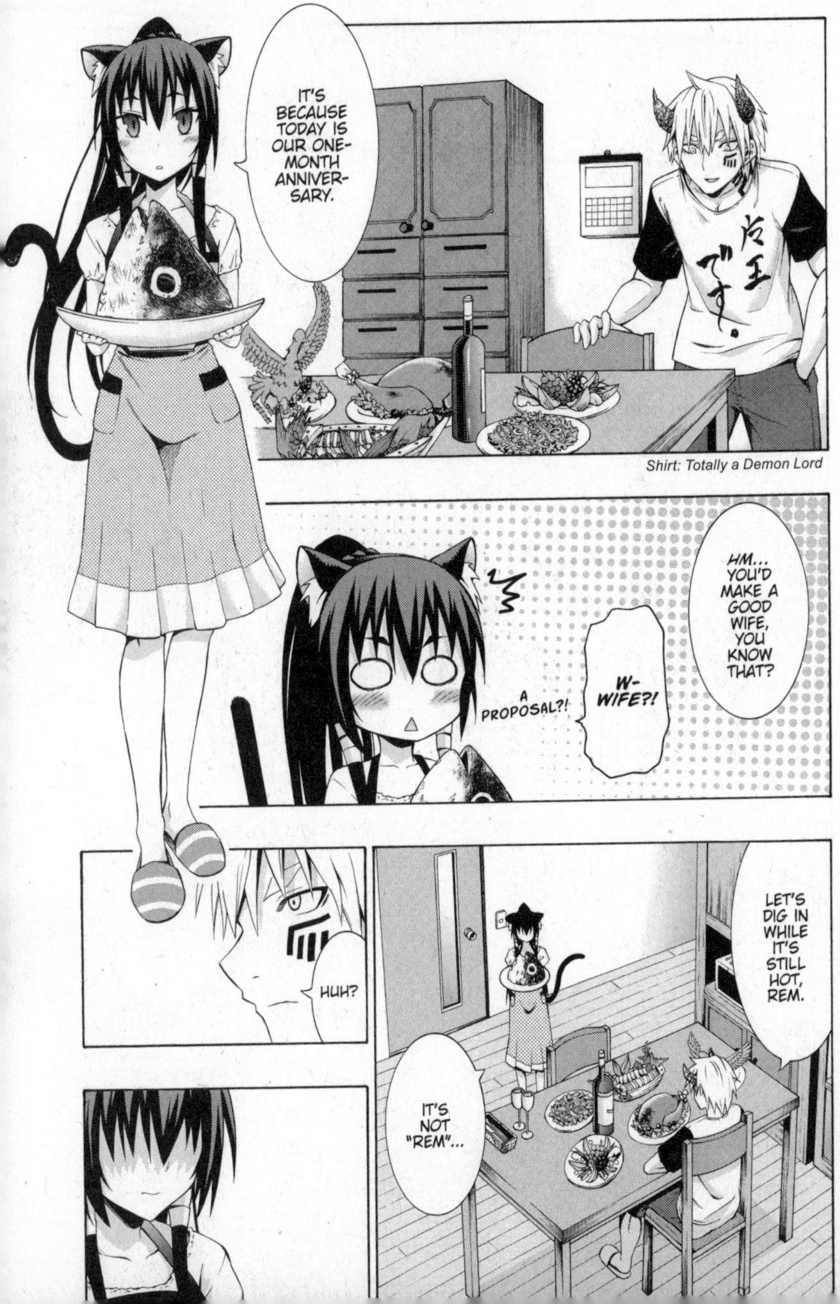
IT'S BECAUSE TODAY IS OUR ONE-MONTH ANNIVERSARY.
Shirt: Totally a Demon Lord
HM... YOU'D MAKE A GOOD WIFE, YOU KNOW THAT?
W-WIFE?!
A PROPOSAL?!
LET'S DIG IN WHILE IT'S STILL HOT, REM.
IT'S NOT "REM"...
HUH?

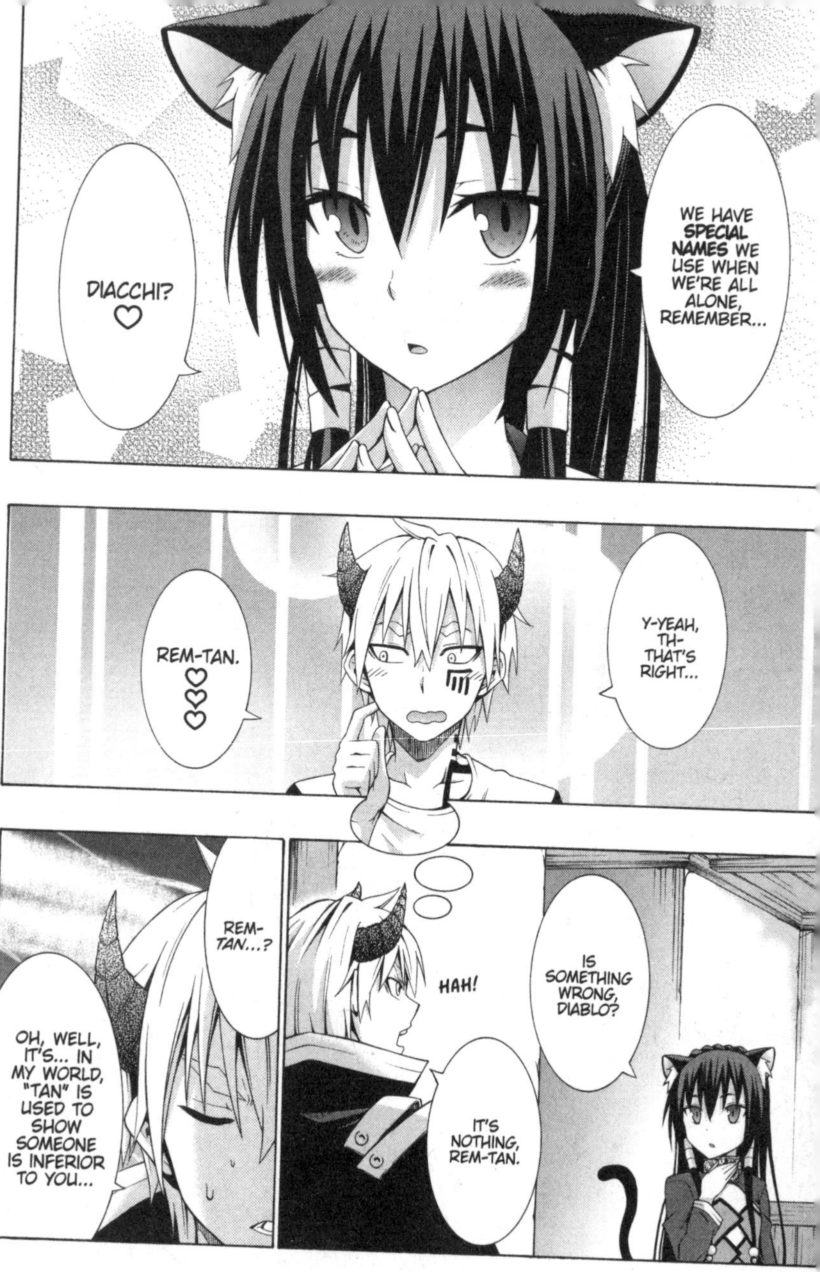
WE HAVE **SPECIAL NAMES** WE USE WHEN WE'RE ALL ALONE, REMEMBER...
DIACCHI? ♡
Y-YEAH, TH-THAT'S RIGHT...
REM-TAN. ♡♡♡
IS SOMETHING WRONG, DIABLO?
HAH!
IT'S NOTHING, REM-TAN.
REM-TAN...?
OH, WELL, IT'S... IN MY WORLD, "TAN" IS USED TO SHOW SOMEONE IS INFERIOR TO YOU...

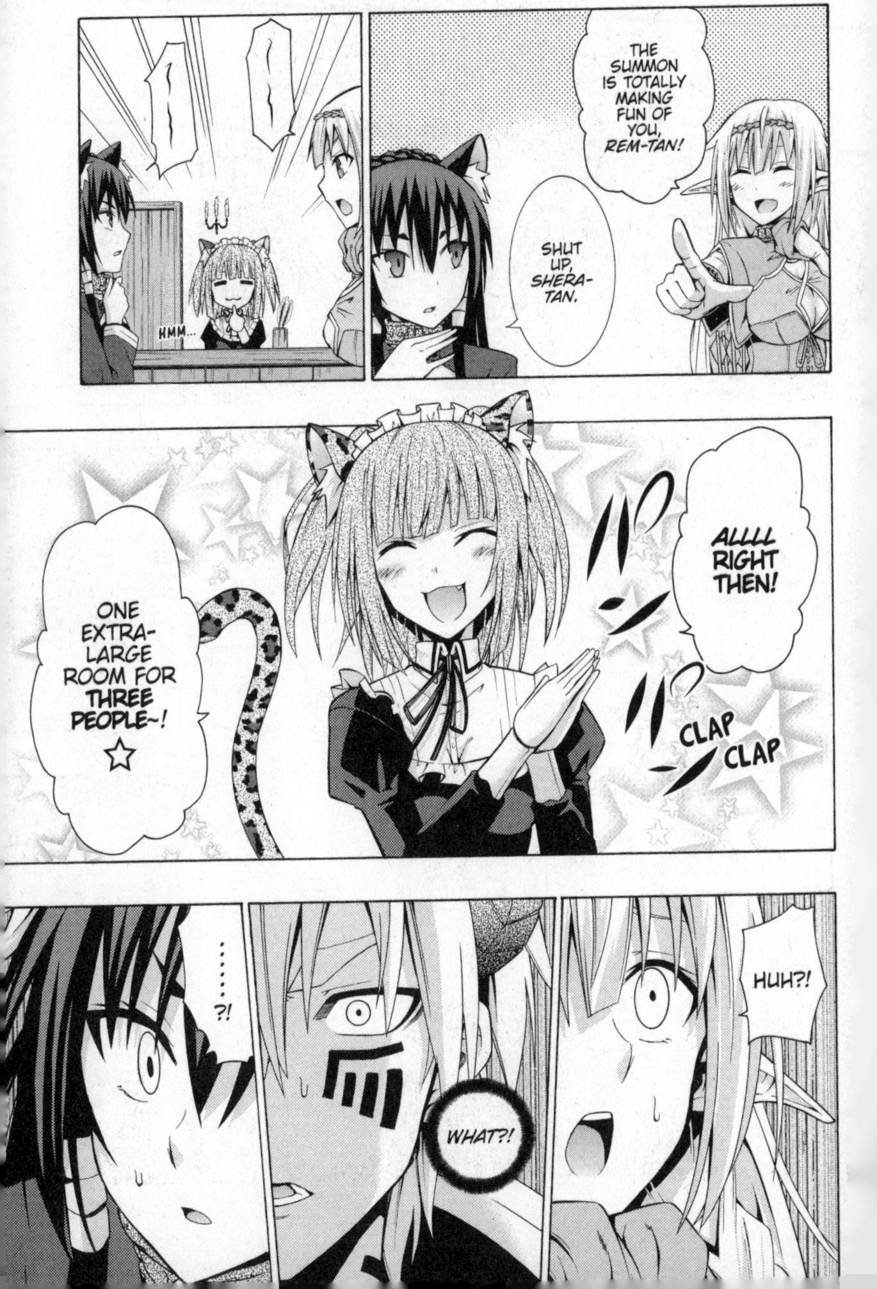
THE SUMMON IS TOTALLY MAKING FUN OF YOU, REM-TAN!
SHUT UP, SHERA-TAN.
HMM...
ALLLL RIGHT THEN!
CLAP CLAP
ONE EXTRA-LARGE ROOM FOR THREE PEOPLE~! ☆
HUH?!
WHAT?!
......?!

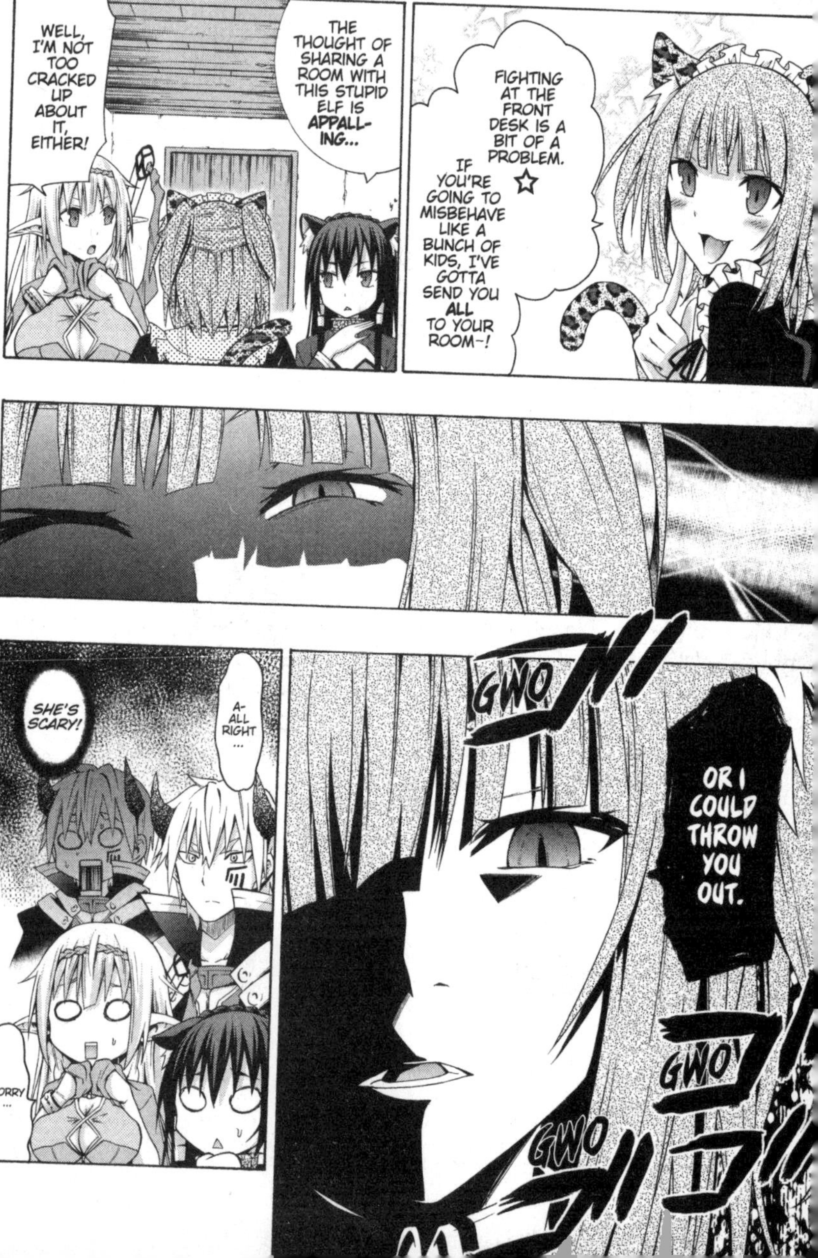
FIGHTING AT THE FRONT DESK IS A BIT OF A PROBLEM. ☆
IF YOU'RE GOING TO MISBEHAVE LIKE A BUNCH OF KIDS, I'VE GOTTA SEND YOU ALL TO YOUR ROOM~!
THE THOUGHT OF SHARING A ROOM WITH THIS STUPID ELF IS APPALL-ING...
WELL, I'M NOT TOO CRACKED UP ABOUT IT, EITHER!
GWO
OR I COULD THROW YOU OUT.
GWO
GWO
A- ALL RIGHT ...
SHE'S SCARY!
SORRY ...

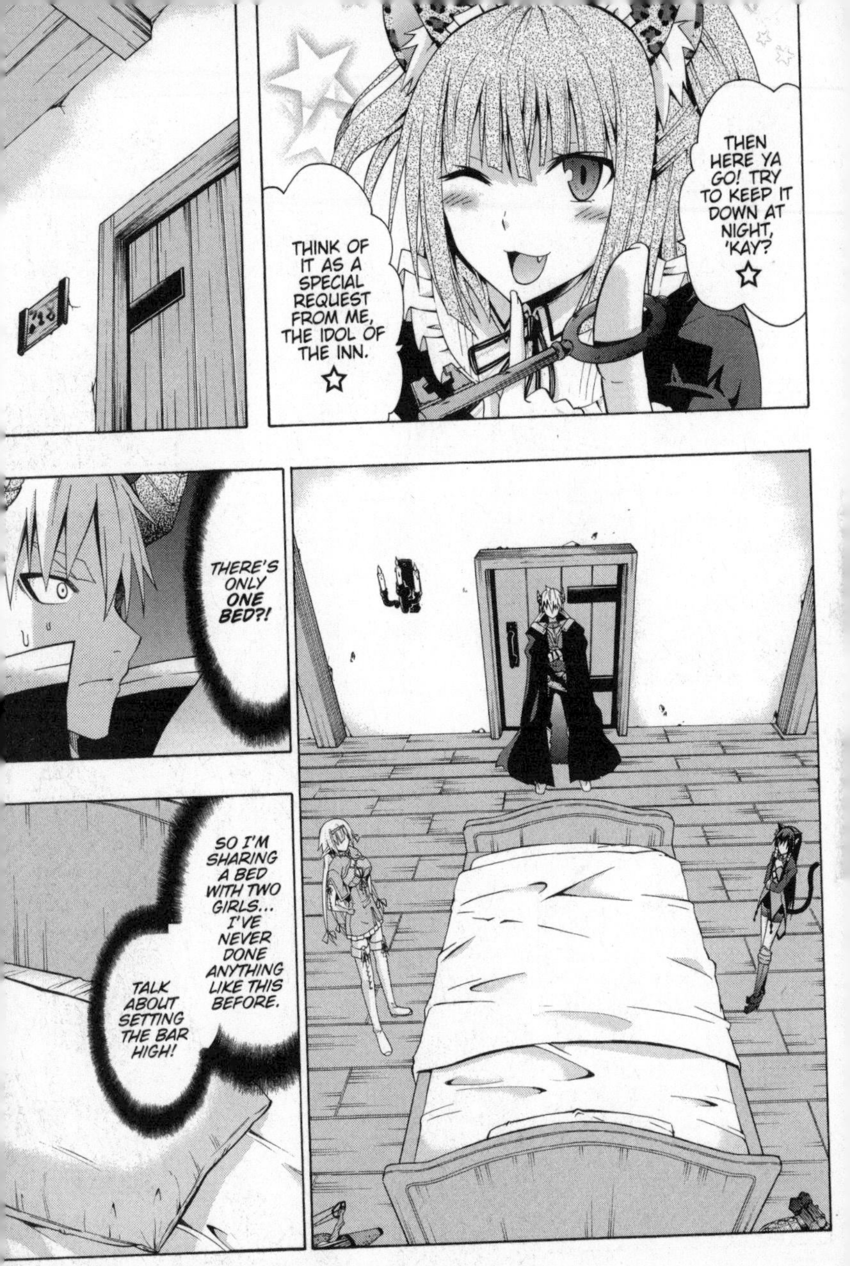
THEN HERE YA GO! TRY TO KEEP IT DOWN AT NIGHT, 'KAY? ☆
THINK OF IT AS A SPECIAL REQUEST FROM ME, THE IDOL OF THE INN. ☆
THERE'S ONLY ONE BED?!
SO I'M SHARING A BED WITH TWO GIRLS... I'VE NEVER DONE ANYTHING LIKE THIS BEFORE.
TALK ABOUT SETTING THE BAR HIGH!

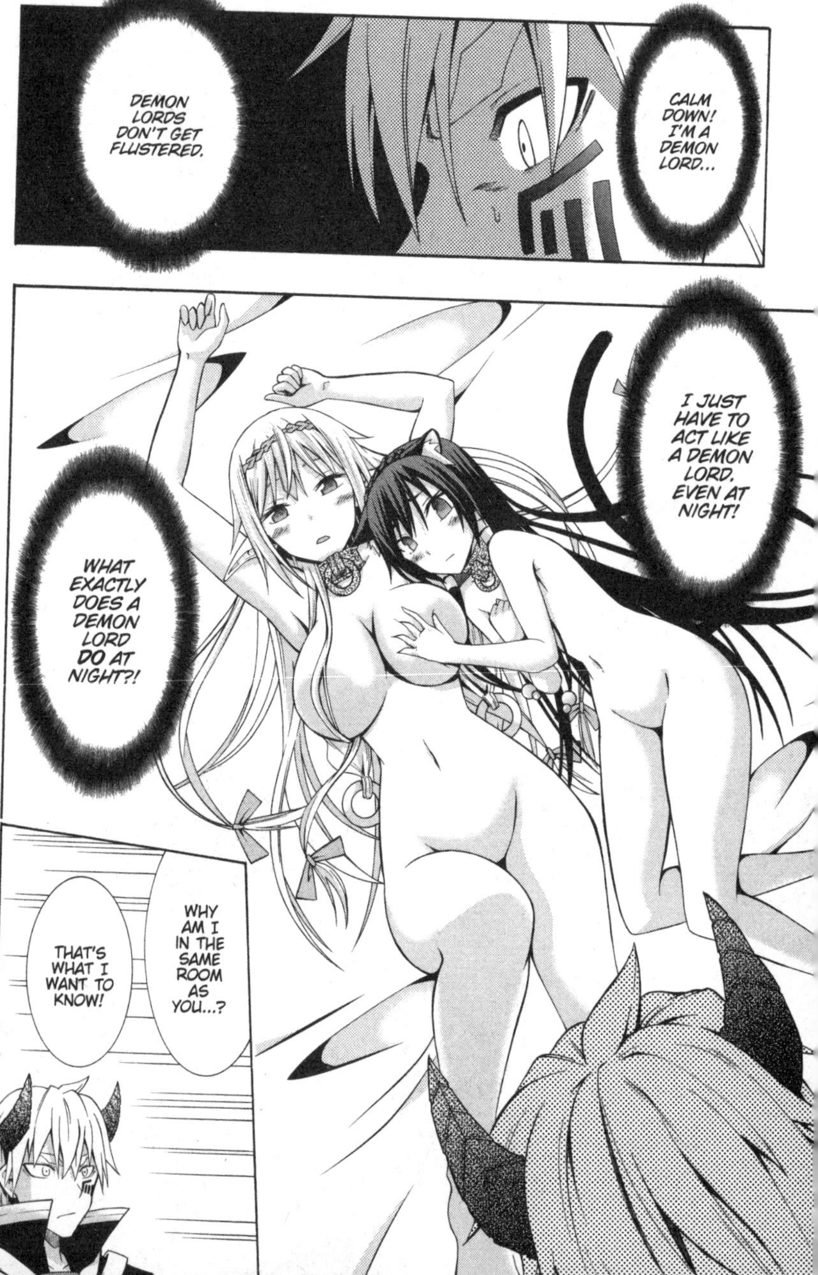
CALM DOWN! I'M A DEMON LORD...
DEMON LORDS DON'T GET FLUSTERED.
I JUST HAVE TO ACT LIKE A DEMON LORD. EVEN AT NIGHT!
WHAT EXACTLY DOES A DEMON LORD DO AT NIGHT?!
WHY AM I IN THE SAME ROOM AS YOU...?
THAT'S WHAT I WANT TO KNOW!

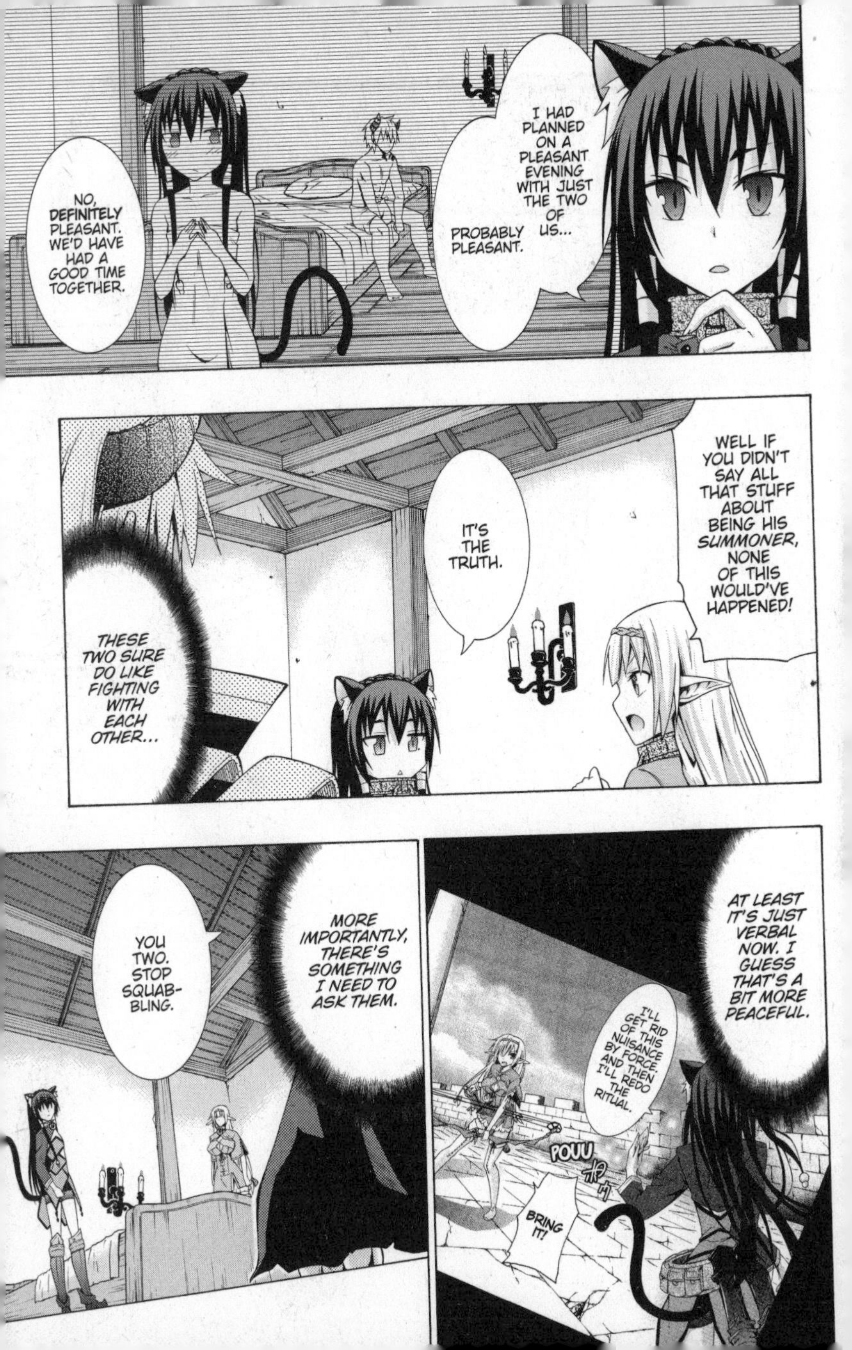
I HAD PLANNED ON A PLEASANT EVENING WITH JUST THE TWO OF US...
PROBABLY PLEASANT.
NO, DEFINITELY PLEASANT. WE'D HAVE HAD A GOOD TIME TOGETHER.
WELL IF YOU DIDN'T SAY ALL THAT STUFF ABOUT BEING HIS *SUMMONER*, NONE OF THIS WOULD'VE HAPPENED!
IT'S THE TRUTH.
THESE TWO SURE DO LIKE FIGHTING WITH EACH OTHER...
AT LEAST IT'S JUST VERBAL NOW. I GUESS THAT'S A BIT MORE PEACEFUL.
I'LL GET RID OF THIS NUISANCE BY FORCE. AND THEN I'LL REDO THE RITUAL.
POUU
BRING IT!
MORE IMPORTANTLY, THERE'S SOMETHING I NEED TO ASK THEM.
YOU TWO. STOP SQUABBLING.

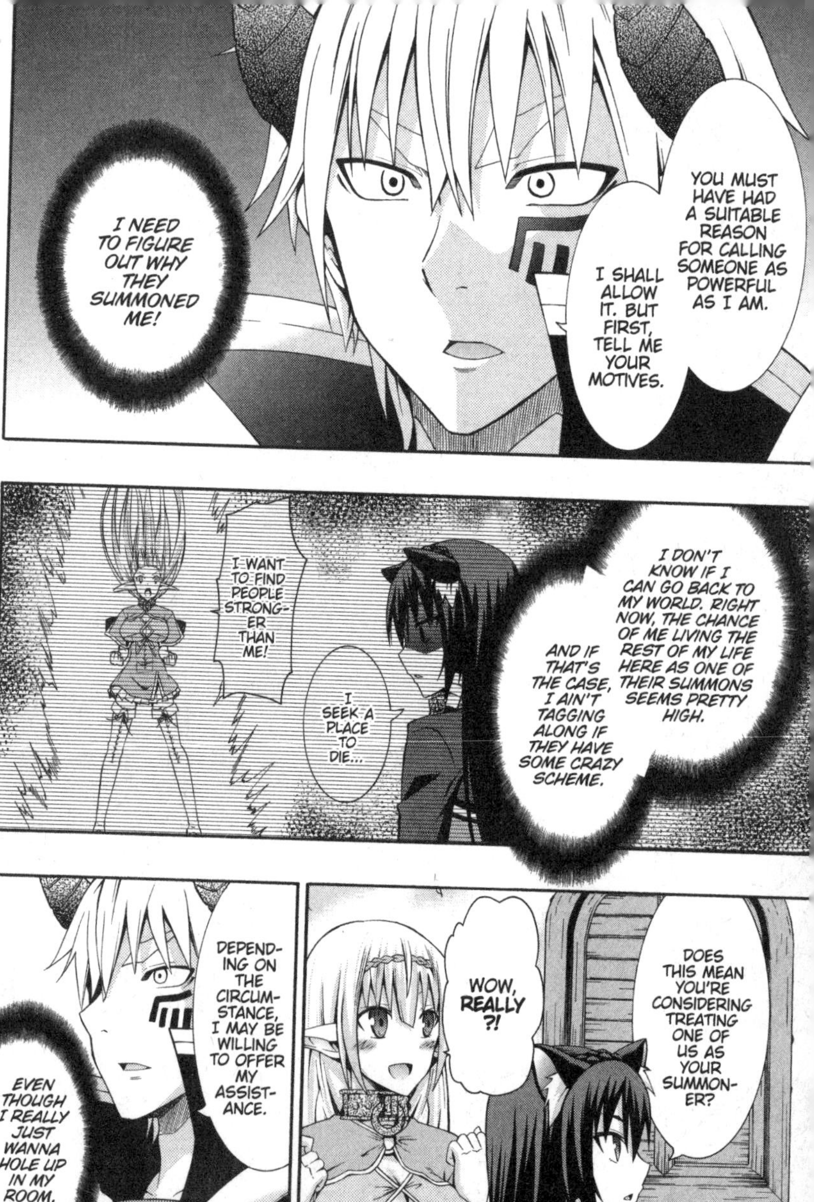
YOU MUST HAVE HAD A SUITABLE REASON FOR CALLING SOMEONE AS POWERFUL AS I AM.
I SHALL ALLOW IT. BUT FIRST, TELL ME YOUR MOTIVES.
I NEED TO FIGURE OUT WHY THEY SUMMONED ME!
I DON'T KNOW IF I CAN GO BACK TO MY WORLD. RIGHT NOW, THE CHANCE OF ME LIVING THE REST OF MY LIFE HERE AS ONE OF THEIR SUMMONS SEEMS PRETTY HIGH.
AND IF THAT'S THE CASE, I AIN'T TAGGING ALONG IF THEY HAVE SOME CRAZY SCHEME.
I SEEK A PLACE TO DIE...
I WANT TO FIND PEOPLE STRONGER THAN ME!
DOES THIS MEAN YOU'RE CONSIDERING TREATING ONE OF US AS YOUR SUMMONER?
WOW, REALLY?!
DEPENDING ON THE CIRCUMSTANCE, I MAY BE WILLING TO OFFER MY ASSISTANCE.
EVEN THOUGH I REALLY JUST WANNA HOLE UP IN MY ROOM.

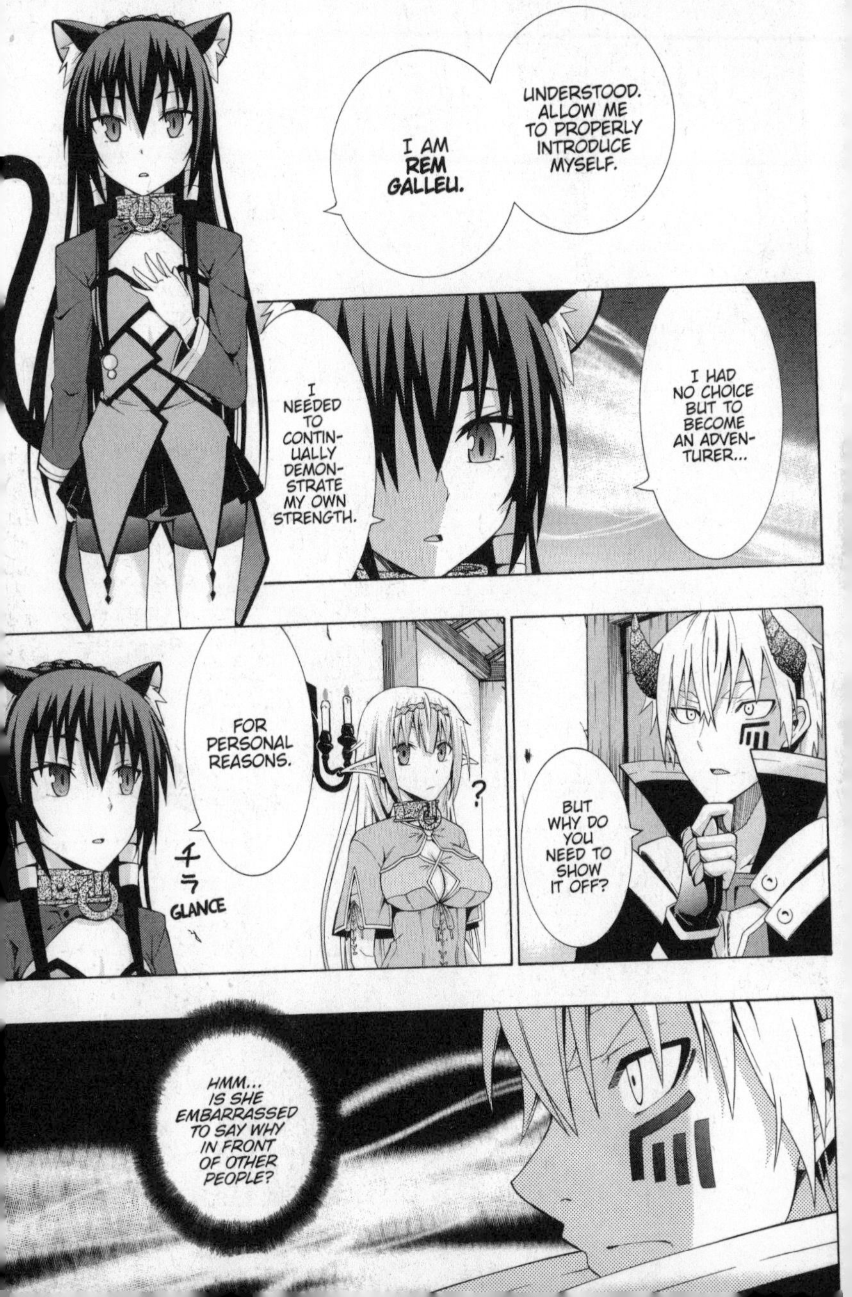
UNDERSTOOD. ALLOW ME TO PROPERLY INTRODUCE MYSELF.
I AM REM GALLEU.
I HAD NO CHOICE BUT TO BECOME AN ADVEN-TURER...
I NEEDED TO CONTIN-UALLY DEMON-STRATE MY OWN STRENGTH.
BUT WHY DO YOU NEED TO SHOW IT OFF?
?
FOR PERSONAL REASONS.
チラ
GLANCE
HMM... IS SHE EMBARRASSED TO SAY WHY IN FRONT OF OTHER PEOPLE?

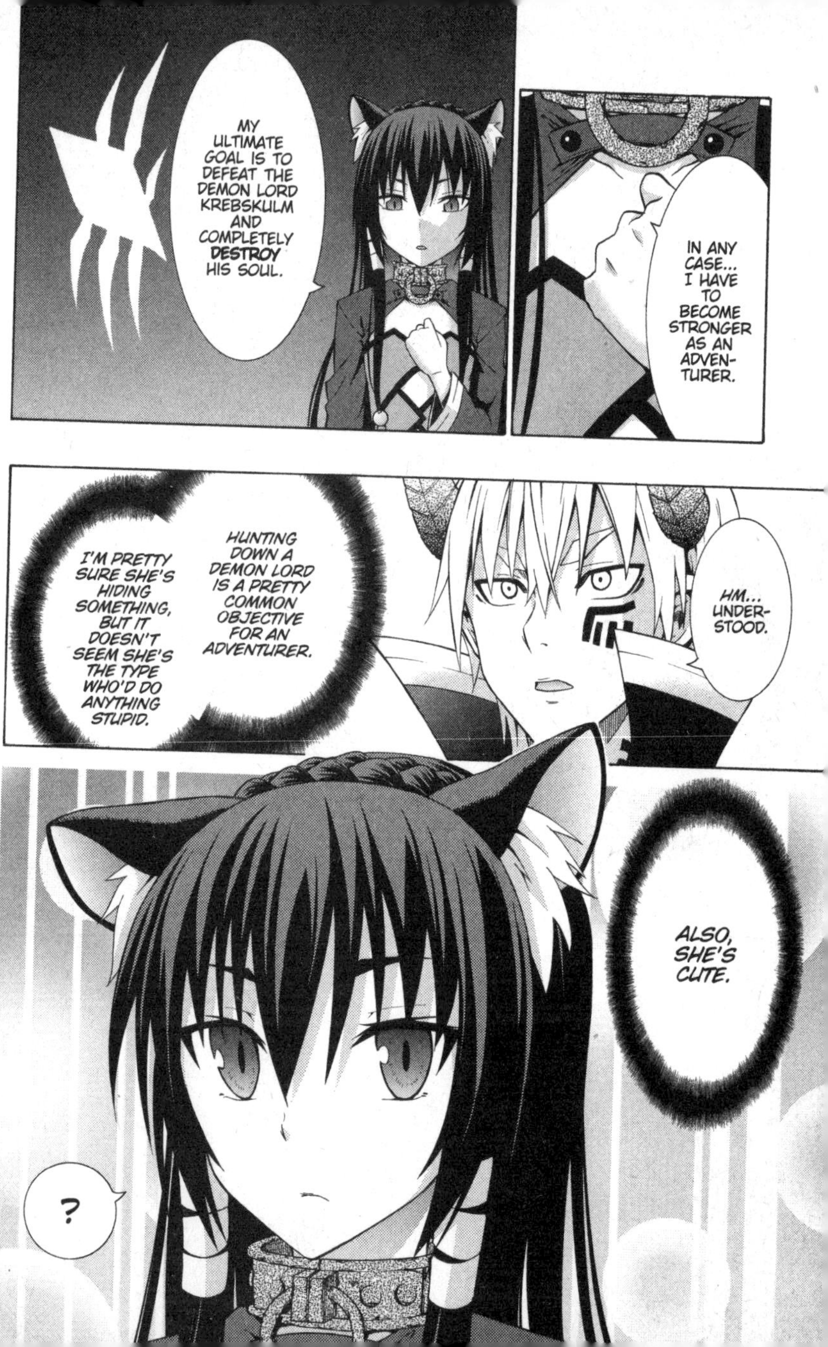
IN ANY CASE... I HAVE TO BECOME STRONGER AS AN ADVENTURER.
MY ULTIMATE GOAL IS TO DEFEAT THE DEMON LORD KREBSKULM AND COMPLETELY **DESTROY** HIS SOUL.
HM... UNDERSTOOD.
HUNTING DOWN A DEMON LORD IS A PRETTY COMMON OBJECTIVE FOR AN ADVENTURER.
I'M PRETTY SURE SHE'S HIDING SOMETHING, BUT IT DOESN'T SEEM SHE'S THE TYPE WHO'D DO ANYTHING STUPID.
ALSO, SHE'S CUTE.
?

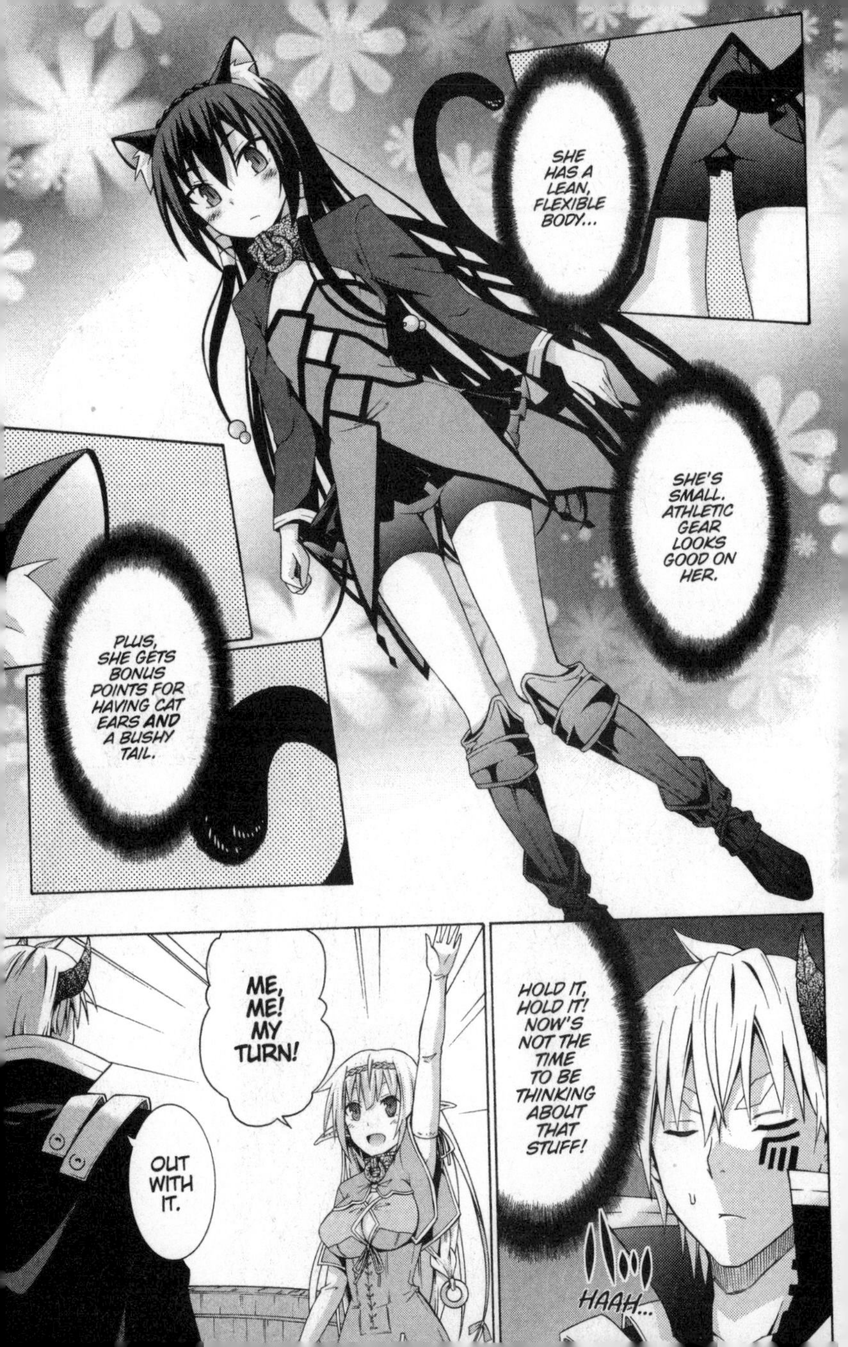
SHE HAS A LEAN, FLEXIBLE BODY...
SHE'S SMALL. ATHLETIC GEAR LOOKS GOOD ON HER.
PLUS, SHE GETS BONUS POINTS FOR HAVING CAT EARS AND A BUSHY TAIL.
HOLD IT, HOLD IT! NOW'S NOT THE TIME TO BE THINKING ABOUT THAT STUFF!
HAAH...
ME, ME! MY TURN!
OUT WITH IT.

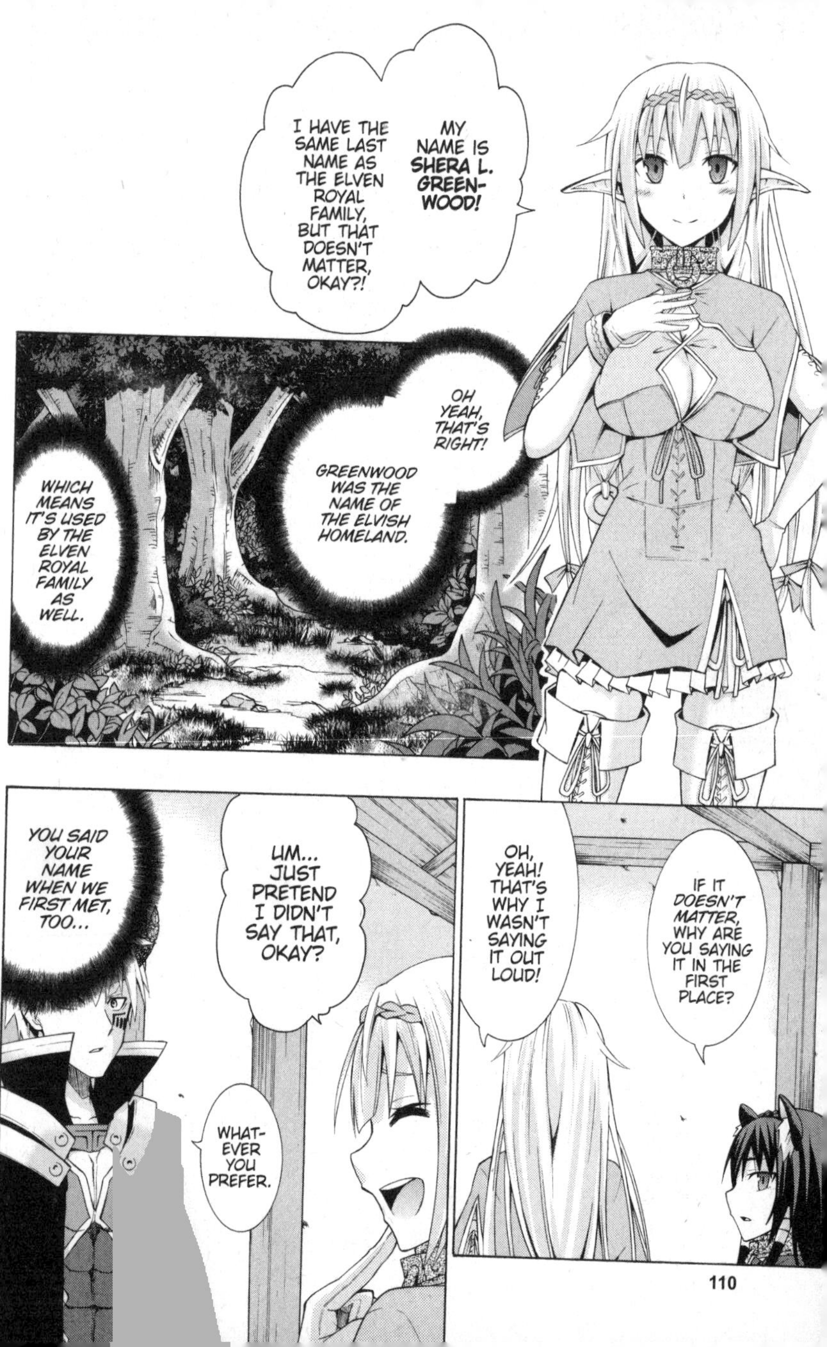
MY NAME IS SHERA L. GREENWOOD!
I HAVE THE SAME LAST NAME AS THE ELVEN ROYAL FAMILY, BUT THAT DOESN'T MATTER, OKAY?!
OH YEAH, THAT'S RIGHT!
GREENWOOD WAS THE NAME OF THE ELVISH HOMELAND.
WHICH MEANS IT'S USED BY THE ELVEN ROYAL FAMILY AS WELL.
IF IT DOESN'T MATTER, WHY ARE YOU SAYING IT IN THE FIRST PLACE?
OH, YEAH! THAT'S WHY I WASN'T SAYING IT OUT LOUD!
UM... JUST PRETEND I DIDN'T SAY THAT, OKAY?
YOU SAID YOUR NAME WHEN WE FIRST MET, TOO...
WHAT-EVER YOU PREFER.

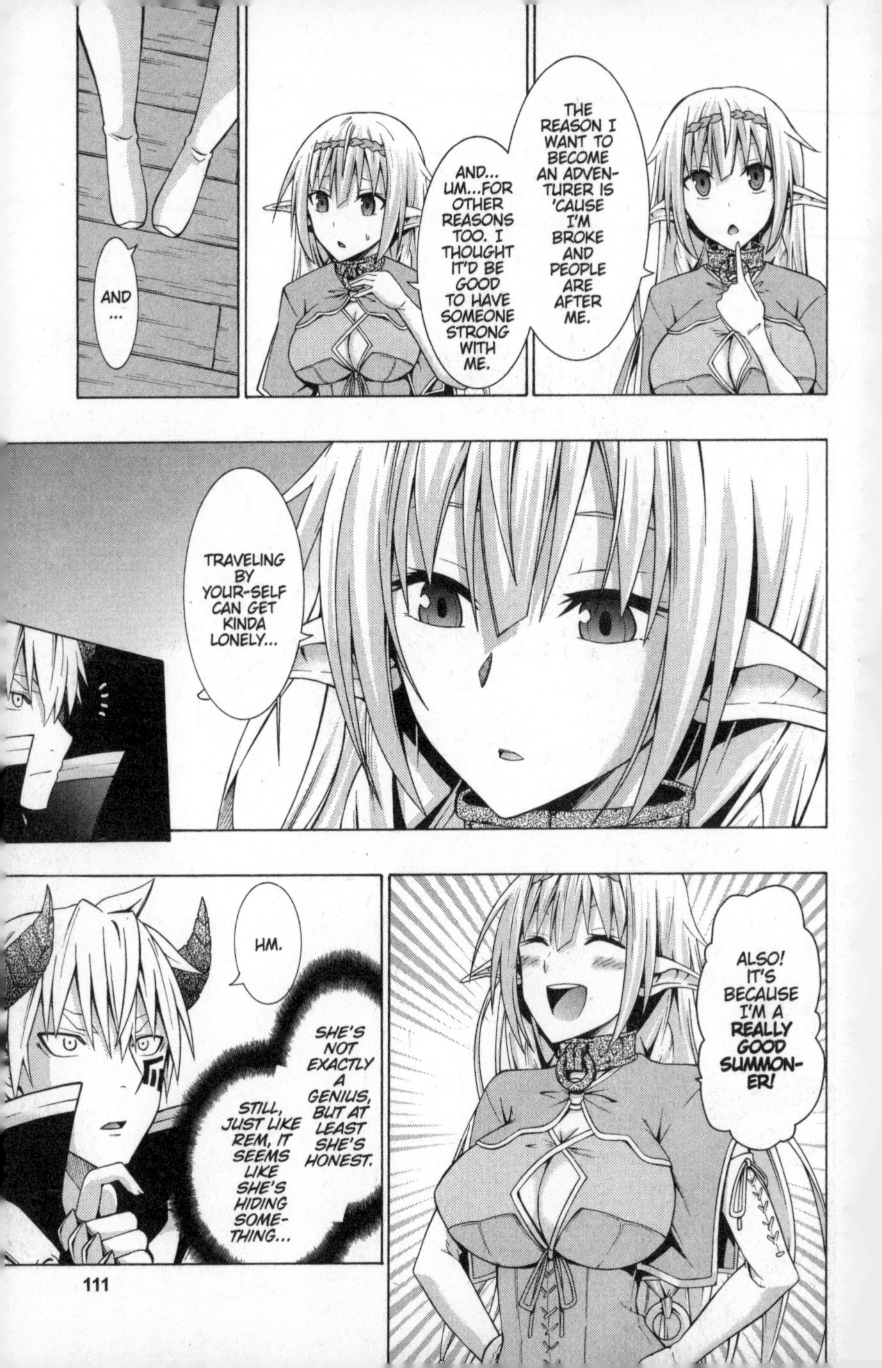
THE REASON I WANT TO BECOME AN ADVEN-TURER IS 'CAUSE I'M BROKE AND PEOPLE ARE AFTER ME.
AND... UM...FOR OTHER REASONS TOO. I THOUGHT IT'D BE GOOD TO HAVE SOMEONE STRONG WITH ME.
AND ...
TRAVELING BY YOUR-SELF CAN GET KINDA LONELY...
ALSO! IT'S BECAUSE I'M A REALLY GOOD SUMMON-ER!
HM.
SHE'S NOT EXACTLY A GENIUS, BUT AT LEAST SHE'S HONEST.
STILL, JUST LIKE REM, IT SEEMS LIKE SHE'S HIDING SOME-THING...

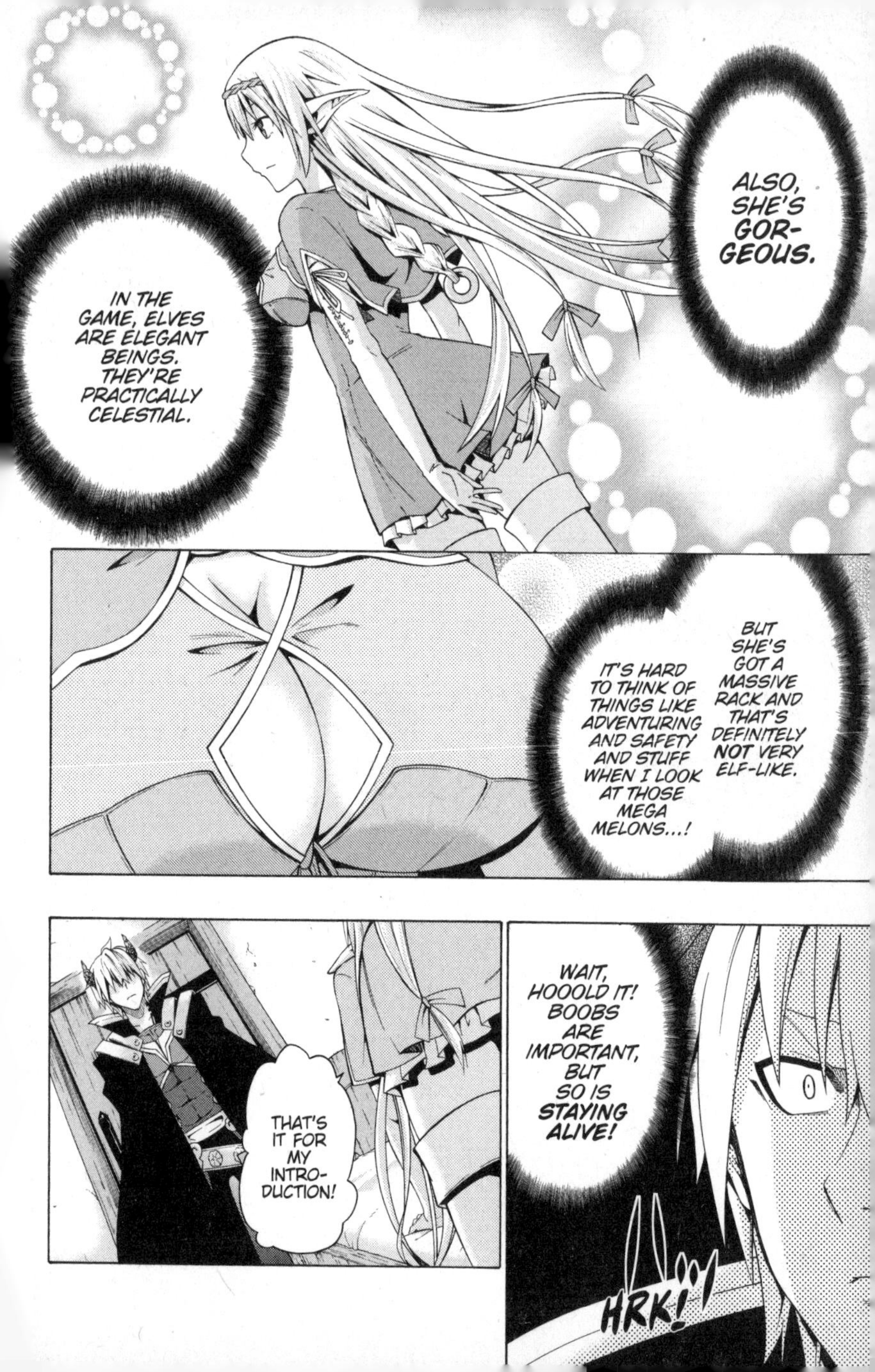
ALSO, SHE'S GORGEOUS.
IN THE GAME, ELVES ARE ELEGANT BEINGS. THEY'RE PRACTICALLY CELESTIAL.
BUT SHE'S GOT A MASSIVE RACK AND THAT'S DEFINITELY **NOT** VERY ELF-LIKE.
IT'S HARD TO THINK OF THINGS LIKE ADVENTURING AND SAFETY AND STUFF WHEN I LOOK AT THOSE MEGA MELONS...!
WAIT, HOOOLD IT! BOOBS ARE IMPORTANT, BUT SO IS **STAYING ALIVE!**
HRK!!
THAT'S IT FOR MY INTRO-DUCTION!

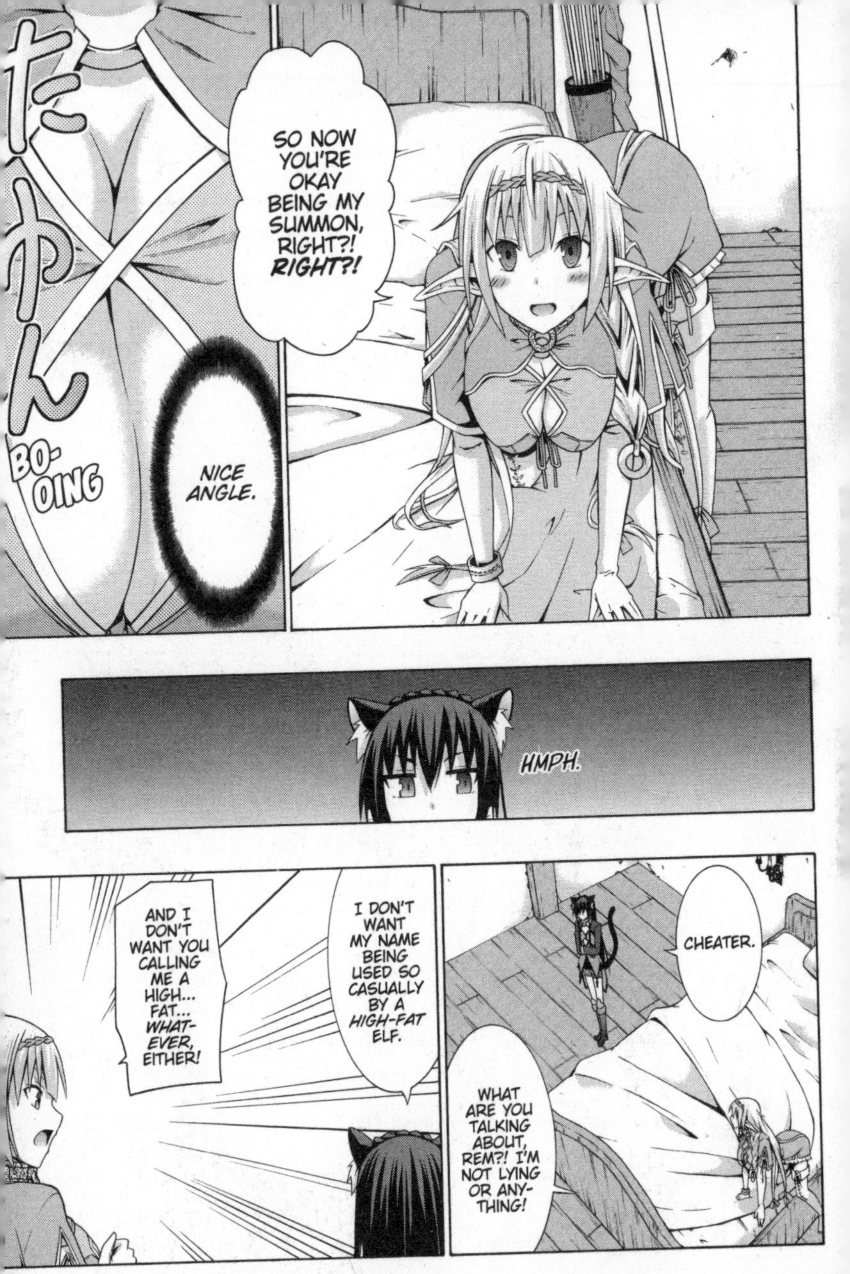
SO NOW YOU'RE OKAY BEING MY SUMMON, RIGHT?! *RIGHT?!*
たゆん
BO-OING
NICE ANGLE.
HMPH.
CHEATER.
WHAT ARE YOU TALKING ABOUT, REM?! I'M NOT LYING OR ANY-THING!
I DON'T WANT MY NAME BEING USED SO CASUALLY BY A *HIGH-FAT* ELF.
AND I DON'T WANT YOU CALLING ME A HIGH... FAT... *WHAT-EVER,* EITHER!

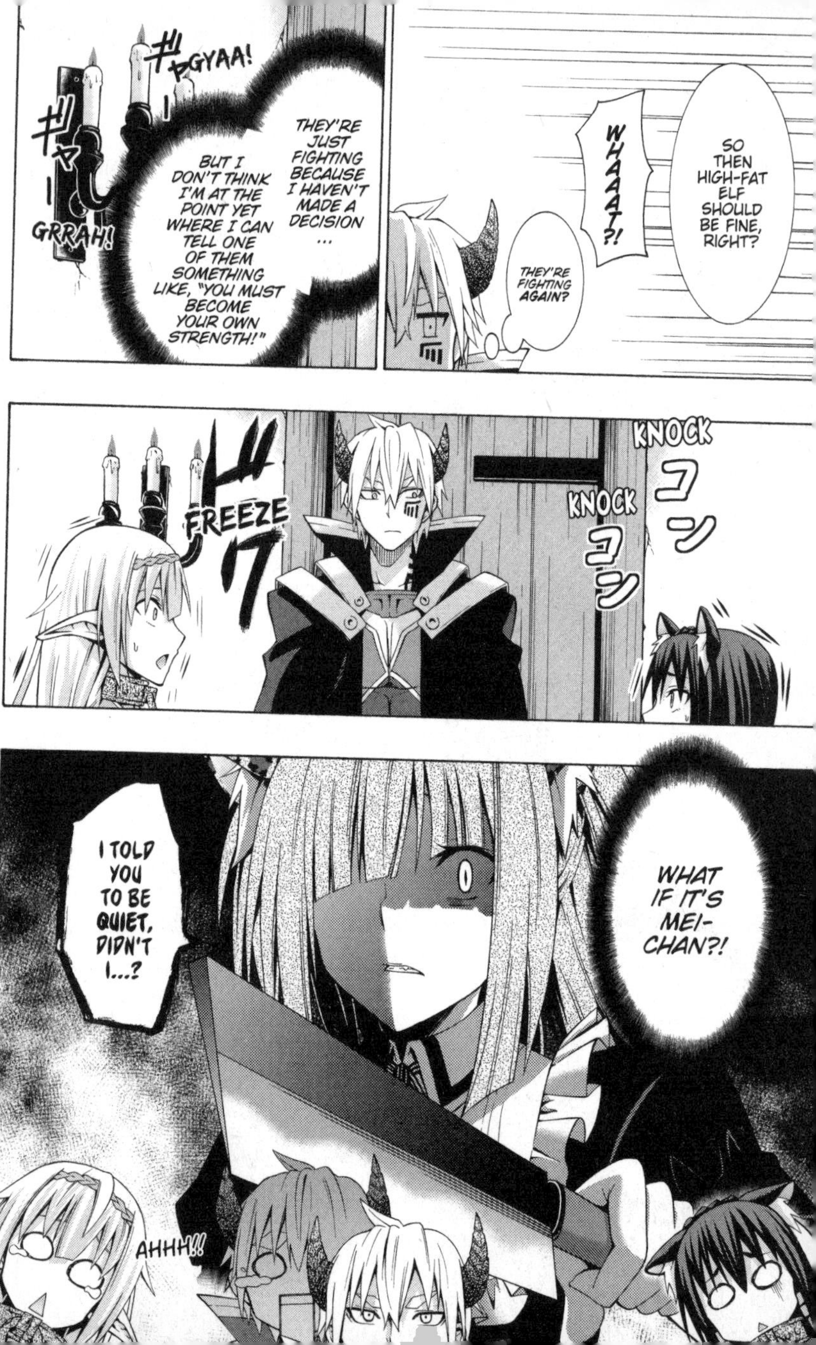
SO THEN HIGH-FAT ELF SHOULD BE FINE, RIGHT?
WHAAAAT?!
THEY'RE FIGHTING AGAIN?
THEY'RE JUST FIGHTING BECAUSE I HAVEN'T MADE A DECISION...
BUT I DON'T THINK I'M AT THE POINT YET WHERE I CAN TELL ONE OF THEM SOMETHING LIKE, "YOU MUST BECOME YOUR OWN STRENGTH!"
GYAA!
GRRAH!
KNOCK
KNOCK
FREEZE
WHAT IF IT'S MEI-CHAN?!
I TOLD YOU TO BE QUIET, DIDN'T I...?
AHHH!!

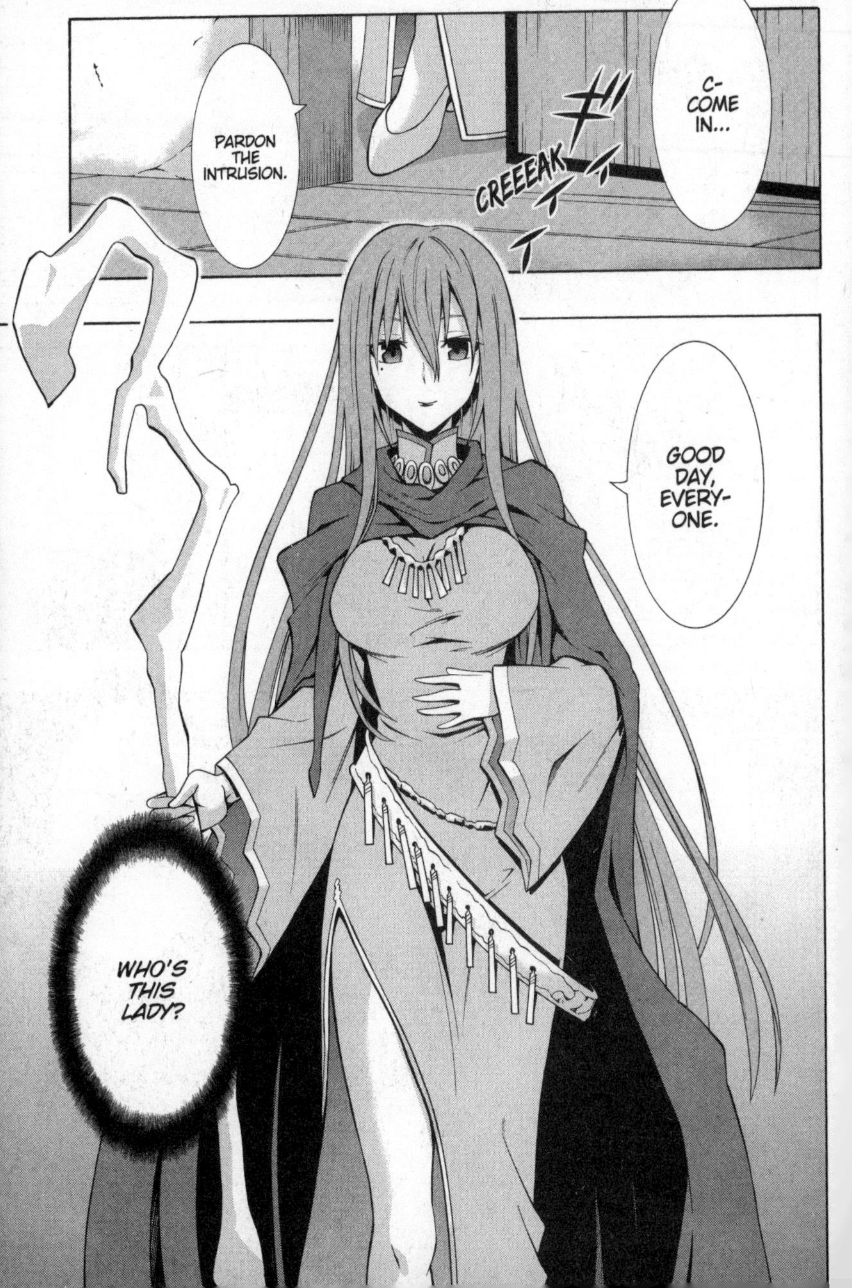
C-COME IN...
CREEEAK
PARDON THE INTRUSION.
GOOD DAY, EVERY-ONE.
WHO'S THIS LADY?

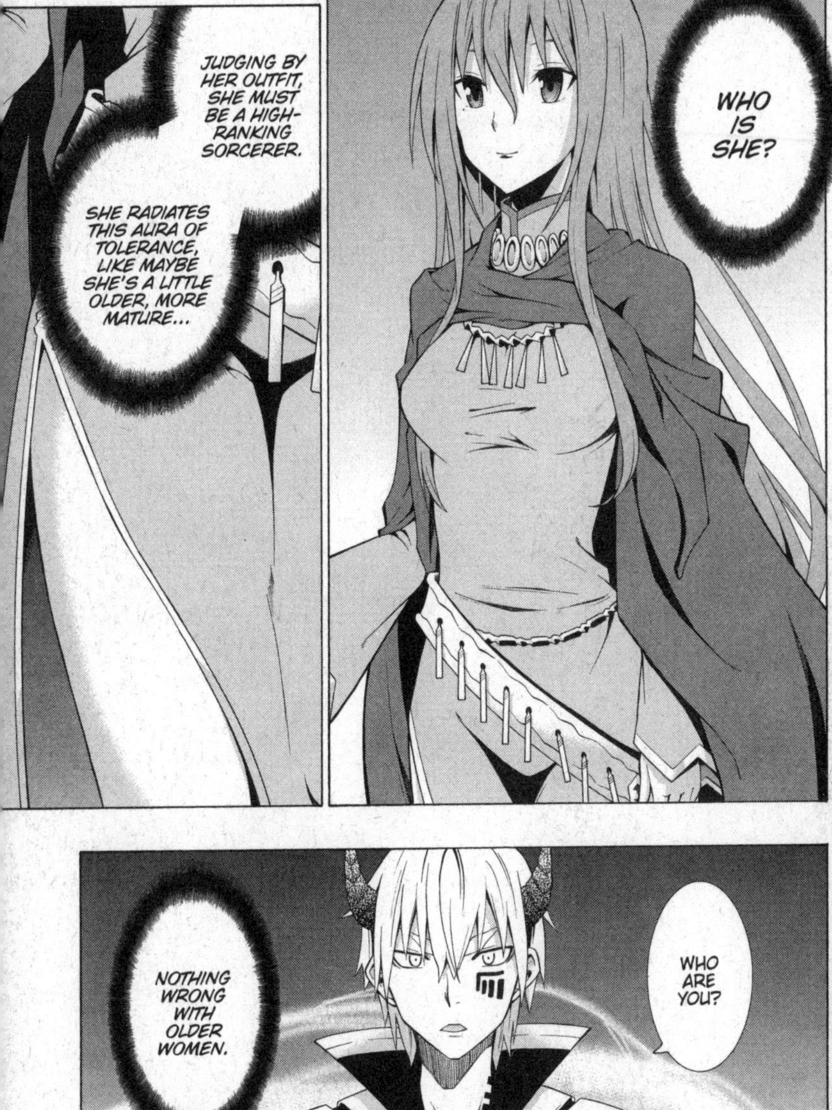
WHO IS SHE?
JUDGING BY HER OUTFIT, SHE MUST BE A HIGH-RANKING SORCERER.
SHE RADIATES THIS AURA OF TOLERANCE, LIKE MAYBE SHE'S A LITTLE OLDER, MORE MATURE...
WHO ARE YOU?
NOTHING WRONG WITH OLDER WOMEN.

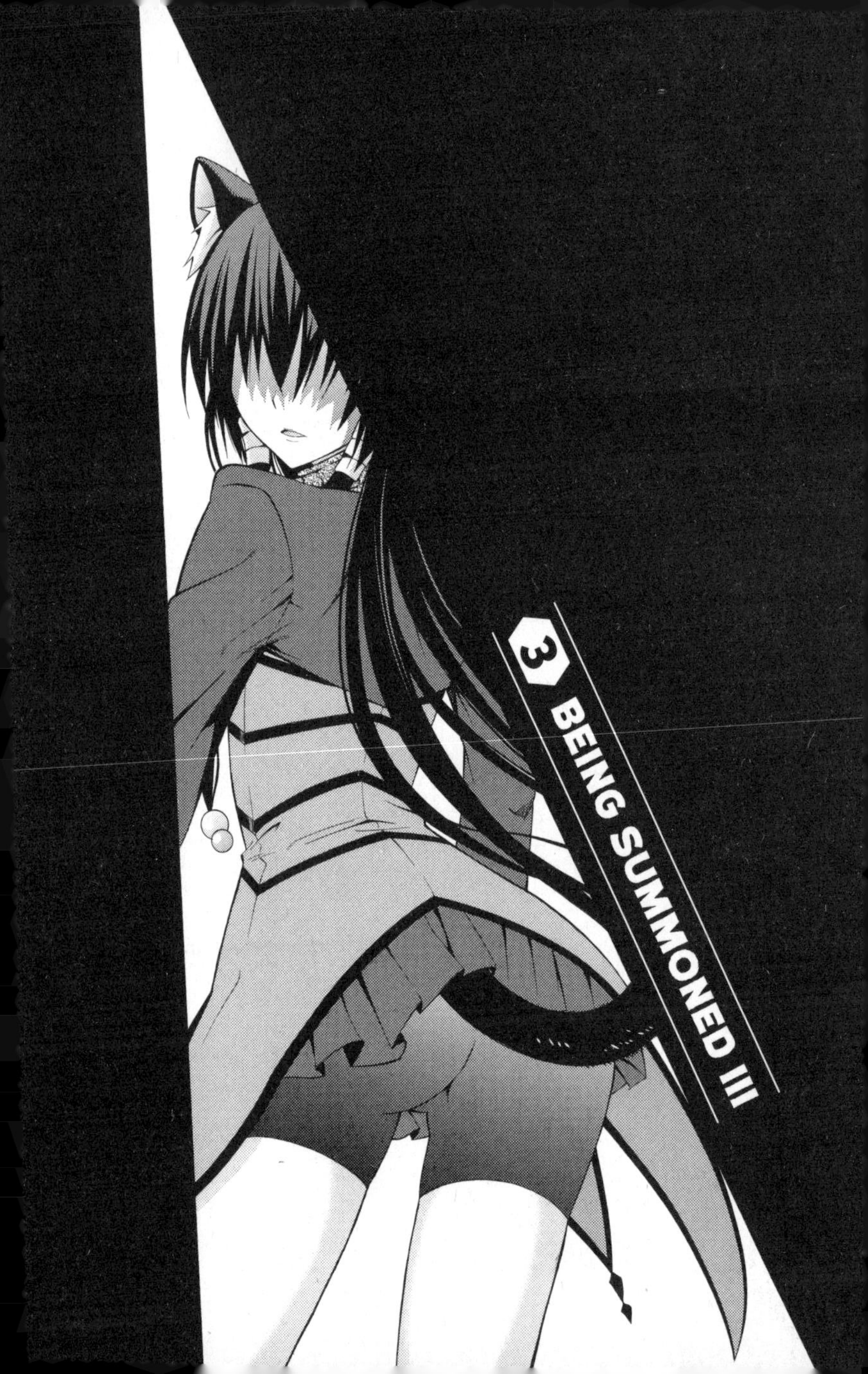
3 BEING SUMMONED III

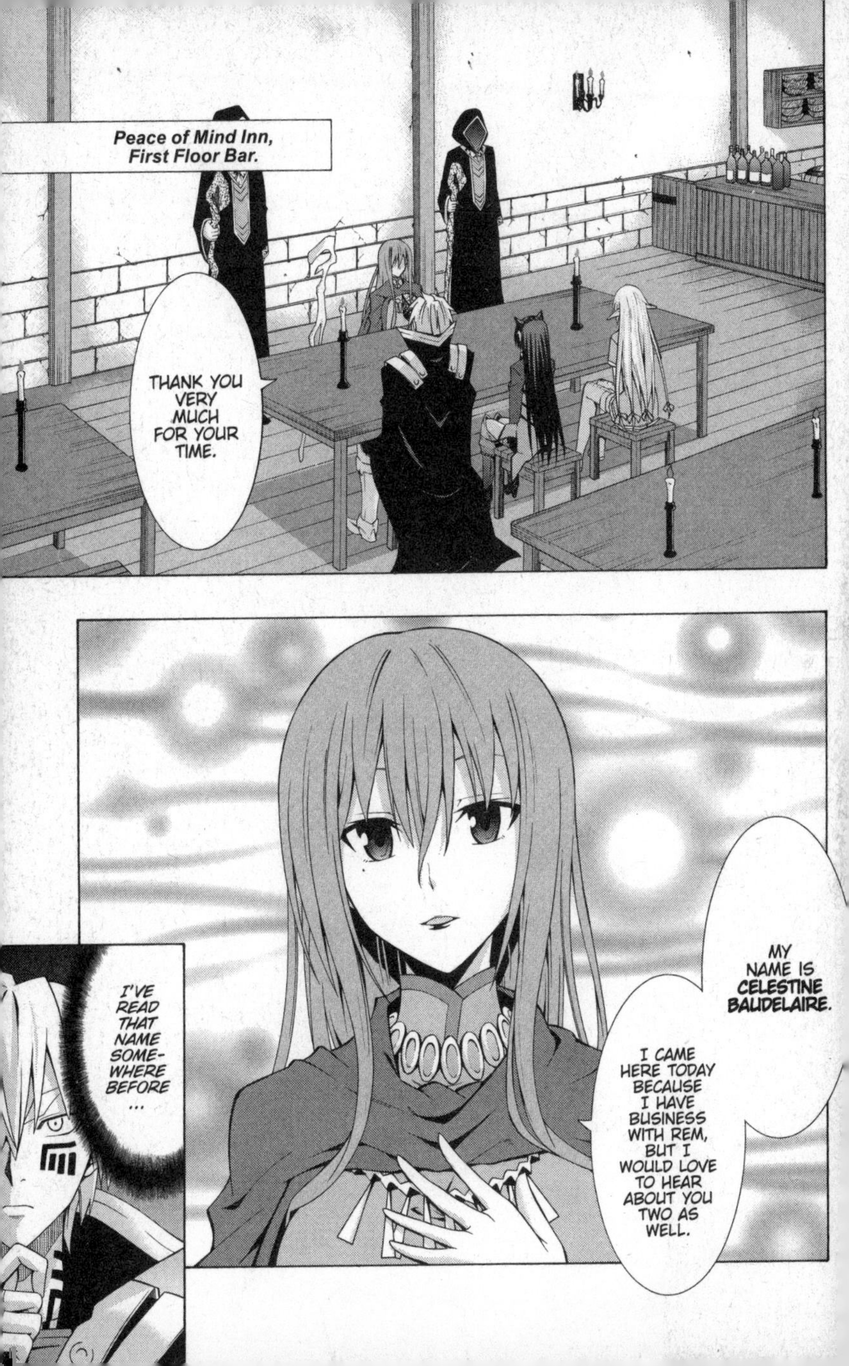
Peace of Mind Inn, First Floor Bar.
THANK YOU VERY MUCH FOR YOUR TIME.
MY NAME IS CELESTINE BAUDELAIRE.
I CAME HERE TODAY BECAUSE I HAVE BUSINESS WITH REM, BUT I WOULD LOVE TO HEAR ABOUT YOU TWO AS WELL.
I'VE READ THAT NAME SOMEWHERE BEFORE...

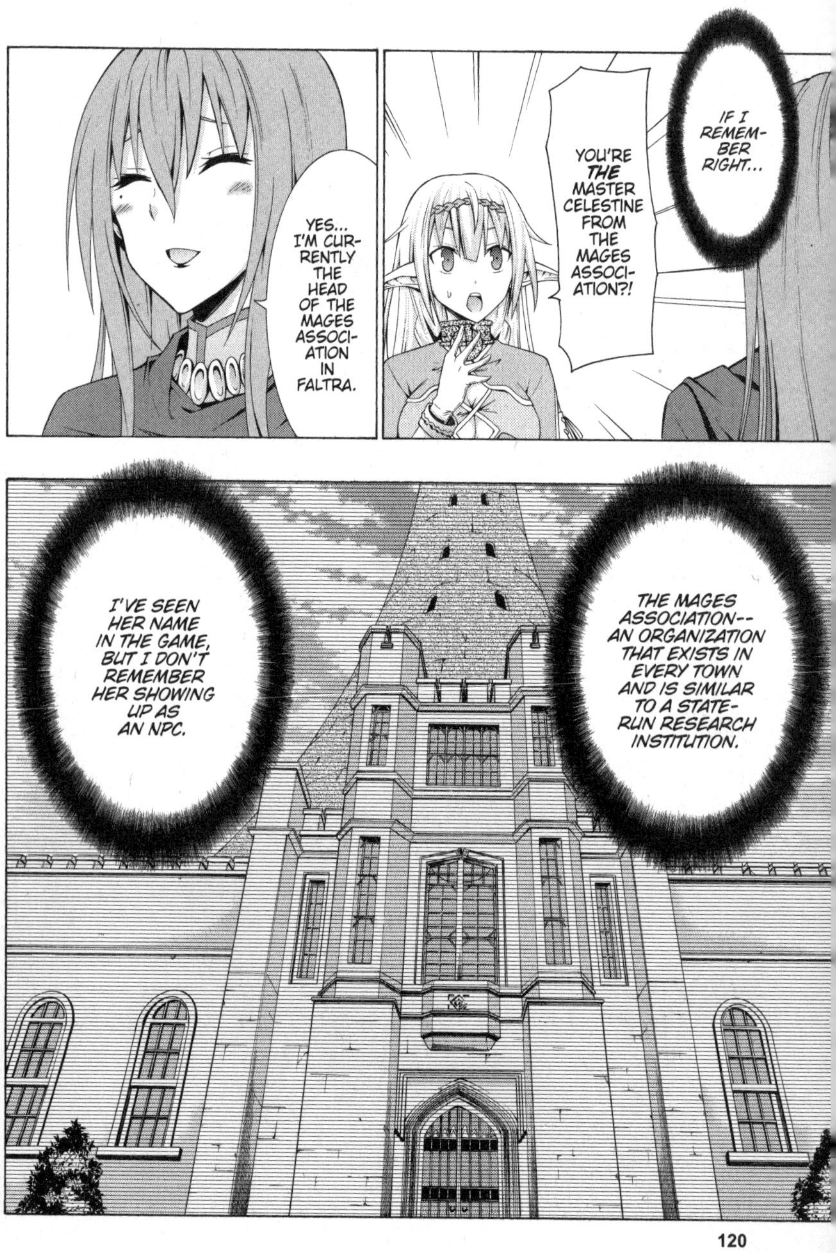
IF I REMEMBER RIGHT...
YOU'RE THE MASTER CELESTINE FROM THE MAGES ASSOCIATION?!
YES... I'M CURRENTLY THE HEAD OF THE MAGES ASSOCIATION IN FALTRA.
THE MAGES ASSOCIATION-- AN ORGANIZATION THAT EXISTS IN EVERY TOWN AND IS SIMILAR TO A STATE-RUN RESEARCH INSTITUTION.
I'VE SEEN HER NAME IN THE GAME, BUT I DON'T REMEMBER HER SHOWING UP AS AN NPC.

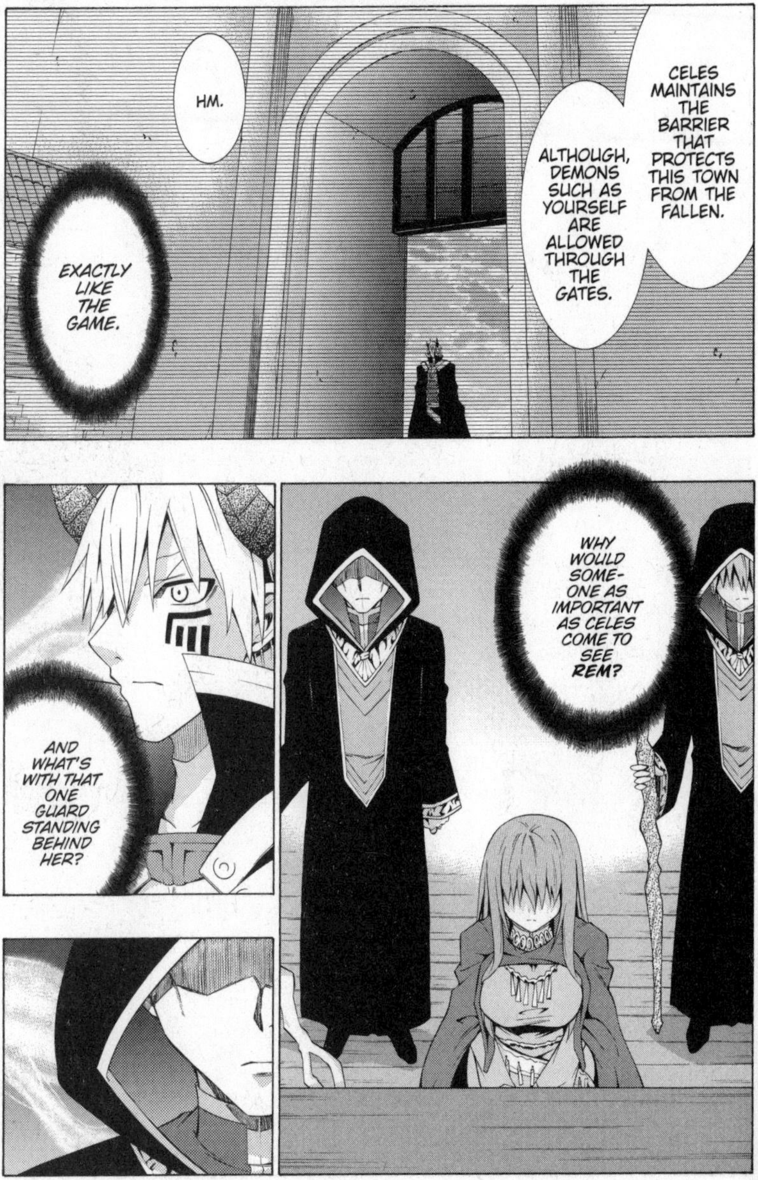
CELES MAINTAINS THE BARRIER THAT PROTECTS THIS TOWN FROM THE FALLEN.
ALTHOUGH, DEMONS SUCH AS YOURSELF ARE ALLOWED THROUGH THE GATES.
HM.
EXACTLY LIKE THE GAME.
WHY WOULD SOME-ONE AS IMPORTANT AS CELES COME TO SEE **REM?**
AND WHAT'S WITH THAT ONE GUARD STANDING BEHIND HER?

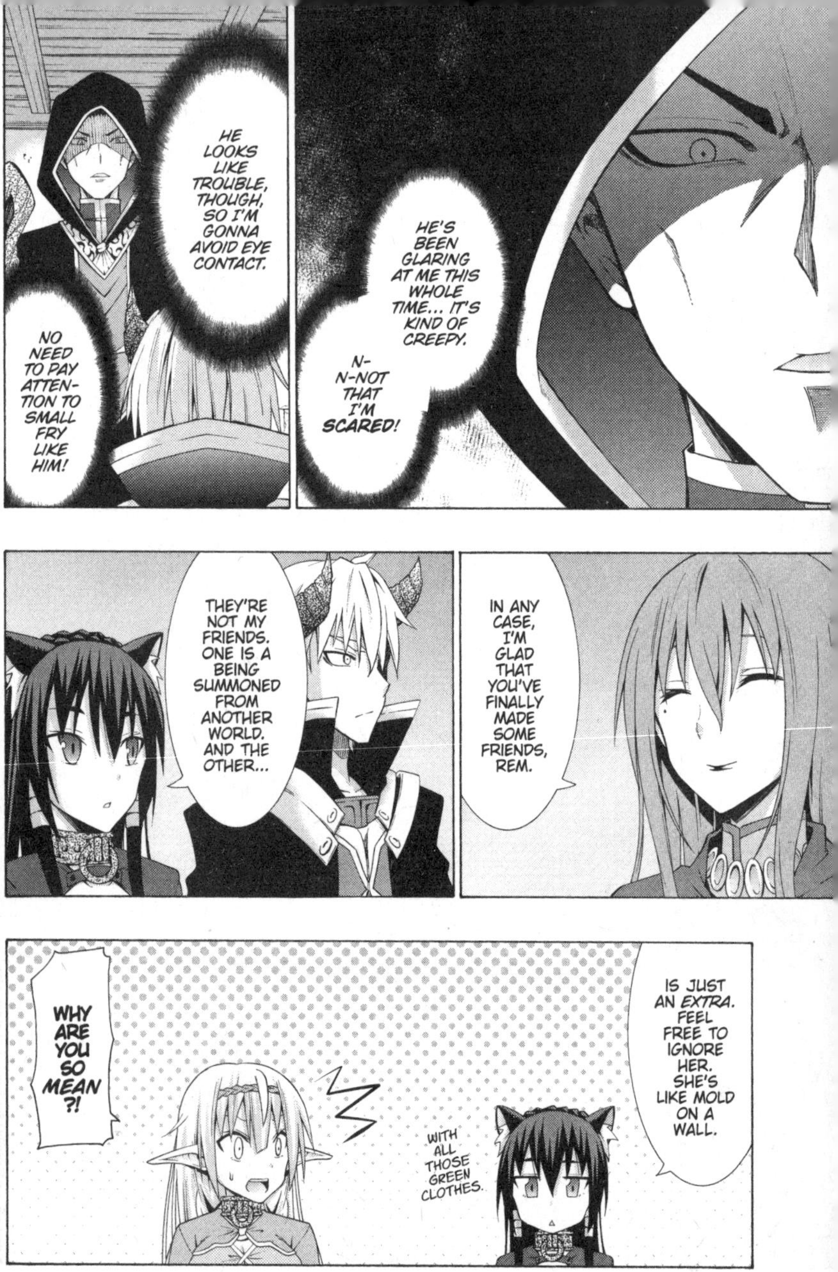
HE'S BEEN GLARING AT ME THIS WHOLE TIME... IT'S KIND OF CREEPY.
N-N-NOT THAT I'M *SCARED!*
HE LOOKS LIKE TROUBLE, THOUGH, SO I'M GONNA AVOID EYE CONTACT.
NO NEED TO PAY ATTEN-TION TO SMALL FRY LIKE HIM!
IN ANY CASE, I'M GLAD THAT YOU'VE FINALLY MADE SOME FRIENDS, REM.
THEY'RE NOT MY FRIENDS. ONE IS A BEING SUMMONED FROM ANOTHER WORLD. AND THE OTHER...
IS JUST AN *EXTRA*. FEEL FREE TO IGNORE HER. SHE'S LIKE MOLD ON A WALL.
WITH ALL THOSE GREEN CLOTHES.
WHY ARE YOU SO MEAN?!

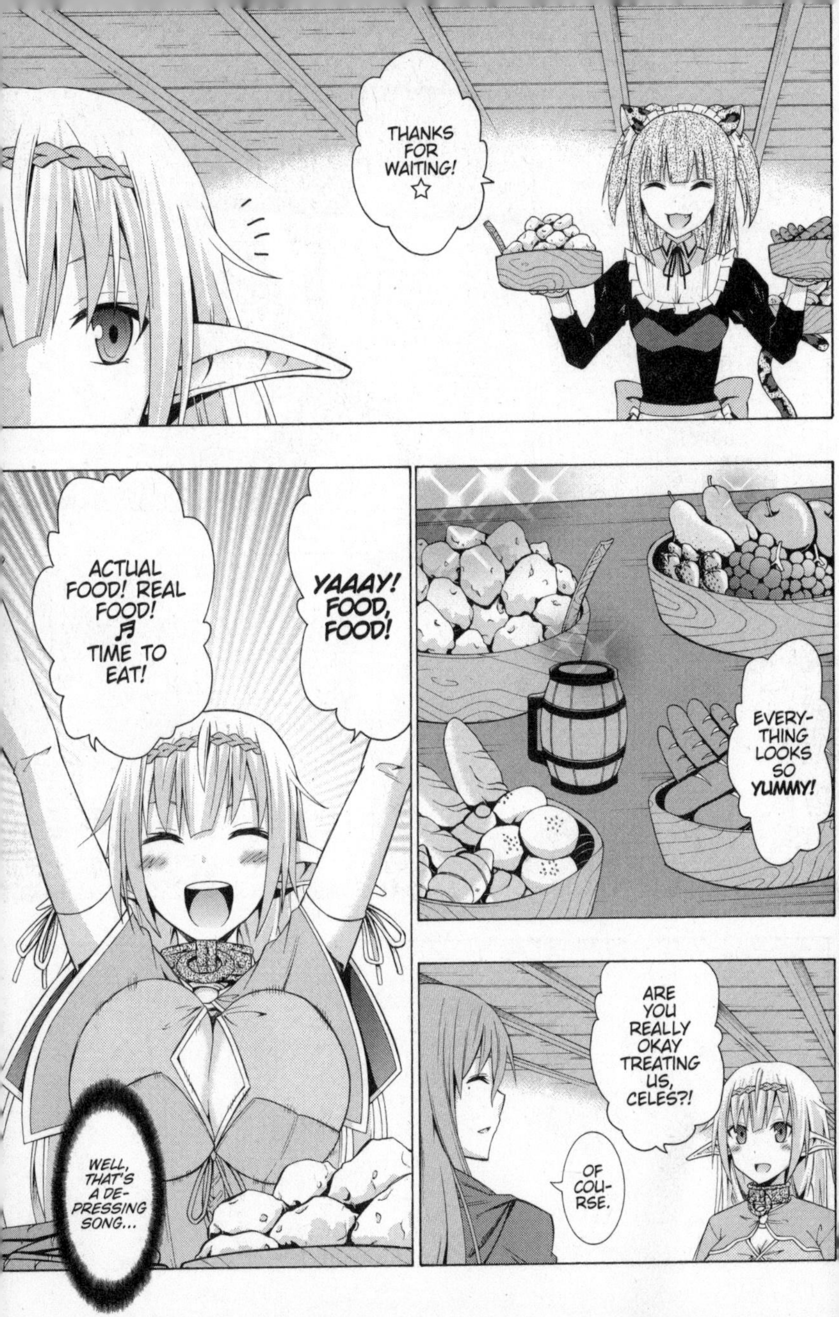
THANKS FOR WAITING! ☆
EVERY-THING LOOKS SO YUMMY!
ARE YOU REALLY OKAY TREATING US, CELES?!
OF COU-RSE.
YAAAY! FOOD, FOOD!
ACTUAL FOOD! REAL FOOD! ♬ TIME TO EAT!
WELL, THAT'S A DE-PRESSING SONG...

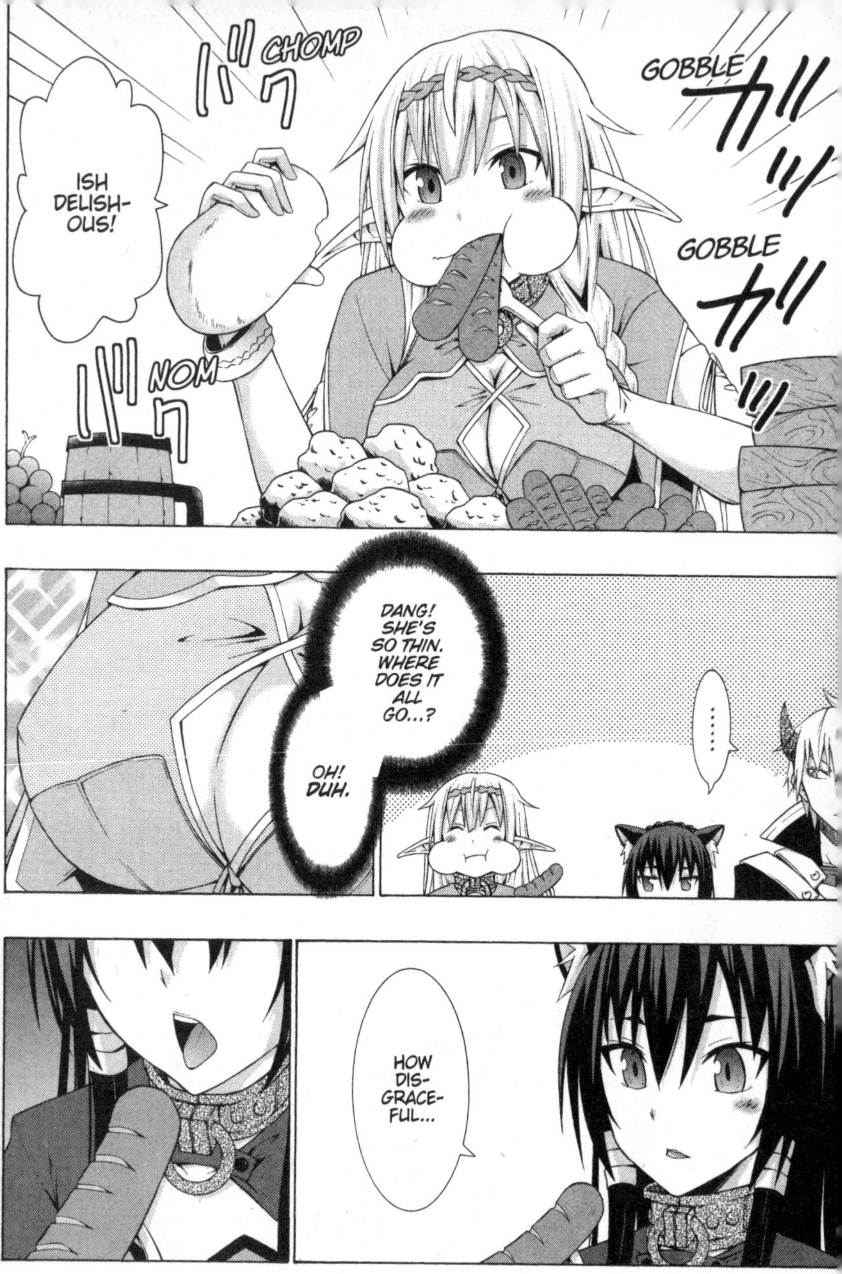
GOBBLE
GOBBLE
CHOMP
ISH DELISH-OUS!
NOM
......
DANG! SHE'S SO THIN. WHERE DOES IT ALL GO...?
OH! DUH.
HOW DIS-GRACE-FUL...

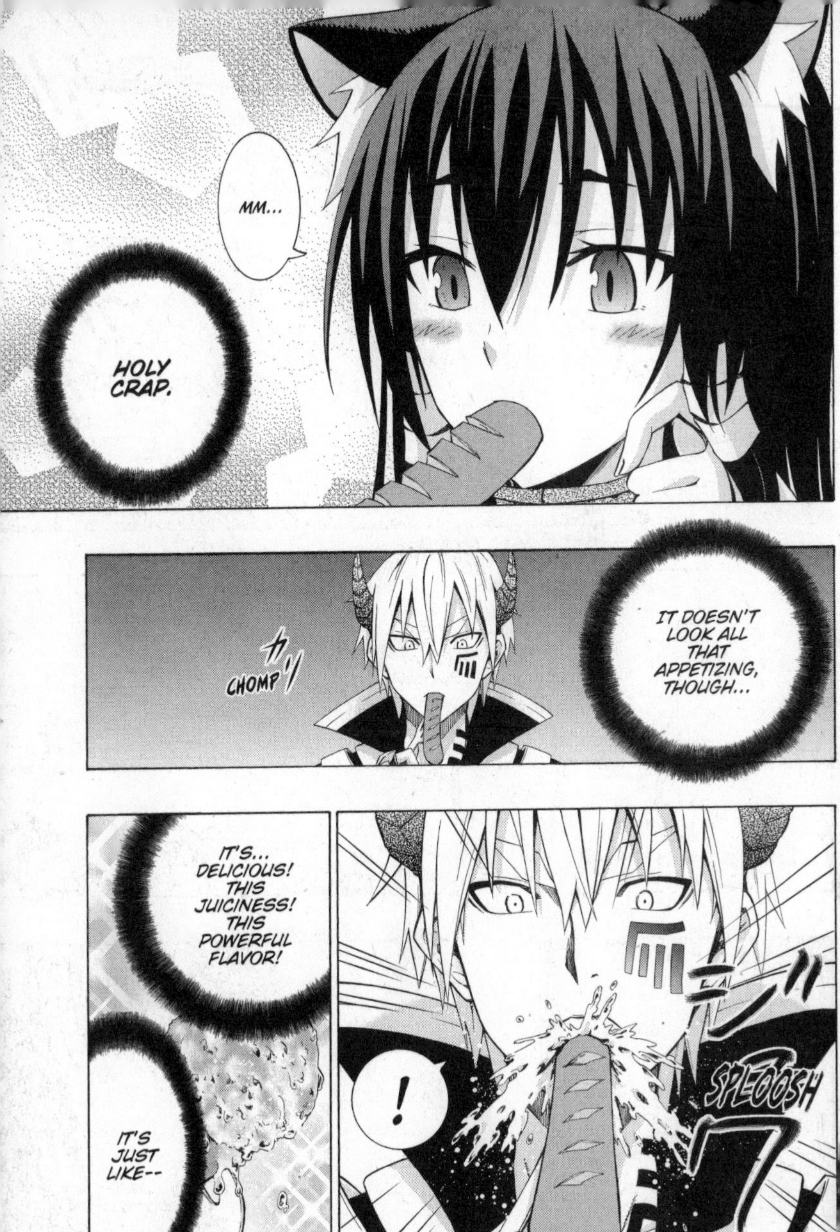
MM...
HOLY CRAP.
IT DOESN'T LOOK ALL THAT APPETIZING, THOUGH...
CHOMP
!
SPLOOSH
IT'S... DELICIOUS! THIS JUICINESS! THIS POWERFUL FLAVOR!
IT'S JUST LIKE--

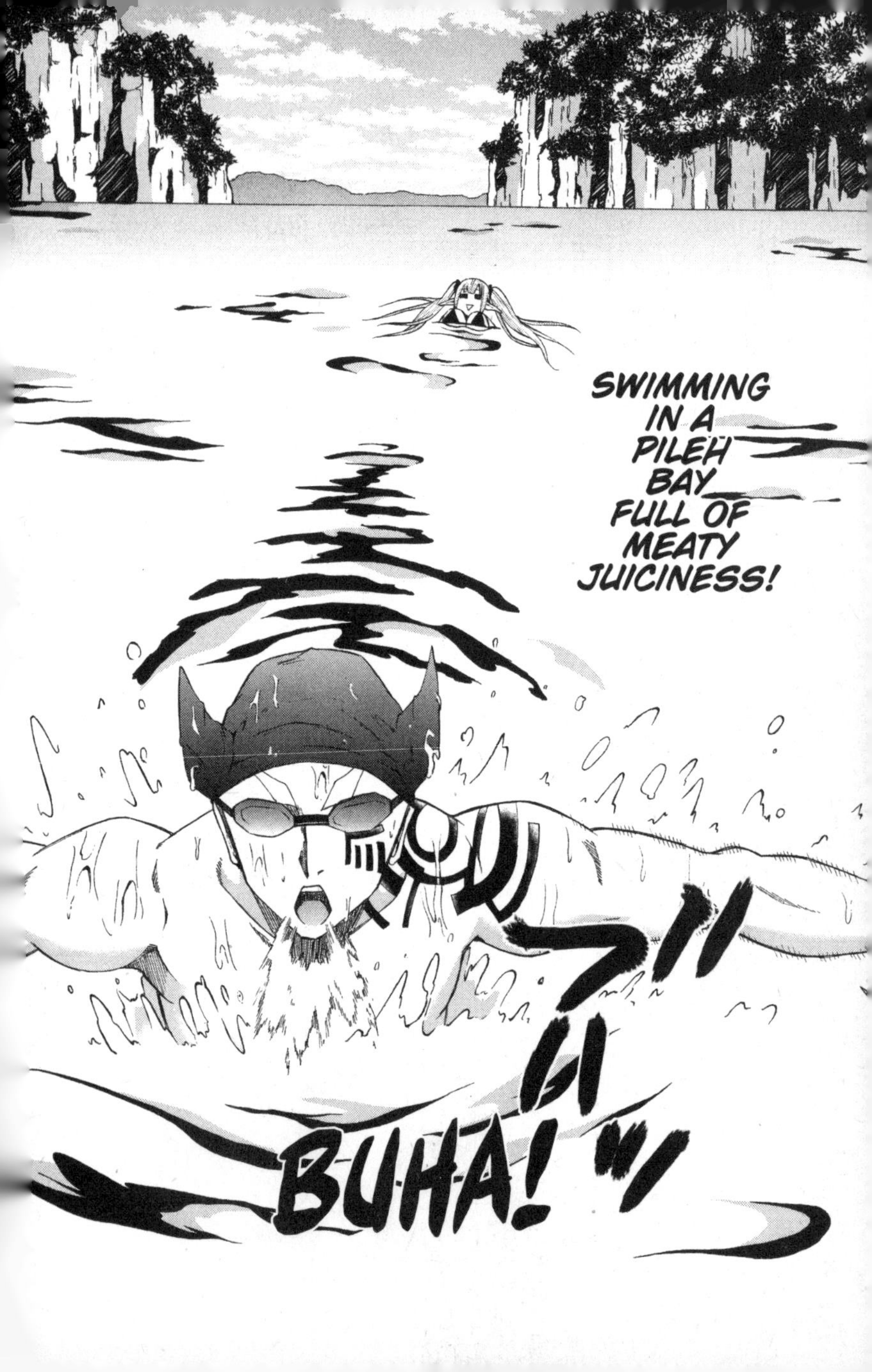
SWIMMING IN A PILEH BAY FULL OF MEATY JUICINESS!
BUHA!

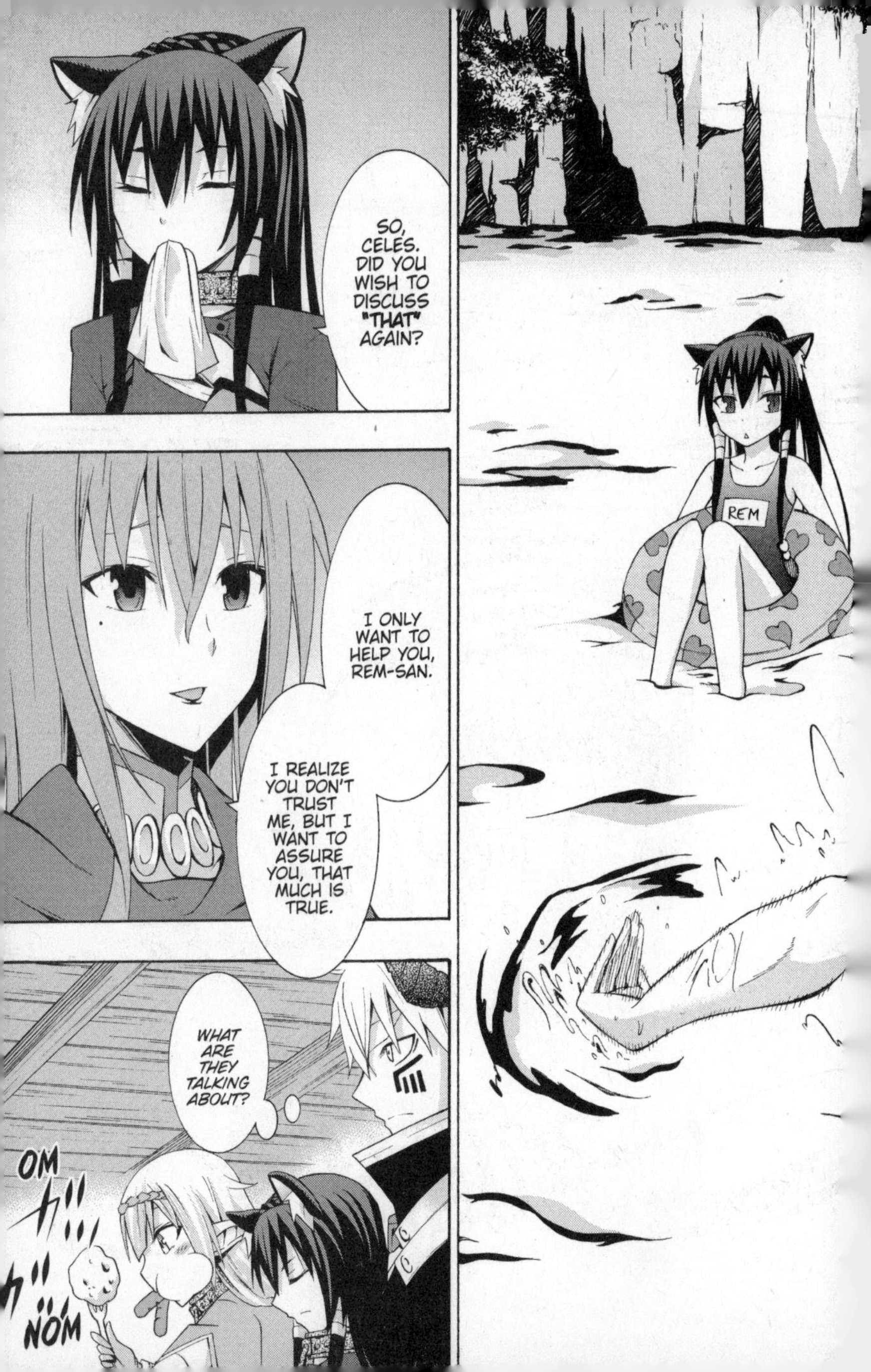
REM
SO, CELES. DID YOU WISH TO DISCUSS "THAT" AGAIN?
I ONLY WANT TO HELP YOU, REM-SAN.
I REALIZE YOU DON'T TRUST ME, BUT I WANT TO ASSURE YOU, THAT MUCH IS TRUE.
WHAT ARE THEY TALKING ABOUT?
OM
NOM

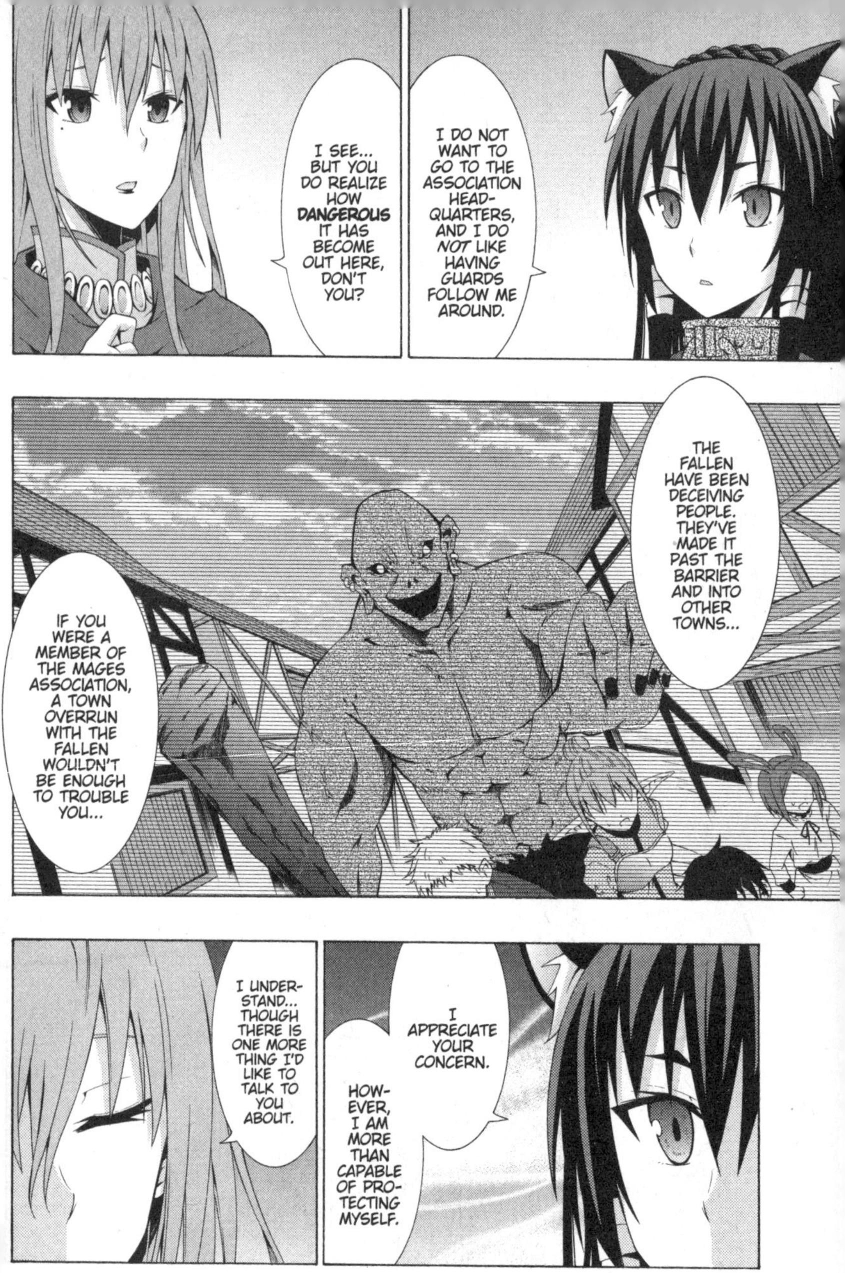
I DO NOT WANT TO GO TO THE ASSOCIATION HEADQUARTERS, AND I DO *NOT* LIKE HAVING GUARDS FOLLOW ME AROUND.
I SEE... BUT YOU DO REALIZE HOW **DANGEROUS** IT HAS BECOME OUT HERE, DON'T YOU?
THE FALLEN HAVE BEEN DECEIVING PEOPLE. THEY'VE MADE IT PAST THE BARRIER AND INTO OTHER TOWNS...
IF YOU WERE A MEMBER OF THE MAGES ASSOCIATION, A TOWN OVERRUN WITH THE FALLEN WOULDN'T BE ENOUGH TO TROUBLE YOU...
I APPRECIATE YOUR CONCERN.
HOWEVER, I AM MORE THAN CAPABLE OF PROTECTING MYSELF.
I UNDERSTAND... THOUGH THERE IS ONE MORE THING I'D LIKE TO TALK TO YOU ABOUT.

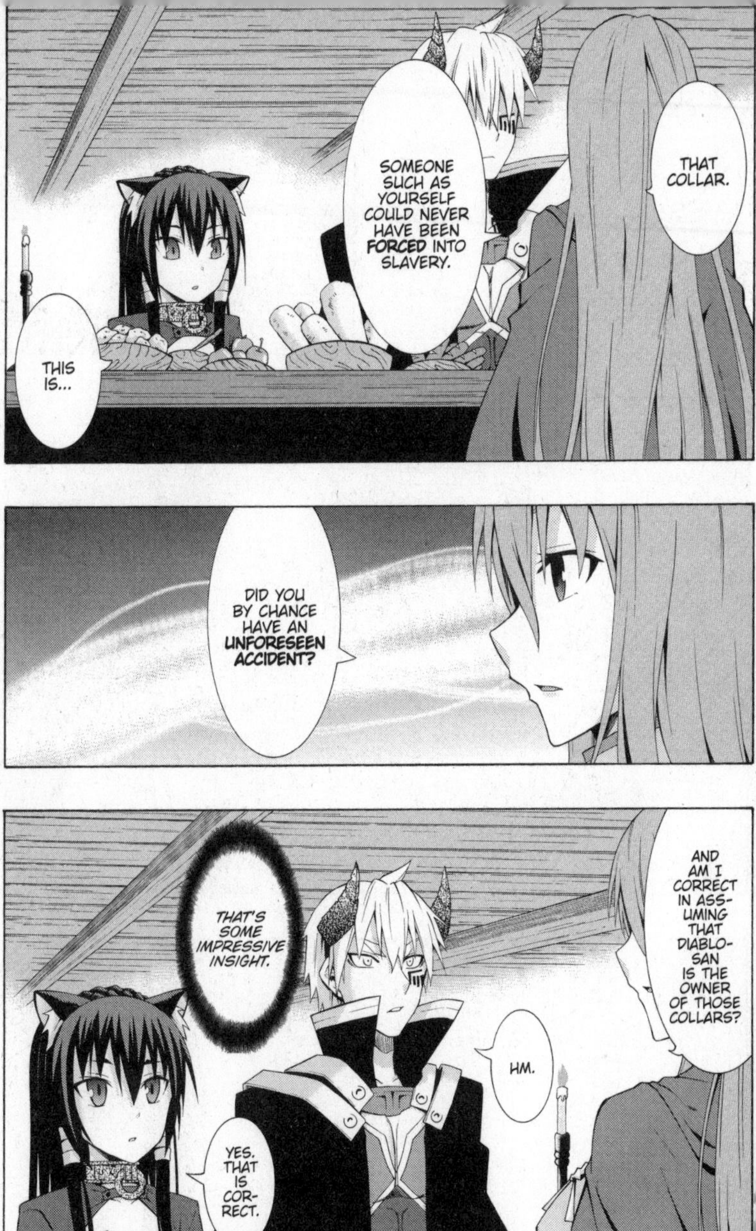
THAT COLLAR.
SOMEONE SUCH AS YOURSELF COULD NEVER HAVE BEEN **FORCED** INTO SLAVERY.
THIS IS...
DID YOU BY CHANCE HAVE AN **UNFORESEEN ACCIDENT?**
AND AM I CORRECT IN ASS-UMING THAT DIABLO-SAN IS THE OWNER OF THOSE COLLARS?
THAT'S SOME IMPRESSIVE INSIGHT.
HM.
YES. THAT IS COR-RECT.

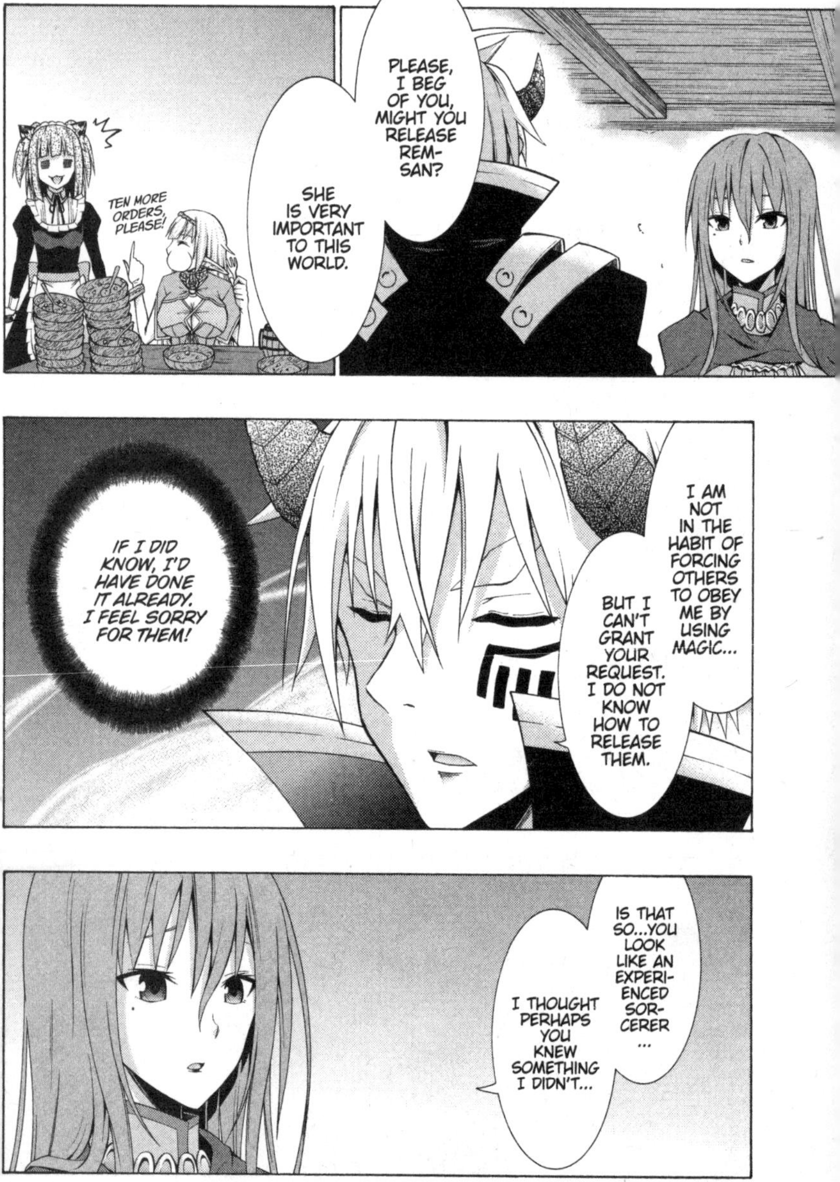
PLEASE, I BEG OF YOU, MIGHT YOU RELEASE REM-SAN?
SHE IS VERY IMPORTANT TO THIS WORLD.
TEN MORE ORDERS, PLEASE!
I AM NOT IN THE HABIT OF FORCING OTHERS TO OBEY ME BY USING MAGIC...
BUT I CAN'T GRANT YOUR REQUEST. I DO NOT KNOW HOW TO RELEASE THEM.
IF I DID KNOW, I'D HAVE DONE IT ALREADY. I FEEL SORRY FOR THEM!
IS THAT SO...YOU LOOK LIKE AN EXPERIENCED SORCERER...
I THOUGHT PERHAPS YOU KNEW SOMETHING I DIDN'T...

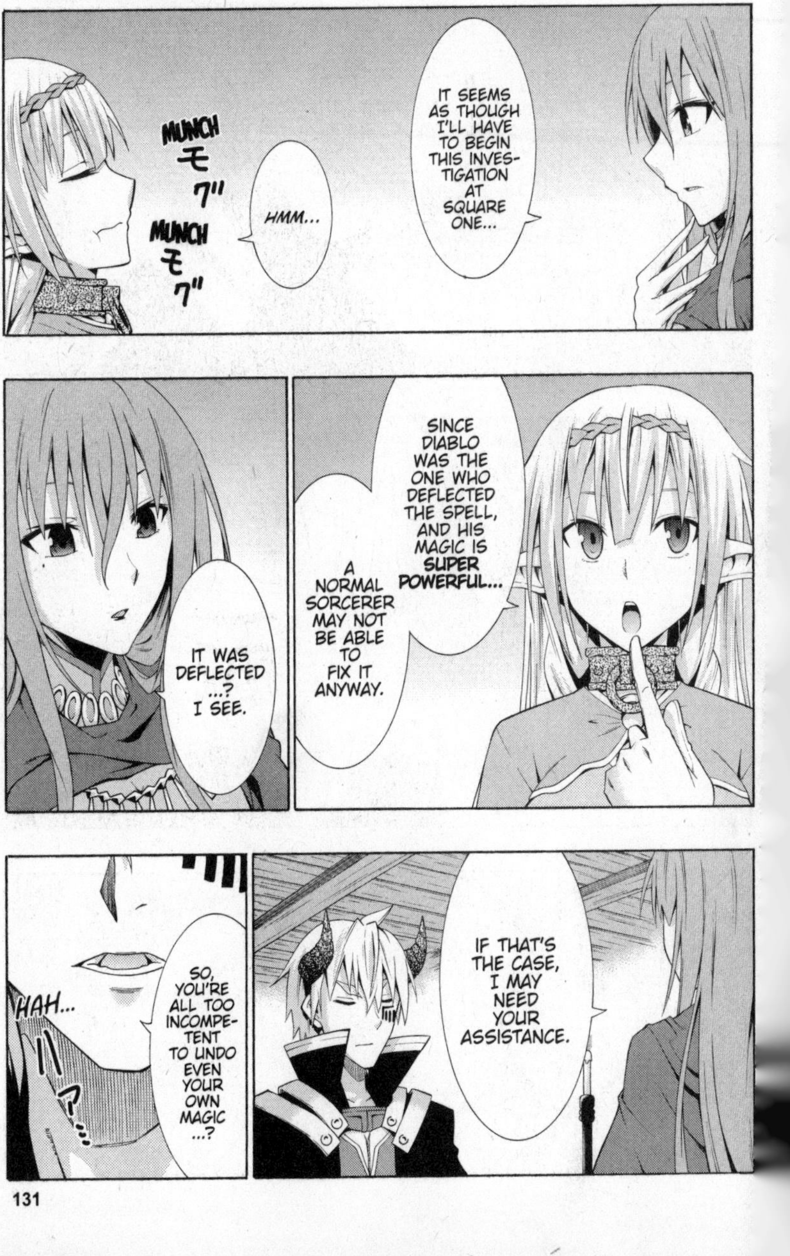
IT SEEMS AS THOUGH I'LL HAVE TO BEGIN THIS INVESTIGATION AT SQUARE ONE...
HMM...
MUNCH モグ
MUNCH モグ
SINCE DIABLO WAS THE ONE WHO DEFLECTED THE SPELL, AND HIS MAGIC IS **SUPER POWERFUL...**
A NORMAL SORCERER MAY NOT BE ABLE TO FIX IT ANYWAY.
IT WAS DEFLECTED ...? I SEE.
IF THAT'S THE CASE, I MAY NEED YOUR ASSISTANCE.
SO, YOU'RE ALL TOO INCOMPETENT TO UNDO EVEN YOUR OWN MAGIC ...?
HAH... ハァ...

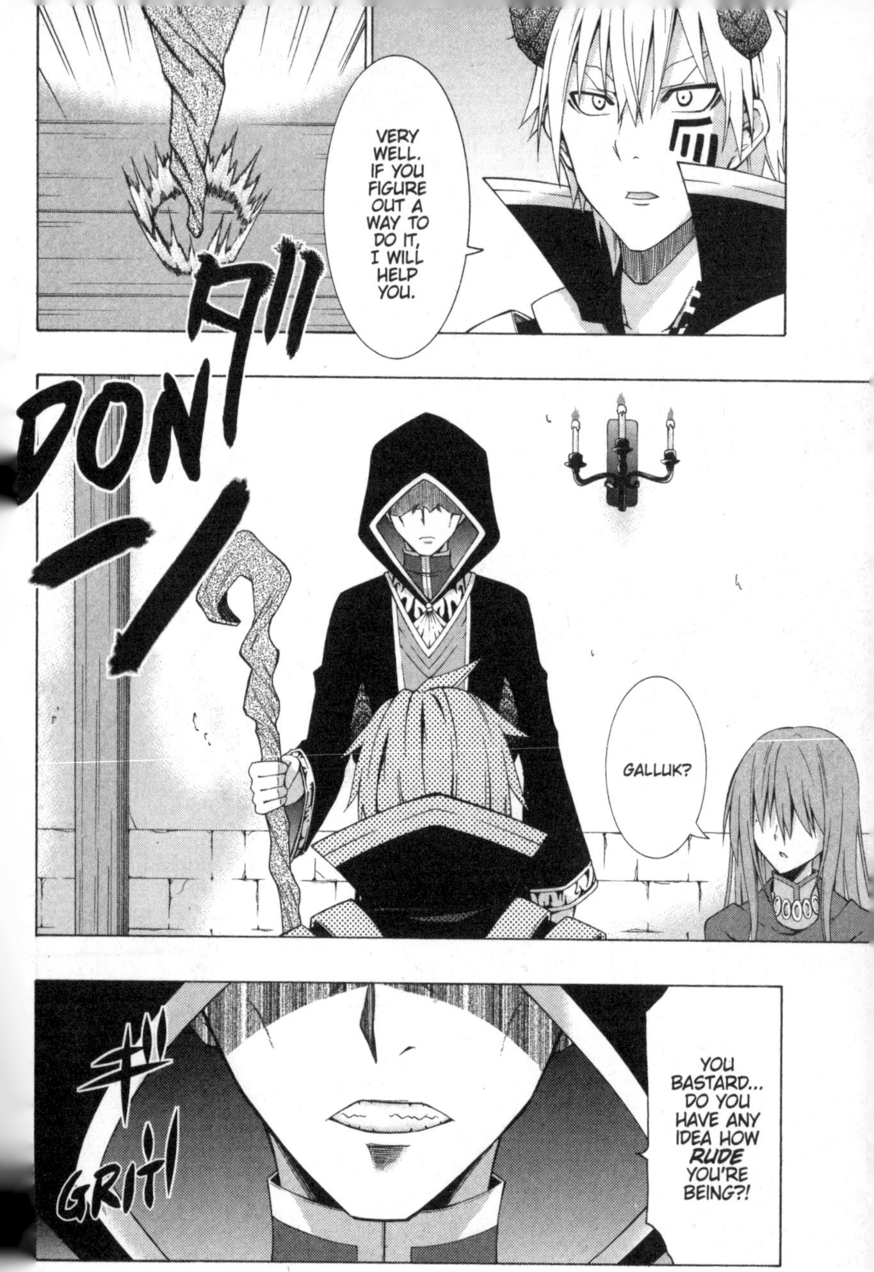
VERY WELL. IF YOU FIGURE OUT A WAY TO DO IT, I WILL HELP YOU.
DON!
GALLUK?
YOU BASTARD... DO YOU HAVE ANY IDEA HOW RUDE YOU'RE BEING?!
GRIT!

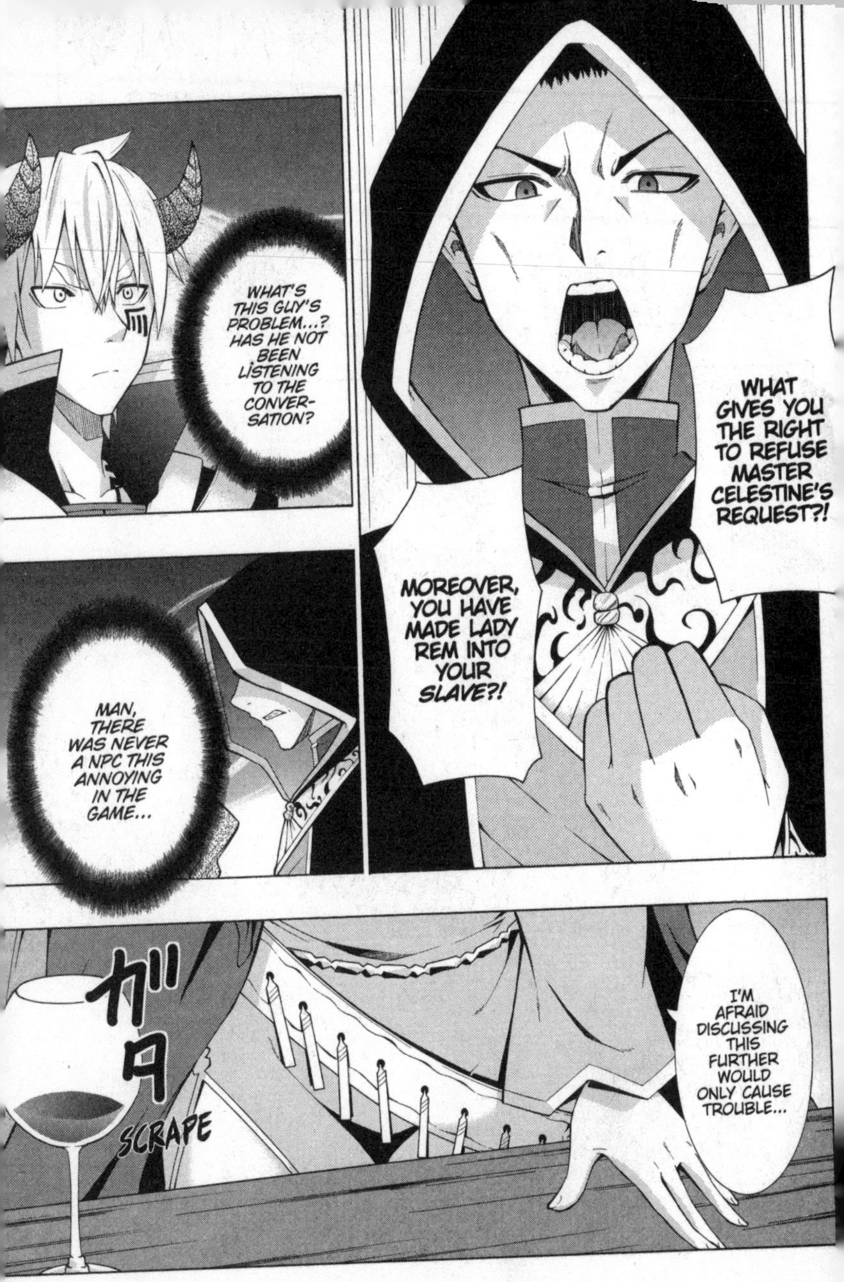
WHAT GIVES YOU THE RIGHT TO REFUSE MASTER CELESTINE'S REQUEST?!
MOREOVER, YOU HAVE MADE LADY REM INTO YOUR SLAVE?!
WHAT'S THIS GUY'S PROBLEM...? HAS HE NOT BEEN LISTENING TO THE CONVER-SATION?
MAN, THERE WAS NEVER A NPC THIS ANNOYING IN THE GAME...
I'M AFRAID DISCUSSING THIS FURTHER WOULD ONLY CAUSE TROUBLE...
ガタ
SCRAPE

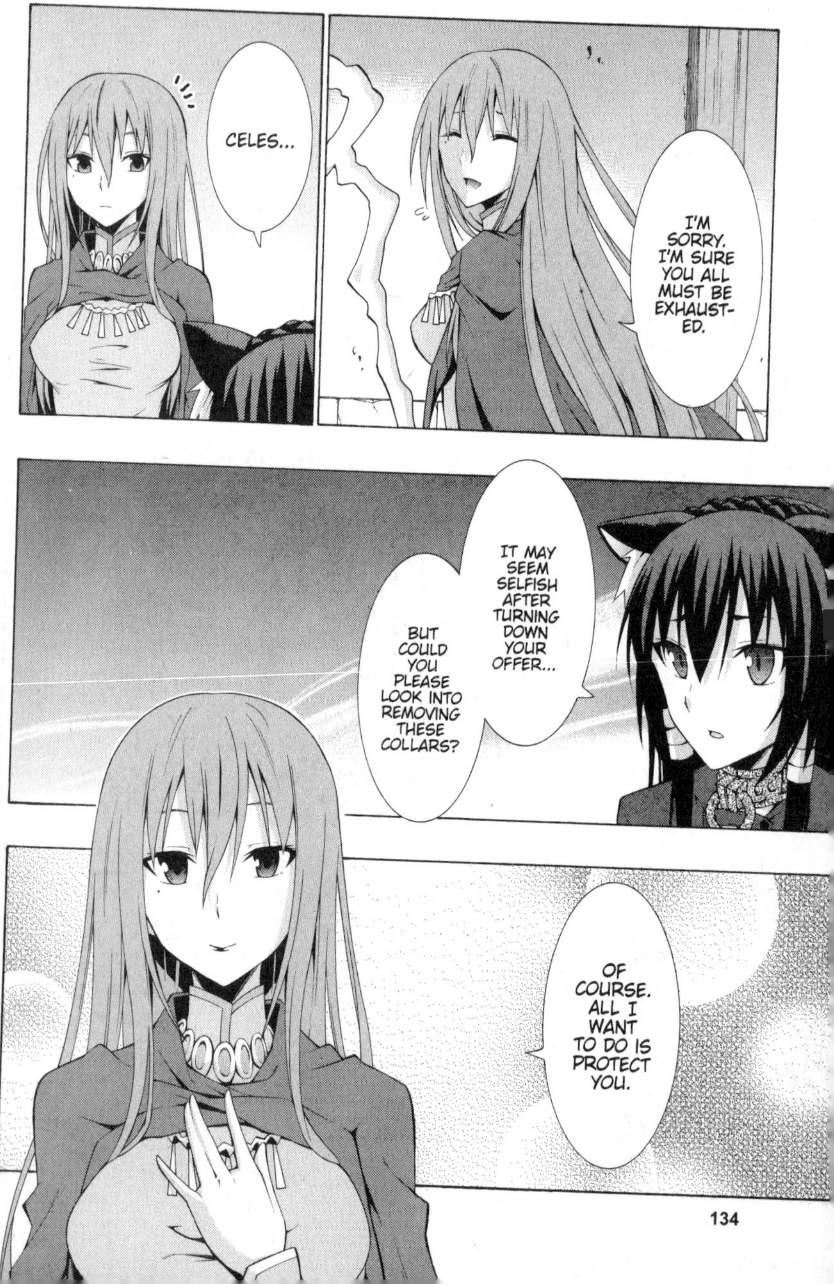
I'M SORRY. I'M SURE YOU ALL MUST BE EXHAUST-ED.
CELES...
IT MAY SEEM SELFISH AFTER TURNING DOWN YOUR OFFER...
BUT COULD YOU PLEASE LOOK INTO REMOVING THESE COLLARS?
OF COURSE. ALL I WANT TO DO IS PROTECT YOU.

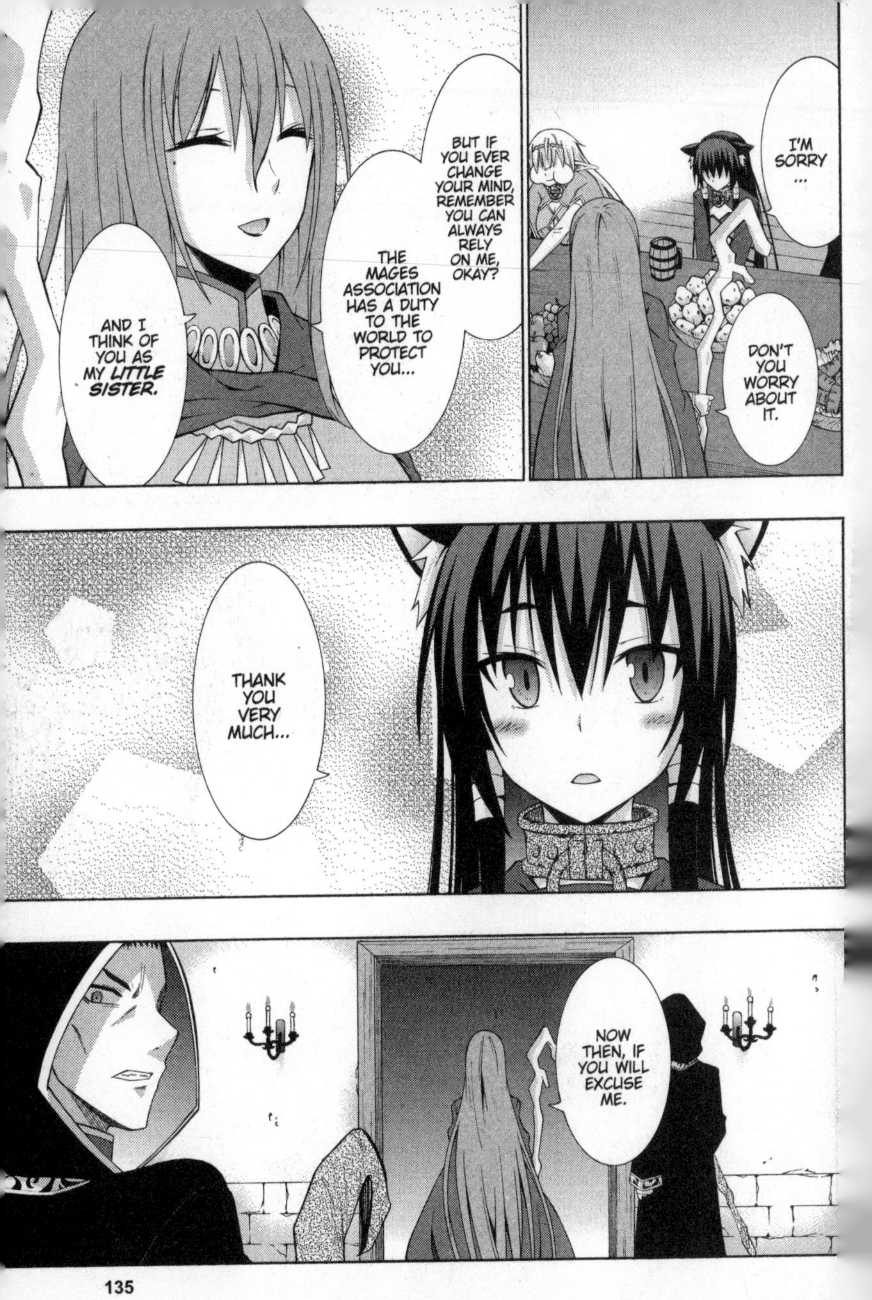
I'M SORRY...
DON'T YOU WORRY ABOUT IT.
THE MAGES ASSOCIATION HAS A DUTY TO THE WORLD TO PROTECT YOU... BUT IF YOU EVER CHANGE YOUR MIND, REMEMBER YOU CAN ALWAYS RELY ON ME, OKAY?
AND I THINK OF YOU AS MY ***LITTLE SISTER.***
THANK YOU VERY MUCH...
NOW THEN, IF YOU WILL EXCUSE ME.

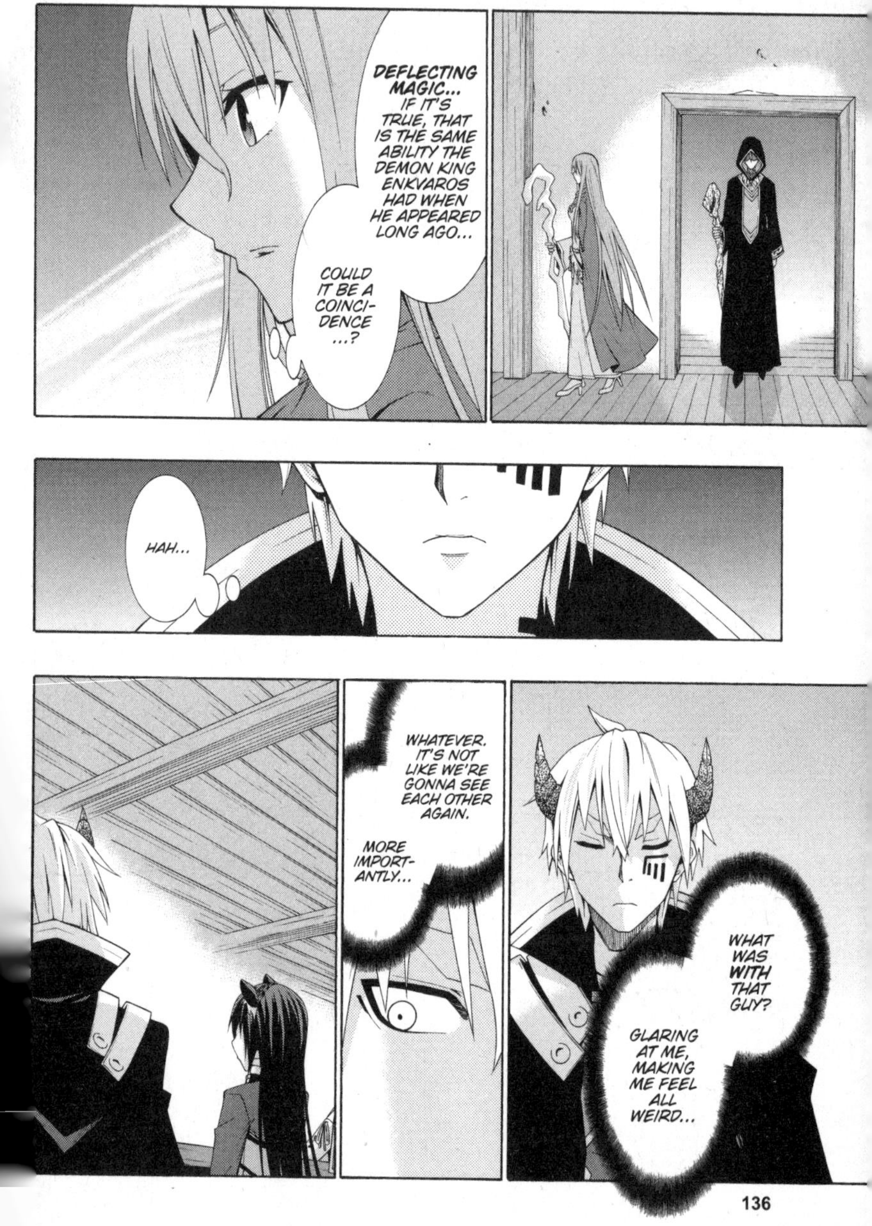
DEFLECTING MAGIC... IF IT'S TRUE, THAT IS THE SAME ABILITY THE DEMON KING ENKVAROS HAD WHEN HE APPEARED LONG AGO...
COULD IT BE A COINCIDENCE...?
HAH...
WHAT WAS WITH THAT GUY?
GLARING AT ME, MAKING ME FEEL ALL WEIRD...
WHATEVER. IT'S NOT LIKE WE'RE GONNA SEE EACH OTHER AGAIN.
MORE IMPORTANTLY...

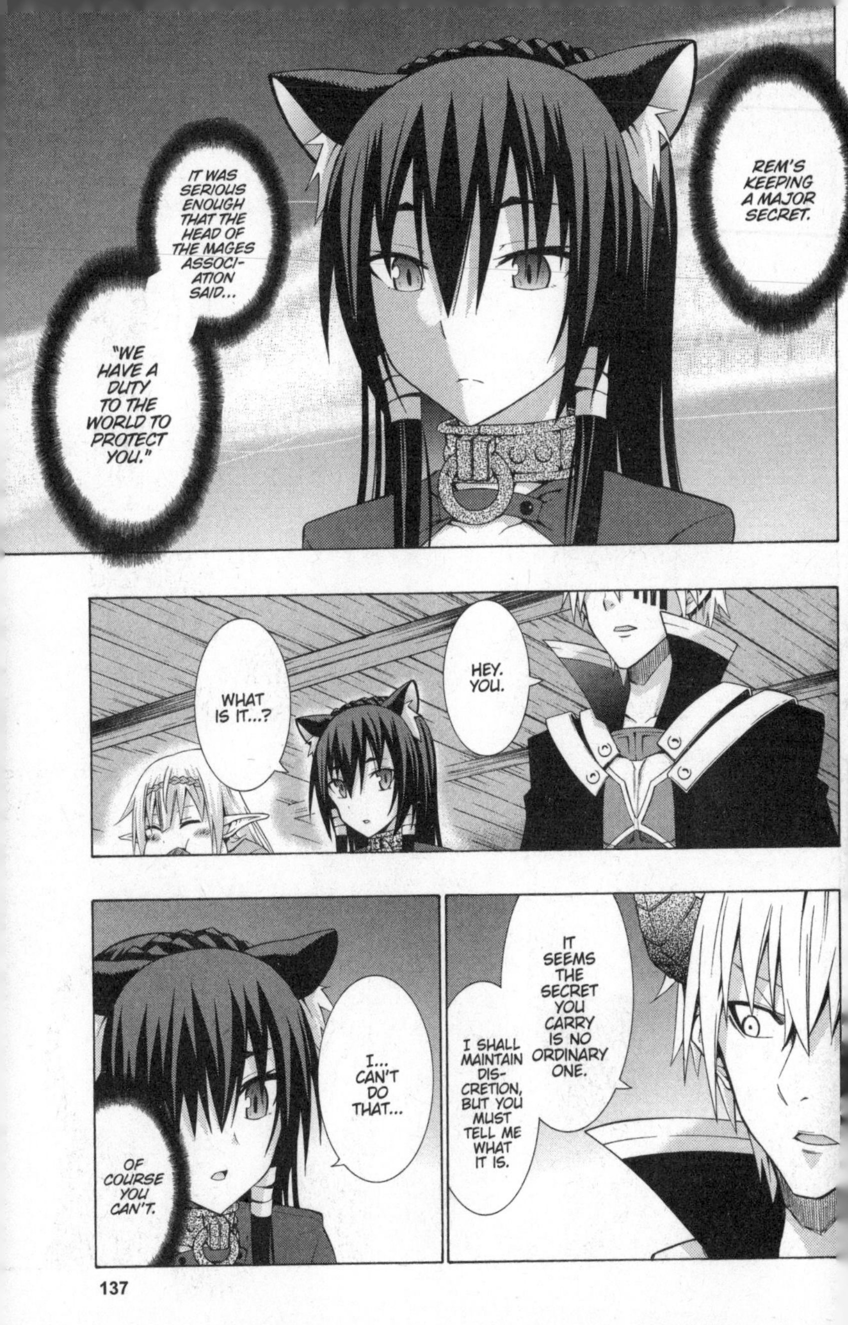
REM'S KEEPING A MAJOR SECRET.
IT WAS SERIOUS ENOUGH THAT THE HEAD OF THE MAGES ASSOCIATION SAID...
"WE HAVE A DUTY TO THE WORLD TO PROTECT YOU."
HEY. YOU.
WHAT IS IT...?
IT SEEMS THE SECRET YOU CARRY IS NO ORDINARY ONE.
I SHALL MAINTAIN DISCRETION, BUT YOU MUST TELL ME WHAT IT IS.
I... CAN'T DO THAT...
OF COURSE YOU CAN'T.

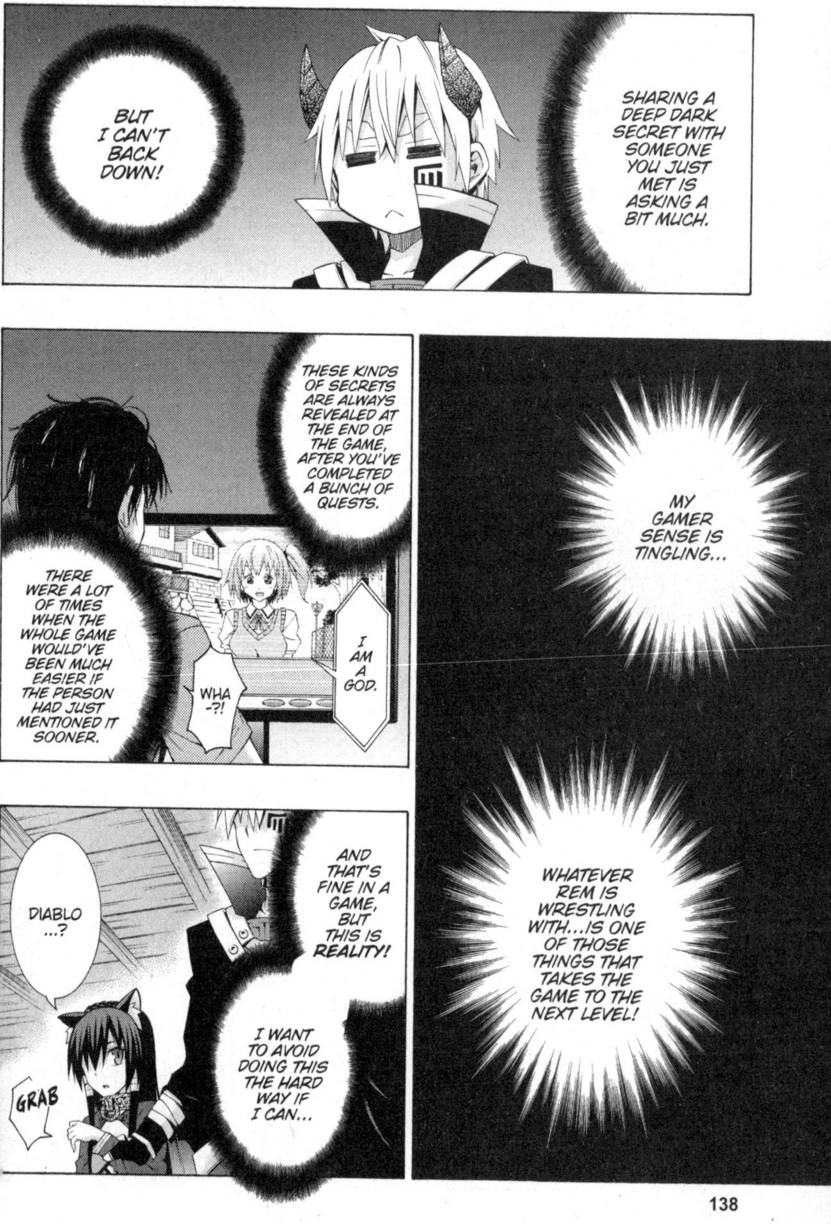
SHARING A DEEP DARK SECRET WITH SOMEONE YOU JUST MET IS ASKING A BIT MUCH.
BUT I CAN'T BACK DOWN!
MY GAMER SENSE IS TINGLING...
WHATEVER REM IS WRESTLING WITH...IS ONE OF THOSE THINGS THAT TAKES THE GAME TO THE NEXT LEVEL!
THESE KINDS OF SECRETS ARE ALWAYS REVEALED AT THE END OF THE GAME, AFTER YOU'VE COMPLETED A BUNCH OF QUESTS.
THERE WERE A LOT OF TIMES WHEN THE WHOLE GAME WOULD'VE BEEN MUCH EASIER IF THE PERSON HAD JUST MENTIONED IT SOONER.
I AM A GOD.
WHA-?!
AND THAT'S FINE IN A GAME, BUT THIS IS **REALITY**!
I WANT TO AVOID DOING THIS THE HARD WAY IF I CAN...
DIABLO ...?
GRAB

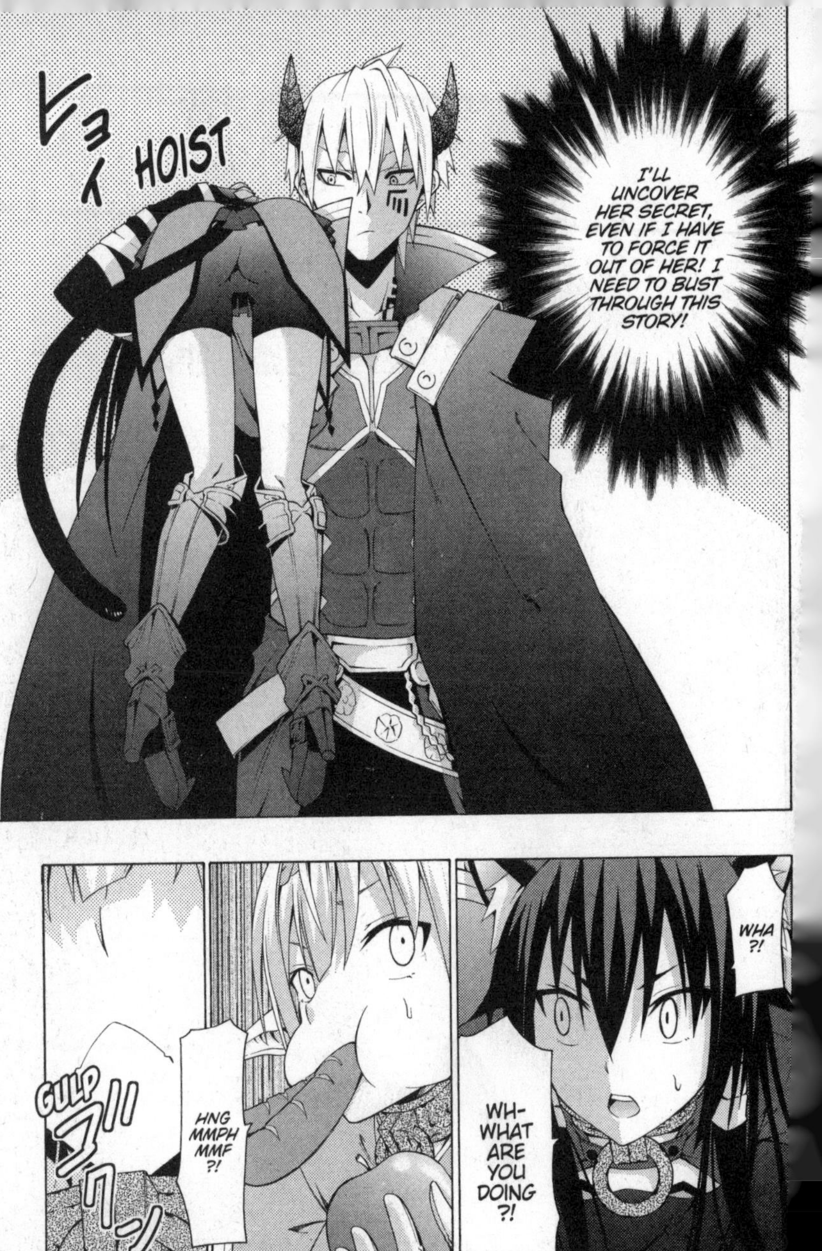
HOIST
I'LL UNCOVER HER SECRET, EVEN IF I HAVE TO FORCE IT OUT OF HER! I NEED TO BUST THROUGH THIS STORY!
WHA?!
WH-WHAT ARE YOU DOING?!
HNG MMPH MMF?!
GULP

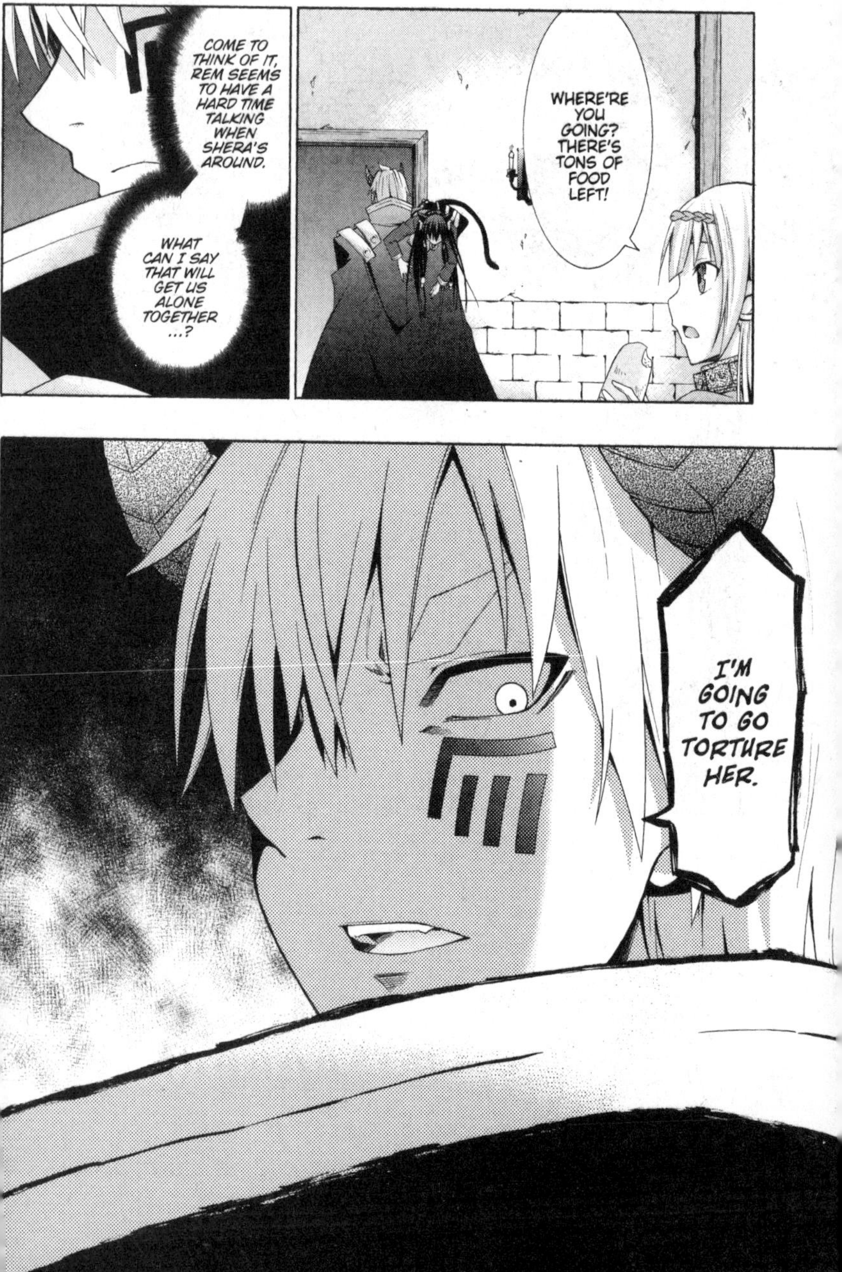
WHERE'RE YOU GOING? THERE'S TONS OF FOOD LEFT!
COME TO THINK OF IT, REM SEEMS TO HAVE A HARD TIME TALKING WHEN SHERA'S AROUND.
WHAT CAN I SAY THAT WILL GET US ALONE TOGETHER ...?
I'M GOING TO GO TORTURE HER.

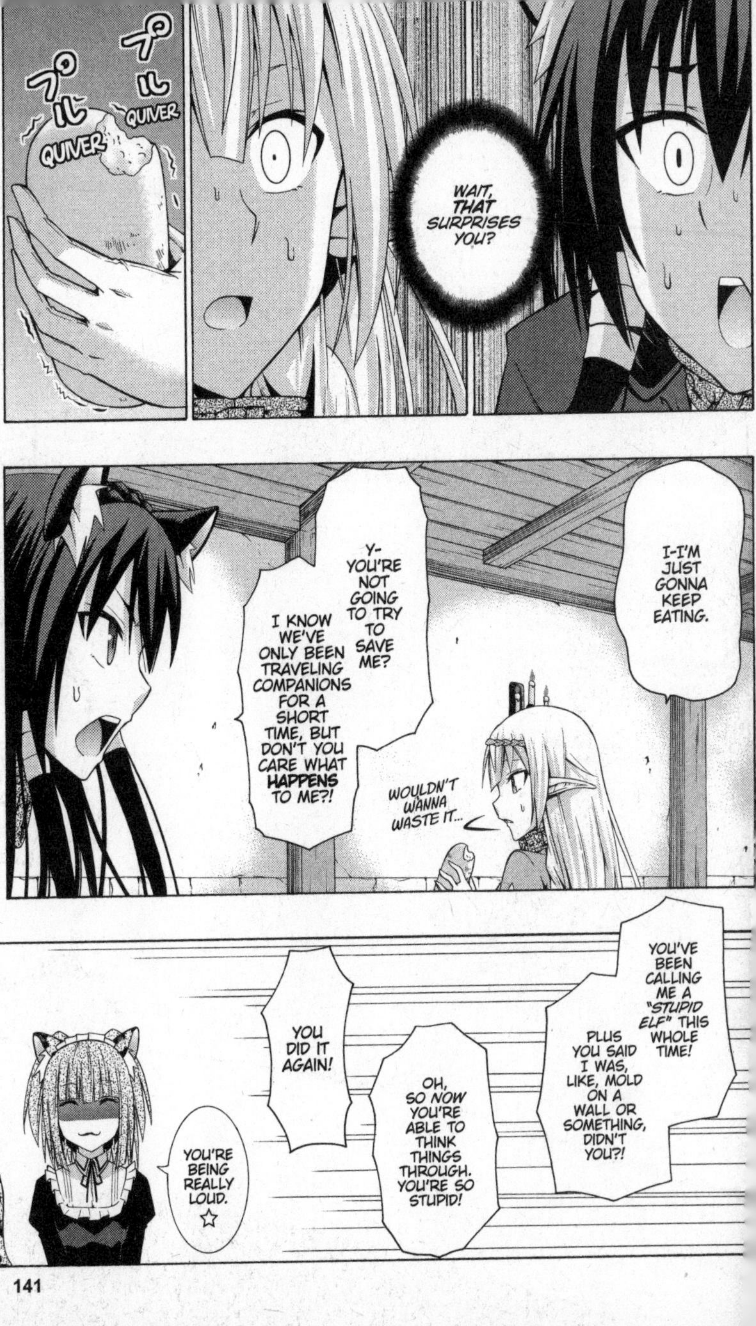
WAIT, THAT SURPRISES YOU?
プル QUIVER
プル QUIVER
I-I'M JUST GONNA KEEP EATING.
WOULDN'T WANNA WASTE IT...
Y-YOU'RE NOT GOING TO TRY TO SAVE ME?
I KNOW WE'VE ONLY BEEN TRAVELING COMPANIONS FOR A SHORT TIME, BUT DON'T YOU CARE WHAT HAPPENS TO ME?!
YOU'VE BEEN CALLING ME A "STUPID ELF" THIS WHOLE TIME!
PLUS YOU SAID I WAS, LIKE, MOLD ON A WALL OR SOMETHING, DIDN'T YOU?!
YOU DID IT AGAIN!
OH, SO NOW YOU'RE ABLE TO THINK THINGS THROUGH. YOU'RE SO STUPID!
YOU'RE BEING REALLY LOUD. ☆

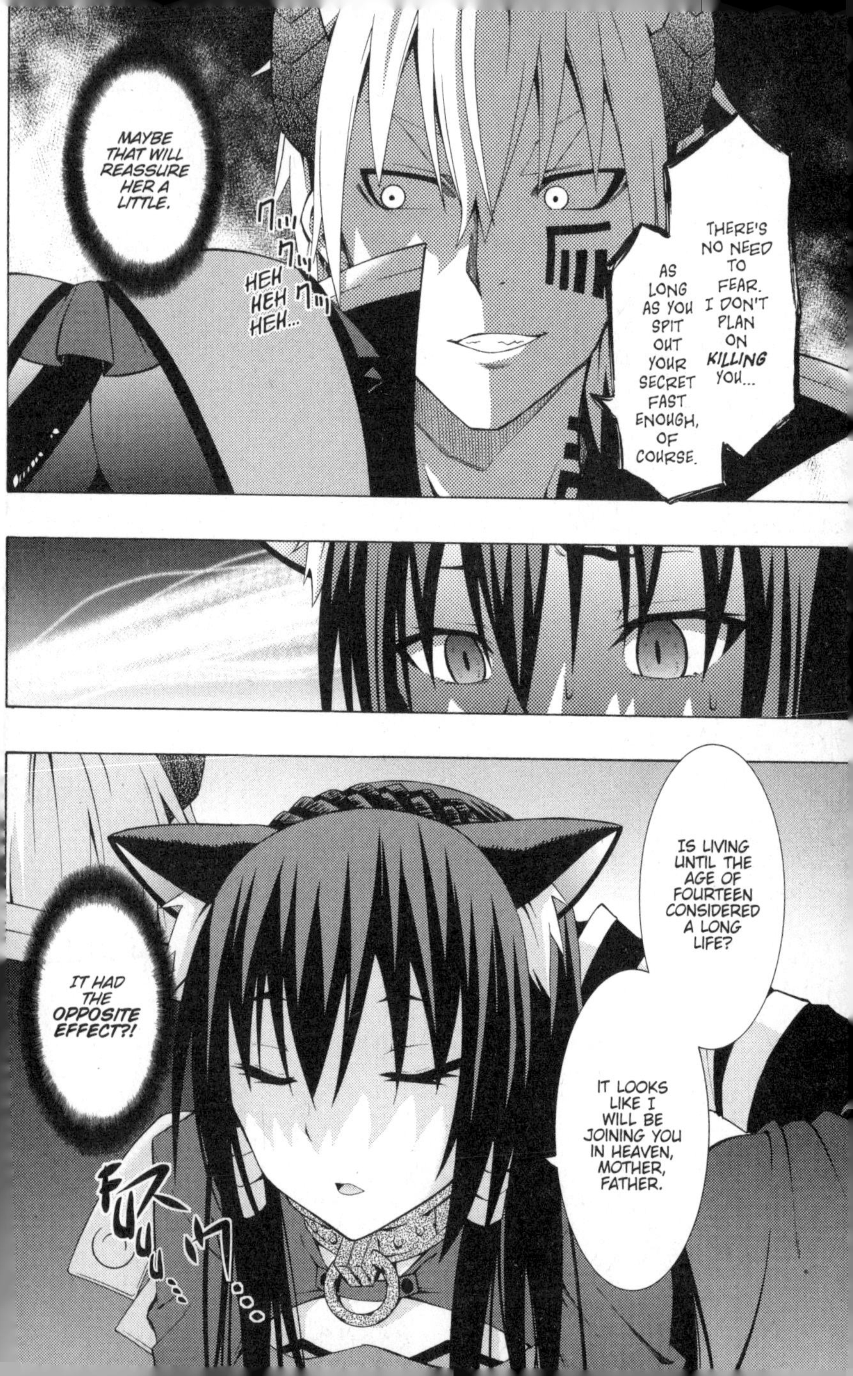
THERE'S NO NEED TO FEAR. I DON'T PLAN ON **KILLING** YOU...
AS LONG AS YOU SPIT OUT YOUR SECRET FAST ENOUGH, OF COURSE.
HEH HEH HEH...
MAYBE THAT WILL REASSURE HER A LITTLE.
IS LIVING UNTIL THE AGE OF FOURTEEN CONSIDERED A LONG LIFE?
IT LOOKS LIKE I WILL BE JOINING YOU IN HEAVEN, MOTHER, FATHER.
IT HAD THE **OPPOSITE EFFECT?!**
FUUU...

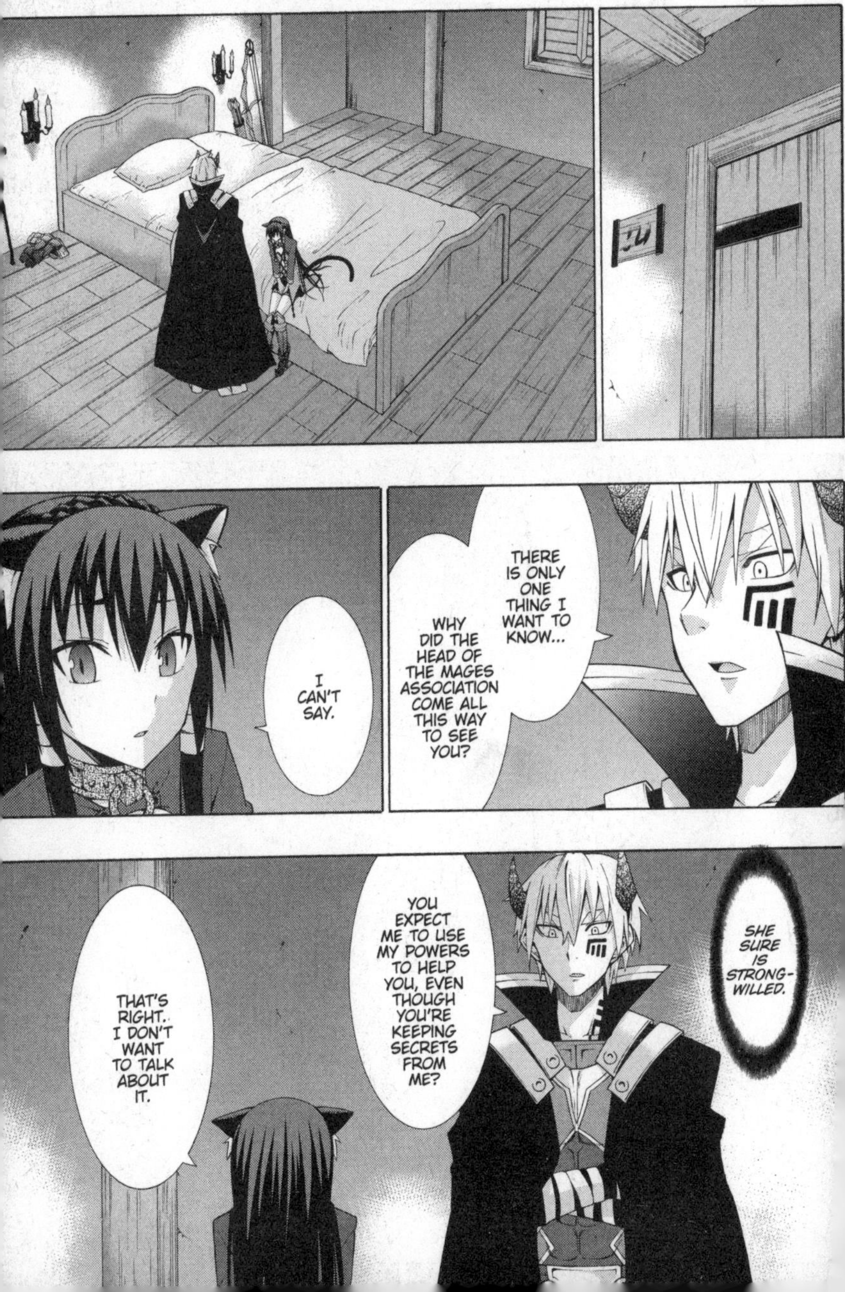
THERE IS ONLY ONE THING I WANT TO KNOW...
WHY DID THE HEAD OF THE MAGES ASSOCIATION COME ALL THIS WAY TO SEE YOU?
I CAN'T SAY.
SHE SURE IS STRONG-WILLED.
YOU EXPECT ME TO USE MY POWERS TO HELP YOU, EVEN THOUGH YOU'RE KEEPING SECRETS FROM ME?
THAT'S RIGHT. I DON'T WANT TO TALK ABOUT IT.

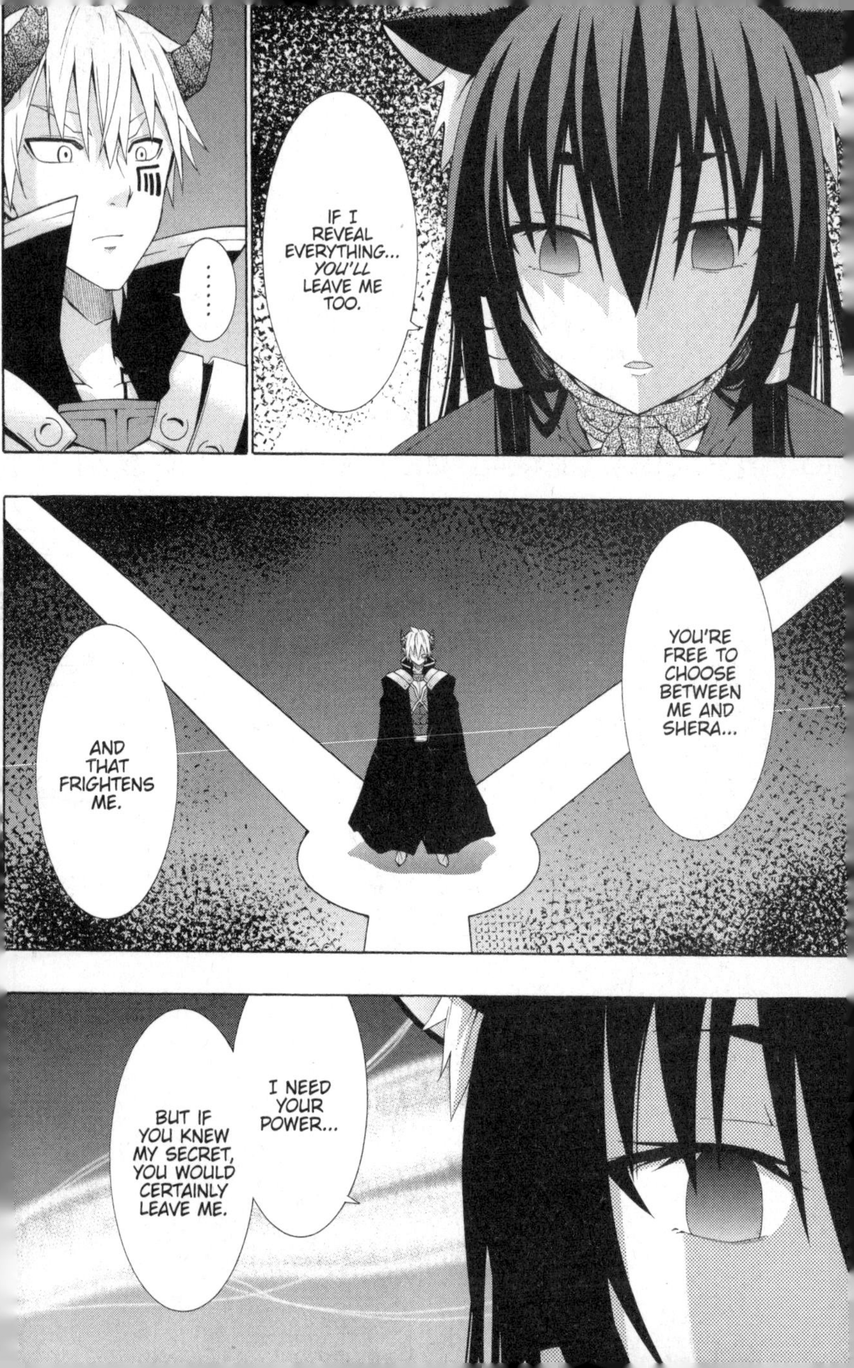
IF I REVEAL EVERYTHING... YOU'LL LEAVE ME TOO.
......
YOU'RE FREE TO CHOOSE BETWEEN ME AND SHERA...
AND THAT FRIGHTENS ME.
I NEED YOUR POWER...
BUT IF YOU KNEW MY SECRET, YOU WOULD CERTAINLY LEAVE ME.

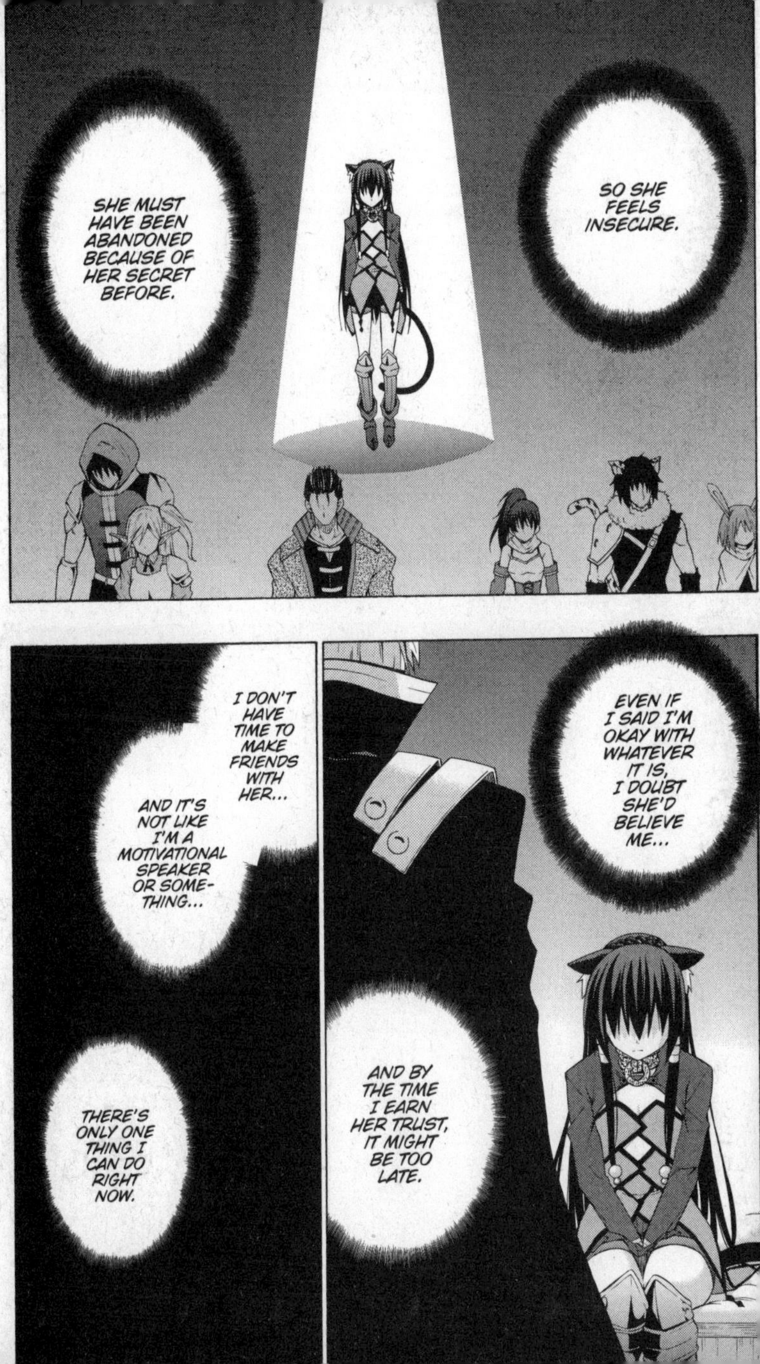
SO SHE FEELS INSECURE.
SHE MUST HAVE BEEN ABANDONED BECAUSE OF HER SECRET BEFORE.
EVEN IF I SAID I'M OKAY WITH WHATEVER IT IS, I DOUBT SHE'D BELIEVE ME...
AND BY THE TIME I EARN HER TRUST, IT MIGHT BE TOO LATE.
I DON'T HAVE TIME TO MAKE FRIENDS WITH HER...
AND IT'S NOT LIKE I'M A MOTIVATIONAL SPEAKER OR SOME-THING...
THERE'S ONLY ONE THING I CAN DO RIGHT NOW.

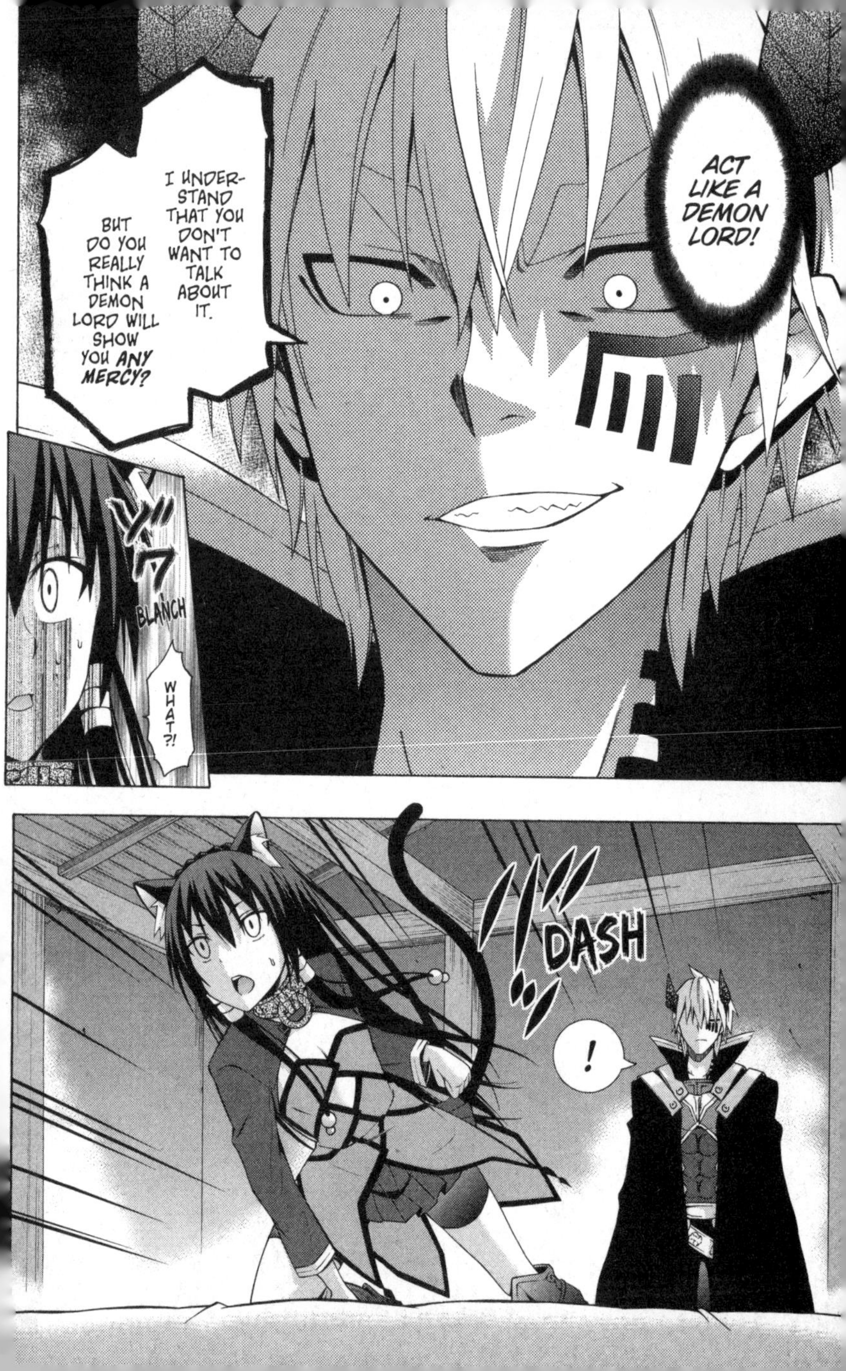

ACT LIKE A DEMON LORD!
I UNDERSTAND THAT YOU DON'T WANT TO TALK ABOUT IT.
BUT DO YOU REALLY THINK A DEMON LORD WILL SHOW YOU ANY MERCY?
ゾワ
BLANCH
WHAT?!
DASH
!

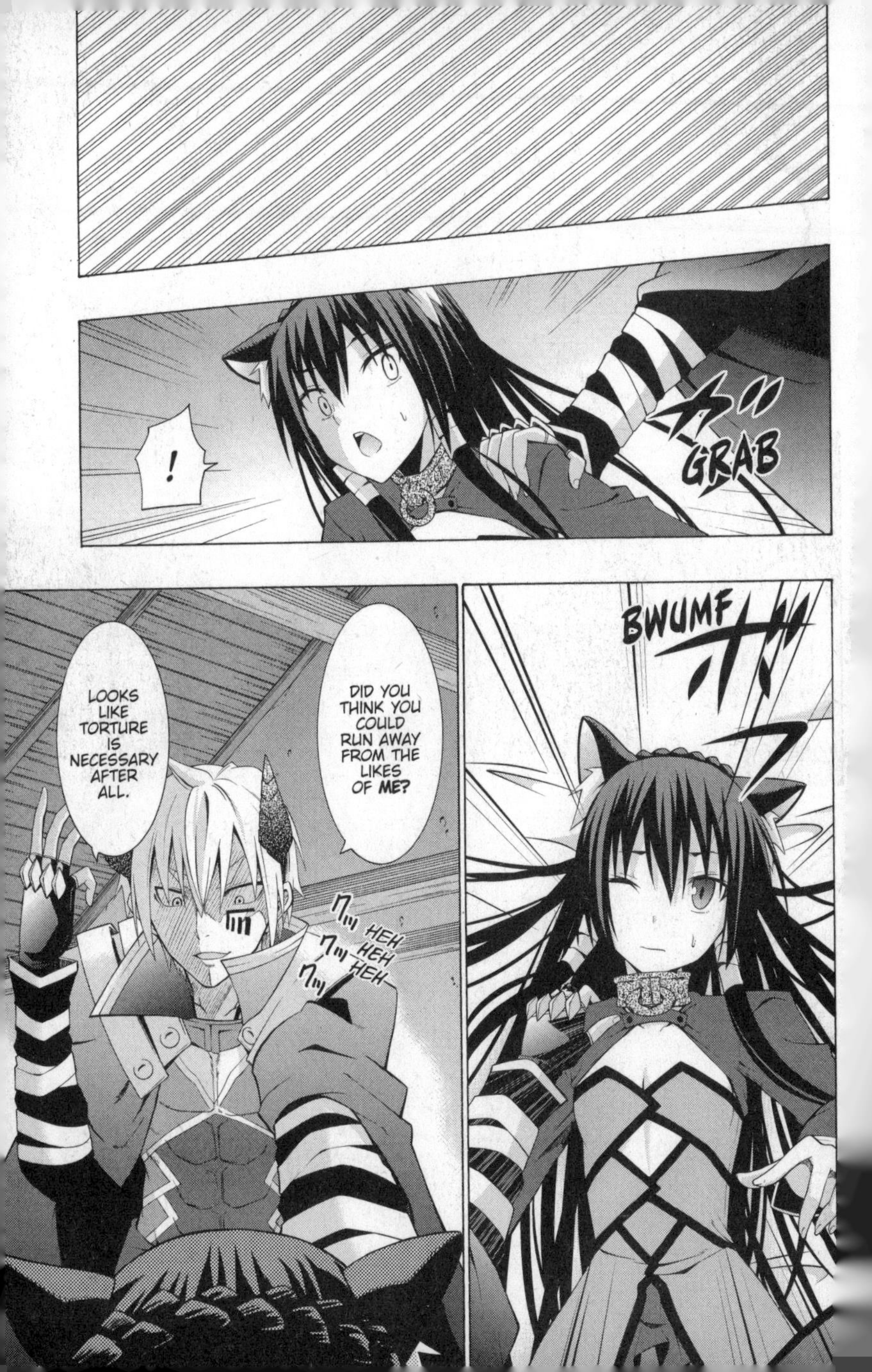
GRAB
!
BWUMF
DID YOU THINK YOU COULD RUN AWAY FROM THE LIKES OF ME?
LOOKS LIKE TORTURE IS NECESSARY AFTER ALL.
HEH HEH HEH

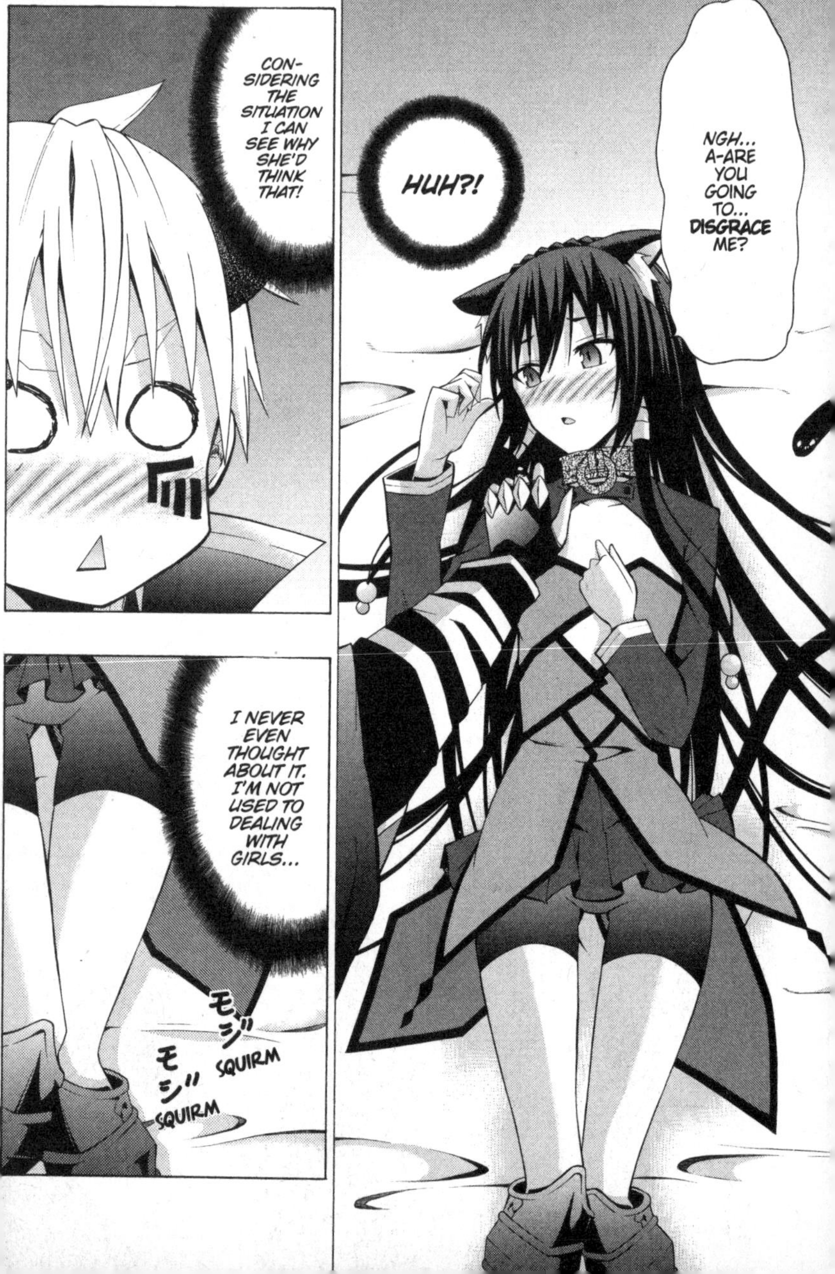
NGH... A-ARE YOU GOING TO... DISGRACE ME?
HUH?!
CON-SIDERING THE SITUATION I CAN SEE WHY SHE'D THINK THAT!
I NEVER EVEN THOUGHT ABOUT IT. I'M NOT USED TO DEALING WITH GIRLS...
モジ SQUIRM
モジ SQUIRM

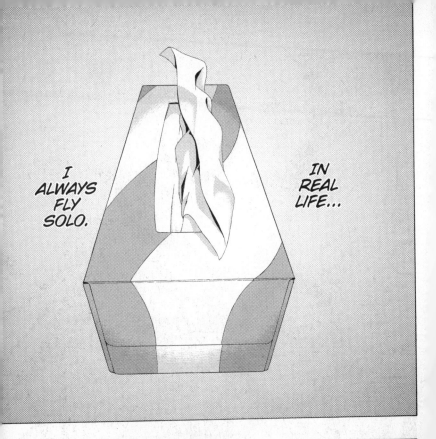

I ALWAYS FLY SOLO.

IN REAL LIFE...

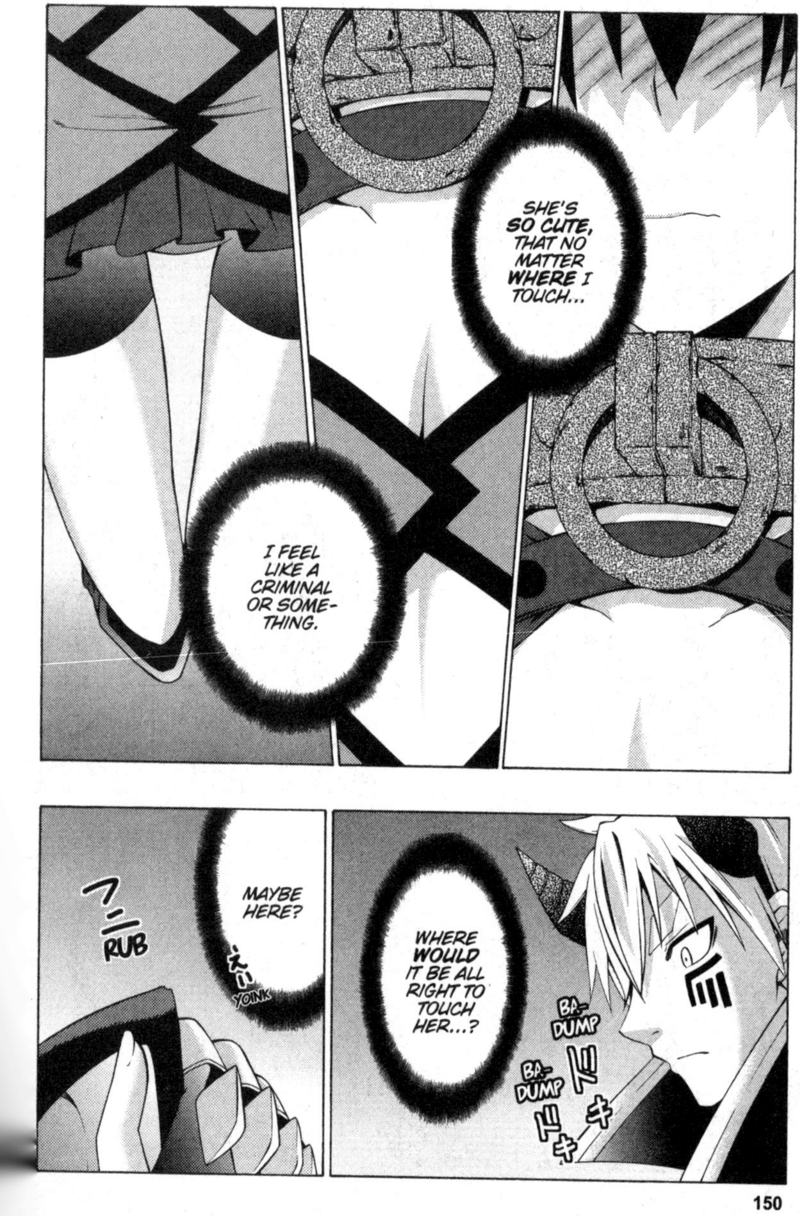
SHE'S **SO CUTE,** THAT NO MATTER **WHERE** I TOUCH...
I FEEL LIKE A CRIMINAL OR SOME-THING.
WHERE **WOULD** IT BE ALL RIGHT TO TOUCH HER...?
BA-DUMP
BA-DUMP
MAYBE HERE?
YOINK
RUB

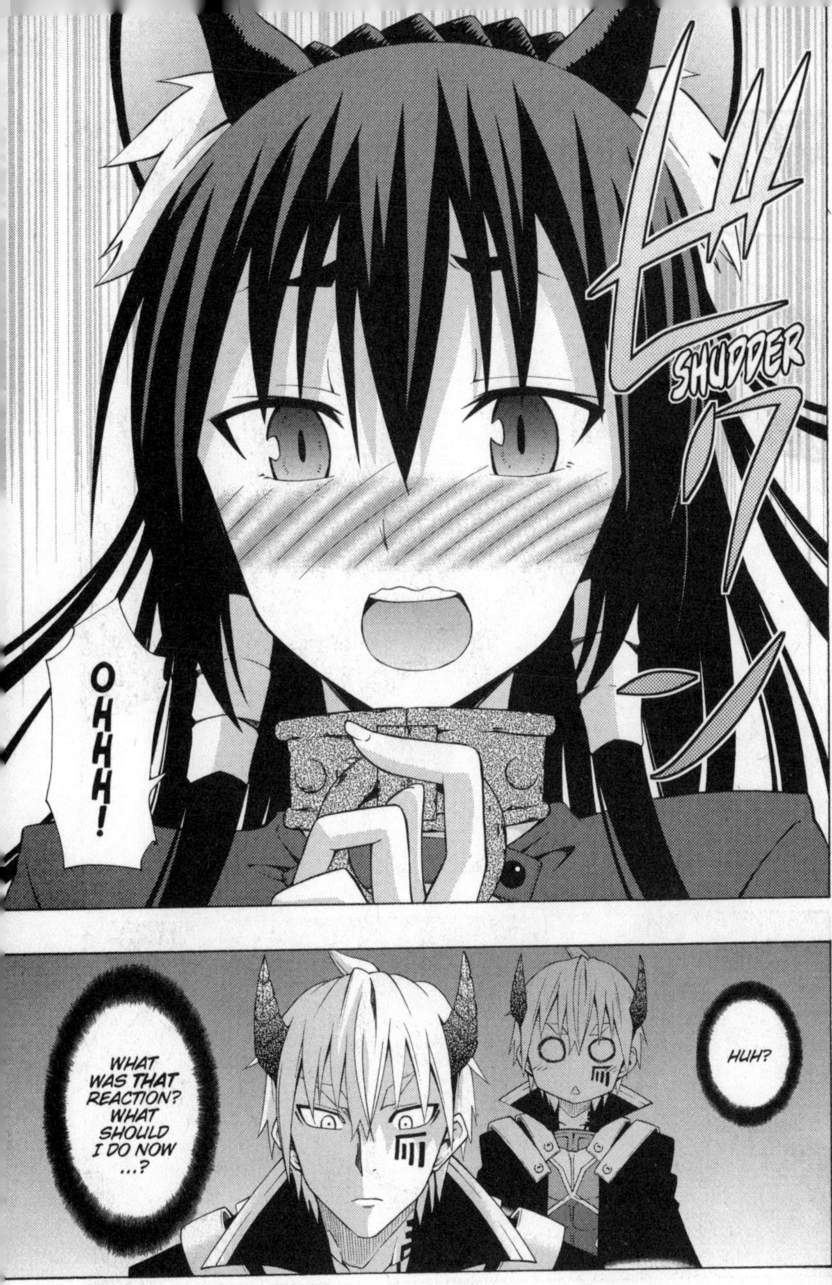
SHUDDER
OHHHH!
HUH?
WHAT WAS THAT REACTION? WHAT SHOULD I DO NOW ...?

4 BEING SUMMONED IV

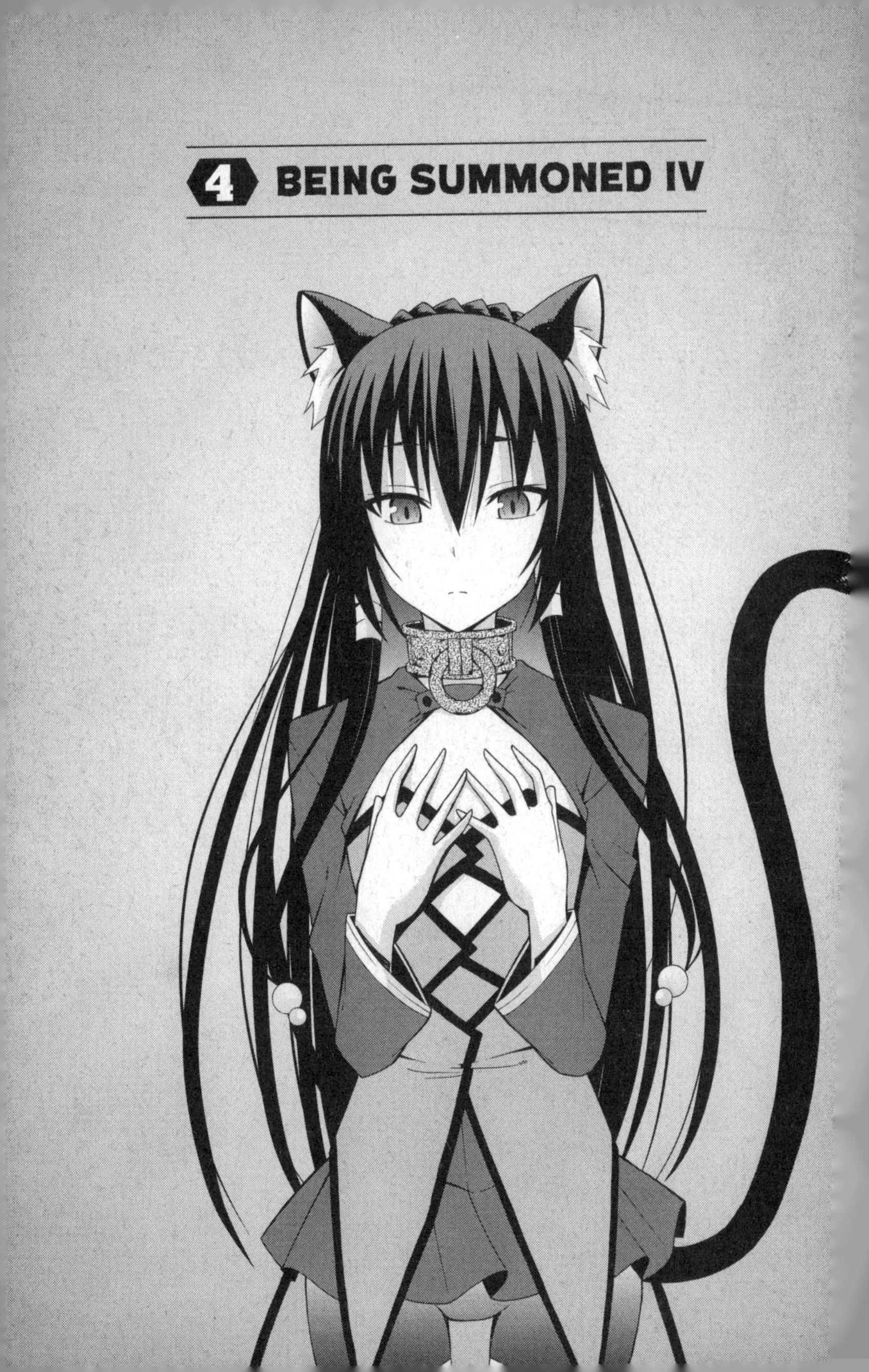

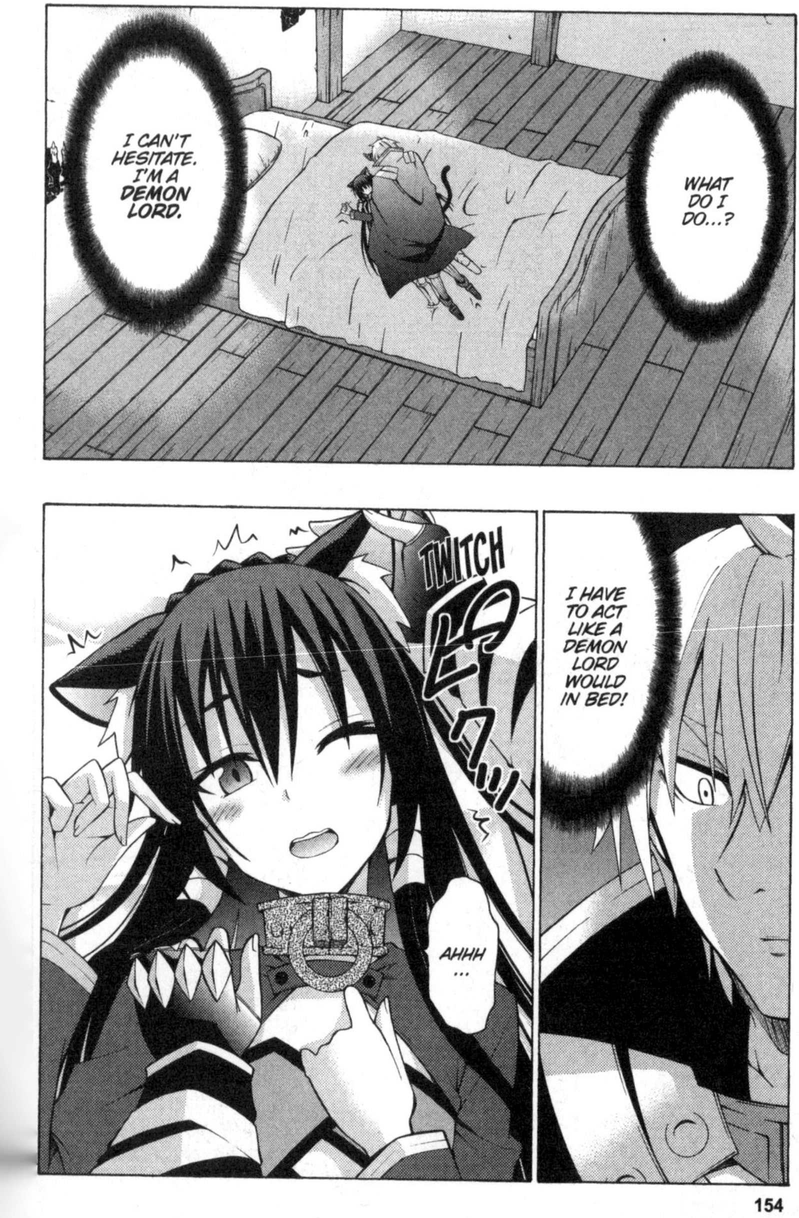
WHAT DO I DO...?
I CAN'T HESITATE. I'M A DEMON LORD.
I HAVE TO ACT LIKE A DEMON LORD WOULD IN BED!
TWITCH
AHHH ...

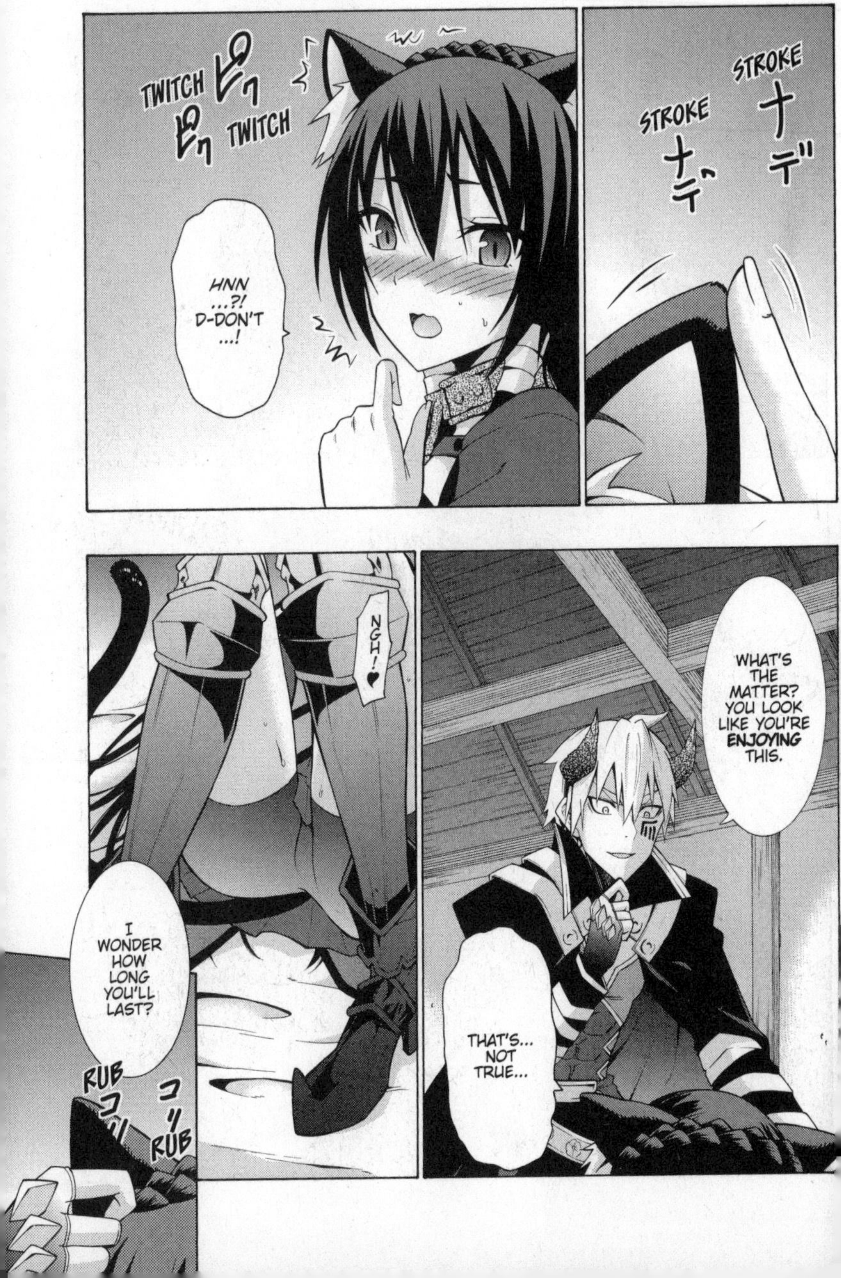
STROKE ナデ
STROKE ナデ
TWITCH ピク
ピク TWITCH
HNN ...?! D-DON'T ...!
WHAT'S THE MATTER? YOU LOOK LIKE YOU'RE **ENJOYING** THIS.
THAT'S... NOT TRUE...
NGH!♥
I WONDER HOW LONG YOU'LL LAST?
RUB コリ
コリ RUB

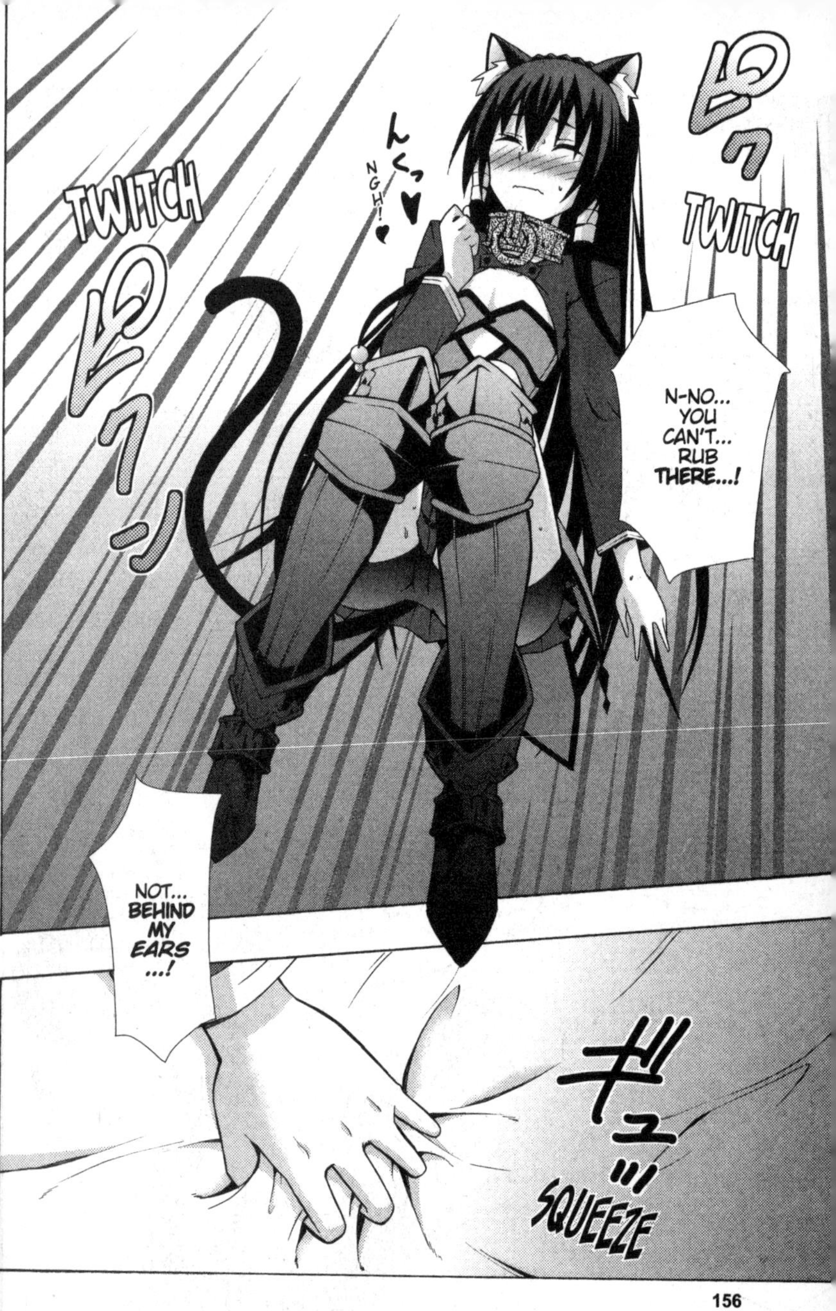
ピクッ
TWITCH
んくっ
NGH!
N-NO... YOU CAN'T... RUB THERE...!
TWITCH
NOT... BEHIND MY EARS...!
ギュッ
SQUEEZE

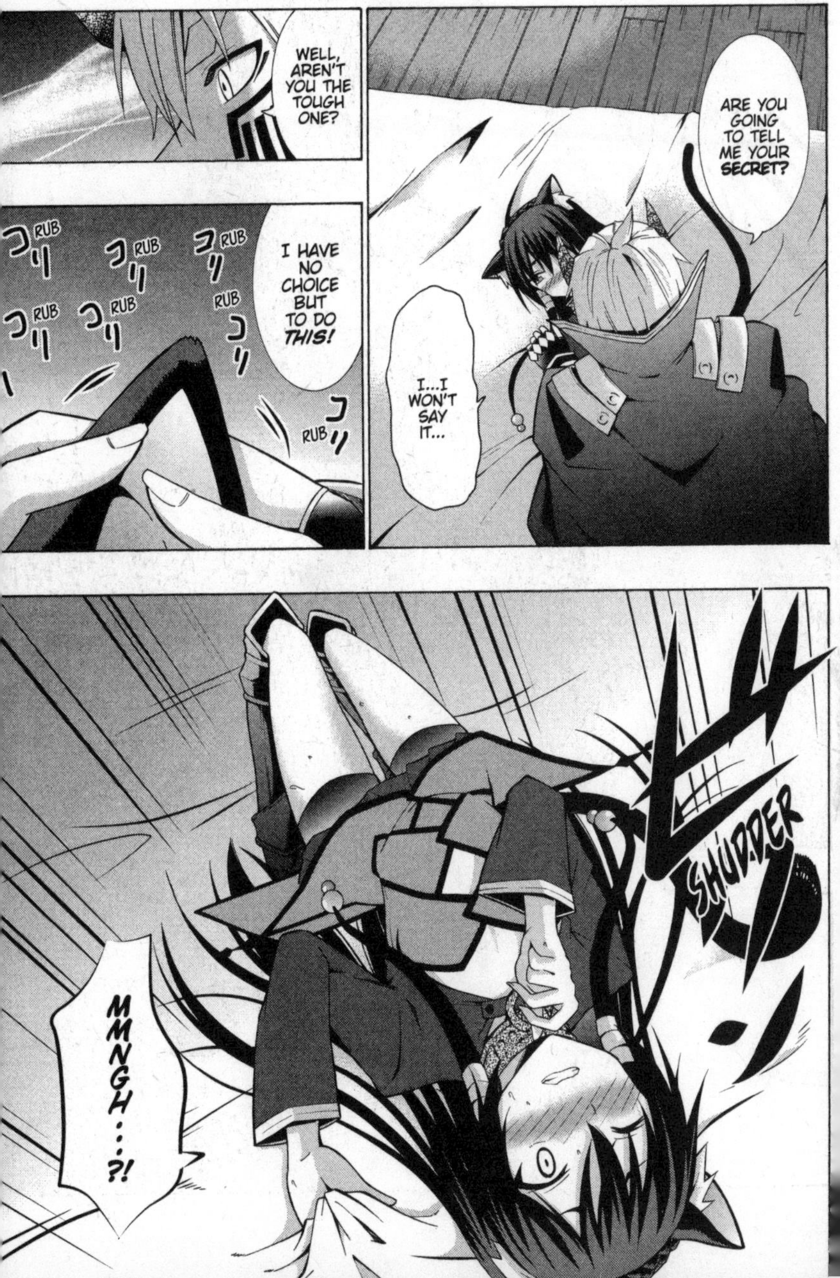
ARE YOU GOING TO TELL ME YOUR SECRET?
I...I WON'T SAY IT...
WELL, AREN'T YOU THE TOUGH ONE?
I HAVE NO CHOICE BUT TO DO THIS!
コリ RUB
コリ RUB
コリ RUB
コリ RUB
コリ RUB
コリ RUB
コリ RUB
SHUDDER
MMNGH...?!

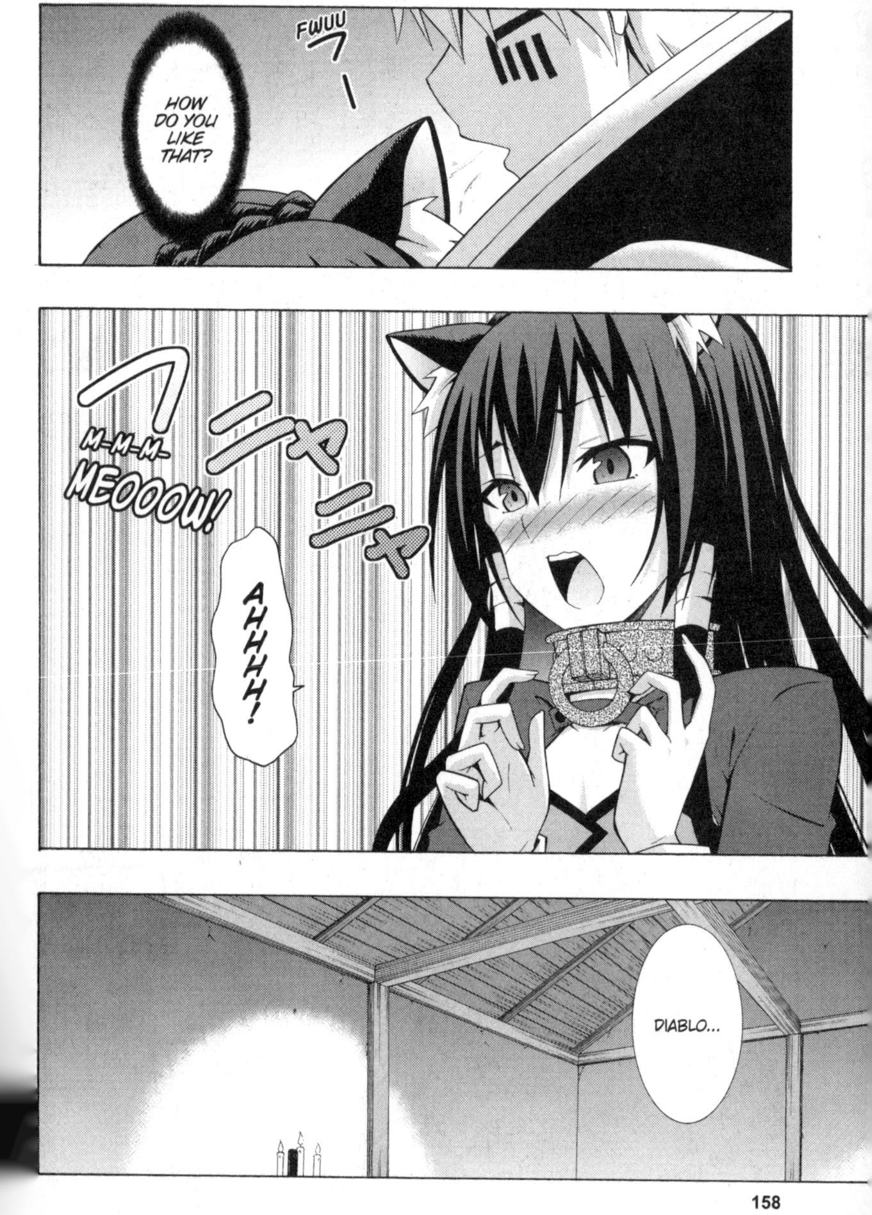
FWUU
HOW DO YOU LIKE THAT?
M-M-M-MEOOOW!
AHHHH!
DIABLO...

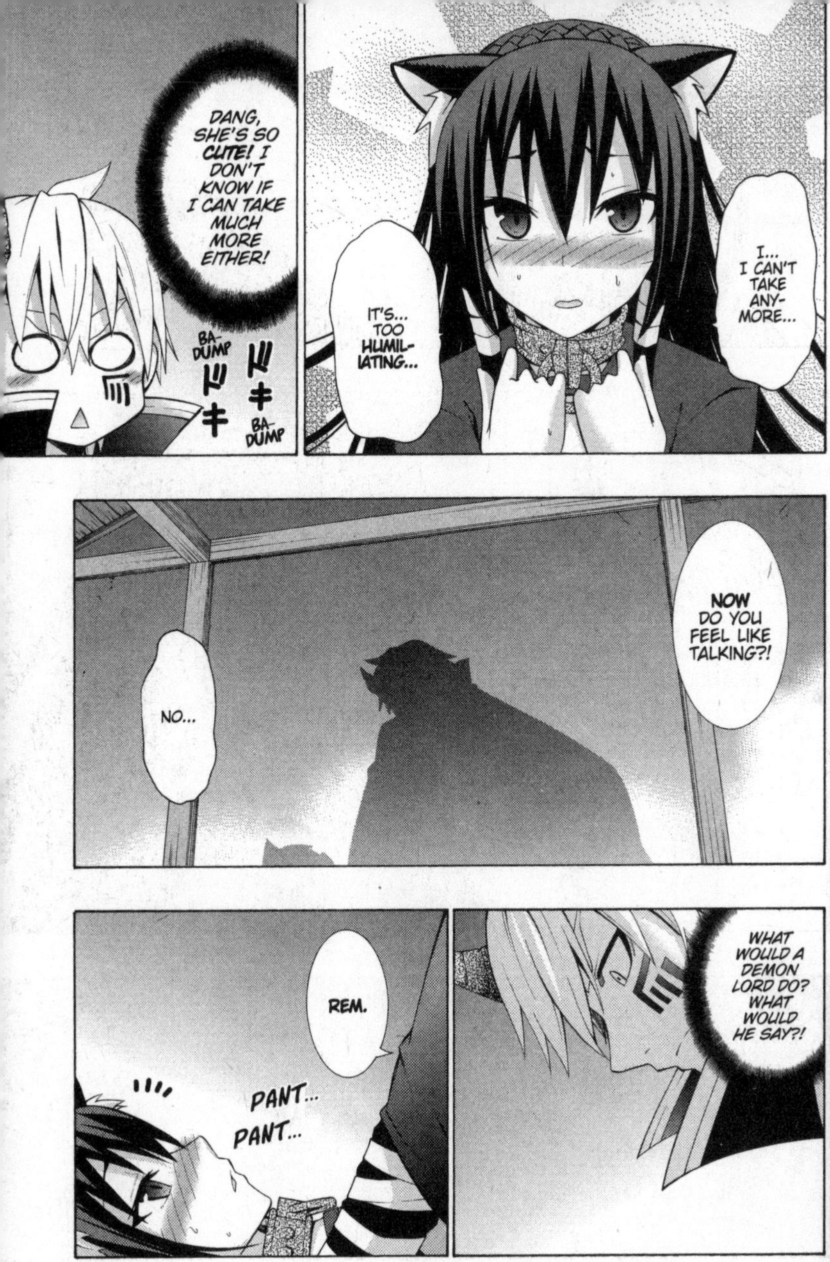
I... I CAN'T TAKE ANY-MORE...
IT'S... TOO HUMIL-IATING...
DANG, SHE'S SO CUTE! I DON'T KNOW IF I CAN TAKE MUCH MORE EITHER!
ドキ
BA-DUMP
ドキ
BA-DUMP
NOW DO YOU FEEL LIKE TALKING?!
NO...
WHAT WOULD A DEMON LORD DO? WHAT WOULD HE SAY?!
REM.
!!!
PANT... PANT...

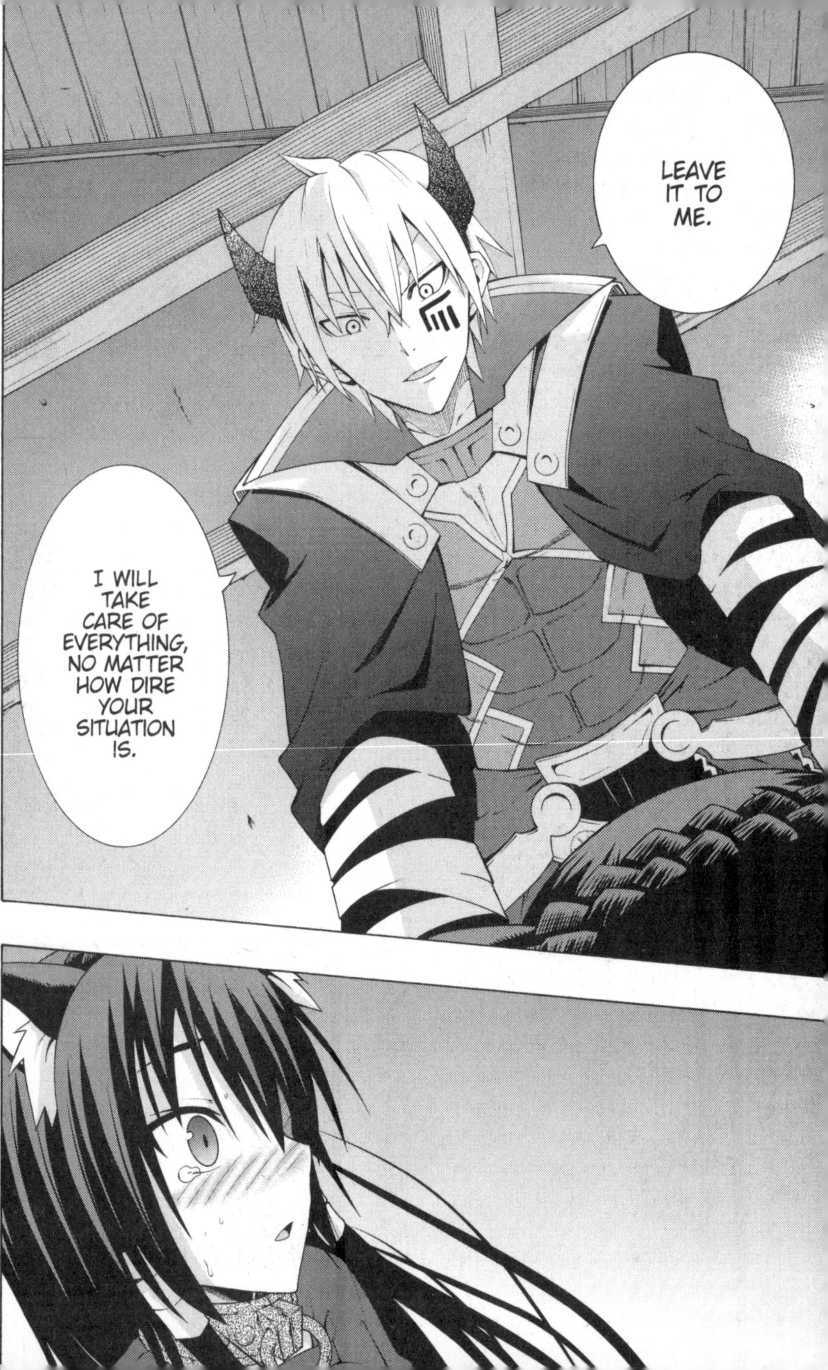
LEAVE IT TO ME.
I WILL TAKE CARE OF EVERYTHING, NO MATTER HOW DIRE YOUR SITUATION IS.

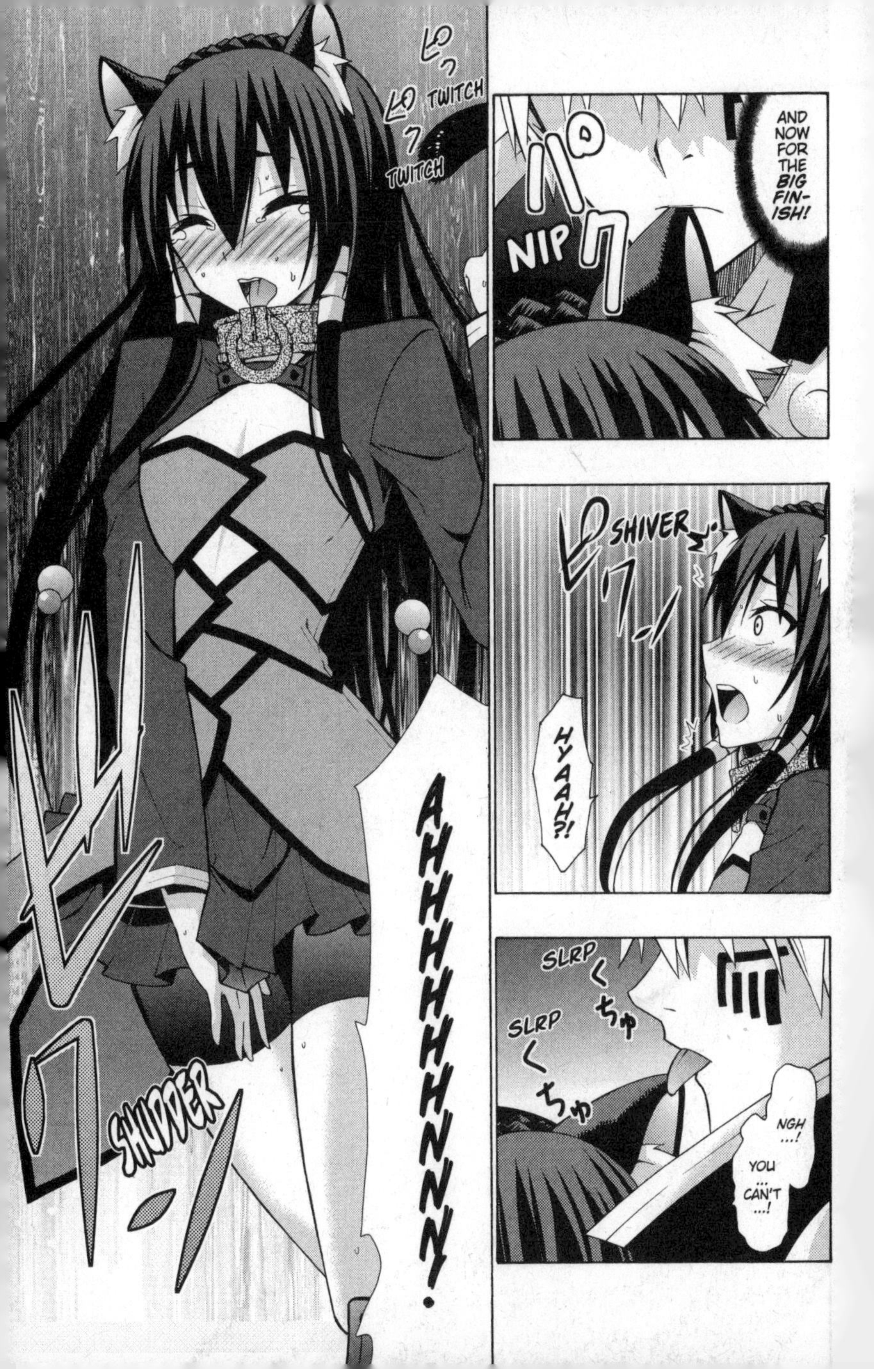
AND NOW FOR THE BIG FIN-ISH!
NIP
パクッ
ビクッ
SHIVER
HYAAAH?!
SLRP
くちゅ
SLRP
くちゅ
NGH ...!
YOU ... CAN'T ...!
ぴっ
ぴっ
TWITCH
TWITCH
AHHHHHHNNN!
ビクッ
SHUDDER

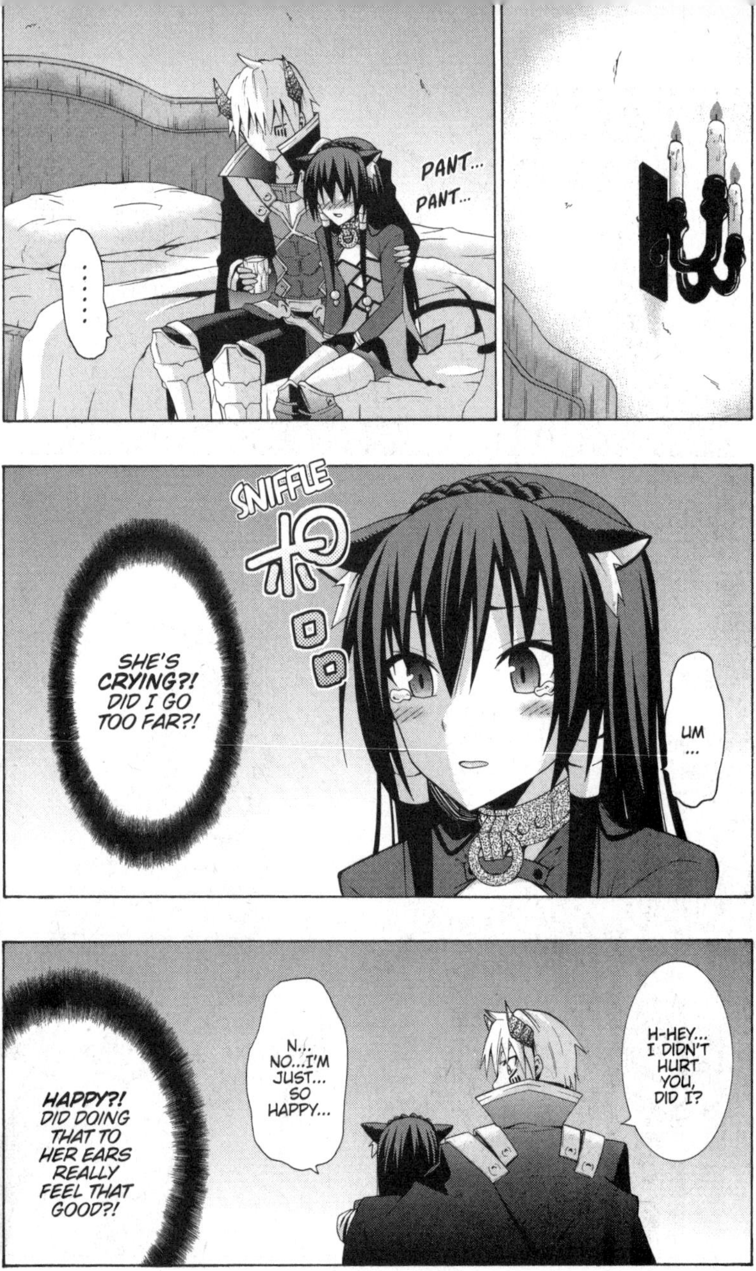
PANT...
PANT...
......
SNIFFLE
ポロ
UM ...
SHE'S CRYING?! DID I GO TOO FAR?!
H-HEY... I DIDN'T HURT YOU, DID I?
N... NO...I'M JUST... SO HAPPY...
HAPPY?! DID DOING THAT TO HER EARS REALLY FEEL THAT GOOD?!

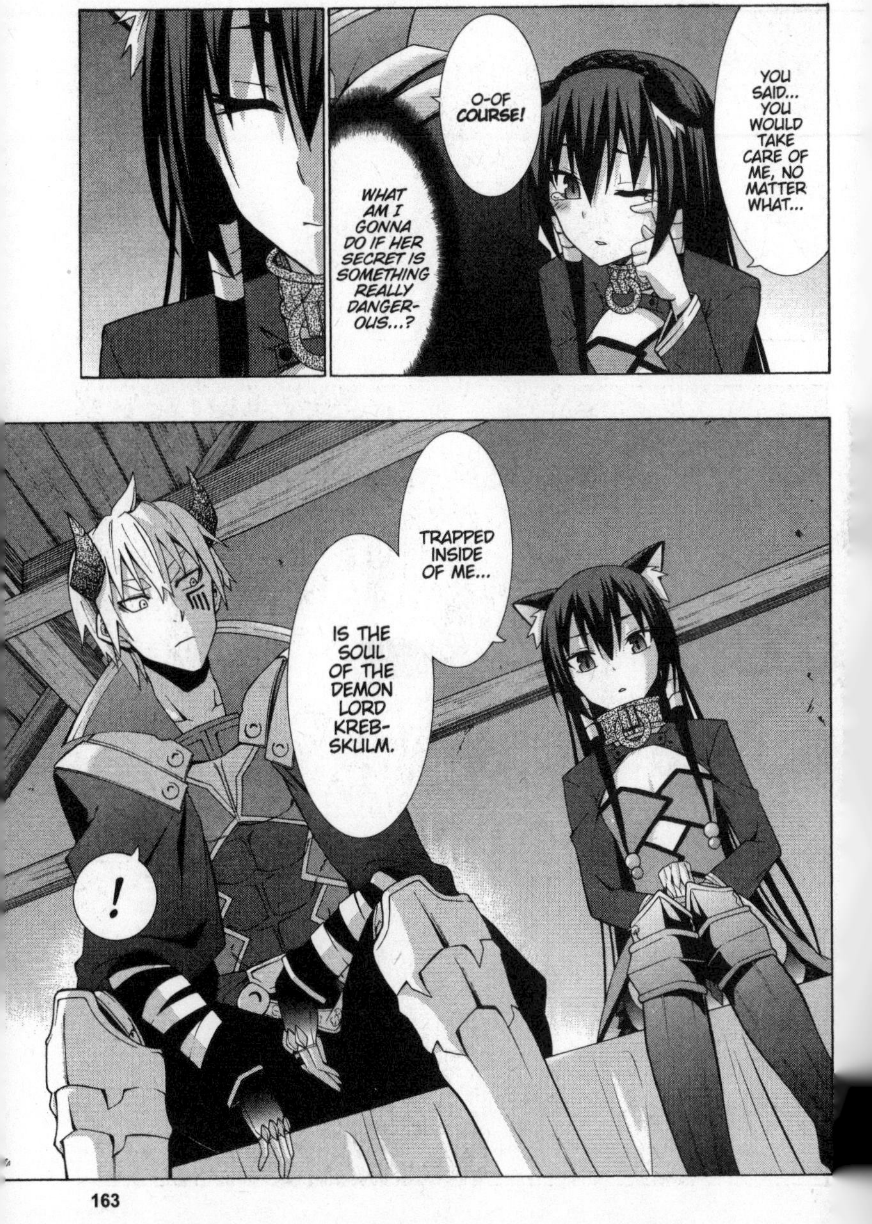
YOU SAID... YOU WOULD TAKE CARE OF ME, NO MATTER WHAT...
O-OF COURSE!
WHAT AM I GONNA DO IF HER SECRET IS SOMETHING REALLY DANGER-OUS...?
TRAPPED INSIDE OF ME...
IS THE SOUL OF THE DEMON LORD KREB-SKULM.
!

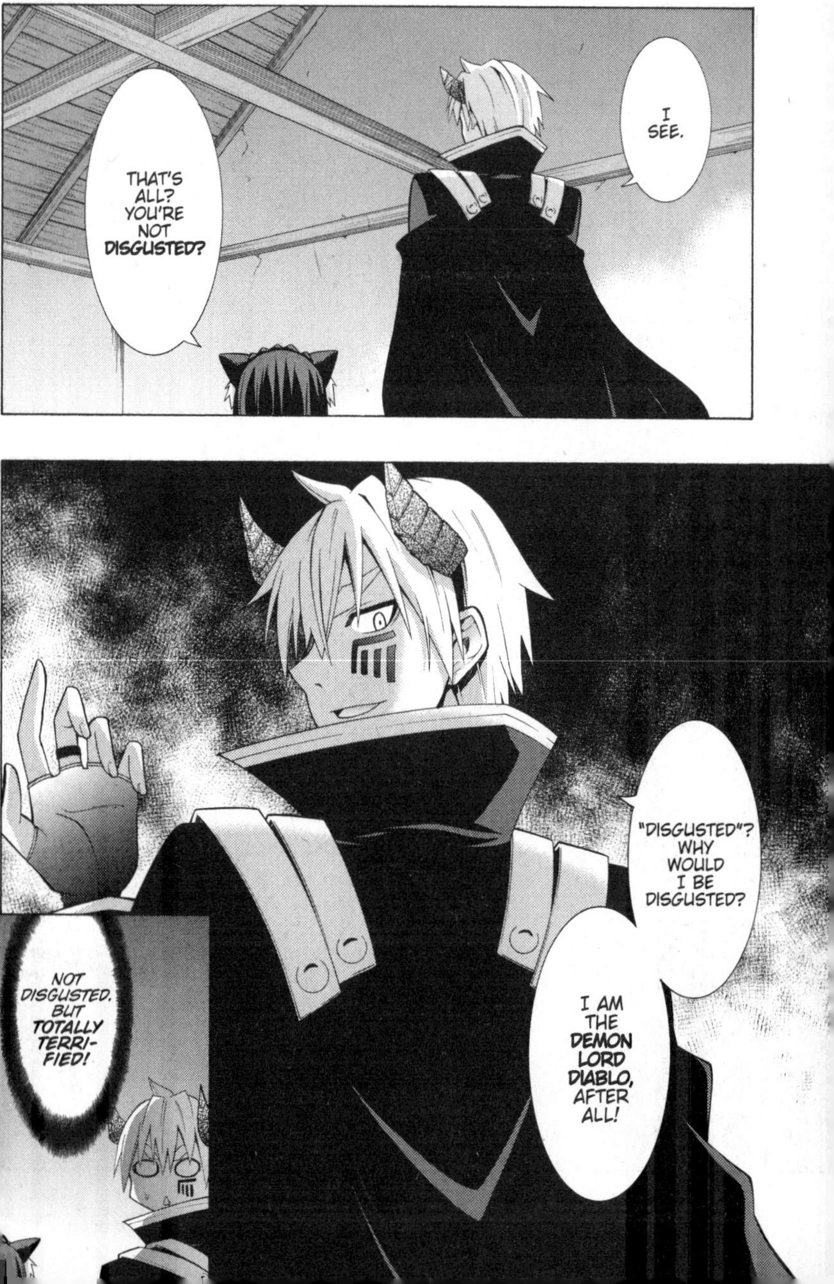
I SEE.
THAT'S ALL? YOU'RE NOT DISGUSTED?
"DISGUSTED"? WHY WOULD I BE DISGUSTED?
I AM THE DEMON LORD DIABLO, AFTER ALL!
NOT DISGUSTED. BUT TOTALLY TERRI-FIED!

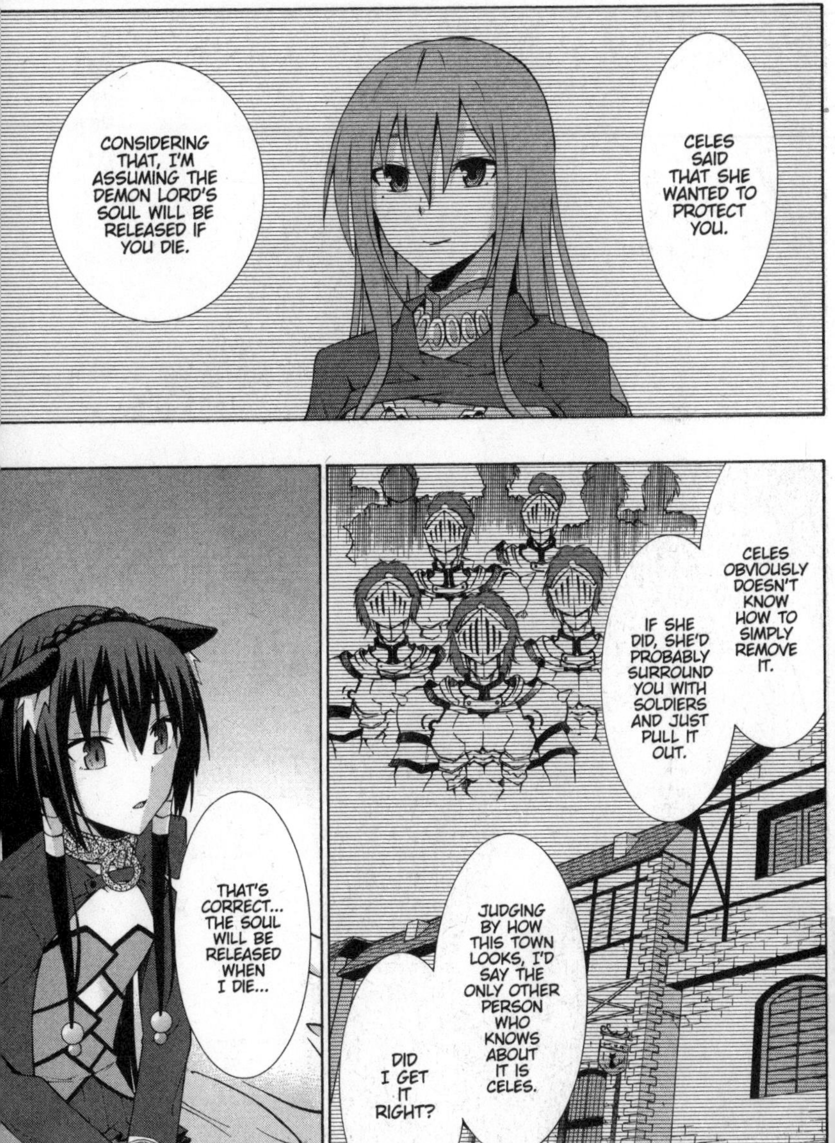
CELES SAID THAT SHE WANTED TO PROTECT YOU.
CONSIDERING THAT, I'M ASSUMING THE DEMON LORD'S SOUL WILL BE RELEASED IF YOU DIE.
CELES OBVIOUSLY DOESN'T KNOW HOW TO SIMPLY REMOVE IT.
IF SHE DID, SHE'D PROBABLY SURROUND YOU WITH SOLDIERS AND JUST PULL IT OUT.
JUDGING BY HOW THIS TOWN LOOKS, I'D SAY THE ONLY OTHER PERSON WHO KNOWS ABOUT IT IS CELES.
DID I GET IT RIGHT?
THAT'S CORRECT... THE SOUL WILL BE RELEASED WHEN I DIE...

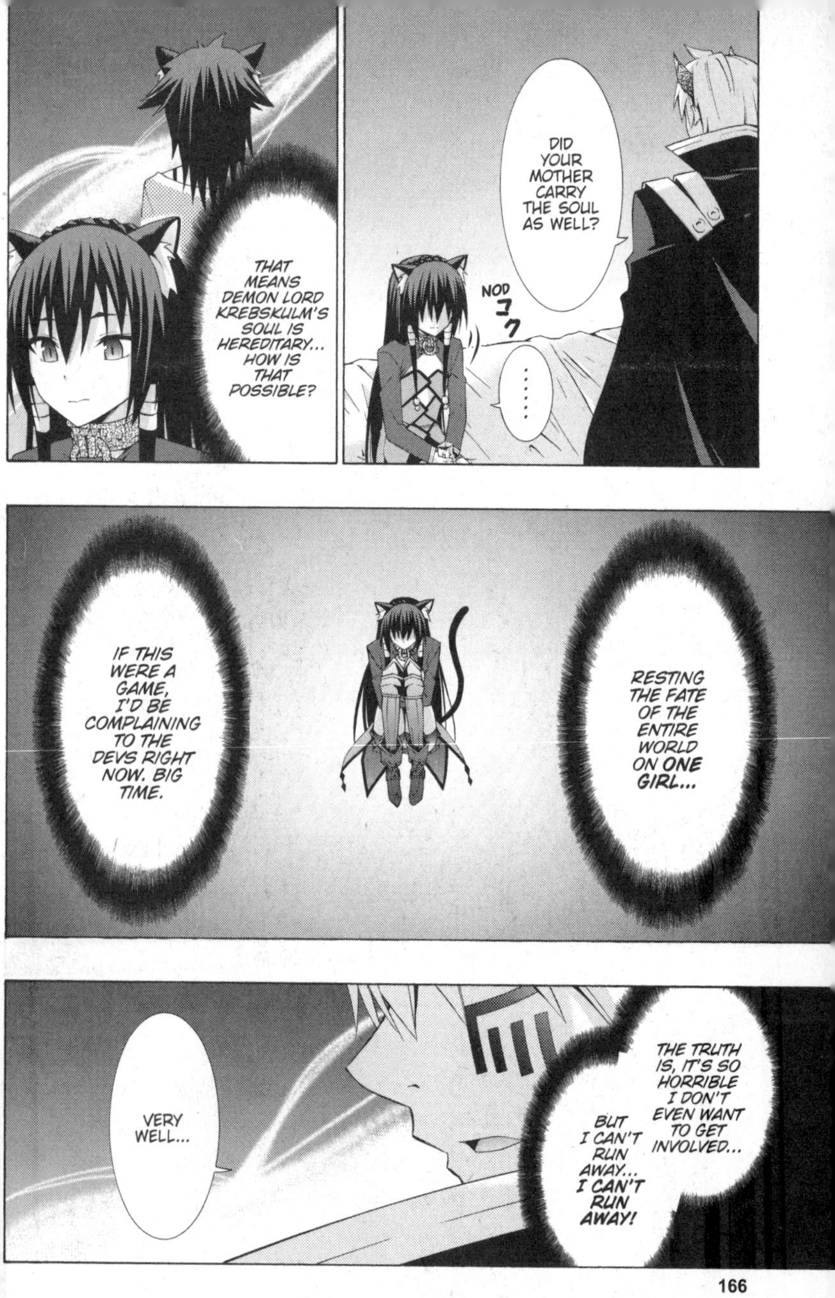
DID YOUR MOTHER CARRY THE SOUL AS WELL?
NOD コク
......
THAT MEANS DEMON LORD KREBSKULM'S SOUL IS HEREDITARY... HOW IS THAT POSSIBLE?
RESTING THE FATE OF THE ENTIRE WORLD ON ONE GIRL...
IF THIS WERE A GAME, I'D BE COMPLAINING TO THE DEVS RIGHT NOW. BIG TIME.
THE TRUTH IS, IT'S SO HORRIBLE I DON'T EVEN WANT TO GET INVOLVED...
BUT I CAN'T RUN AWAY... I CAN'T RUN AWAY!
VERY WELL...

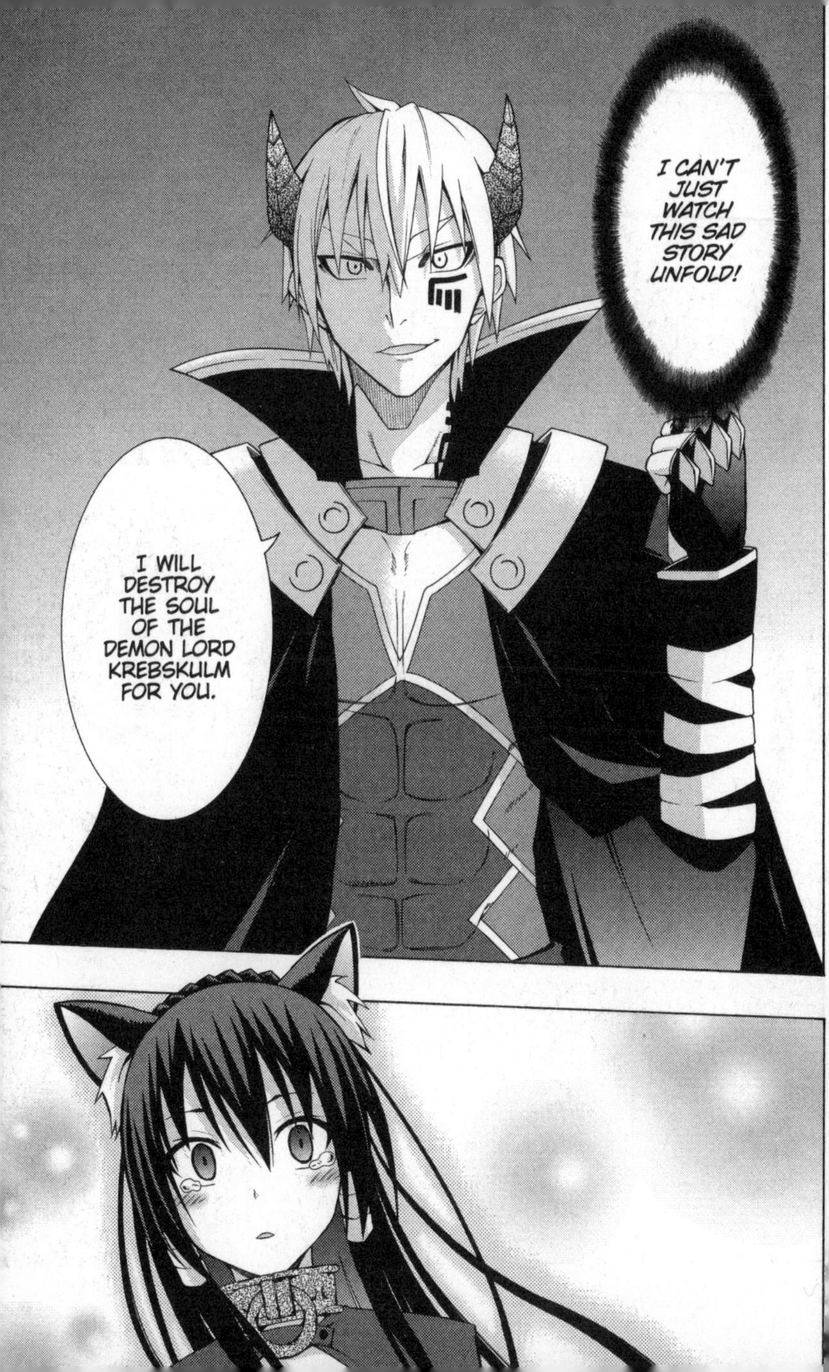
I CAN'T JUST WATCH THIS SAD STORY UNFOLD!
I WILL DESTROY THE SOUL OF THE DEMON LORD KREBSKULM FOR YOU.

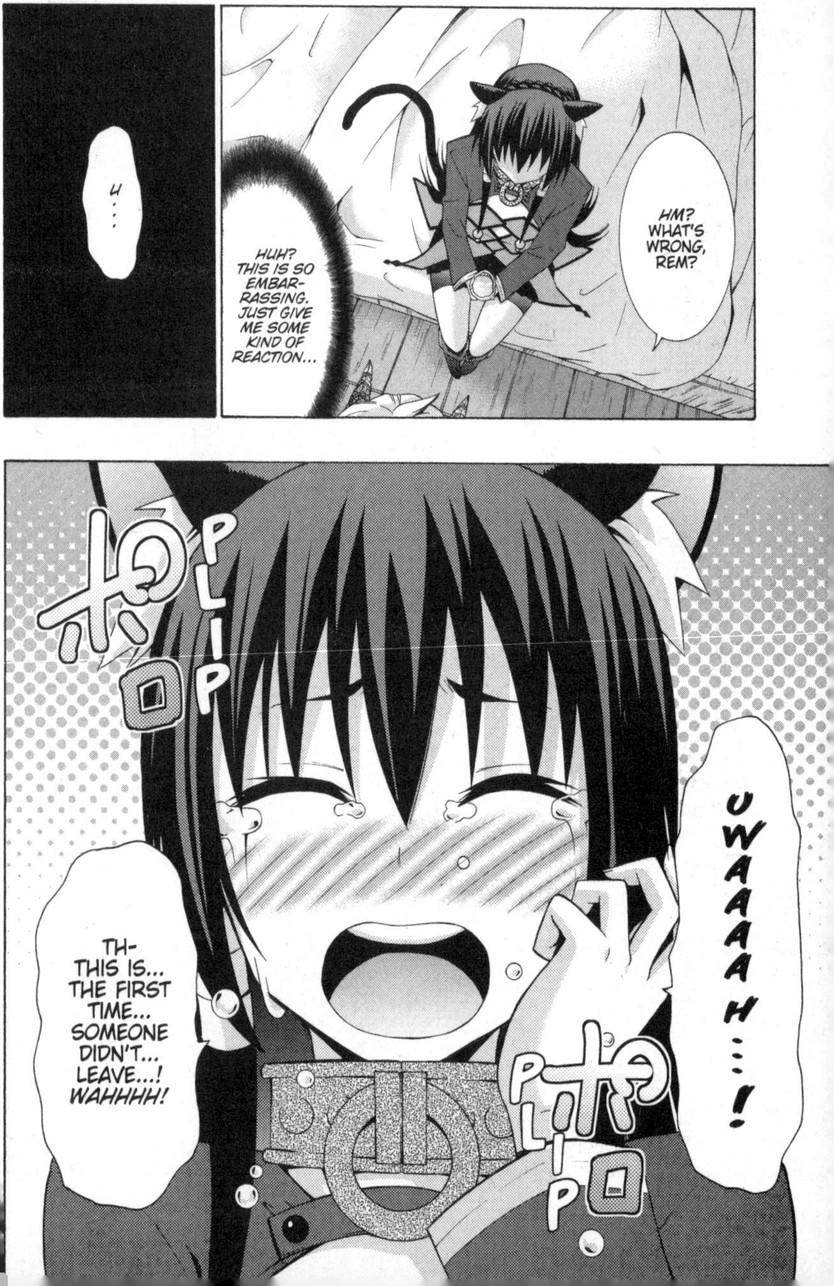
HM? WHAT'S WRONG, REM?
HUH? THIS IS SO EMBARRASSING. JUST GIVE ME SOME KIND OF REACTION...
U...
UWAAAAAH...!
PLIP PLIP
TH-THIS IS... THE FIRST TIME... SOMEONE DIDN'T... LEAVE...! WAHHHH!
PLIP PLIP

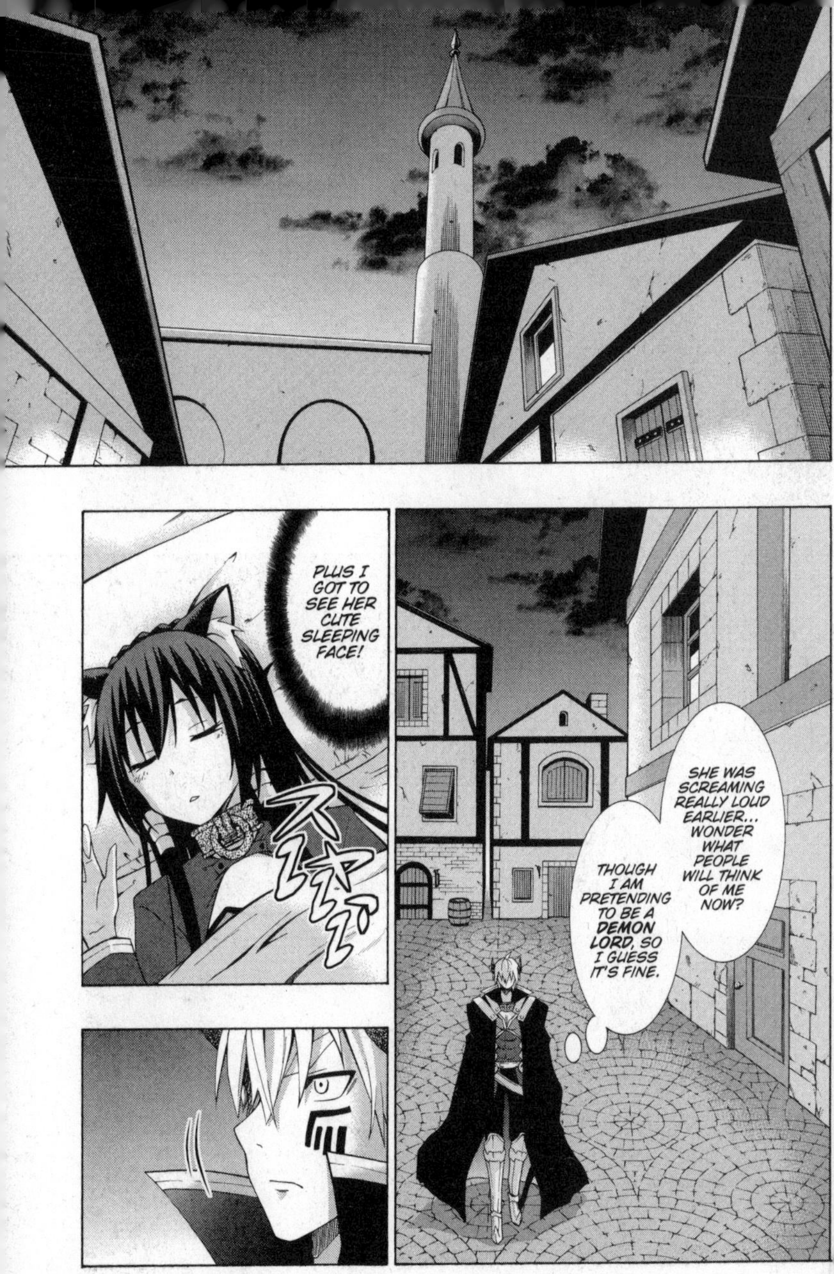
SHE WAS SCREAMING REALLY LOUD EARLIER... WONDER WHAT PEOPLE WILL THINK OF ME NOW?
THOUGH I AM PRETENDING TO BE A **DEMON LORD**, SO I GUESS IT'S FINE.
PLUS I GOT TO SEE HER CUTE SLEEPING FACE!

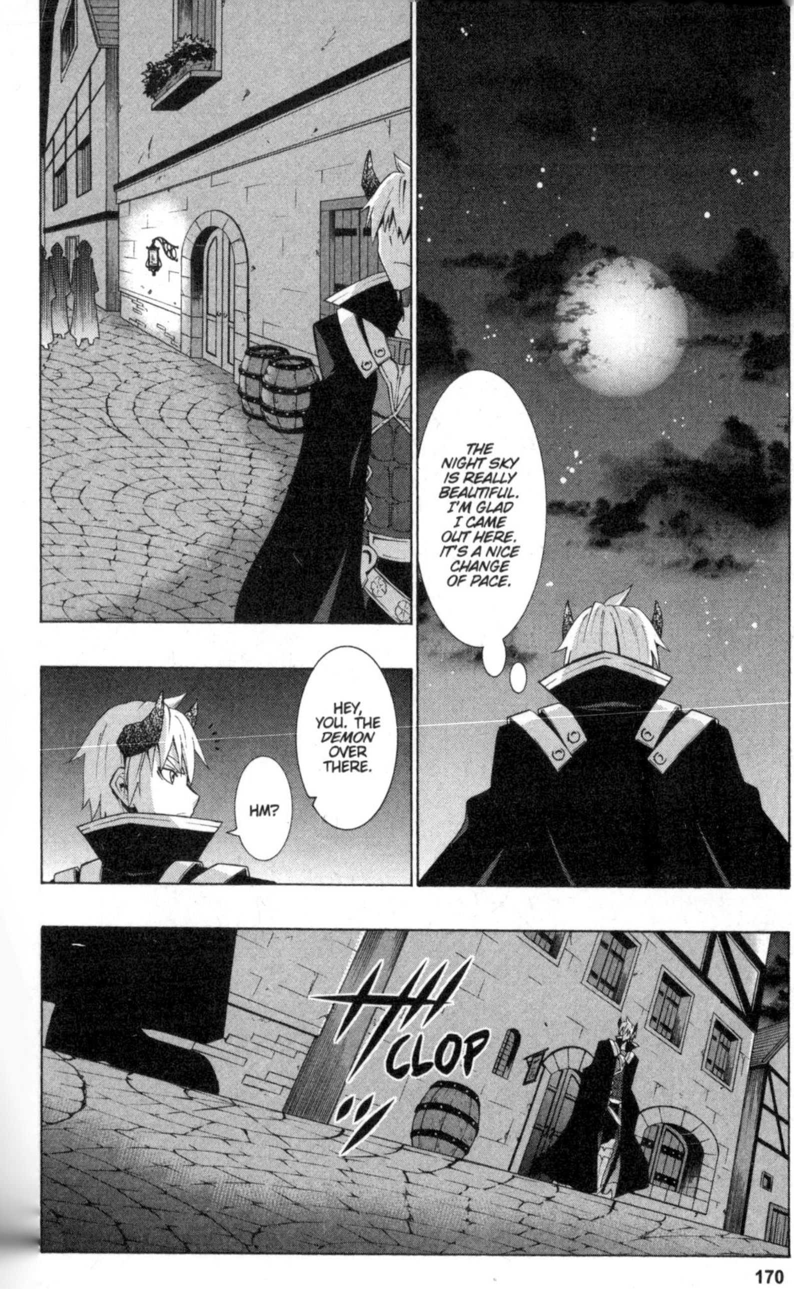
THE NIGHT SKY IS REALLY BEAUTIFUL. I'M GLAD I CAME OUT HERE. IT'S A NICE CHANGE OF PACE.
HEY, YOU. THE DEMON OVER THERE.
HM?
CLOP

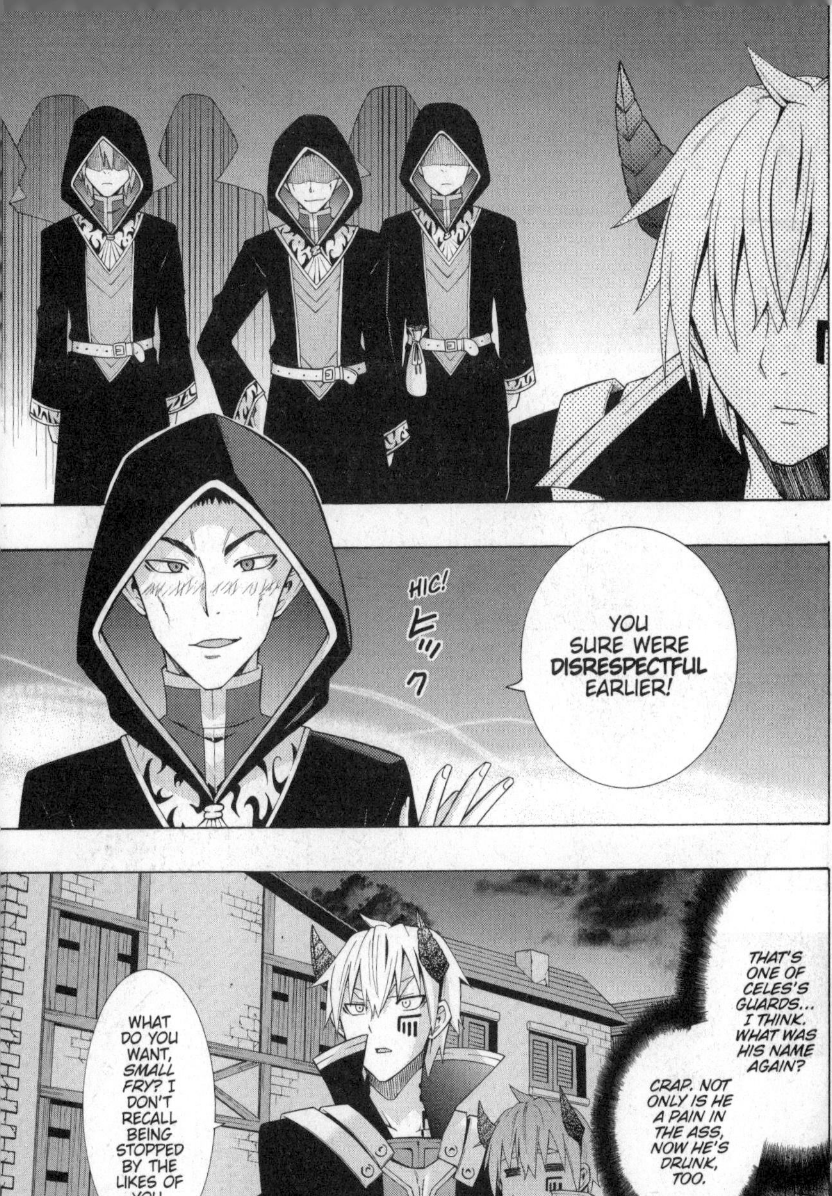
YOU SURE WERE DISRESPECTFUL EARLIER!
HIC!
ヒック
THAT'S ONE OF CELES'S GUARDS... I THINK. WHAT WAS HIS NAME AGAIN?
CRAP. NOT ONLY IS HE A PAIN IN THE ASS, NOW HE'S DRUNK, TOO.
WHAT DO YOU WANT, SMALL FRY? I DON'T RECALL BEING STOPPED BY THE LIKES OF YOU.

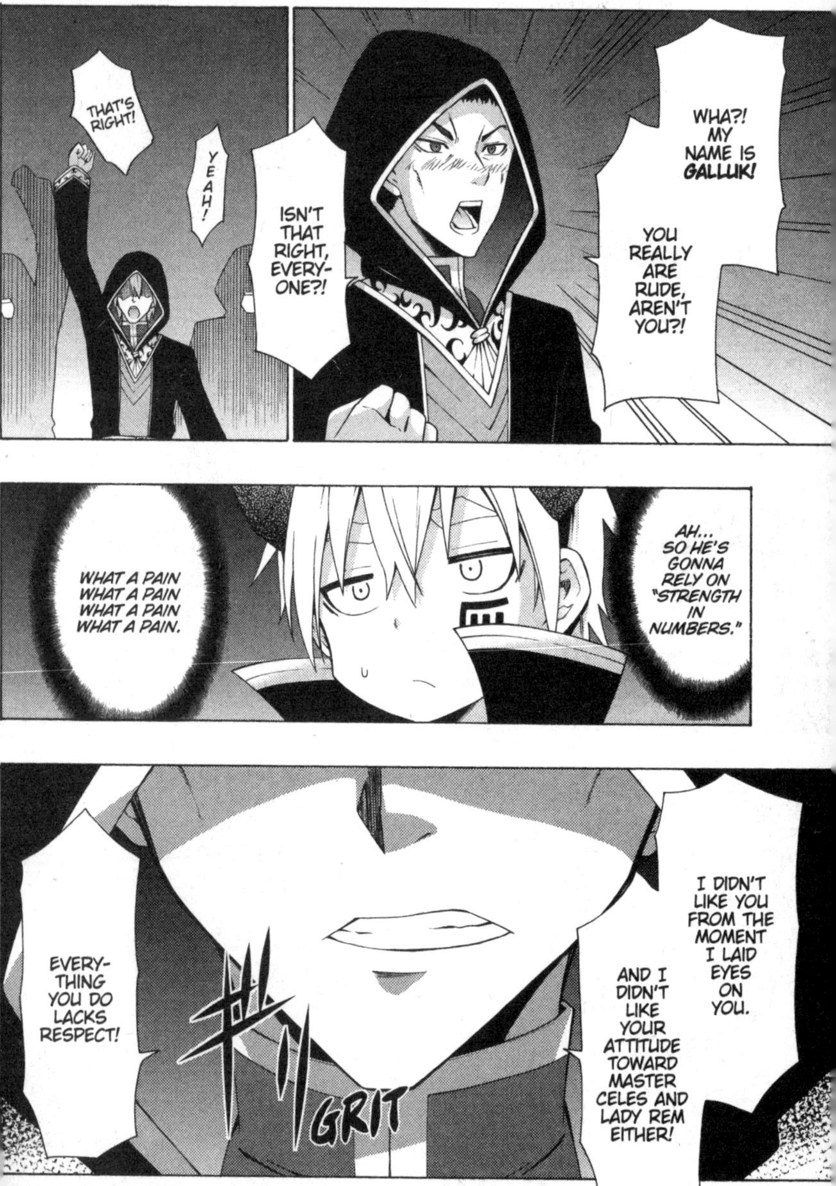
WHA?! MY NAME IS **GALLUK!**
YOU REALLY ARE RUDE, AREN'T YOU?!
ISN'T THAT RIGHT, EVERY-ONE?!
YEAH!
THAT'S RIGHT!
AH... SO HE'S GONNA RELY ON "STRENGTH IN NUMBERS."
WHAT A PAIN WHAT A PAIN WHAT A PAIN WHAT A PAIN.
I DIDN'T LIKE YOU FROM THE MOMENT I LAID EYES ON YOU.
AND I DIDN'T LIKE YOUR ATTITUDE TOWARD MASTER CELES AND LADY REM EITHER!
GRIT
EVERY-THING YOU DO LACKS RESPECT!

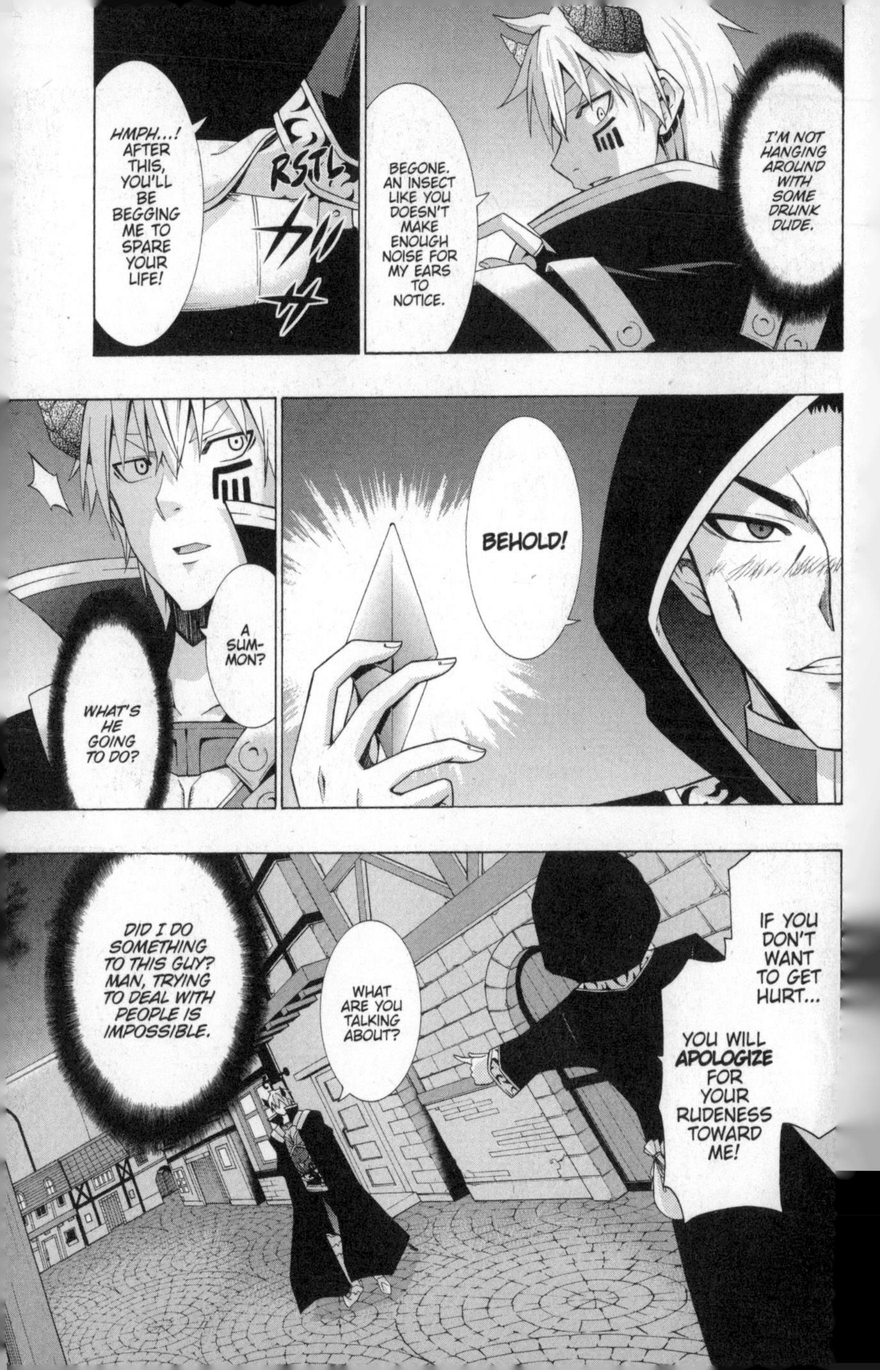
I'M NOT HANGING AROUND WITH SOME DRUNK DUDE.
BEGONE. AN INSECT LIKE YOU DOESN'T MAKE ENOUGH NOISE FOR MY EARS TO NOTICE.
HMPH...! AFTER THIS, YOU'LL BE BEGGING ME TO SPARE YOUR LIFE!
RSTL
BEHOLD!
A SUM-MON?
WHAT'S HE GOING TO DO?
IF YOU DON'T WANT TO GET HURT...
YOU WILL **APOLOGIZE** FOR YOUR RUDENESS TOWARD ME!
WHAT ARE YOU TALKING ABOUT?
DID I DO SOMETHING TO THIS GUY? MAN, TRYING TO DEAL WITH PEOPLE IS IMPOSSIBLE.

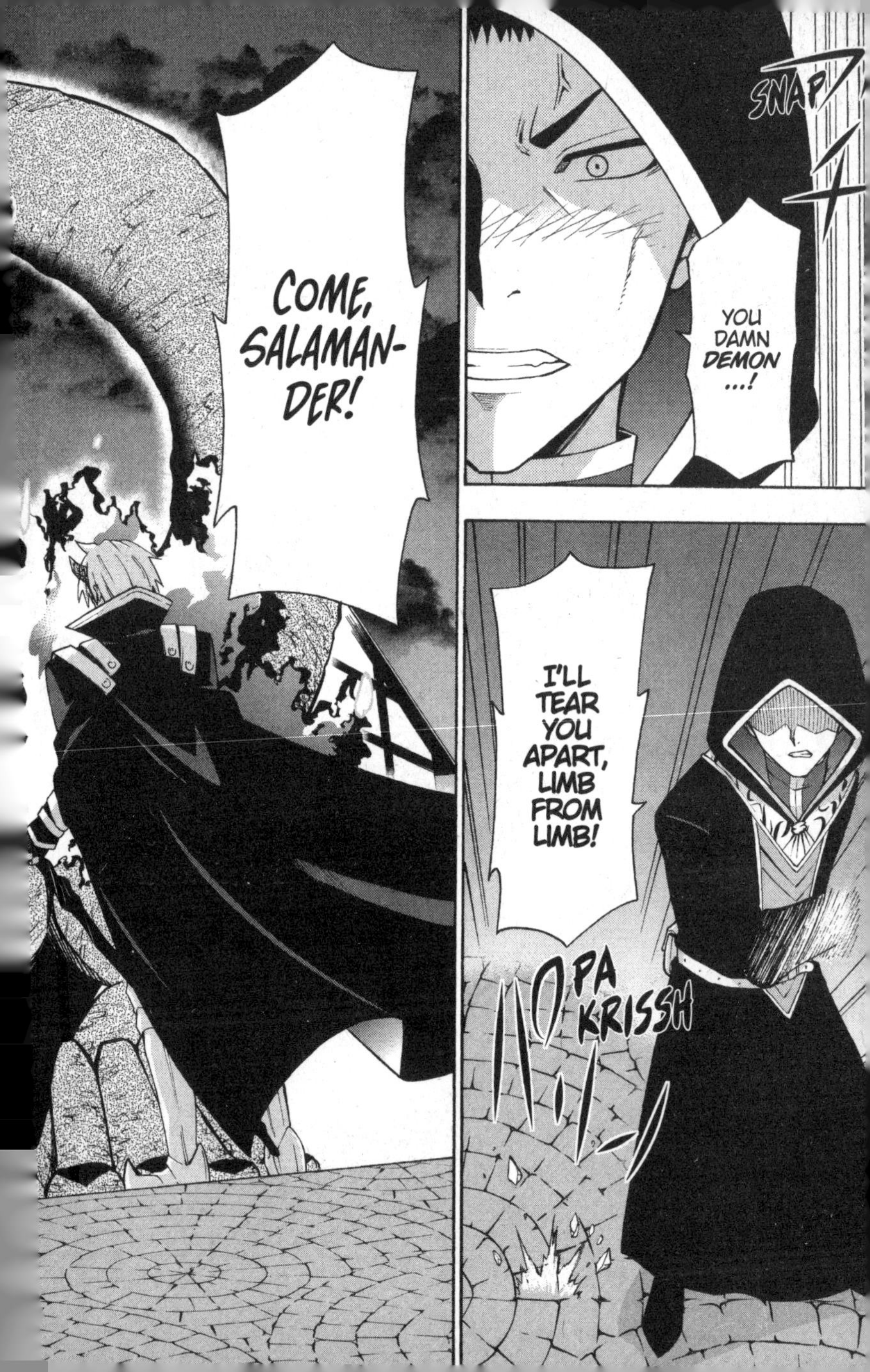
SNAP
YOU DAMN DEMON ...!
I'LL TEAR YOU APART, LIMB FROM LIMB!
PA KRISSH
COME, SALAMAN-DER!

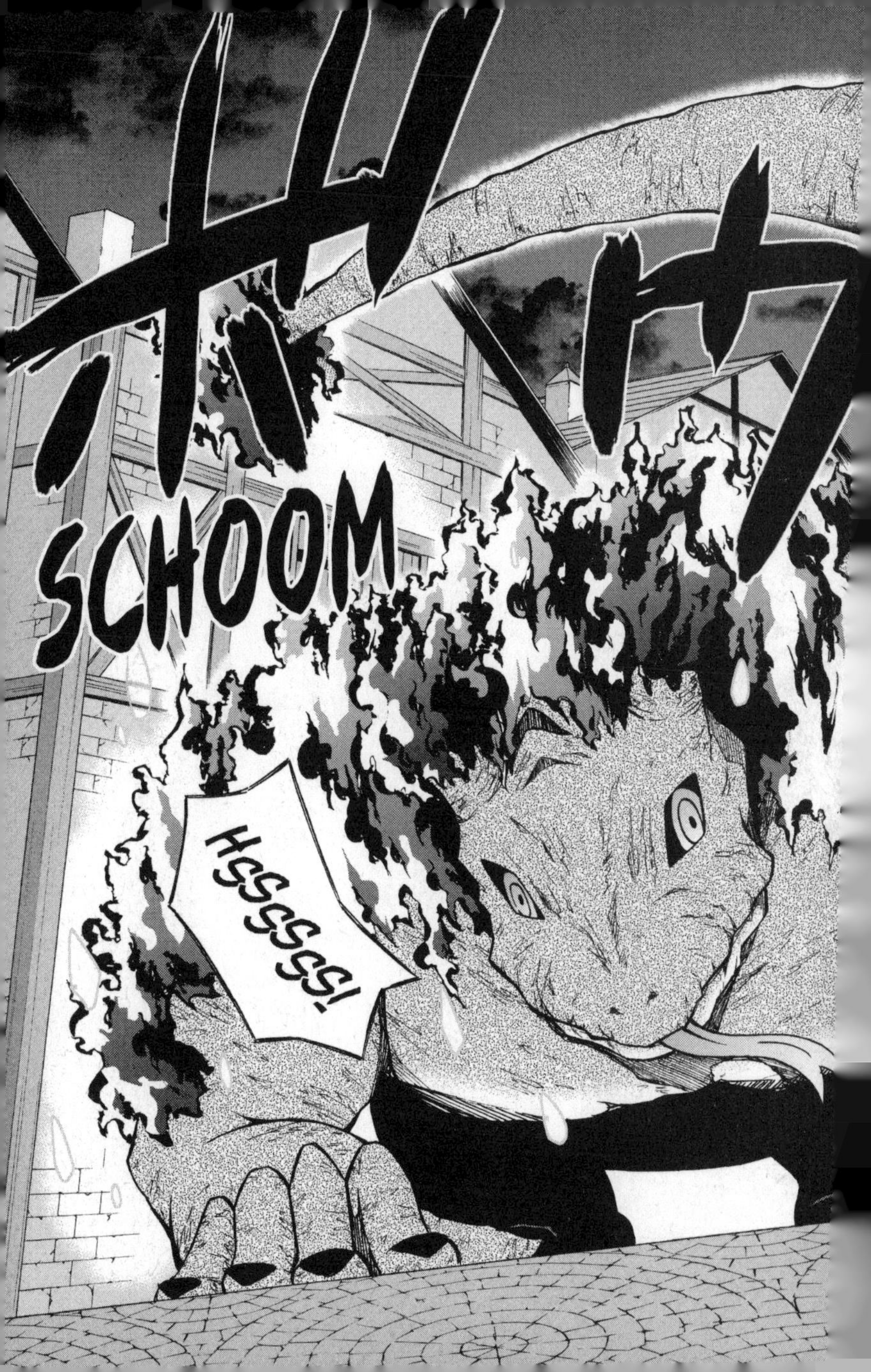
SCHOOM
HSSSSSS!

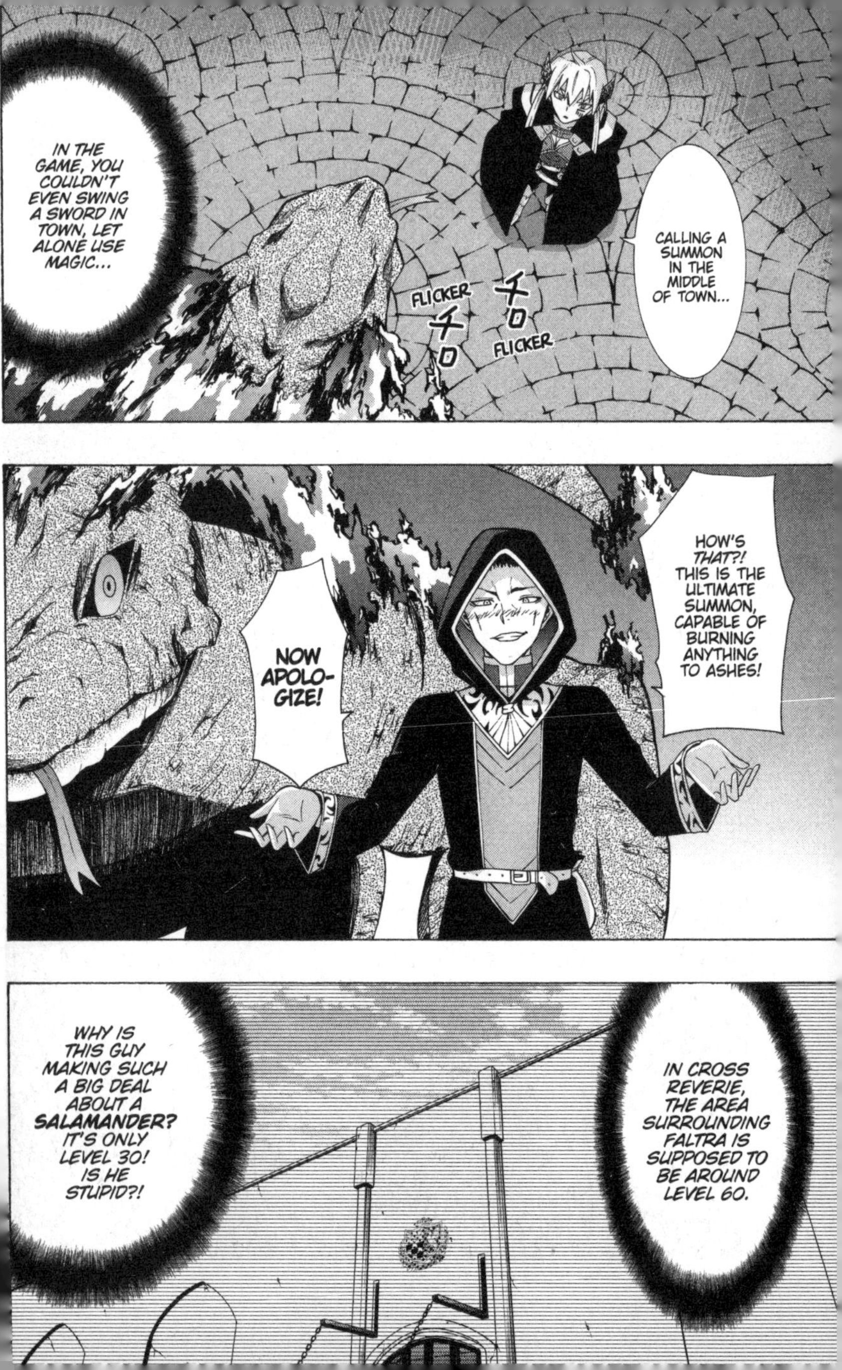
CALLING A SUMMON IN THE MIDDLE OF TOWN...
FLICKER
FLICKER
IN THE GAME, YOU COULDN'T EVEN SWING A SWORD IN TOWN, LET ALONE USE MAGIC...
HOW'S *THAT?!* THIS IS THE ULTIMATE SUMMON, CAPABLE OF BURNING ANYTHING TO ASHES!
NOW APOLO-GIZE!
IN CROSS REVERIE, THE AREA SURROUNDING FALTRA IS SUPPOSED TO BE AROUND LEVEL 60.
WHY IS THIS GUY MAKING SUCH A BIG DEAL ABOUT A **SALAMANDER?** IT'S ONLY LEVEL 30! IS HE STUPID?!

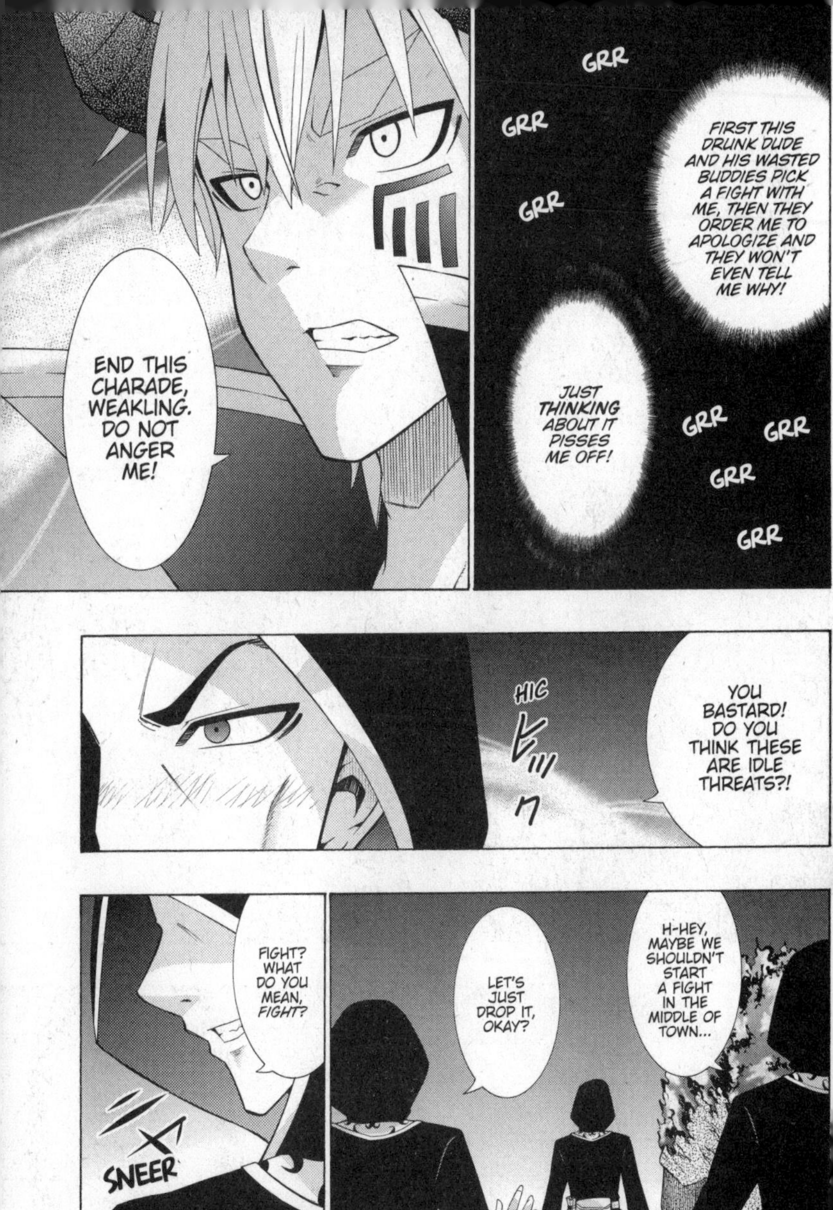
GRR
GRR
GRR
FIRST THIS DRUNK DUDE AND HIS WASTED BUDDIES PICK A FIGHT WITH ME, THEN THEY ORDER ME TO APOLOGIZE AND THEY WON'T EVEN TELL ME WHY!
JUST THINKING ABOUT IT PISSES ME OFF!
GRR
GRR
GRR
GRR
END THIS CHARADE, WEAKLING. DO NOT ANGER ME!
YOU BASTARD! DO YOU THINK THESE ARE IDLE THREATS?!
HIC
ヒック
H-HEY, MAYBE WE SHOULDN'T START A FIGHT IN THE MIDDLE OF TOWN...
LET'S JUST DROP IT, OKAY?
FIGHT? WHAT DO YOU MEAN, FIGHT?
SNEER

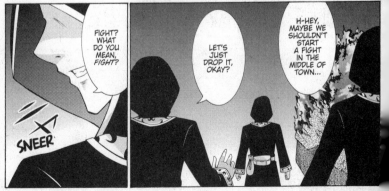

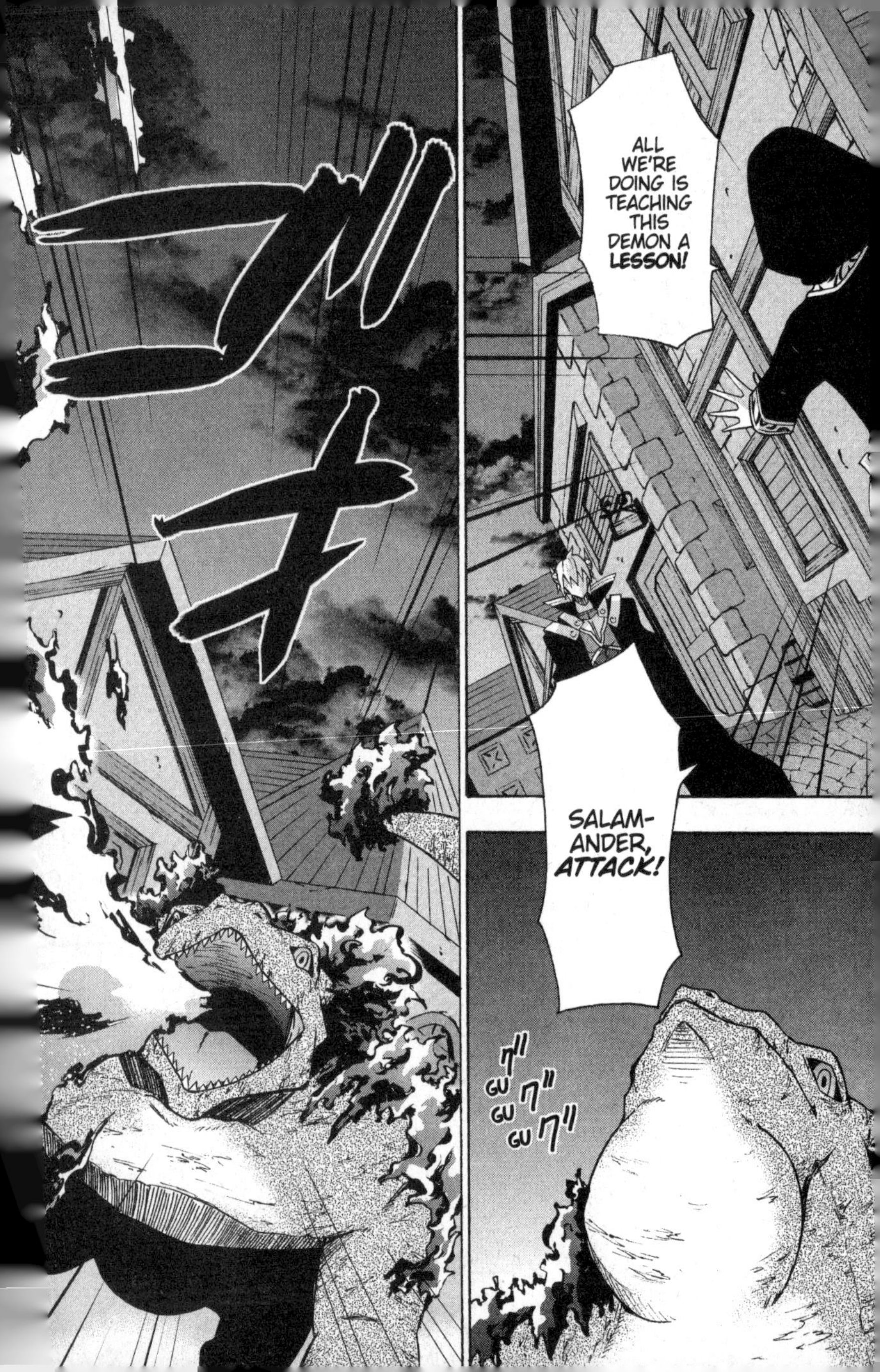
ALL WE'RE DOING IS TEACHING THIS DEMON A **LESSON!**
SALAM-ANDER, ***ATTACK!***
GU GU GU

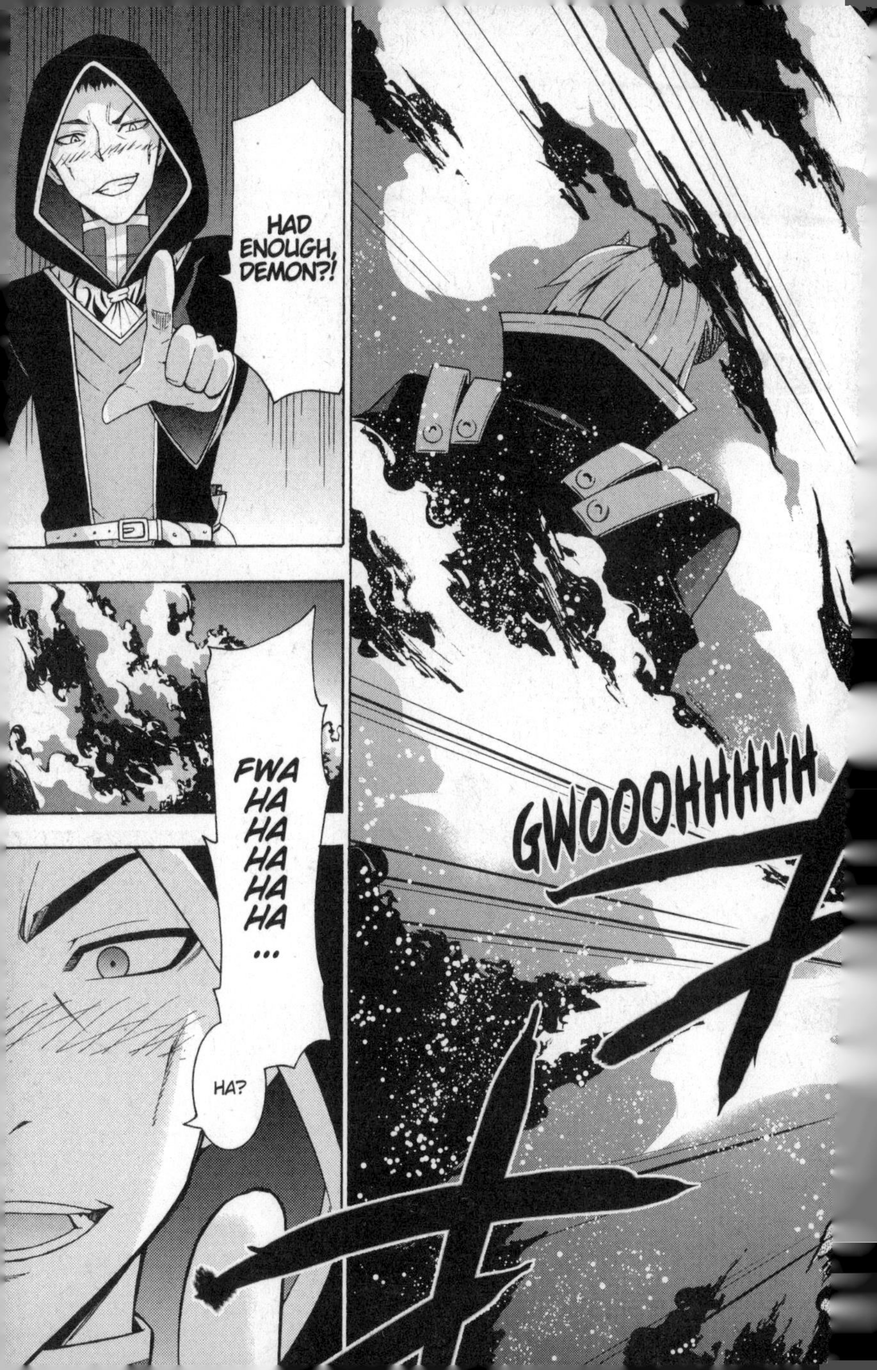
GWOOOHHHHH
HAD ENOUGH, DEMON?!
FWA HA HA HA HA HA...
HA?

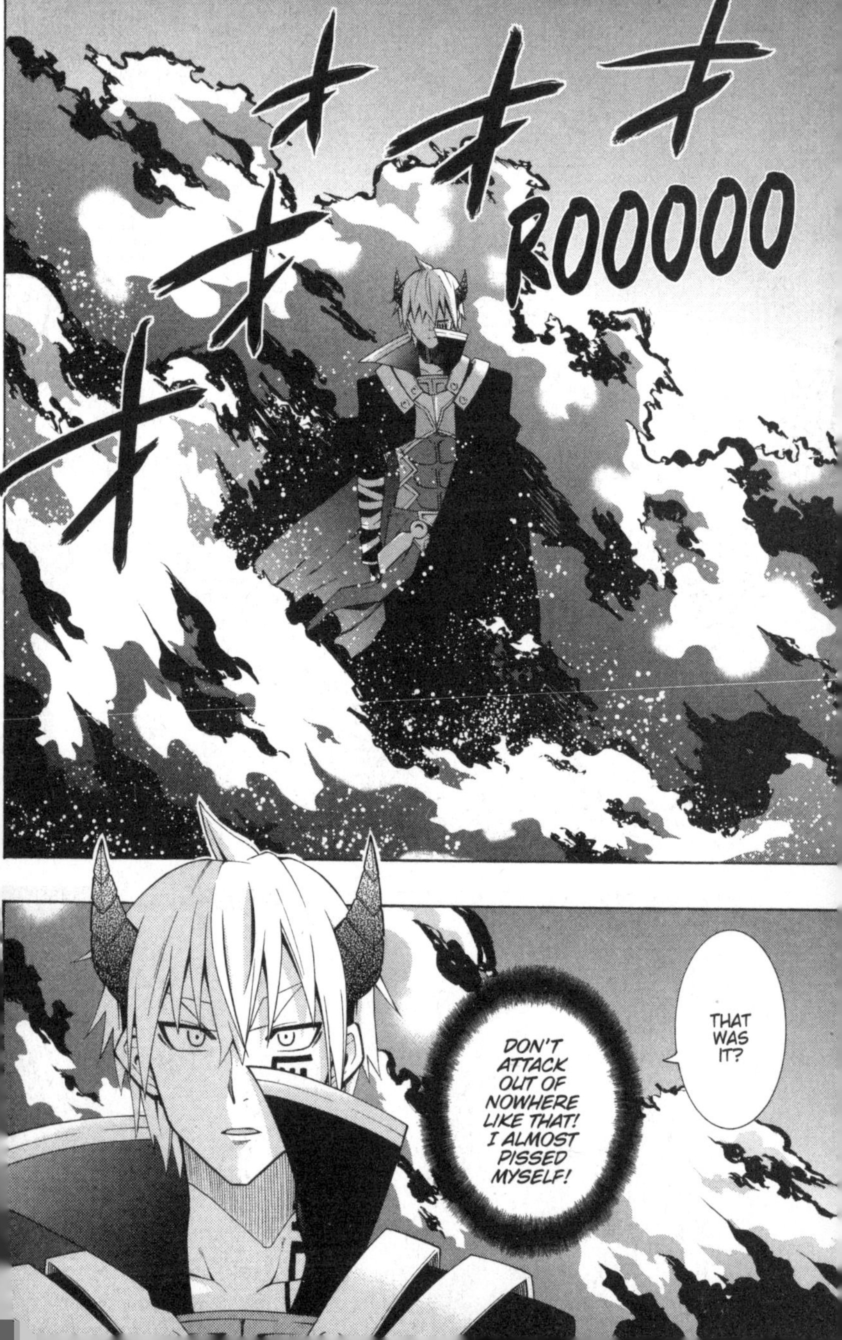
オオオオオ
ROOOOO
THAT WAS IT?
DON'T ATTACK OUT OF NOWHERE LIKE THAT! I ALMOST PISSED MYSELF!

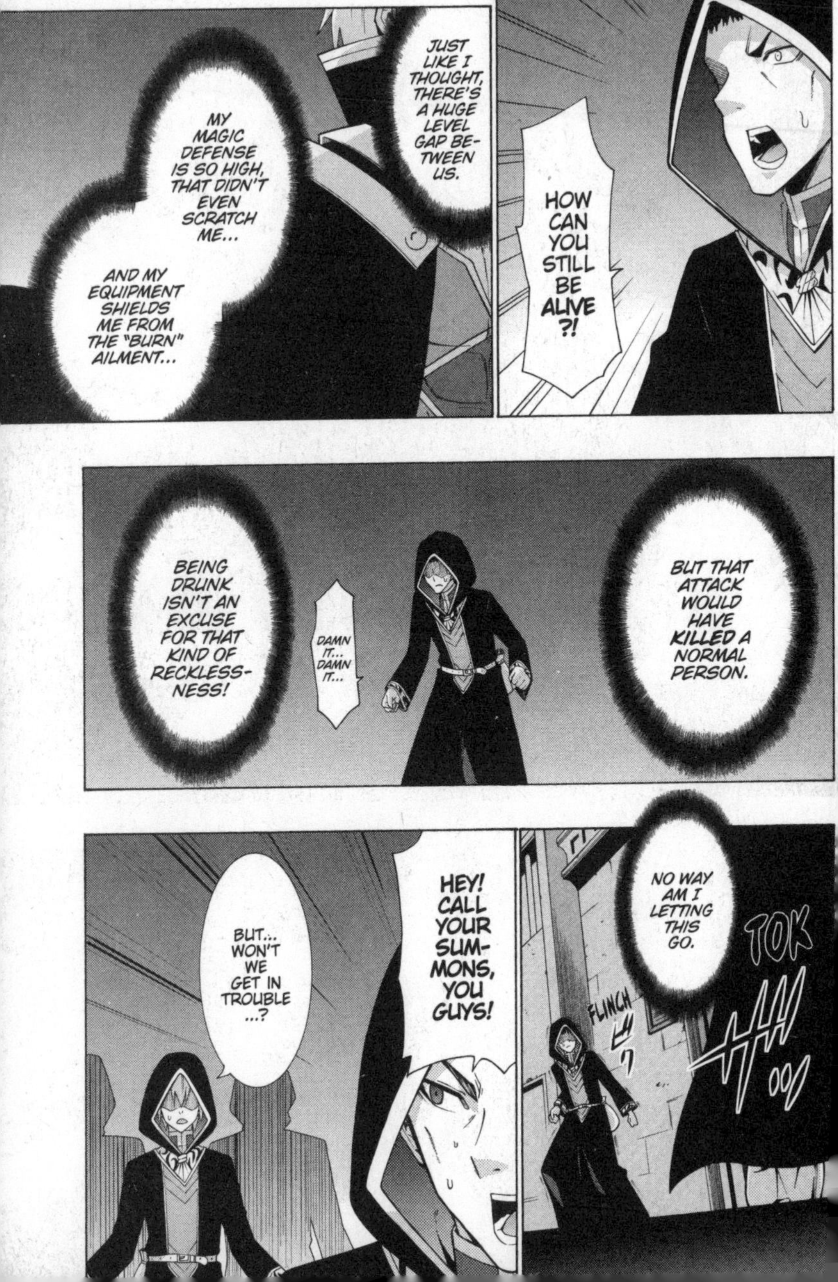
HOW CAN YOU STILL BE ALIVE?!
JUST LIKE I THOUGHT, THERE'S A HUGE LEVEL GAP BE-TWEEN US.
MY MAGIC DEFENSE IS SO HIGH, THAT DIDN'T EVEN SCRATCH ME...
AND MY EQUIPMENT SHIELDS ME FROM THE "BURN" AILMENT...
BUT THAT ATTACK WOULD HAVE KILLED A NORMAL PERSON.
DAMN IT... DAMN IT...
BEING DRUNK ISN'T AN EXCUSE FOR THAT KIND OF RECKLESS-NESS!
NO WAY AM I LETTING THIS GO.
TOK
FLINCH
HEY! CALL YOUR SUM-MONS, YOU GUYS!
BUT... WON'T WE GET IN TROUBLE ...?

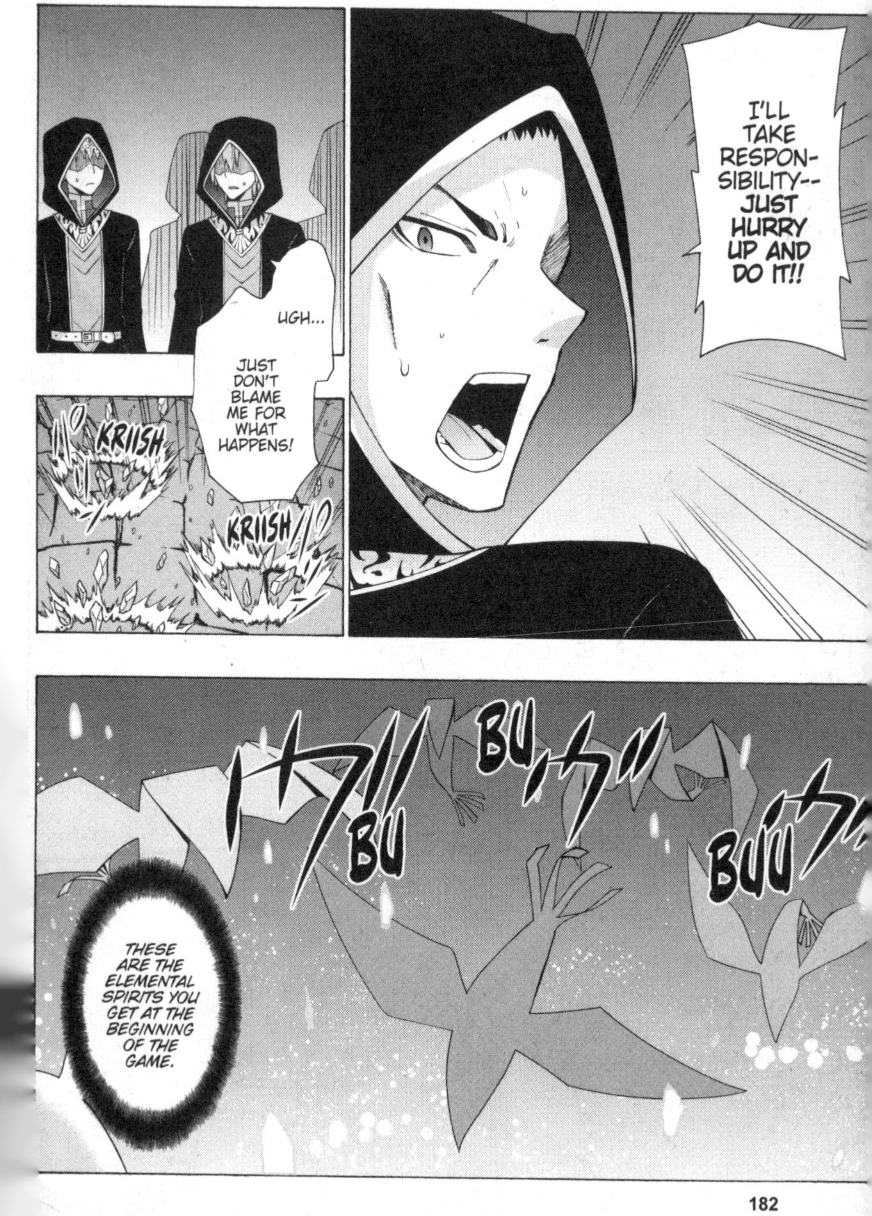
I'LL TAKE RESPON-SIBILITY-- JUST HURRY UP AND DO IT!!
UGH...
JUST DON'T BLAME ME FOR WHAT HAPPENS!
KRIISH
KRIISH
BU
BU
BUU
THESE ARE THE ELEMENTAL SPIRITS YOU GET AT THE BEGINNING OF THE GAME.

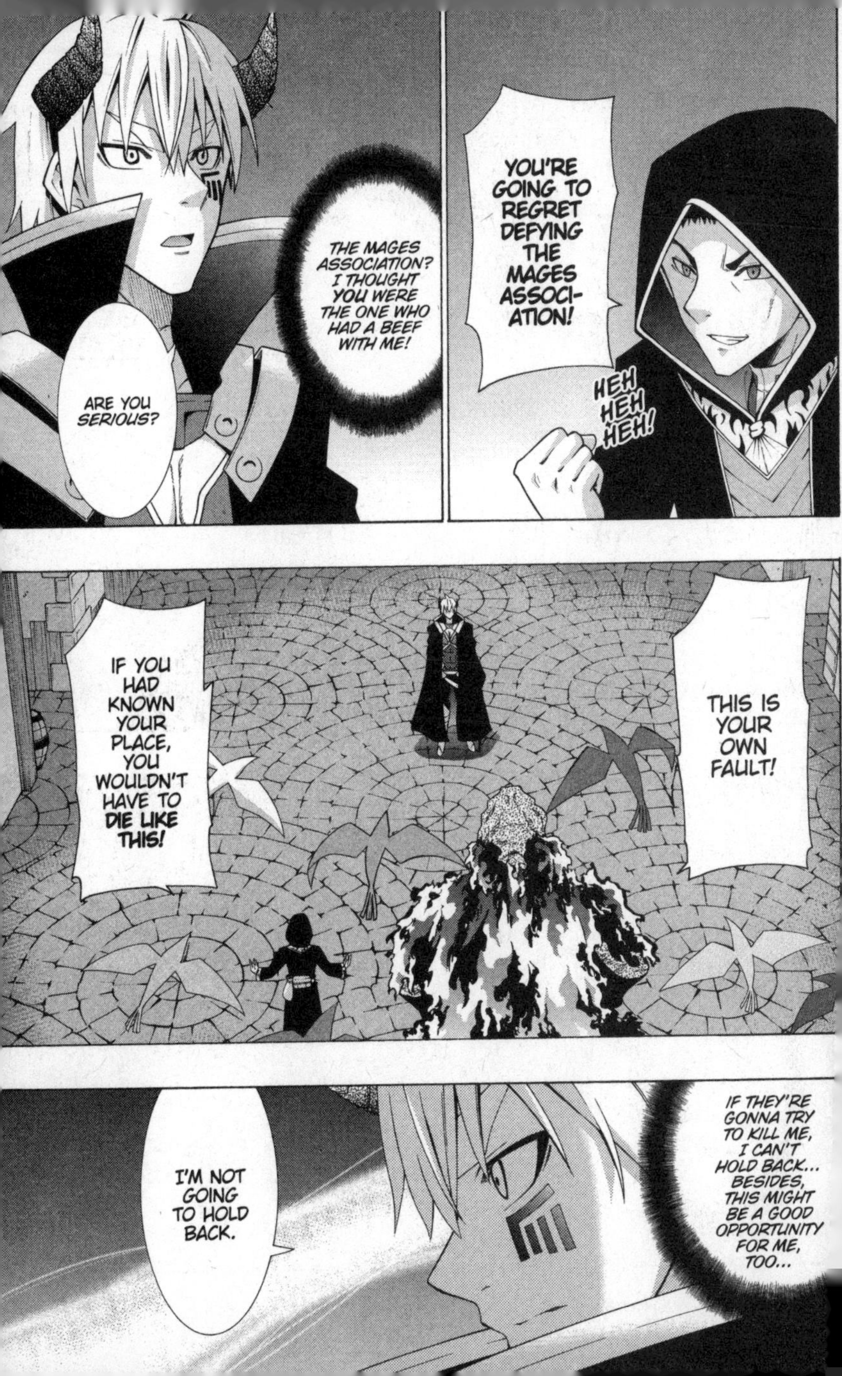
YOU'RE GOING TO REGRET DEFYING THE MAGES ASSOCIATION!
HEH HEH HEH!
THE MAGES ASSOCIATION? I THOUGHT YOU WERE THE ONE WHO HAD A BEEF WITH ME!
ARE YOU SERIOUS?
THIS IS YOUR OWN FAULT!
IF YOU HAD KNOWN YOUR PLACE, YOU WOULDN'T HAVE TO DIE LIKE THIS!
IF THEY'RE GONNA TRY TO KILL ME, I CAN'T HOLD BACK... BESIDES, THIS MIGHT BE A GOOD OPPORTUNITY FOR ME, TOO...
I'M NOT GOING TO HOLD BACK.

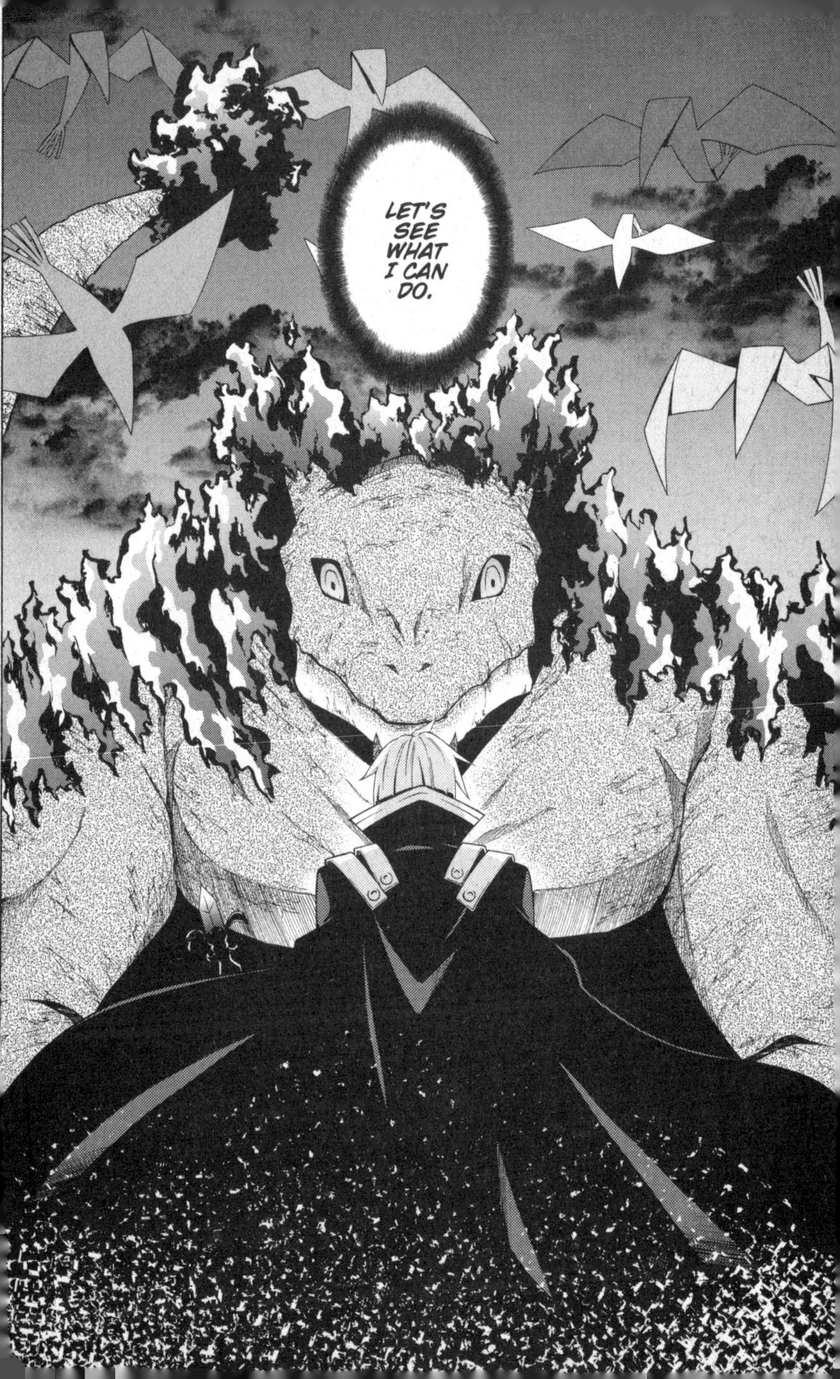
LET'S SEE WHAT I CAN DO.

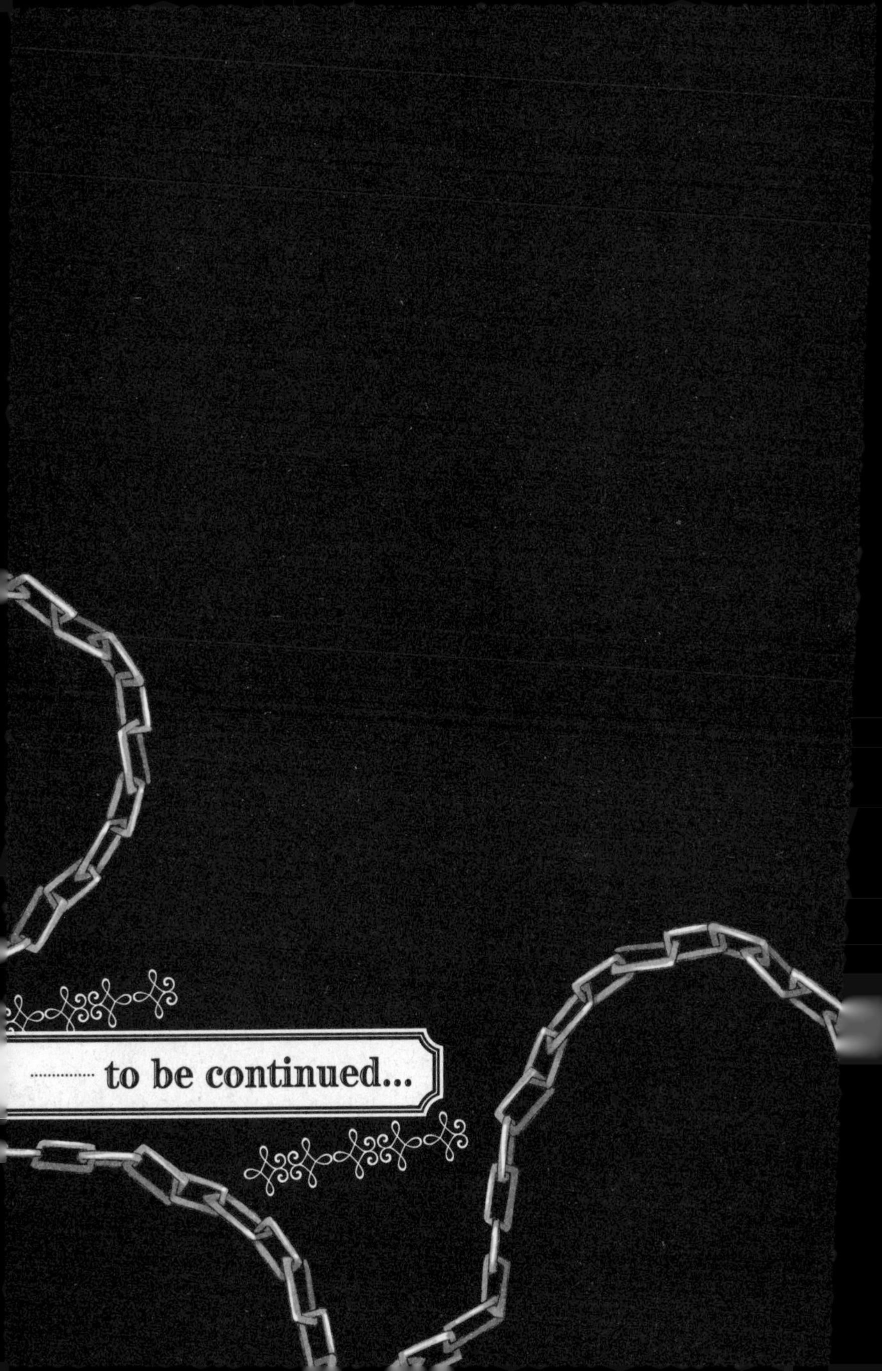
to be continued...

SPECIAL THANKS FOR VOLUME 1

YUKIYA MURASAKI

TAKAHIRO TSURUSAKI

ASSISTANTS:

YOSHITSUGU OHARA

TAKUYA NISHIDA

DAIKI HARAGUCHI

MINAMI YAITA

K

YUU TAKIGAWA

AKARI MATSUURA

THANK YOU FOR READING!

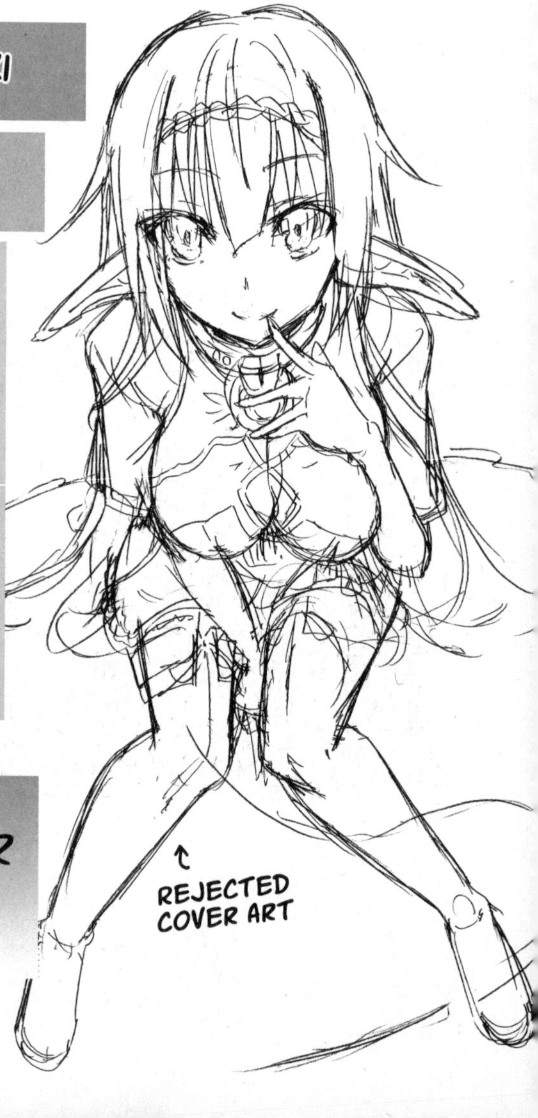

↑ REJECTED COVER ART

CHARACTER INTRODUCTION 1

DIABLO (DEMON, LEVEL 150)

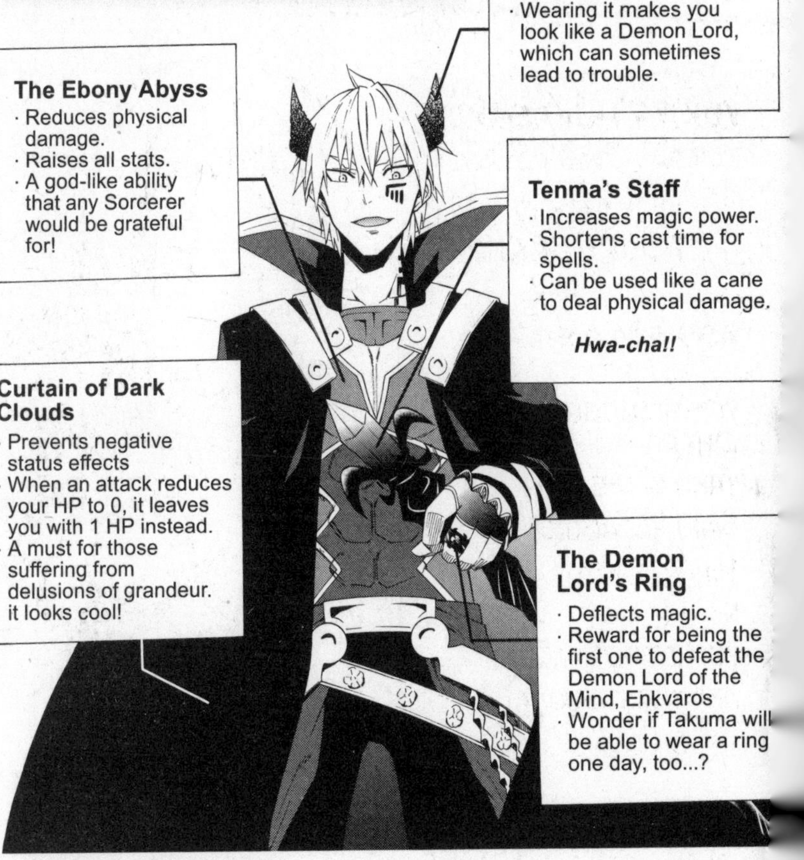
The Distorted Crown
· Automatic HP recovery.
· Wearing it makes you look like a Demon Lord, which can sometimes lead to trouble.
The Ebony Abyss
· Reduces physical damage.
· Raises all stats.
· A god-like ability that any Sorcerer would be grateful for!
Tenma's Staff
· Increases magic power.
· Shortens cast time for spells.
· Can be used like a cane to deal physical damage.
Hwa-cha!!
Curtain of Dark Clouds
· Prevents negative status effects
· When an attack reduces your HP to 0, it leaves you with 1 HP instead.
· A must for those suffering from delusions of grandeur. it looks cool!
The Demon Lord's Ring
· Deflects magic.
· Reward for being the first one to defeat the Demon Lord of the Mind, Enkvaros
· Wonder if Takuma will be able to wear a ring one day, too...?

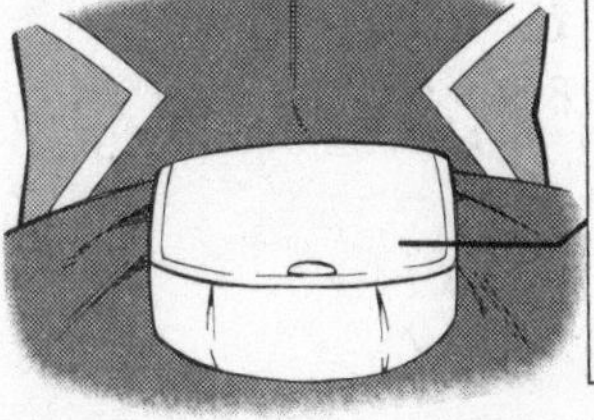
CARRIES A POUCH FILLED WITH POTIONS AROUND HIS WAIST. IT ALSO CONTAINS AN EXTREMELY RARE ITEM THAT TAKUMA PLANS ON GIVING TO WHOEVER DEFEATS "DEMON LORD DIABLO" TO COMMEMORATE THE OCCASION.

As we get ready for the publication of Volume 1 of *How NOT to Summon a Demon Lord.*

Congratulations on the release of the first volume of *How* NOT *to Summon a Demon Lord!* I'm Murasaki Yukiya, the original creator and author of the light novels. Fukuda Naoto-sensei is a very skilled manga artist, and I think his drawings truly bring the story to life. Having someone like him turn the series into a manga has definitely made for a wonderful end product, which I really appreciate. I love it so much that I've read it over and over again and I'm looking forward to what comes next! To all of you who have read the manga version of *How NOT to Summon a Demon Lord*, thank you very much!

Yukiya Murasaki

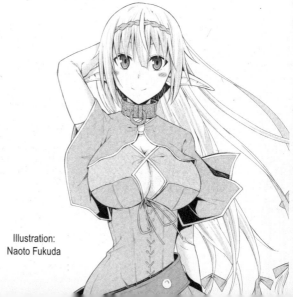

Illustration:
Naoto Fukuda

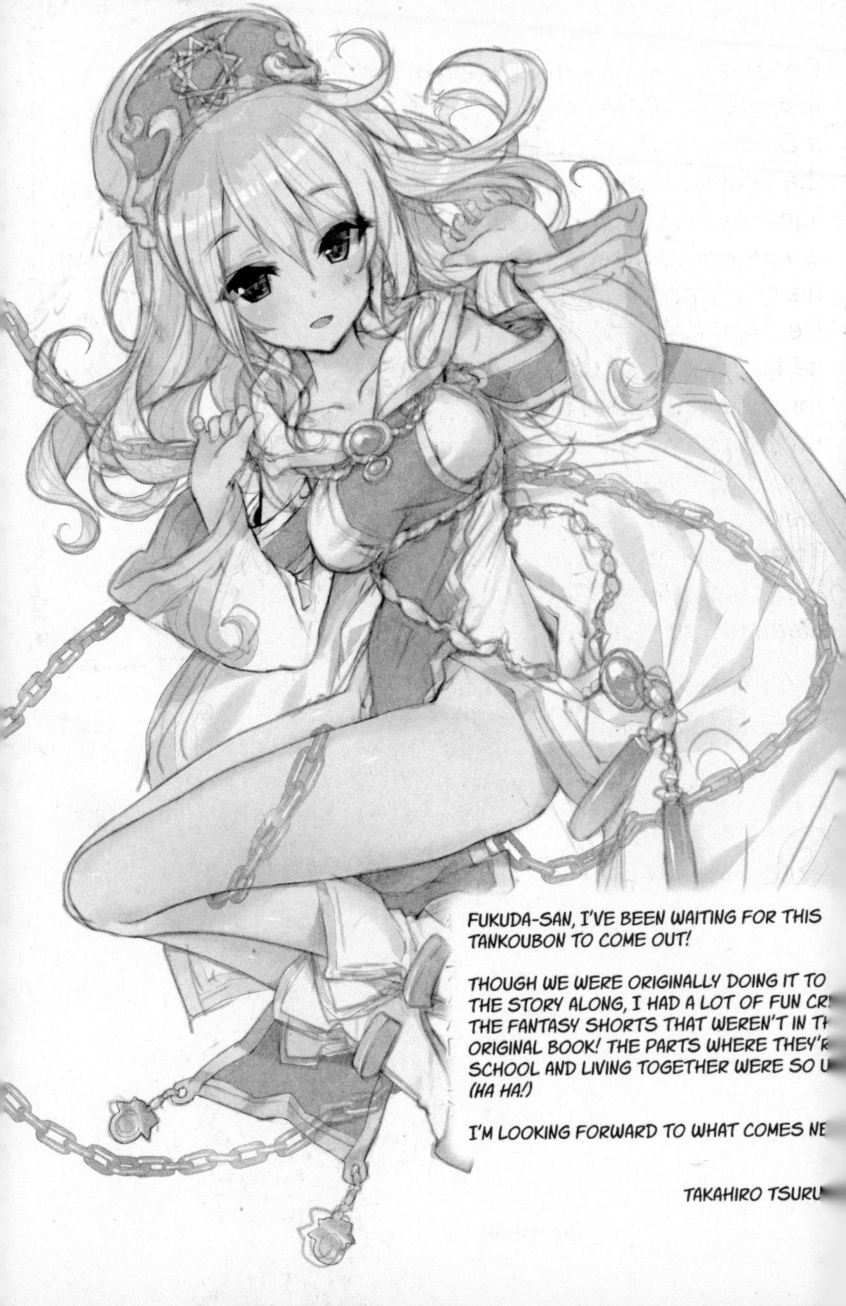

FUKUDA-SAN, I'VE BEEN WAITING FOR THIS TANKOUBON TO COME OUT!

THOUGH WE WERE ORIGINALLY DOING IT TO THE STORY ALONG, I HAD A LOT OF FUN CR THE FANTASY SHORTS THAT WEREN'T IN TH ORIGINAL BOOK! THE PARTS WHERE THEY'R SCHOOL AND LIVING TOGETHER WERE SO U (HA HA!)

I'M LOOKING FORWARD TO WHAT COMES NE

TAKAHIRO TSURU

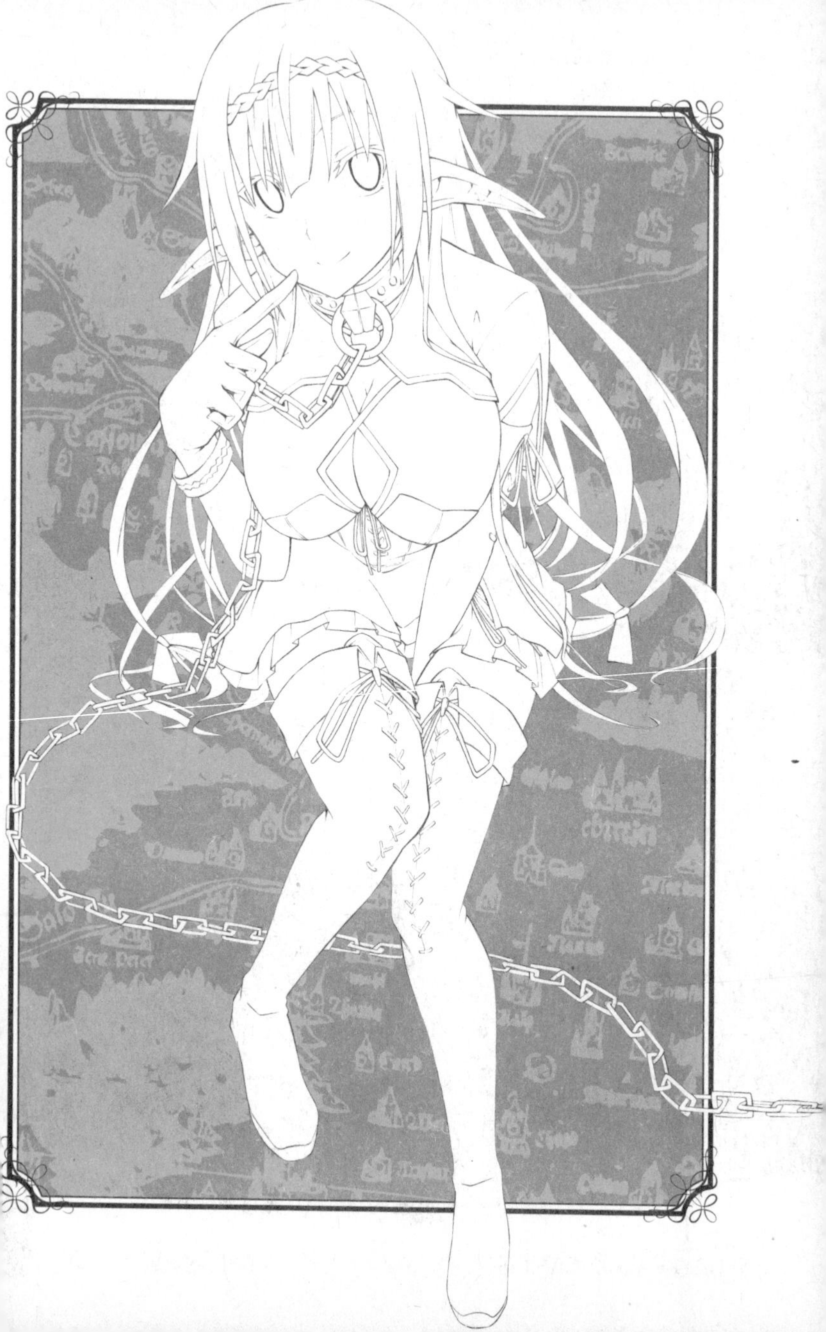